Marco Cantù

Delphi 2009 Handbook

Piacenza, Italy, November 2008

Author: Marco Cantù

Publisher: Wintech Italia Srl, Italy

Editor: Peter W A Wood

Tech Editors: Holger Flick, Jeroen Pluimers, Jan Goyvaerts, Jeremy North, Marco Breveglieri

Cover Designer: Fabrizio Schiavi

Copyright 2008 Marco Cantù, Piacenza, Italy. World rights reserved.

The author created example code in this publication expressly for the free use by its readers. The source code for this book is copyrighted freeware, distributed via the web site `http://www.marcocantu.com`. The copyright prevents you from republishing the code in print media without permission. Readers are granted limited permission to use this code in their applications, as long at the code itself is not distributed, sold, or commercially exploited as a stand-alone product.

Aside from this specific exception concerning source code, no part of this publication may be stored in a retrieval system, transmitted, or reproduced in any way, in the original or in a translated language, including but not limited to photocopy, photograph, magnetic, or other record, without the prior agreement and written permission of the publisher.

ISBN: 1440480095   (EAN-13 9781440480096)

Delphi is a trademark of CodeGear, a subsidiary of Embarcadero Technologies. Windows Vista is a trademarks of Microsoft. Other trademarks are of the respective owners, as referenced in the text. The author and publisher have made their best efforts to prepare this book, and the content is based upon the final release of the software whenever possible. The author and publisher make no representation or warranties of any kind with regard to the completeness or accuracy of the contents herein and accepts no liability of any kind including but not limited to performance, merchantability, fitness for any particular purpose, or any losses or damages of any kind caused or alleged to be caused directly or indirectly from this book.

Edition 2, Revision 1. April 15th 2009.
Printed by CreateSpace (a DBA of On-Demand Publishing LLC) in USA.

Printed copies of this book are on sale on `http://www.amazon.com`
More information on `http://www.marcocantu.com/dh2009`

Marco Cantù, Delphi 2009 Handbook

Preface

To my wife Lella, with love, encouragement, passion, dedication, and patience

This is a book about CodeGear Delphi 2009.

You won't find an introduction to Delphi programming, its Object Pascal language or its Visual Component Library in it. In this book you can read only about *new features of Delphi 2009 for Win32* in each of these areas.

The book covers Delphi 2009 Unicode support, the new language features (such as generics and anonymous methods), the improvements of the IDE, the new classes of the Run Time Library, the new components of the VCL (including the Ribbon control), and the extensions to the database architecture and the DataSnap multi-tier technology.

As usual for my books, I'm covering the theory but also showing you dozens of examples, you can download and play with on your computer. If you still don't own Delphi 2009, you can download the trial version and also look at the actual programs in action in a series of videos linked from the web page:

http://www.marcocantu.com/dh2009/videos.html

Marco Cantù, Delphi 2009 Handbook

4 - Preface

This book is a sequel to Delphi 2007 Handbook, as it doesn't repeat its content at all. If you are interested in new features of Delphi 2009 since Delphi 7 (or a similar old version), you can buy both of my Handbooks.

If you are looking for an introduction to Delphi, instead, you can refer to my "Essential Pascal" for the language foundations and to the books in "Mastering Delphi" series (in particular either "Mastering Delphi 7" or "Mastering Delphi 2005"). While my recent Handbooks and "Essential Pascal" are available on Lulu.com, the Mastering series was published in a more traditional way and can be found in physical or online bookstores.

You can find more details about all of my books at my personal website:

```
http://www.marcocantu.com
```

As usual, writing this book was quite an effort, and I have to thank many developers from the Delphi community who supported me in various ways, starting with the tech reviewers and Delphi product managers and R&D team members. A big thank you goes to my wife and kids for their patience and encouragement.

I hope you enjoy the result, like I've enjoyed writing it. And I hope you like Delphi 2009, one of the best versions of Delphi ever, as I did.

Table Of Contents

Preface..3
Introduction..13
    The Status of Delphi..14
        Why Win32 Matters..14
    This Book..15
    The Author...16
        Contact Information..17

Part I:
Unicode..19

Chapter 1: What is Unicode?..21
    Characters from the Past: from ASCII to ISO Encodings..............22
    Unicode: An Alphabet for the Entire World....................................24
        From Code Points to Bytes...27
        Unicode Code Points and Graphemes..27

6 - Table of Contents

    Unicode Transformation Formats (UTF)...28
    Looking at UTF-16..29
    Unicode Code Point Descriptions..32
    Byte Order Mark..34
Unicode in Win32...34
    Unicode API Call Speed..37
    UnicodeString Parameters in API calls...38
    Unicode and Fonts and APIs...39
    Unicode Before Delphi 2009..41
What's Next..41

Chapter 2: The Unicode String Type..43
From AnsiChar to WideChar..44
    Char as an Ordinal Type..44
    Converting with Chr..46
    32-bit Characters...46
    The New Character Unit...47
Of String and UnicodeString..49
    The Internal Structure of Strings..50
    UnicodeString and Unicode..52
    The UCS4String type..54
The Many String Types...54
    The New AnsiString Type...55
    Creating a Custom String Type...56
    Managing UTF-8 Strings...60
Converting Strings..61
    Conversions Slow Down the Code..62
    The Ensure Calls..64
    Watch Out for Literals in Concatenation..65
    Using RawByteString..66
    New UTF-8 Conversion Functions...70
String and Character Literals...70
Streams and Encodings..72
    Streaming Strings Lists...73
    Defining a Custom Encoding..76
Unicode and the VCL...79
    A Growing Core RTL?..80
    Unicode in DFM Files...80
    Localizing the VCL...81
What's Next..82

Chapter 3: Porting to Unicode...83
Char Operations That Fail...84
    Watch Out for Set of Char..84
    Avoid FillChar for Characters...86

String Operations That Fail or Slow Down..........87
    Turn on All String Conversion Warnings..........88
    Don't Move String Data..........89
    Reading and Writing Buffers..........91
    Appending and Concatenating Strings..........92
    Strings are... Strings (not Bookmarks)..........93
    Actual Troublesome "Porting" Cases..........93
    InliningTest used AnsiString..........94
    Calling Ansi-prefixed Functions..........95
Unicode Strings and Win32..........97
    Win32 Console Applications..........98
PChar and Pointer Math..........99
    The Problem with PChar..........100
    From PChar to PByte..........101
    PInteger and the POINTERMATH Directive..........102
    Don't use PChar for Pointer Math..........103
Variants and Open Arrays Parameters..........103
What's Next..........104

Part II:
Delphi 2009 and Its Compiler..........105

Chapter 4: New IDE Features..........107

Installing and Running..........108
    .NET SDK Not Needed..........108
    Windows Install Clean Up..........109
    The -idecaption Flag..........109
Managing Delphi Projects..........110
    Upgrading Project Configuration Files..........110
    Project Options Dialog Redesigned..........113
    New Project Options for the Compiler..........114
    Other New Project Options..........116
    Default Projects Location..........116
The Project Manager..........117
    Project Manager Views..........118
    Build Configurations and Configuration Settings..........119
    Project Configuration Manager..........122
Managing Resources in the IDE..........123
    A "New" Resource Compiler..........126
The Delphi Class Explorer..........127
Other New Features..........129
    Tool Palette Search Box..........130
    Updated Components Wizards..........131

8 - Table of Contents

Anything New in the Editor?..132
Debugger..133
    Debugging and New Language Features.....................................134
What's Next...134

Chapter 5: Generics...135
Generic Key-Value Pairs..136
    Type Rules on Generics..139
Generics in Delphi..140
    Generic Types Compatibility Rules..141
    Generic Global Functions (Well, Almost)...................................143
    Generic Type Instantiation..144
    Generic Type Functions...145
Generic Constraints...148
    Class Constraints..149
    Specific Class Constraints...151
    Interface Constraints...151
    Interface References vs. Generic Interface Constraints...........154
    Default Constructor Constraint...155
    Generic Constraints Summary and Combining Them.............156
Predefined Generic Containers..157
    Using TList<T>...158
    Sorting a TList<T>..159
    Sorting with an Anonymous Method..161
    Object Containers...163
    Using a Generic Dictionary...164
Generic Interfaces..167
    Predefined Generic Interfaces..170
Smart Pointers in Delphi...171
    What's Next..176

Chapter 6: Anonymous Methods..177
Syntax and Semantic of Anonymous Methods..................................178
    An Anonymous Method Variable...179
    An Anonymous Method Parameter...179
Using Local Variables..180
    Extending the Lifetime of Local Variables.................................181
More on Anonymous Methods...183
    The (Potentially) Missing Parenthesis..183
    Behind Anonymous Methods...185
    Ready To Use Reference Types..186
Anonymous Methods in the Real World...187
    Anonymous Event Handlers...188
    Timing Anonymous Methods...190
    Thread Synchronization with the VCL..193

Marco Cantù, Delphi 2009 Handbook

Parallel For Loop...196
　　　AJAX in Delphi..200
　　　　Debating the AJAX Demo..204
　What's Next..206

Chapter 7: More Language and RTL Changes..................................207
　Other New Language Features..208
　　Compiler Version..208
　　A Commented Deprecated Directive..209
　　Exit with a Value...210
　　Setting Properties by Reference..211
　　Changes in Overloading 212
　　Code That Triggers a Compiler Error..213
　　Code That Calls a Different Method..214
　　New and Aliased Integral Types...214
　TObject's New Methods..216
　　The ToString Method..216
　　The Equals Method...217
　　The GetHashCode Method..217
　　The UnitName Method..218
　　Porting an Example from .NET...218
　　TObject Class Summary..221
　　Unicode and Class Names..222
　Changes in Threading Support..223
　Building Strings...226
　　Methods Chaining in StringBuilder..228
　　The Speed of Building Strings..229
　　Porting a Delphi for .NET Example..231
　Using Readers and Writers...232
　Exception(al) Enhancements..236
　　The InnerException Mechanism...237
　　Preprocessing Exceptions...241
　　New Exception Classes...242
　Summary of New Units and New RTL Classes...............................243
　　More and Less FastCode..244
　What's Next..244

Part III:
VCL and Databases..245

Chapter 8: VCL Improvements...247
　VCL Core Improvements...248
　　Custom Hints and Balloon Hints..248

Marco Cantù, Delphi 2009 Handbook

10 - Table of Contents

Enhancements to Standard Components..251
   Buttons Get New Features...251
   Glowing Labels and LinkLabels...254
   RadioGroup Text Wrapping..255
   Edits Get Many New Features..256
   ComboBoxes and Text Hints...259
   The New ButtonedEdit Control..259
Updates to Common Controls..262
   Grouping in a ListView..262
   Marquee and More for ProgressBar Controls.................................265
   Check Boxes in a Header..266
   RichEdit 2.0..267
Native VCL Components..269
   The Action Manager Components..269
   About Panels..269
   The New CategoryPanelGroup Control..270
   TrayIcon Update..273
   Default Fonts for Application and Screen Global Objects.............274
   Improved Graphics Support...276
   The Clipboard and Unicode...280
Extended Vista Support...281
What's Next..282

Chapter 9: COM Support in Delphi 2009................................283
IDL, Type Libraries, and RIDL..284
   A Textual RIDL..285
The RIDL Format (COM Servers)..286
   Registering and Calling the Server..290
The New Registered Type Libraries Pane..291
COM and Unicode..293
Returning Features: Active Forms...294
What's Next..297

Chapter 10: The Ribbon..299
Introducing the Fluent User Interface...300
   The Legal Side of the Ribbon..301
   A First Simple Ribbon...301
Actions and The Ribbon..304
   From Events to Actions...305
   The ActionList and ActionManager Components...........................306
   Actions and Ribbon in Practice...307
   Groups And Commands..308
   Application Menu..310
   Quick Access Toolbar..313
   Supporting Key Tips..313

Marco Cantù, Delphi 2009 Handbook

The Ribbon Components...315
Ribbons for Database Applications..319
Using Screen Tips...323
    Screen Tips with No Ribbon..323
    Screen Tips Manager and Actions...325
What's Next..328

Chapter 11: Datasets and dbExpress...329
A Unicode ClientDataSet..330
Unicode in Datasets, Take 2..332
    Unicode String Lists..333
    Bookmarks...334
    Field Types and Strings...335
Other Dataset Enhancements..336
    New Field Types..336
    A More Virtual Dataset...337
    Fields Extensions..341
    BLOB fields Considered ANSI..343
    Parameters Extensions..344
DataSet Internals..344
    Porting a (Simple) Custom Dataset..345
dbExpress in Delphi 2009..346
    Connection Settings and Connection Strings.............................347
    Setting Driver Properties and Delegate Drivers........................349
    Deployment and INI files..350
    Drivers in the Executable..351
    Extended Metadata Support...352
    Data Pumping for dbExpress..356
Data-Aware Controls...357
    From DBImage to Poor Old DBGrid..359
What's Next..359

Chapter 12: DataSnap 2009..361
Building a First DataSnap 2009 Demo...362
    Building a Server...362
    The First Client...364
    From DataSnap to DataSnap 2009...365
    Adding Server Methods..366
Sessions and Threading with a Non-Database DataSnap Server...370
    Server Objects Life Cycle...373
    A Client Starting the Server and Opening Multiple Connections.....374
    Memory Management...377
    Thread Management...378
Porting an Old DataSnap Demo..381
    Porting the Server...381

12 - Table of Contents

Upgrading the Client..382
Advanced Features of ThinPlus2009...383
The DataSnap Administrative Interface..387
Conclusion..390

Index..391

Introduction

First introduced by Borland on February 14th 1995, Delphi has a long and glorious history of success in the Windows development and client/server areas. With millions of applications written in its Object Pascal language, Delphi spawned an entire ecosystem of components, tools, magazines, books, and (of course) web sites and online resources.

Delphi is now in its 12th version, the 20th if you count all the way back to its predecessor Turbo Pascal[1], which was first released 25 years ago. What's new in this version of Delphi is the company owning the product!

With the acquisition of the CodeGear division of Borland on July 1st, 2008, Delphi became a subsidiary of Embarcadero Technologies. This change of ownership happened quite late in the Delphi 2009 development cycle, so the only practical effect of the change is the inclusion of ER/Studio in the Architect version of the product. Since the start of the CodeGear division within Borland, though, there has been a renewed focus (and investment in terms of R&D, QA, and Docs) on Delphi, specifically in its Win32 version. That's why it is relevant to focus for a second on some higher-level *political* issues.

---

[1] The current version of the Delphi compiler, in fact, is 20.00. This is highlighted by the value of the VER200 define, mentioned in the section "Compiler Version" at the beginning of Chapter 7.

Marco Cantù, Delphi 2009 Handbook

The Status of Delphi

As I've just mentioned, the creation of the CodeGear division and then the acquisition of that division by Embarcadero Technology is providing a new foundation for Delphi, and new funding for investing in the product. Even if not aggressively marketed, and off the radar of most publications Delphi still has millions of active users, both in the ISV sector (where its deployment simplicity wins over frameworks-based solutions) and in business client/server environments, where the stability of an investment is worth more than the *coolness* of the platform.

It is true that the Delphi community is smaller than it was a few years back, and that part of it sticks with older versions of the product, but it is certainly still lively in many countries and has actually got back into a nice mood over the last year.

Why Win32 Matters

If you read most of the IT press, follow blogs, or attend to conferences, it looks that only the latest technology (and the latest fad) are worth working on and everything else is either dead or dying away. This is far from true.

From COBOL development to mainframes, from AS/400 computers to DBF databases, there is a ton of legacy technology that's not only maintained but sees significant new investment. It might be for compatibility reasons, but it is also because companies prefer having a proven and reliable technology for their core business rather than risking their business over the most-recently hyped technology.

This doesn't mean, of course, that following trends, providing higher quality, and empowering users is not important. Quite the opposite. If you can keep delivering additional value on solid foundations, you have a win-win situation. Looking at the Windows side of things, for example, Microsoft has certainly created a lot of value with its growing set of libraries and architectures based on the solid foundation of the .NET framework. On the other hand it is true that, despite the robustness and stability of the core, targeting the latest and best .NET technologies is like focusing on a fast moving target, which is not exactly the best thing when you need to build your client/server application that will take a couple of years to create and you hope will last at least for the next ten years or so.

The other extreme is that of Micro ISV, small tools vendors, shareware developers, Internet utility builders. They are in the situation of short life span products and could certainly benefit for staying on the edge... but even they cannot rely on a large and even changing framework for deploying their applications. They need something that works on each and every Windows box out there. This is a situation in which Delphi shines in comparison to most other solutions. The only real exception is Visual C++, but (if you've never tried to do so) developing in it is not a RAD and OOP experience like .NET and VCL development are.

Visual C++ MFC library is only a thin layer on top of the Windows API, while Delphi provides what has been called a platform, with memory management and runtime services, a pretty large class library with lots of insight into user interface creation, Internet support, and database connectivity, to name only the most noticeable areas of the product.

Delphi does such a good job of producing native looking Windows applications like Skype that there is rarely any visible sign that an application has been developed with Delphi.

This Book

Having introduced the status of Delphi, it is about time to talk about this book. Like my recent "Delphi 2007 Handbook" this is not an all encompassing manual covering all of the features of Delphi, as this would probably require close to 4,000 pages[2].

Despite its size, the focus of this book is uniquely on new features found in Delphi 2009, or at least added to Delphi since Delphi 2007 was released (as BlackFish SQL and some of the dbExpress metadata extensions were included in Delphi 2007 updates).

---

2   This figure (4,000 pages) is my estimate of the amount of material I've written in books about Delphi over the last 13 years. That is, without considering chapters that were included in subsequent editions of my Mastering Delphi series.

Marco Cantù, Delphi 2009 Handbook

16 - Introduction

Needless to say I've given a central role to Unicode and to the core language changes (like generics and anonymous methods), but there is also material on updates to the RTL and the VCL, the improved support for Vista, the latest user interface controls, and an in-depth analysis of the improved dbExpress and new DataSnap 2009 multi-tier capabilities of the product.

As in my past books, there is a lot of theory and overview material mixed with countless examples, readily available online at:

```
http://www.marcocantu.com/dh2009
```

As I mentioned in the "Preface", I've also created short demonstration videos (covering how the program works, not how it was written) for most of the examples in the book, available online and listed at:

```
http://www.marcocantu.com/dh2009/videos.html
```

Having published this book through Lulu.com, I could shape it the way I like most, get the help of editors and reviewers I trust, and (hopefully) make it more valuable for you while keeping the price lower than through a traditional channel. When I published "Delphi 2007 Handbook", it was my first experience of publishing via Lulu.com. Now I've learned from mistakes, streamlined some operations, and have reduced some of the publishing headaches to fully focus on writing for quite some time. I hope you find this effort valuable!

The Author

For those of you new to my books, and for those who haven't read a recent one, my name is Marco Cantù, and I've been in the "Delphi book writing" business since the first version of the product, when I released the original "Mastering Delphi" (a hefty tome of 1,500 pages). This was not my first writing experience, as I had previously written works on Borland C++ and the Object Windows Library.

Over the last few years, beside my continuous involvement in the Delphi community, I've also devoted a lot of time to XML-related technologies and XSLT, with web services (including SOAP and REST implementations), JavaScript and AJAX, and other Web 2.0 technologies. After a break, I got back to writing by self-publishing my books, not only on Delphi, as I ended up also with a volume on social networks.

Marco Cantù, Delphi 2009 Handbook

Beside writing, I keep myself busy with consulting (mostly on applications architectures), helping selling Delphi in Italy, doing code reviews, Delphi mentoring, and general consulting for developers.

I'm also a frequent speaker at Delphi and general developer conferences, including the new online CodeGear conferences. If you are interested in inviting me to speak at a public event or give a training session (on Delphi 2009 or any advanced subject) at your company location, feel free to send me a note over email.

Contact Information

Finally, here is some contact information, with my main web sites (my blog, my not-so-up-do-date personal site, my company site):

```
http://blog.marcocantu.com
http://www.marcocantu.com
http://www.wintech-italia.com
```

My personal web site hosts a specific page devoted to the book, including updates, source code downloads, and other information:

```
http://www.marcocantu.com/dh2009
```

I have an online mailing list based on a Google group you can sign up from my web site. I also run an online newsgroup with a section devoted to discuss my books and their content, available on the web (in the section called "marco cantu") at:

```
http://delphi.newswhat.com
```

Finally, feel free to drop me an email at my public address:

```
marco.cantu@gmail.com
```

Part I: Unicode

The first part of this book focuses on Unicode, the international character encoding standard that Delphi 2009 supports for the first time. The three chapters in this part introduce the topic, describe the actual implementation, and address porting and compatibility issues, respectively.

- Chapter 1: What is Unicode?
- Chapter 2: The Unicode String Type
- Chapter 3: Porting to Unicode

Chapter 1: What Is Unicode?

Unicode is the name of an international character set, encompassing the symbols of all written alphabets of the world, of today and of the past, plus a few more[3]. The Unicode standard (formally referenced as "ISO/IEC 10646") is defined and documented by the Unicode Consortium, and contains over 100,000 characters. Their main web site is located at:

    http://www.unicode.org

As the adoption of Unicode is a central element of Delphi 2009 and there are many issues to address, this chapter focuses only on the theory behind Unicode and other character encodings, while the next one will focus on the key elements of Delphi implementation.

---

[3] Unicode includes also technical symbols, punctuations, and many other characters used in writing text, even if not part of any alphabet.

Characters from the Past: from ASCII to ISO Encodings

The American Standard Code for Information Interchange (ASCII) was developed in the early '60s as a standard encoding of computer characters, encompassing the 26 letters of the English alphabet, both lowercase and uppercase, the numbers, common punctuation symbols, and a number of control characters[4].

ASCII uses a 7 bit encoding system to represent 128 different characters. Only characters between #32 (Space) and #126 (Tilde) have a visual representation, as show in the following table:

	0	1	2	3	4	5	6	7	8	9	10	11	12	13	14	15
0																
16																
32		!	"	#	$	%	&	'	(	)	*	+	,	-	.	/
48	0	1	2	3	4	5	6	7	8	9	:	;	<	=	>	?
64	@	A	B	C	D	E	F	G	H	I	J	K	L	M	N	O
80	P	Q	R	S	T	U	V	W	X	Y	Z	[	\	]	^	_
96	`	a	b	c	d	e	f	g	h	i	j	k	l	m	n	o
112	p	q	r	s	t	u	v	w	x	y	z	{			}	~	

While ASCII was certainly a foundation (with its basic set of 128 characters that are still part of the core of Unicode), it was soon superseded by extended versions that used the 8th bit to add another 128 characters to the set.

Now the problem is that with so many languages around the world, there was no simple way to figure out which other characters to include in the set (at times indicated as ASCII-8). To make the story short, Windows adopts a different set of characters, called a *code page*, depending on your locale configuration and version of Windows. Beside Windows code pages there are many other standards based on a similar *paging* approach.

---

[4] While most control characters have lost any meaning (like the File Separator or the Vertical Tab) some like the Carriage Return (#13), Line Feed (#10), Tab (#9), and Backspace (#8) are still in everyday use.

Chapter 1: What is Unicode? - 23

The most relevant is certainly the ISO 8859 standard, which defines several *regional* sets. The most used set (well, the one used in most Western countries to be a little more precise) is the Latin set, referenced as ISO 8859-1. Even if partially similar, Windows 1252 code page doesn't fully conform to the ISO 8859-1 set. Windows adds extra characters like the € symbol, as we'll see later.

If I keep printing all 8-bit characters, on my computer (that uses Windows 1252 code page by default) I get the following output (yours might be different)[5]:

	0	1	2	3	4	5	6	7	8	9	10	11	12	13	14	15
0																
16																
32		!	"	#	$	%	&	'	(	)	*	+	,	-	.	/
48	0	1	2	3	4	5	6	7	8	9	:	;	<	=	>	?
64	@	A	B	C	D	E	F	G	H	I	J	K	L	M	N	O
80	P	Q	R	S	T	U	V	W	X	Y	Z	[	\	]	^	_
96	`	a	b	c	d	e	f	g	h	i	j	k	l	m	n	o
112	p	q	r	s	t	u	v	w	x	y	z	{	|	}	~	
128	€		‚	ƒ	„	…	†	‡	ˆ	‰	Š	‹	Œ		Ž	
144		'	'	"	"	•	–	—	˜	™	š	›	œ		ž	ÿ
160		¡	¢	£	¤	¥	¦	§	¨	©	ª	«	¬	-	®	¯
176	°	±	²	³	´	µ	¶	·	¸	¹	º	»	¼	½	¾	¿
192	À	Á	Â	Ã	Ä	Å	Æ	Ç	È	É	Ê	Ë	Ì	Í	Î	Ï
208	Ð	Ñ	Ò	Ó	Ô	Õ	Ö	×	Ø	Ù	Ú	Û	Ü	Ý	Þ	ß
224	à	á	â	ã	ä	å	æ	ç	è	é	ê	ë	ì	í	î	ï
240	ð	ñ	ò	ó	ô	õ	ö	÷	ø	ù	ú	û	ü	ý	þ	ÿ

How did I get this and the previous image? Using a simple Delphi 2009 program (called FromAsciiToUnicode) that displays characters on a StringGrid component, initially with the number of the corresponding columns and rows painted on the borders. The program forces some type casts to the AnsiChar type[6] to be able to manage *traditional 8-bit* characters (more on this in the next chapter):

---

5   If the system default is a multi-byte code page, the code of this program becomes meaningless, because most of the characters #$80 through #$FF are lead bytes, which can't be displayed on their own.

6   As we'll see in detail in the next chapter, in Delphi 2009 the Char type has changed and the old Char type of Delphi 1 through Delphi 2007 is now called AnsiChar.

Marco Cantù, Delphi 2009 Handbook

```
procedure TForm30.btnAscii8Click(Sender: TObject);
var
  I: Integer;
begin
  ClearGrid;
  for I := 32 to 255 do
  begin
    StringGrid1.Cells [I mod 16 + 1,
      I div 16 + 1] := AnsiChar (I);
  end;
end;
```

In previous versions of Delphi you could obtain the same output by writing the following simpler version (that uses Char rather than AnsiChar for the conversion):

```
for I := 32 to 255 do
begin
  StringGrid1.Cells [I mod 16 + 1,
    I div 16 + 1] := Char (I);
end;
```

I don't think I really need to tell you how messy the situation is with the various ISO 8859 encodings (there are 16 of them, still unable to cover the more complex alphabets), Windows page codes, multi byte representations to cover Chinese and other languages. With Unicode, this is all behind us, even though the *new* standard has its own complexity and potential problems.

Unicode: An Alphabet for the Entire World

As I mentioned, all this changed with the introduction of Unicode. The idea behind Unicode (which is what makes it simple) is that every single character has its own unique number (or *code point*, to use the proper Unicode term). I don't want to delve into the complete theory of Unicode here (if you want to you can refer to the Unicode book with the complete standard [7]), but only highlight its key points.

---

[7] More information on "The Unicode Standard" book can be found at: http://www.unicode.org/book/aboutbook.html.

Chapter 1: What is Unicode? - 25

In any case, I'll start by extending the FromAsciiToUnicode program, which has a third button that displays those same 256 characters (256 minus the initial 32 control characters and the space character). This is what you'll get (and this doesn't depend on your locale or Windows page code):

	0	1	2	3	4	5	6	7	8	9	10	11	12	13	14	15
0																
16																
32		!	"	#	$	%	&	'	(	)	*	+	,	-	.	/
48	0	1	2	3	4	5	6	7	8	9	:	;	<	=	>	?
64	@	A	B	C	D	E	F	G	H	I	J	K	L	M	N	O
80	P	Q	R	S	T	U	V	W	X	Y	Z	[	\	]	^	_
96	`	a	b	c	d	e	f	g	h	i	j	k	l	m	n	o
112	p	q	r	s	t	u	v	w	x	y	z	{	|	}	~	
128																
144																
160		¡	¢	£	¤	¥	¦	§	¨	©	ª	«	¬	-	®	¯
176	°	±	²	³	´	µ	¶	·	¸	¹	º	»	¼	½	¾	¿
192	À	Á	Â	Ã	Ä	Å	Æ	Ç	È	É	Ê	Ë	Ì	Í	Î	Ï
208	Ð	Ñ	Ò	Ó	Ô	Õ	Ö	×	Ø	Ù	Ú	Û	Ü	Ý	Þ	ß
224	à	á	â	ã	ä	å	æ	ç	è	é	ê	ë	ì	í	î	ï
240	ð	ñ	ò	ó	ô	õ	ö	÷	ø	ù	ú	û	ü	ý	þ	ÿ

You might expect to see exactly the same sequence of characters, as everyone knows that the initial portion of the Unicode character set maps the ASCII sequence, right? This is, in fact, quite wrong! Only the original ASCII-7 set has a perfect match in Unicode, and most of the other extended characters also match, but not all of them. The portion between 128 and 160, in fact, is different (although to be more precise it is different from Microsoft own interpretation of the Latin 1 code page). If you look at the previous image[8], you might notice a collection of seldom used symbols... but there is one that (at least in my area of the world) is quite important, the € currency symbol.

To further test the situation, I've added the following code to the same program, again using the two different characters types, AnsiChar and Char:

---

8   For a more lively demo based on this example see the YouTube video "Delphi does Unicode", that I made available in August 2008, during the period that Tiburòn beta testers were allowed to blog about the new features of the product. Following videos cover other examples in this chapter. The link is:
    http://www.youtube.com/watch?v=BJMakOY8qbw

Marco Cantù, Delphi 2009 Handbook

26 - Chapter 1: What is Unicode?

```
procedure TForm30.btnEuroClick(Sender: TObject);
var
   aChar: AnsiChar;
   uChar: Char;
begin
   aChar := '€';
   uChar := '€';
   ShowMessage ('€ for AnsiChar is ' +
      IntToStr (Ord (aChar)));
   ShowMessage ('€ for UnicodeChar is ' +
      IntToStr (Ord (uChar)));
end;
```

Keep in mind that the way this code snippet is compiled depends on the --codepage compiler option, which (if not specified) defaults to the operating system code page[9]. So if you recompile the same code in a different part of the world, without providing an explicit code page, you'll get a different compiled program (not just different output).

Again, the output you'll get might depend on your settings and look somewhat strange... but we'll have to learn to live with it in the Unicode world. This is what I get:

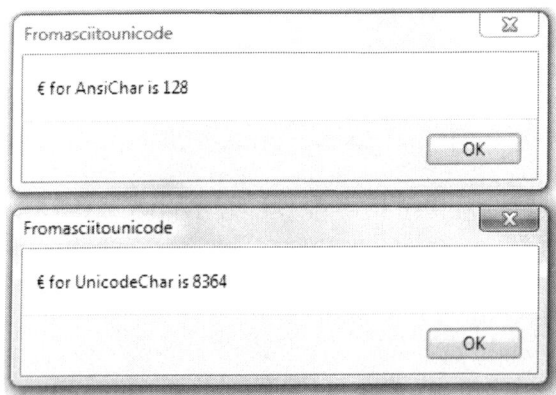

---

[9] The code page used to compile the program affects only the way it manages the AnsiChar character, not the Unicode Char. Unicode characters and strings, in fact, ignore the code page altogether (which is a great reason for using them!)

From Code Points to Bytes

The confusion behind Unicode (what makes it complex) is that there are multiple ways to represent the same code point (or Unicode character numerical value) in terms of actual storage, of physical bytes. If the only way to represent all Unicode code points in a simple and uniform way was to use four bytes for each code point[10] most developers would perceive this as too expensive in memory and processing terms.

One of the options is to use smaller representations with differing number of bytes (at least 1 or 2, but possibly up to 4) for the various code points of the entire Unicode set. This is also called a *variable-length* representation. These encodings have names you've probably heard about, like UTF-8 and UTF-16, and I'll examine them in technical detail in the following section.

There is a common misconception that UTF-16 can map directly all code points with two bytes, but since Unicode defines over 100,000 code points you can easily figure out they won't fit. It is true, however, that at times developers use only a subset of Unicode, to make it fit in a 2-bytes-per-characters fixed-length representation. In the early days, this subset of Unicode was called UCS-2[11], now you often see it referenced as Basic Multilingual Plane (BMP). However, this is only a subset of Unicode (one of many *Planes*).

Unicode Code Points and Graphemes

If I really want to be precise, I should include one more concept beyond that of code points. At times, in fact, multiple code points could be used to represent a single *grapheme* (a visual character). This is generally not a letter, but a combination of letters or letters and symbols. For example, if you have a sequence of the code point representing the Latin letter *a* (#$0061) followed by the code point representing the grave accent (#$0300), this should be displayed as a single accented character.

---

10 In Delphi the Unicode Code Points are represented using the UCS4Char data type, which is covered in the section "32-bit Characters" of Chapter 2.

11 The 2-byte Universal Character Set (UCS-2) is now considered an obsolete character encoding. Still, both UTF-16 and UCS-2, map the code points contained within the BMP in the same way, excluding the 2,048 special surrogate code points.

In Delphi coding terms, if you write the following (also in the FromAsciiToUnicode example):

```
var
  str: String;
begin
  str := #$0061 + #$0300;
  ShowMessage (str);
```

the message will have one single accented character:

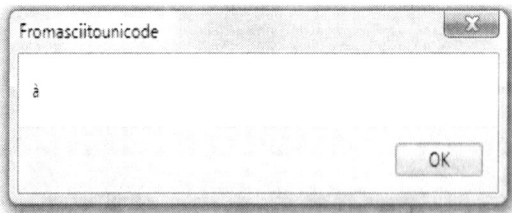

In this case we have two Chars, representing two code points, but only one grapheme. The fact is that while in the Latin alphabet you can use a specific Unicode code point to represent the given grapheme (*letter a with grave accent is code point $00E0*), in other alphabets combining Unicode code points is the only way to obtain a given grapheme (and the correct output).

Unicode Transformation Formats (UTF)

Few people know that the very common "UTF" term is the acronym of Unicode Transformation Format. These are algorithmic *mappings*, part of the Unicode standard, that map each code point (the absolute numeric representation of a character) to a unique sequence of bytes representing the given character. Notice that the mappings can be used in both directions, converting back and forth between different representations.

The standard defines three of these formats, depending on how many bits are used to represent the initial part of the set (the initial 128 characters): 8, 16, or 32. It is interesting to notice that all three forms of encodings need at most 4 bytes of data for each code point.

- **UTF-8** transforms characters into a variable-length encoding of 1 to 4 bytes. UTF-8 is popular for HTML and similar protocols, because it is quite compact when most characters (like tags in HTML) fall within the ASCII subset[12].

- **UTF-16** is popular in many operating systems (including Windows) and development environments. It is quite convenient as most characters fit in two bytes, reasonably compact and fast to process.
- **UTF-32** makes a lot of sense for processing (all code points have the same length), but is memory consuming and has limited use in practice.

A problem relating to multi-byte representations (UTF-16 and UTF-32) is which of the bytes comes first? According to the standard, all forms are allowed, so you can have a UTF-16 BE (big-endian[13]) or LE (little-endian), and the same for UTF-32.

Looking at UTF-16

How do we create a table of Unicode characters like those I displayed earlier for ASCII ones? We can start by displaying code points in the Basic Multilingual Plane above 32 (the usual control characters) and excluding what are called surrogate pairs. Not all numeric values are true UTF-16 code points, since there are some non-valid numerical values for characters (called *surrogates*) used to form a *paired code* and represent code points above 65535.

As displaying a 256 * 256 grid was quite hard, I've actually kept the grid as is and added a TreeView control on the side to let you pick an arbitrary block of 256 code points to display. I've used a TreeView as there are 256 sections (including the surrogates), so I decided to group them at two levels:

```
▲ Char #0 [ ]/Char #3840 ҿ
    Char #0 [ ]/Char #255 [ÿ]
    Char #256 [Ā]/Char #511 [ǿ]
    Char #512 [Ǡ]/Char #767 [˿]
    Char #768 []/Char #1023 [ϯ]
```

---

12 Originally UTF-8 was represented by 1 to 6 bytes, to represent any theoretical Unicode code point of the future, but it was later but restricted to use only the formal Unicode definition up to code point 10FFFF. More information, including a map of the different lengths of code points in UTF-8, on http://en.wikipedia.org/wiki/Utf-8.

13 The big-endian byte serialization has the most significant byte first, the little-endian byte serialization has the least significant byte first. As we'll see soon, the bytes serialization is often marked in files with a header called Byte Order Mark (BOM).

30 - Chapter 1: What is Unicode?

When the program starts, it fills the TreeView with 16 higher level groups, each containing 16 second level subgroups, thus providing 256 items, each of which can display a grid with 256 characters, for a total of 64K code points (again, not considering those excluded):

```
procedure TForm30.FormCreate(Sender: TObject);
var
  nTag: Integer;
  I: Integer;
  J: Integer;
  topNode: TTreeNode;
begin
  for I := 0 to 15 do
  begin
    nTag := I * 16;
    topNode := TreeView1.Items.Add (nil,
      GetCharDescr (nTag * 256) + '/' +
      GetCharDescr ((nTag + 15)* 256));
    for J := nTag to nTag + 15 do
    begin
      if (J < 216) or (J > 223) then
      begin
        TreeView1.Items.AddChildObject (
          topNode,
          GetCharDescr(J*256) + '/' +
            GetCharDescr(J*256+255),
          Pointer (J));
      end
      else
      begin
        TreeView1.Items.AddChildObject (
          topNode,
          'Surrogate Code Points',
          Pointer (J));
      end;
    end;
  end;
end;

// helper function
function GetCharDescr (nChar: Integer): string;
begin
  if nChar < 32 then
    Result := 'Char #' + IntToStr (nChar) + ' [ ]'
  else
    Result := 'Char #' + IntToStr (nChar) +
      ' [' + Char (nChar) + ']';
end;
```

As you can see in the code above, every node of the TreeView gets the number with its page number or starting position as its data field (generally a pointer). This is used whenever you select a second-level element in the TreeView (that is a node that has a parent node) to compute the starting point of the grid:

```
procedure TForm30.TreeView1Click(Sender: TObject);
var
  I, nStart: Integer;
begin
  if (TreeView1.Selected.Parent <> nil) then
  begin
    // a second level node
    nCurrentTab := Integer(TreeView1.Selected.Data);
    nStart := nCurrentTab * 256;
    for I := 0 to 255 do
    begin
      StringGrid1.Cells [I mod 16 + 1, I div 16 + 1] :=
        IfThen (I + nStart >= 32, Char (I + nStart), '');
    end;
  end;
end;
```

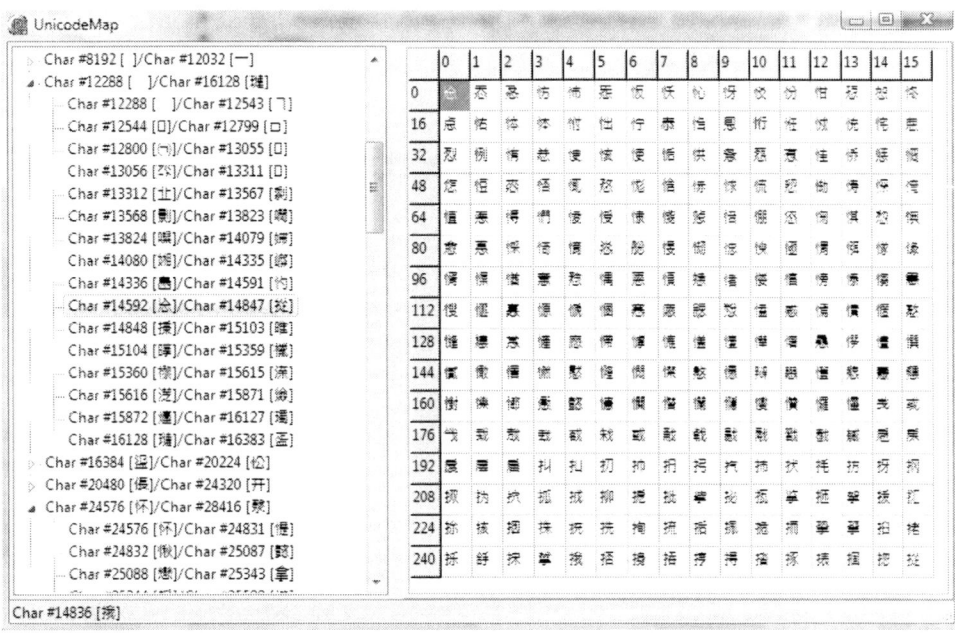

Notice the use of the IfThen function to optionally replace the initial 32 characters with an empty string. The starting point of the current TreeView item is kept in the nCurrentTab form field. This information is needed to display the code point and its value as a user moves the mouse over the cells of the grid:

```
procedure TForm30.StringGrid1MouseMove(Sender: TObject;
  Shift: TShiftState; X, Y: Integer);
var
  gc: TGridCoord;
  nChar: Integer;
begin
  gc := StringGrid1.MouseCoord(X, Y);
  nChar := (gc.Y - 1) * 16 + (gc.X - 1);
  StatusBar1.SimpleText :=
    GetCharDescr (nCurrentTab * 256 + nChar);
end;
```

As you use the program and browse the various pages of code points in the various alphabets, you'll often see characters that aren't displayed properly. This is most probably due to the font you are using as not all fonts provide a proper representation for the entire Unicode character set. That's why I've added to the UnicodeMap program the ability to pick a different font (something achieved by double clicking on the grid). You can find more information about this issue in the section "Unicode and Fonts and APIs" later in this chapter.

Unicode Code Point Descriptions

On the Unicode Consortium web site, you can find a lot of information, including a text file with a written description of a large number of code points (most of them excluding the unified ideographs for Chinese, Japanese, and Korean). I've used this file to create an extended version of the UnicodeMap program, called UnicodeData. The user interface is based on the same structure, but the program reads and parses the UnicodeData.txt[14] file, and adds any available character description to the status bar when moving over the grid:

---

14 The URL for this file is http://unicode.org/Public/UNIDATA/UnicodeData.txt. There is second much larger file (I've not used in the demo) for the unified ideographs, avauilable at http://www.unicode.org/Public/UNIDATA/Unihan.zip.

Chapter 1: What is Unicode? - 33

Parsing the file is not terribly simple, as not all of the Unicode symbols are present. I resorted to creating a StringList with information in the format *charnumber=description*, extracted from the file. The original file uses semicolons for separating fields and a newline character (alone, not combined with line feed) for each record. After loading the entire file into a string, I use the following code to parse it and move the two descriptions to the information section (as at times only one or the other description is relevant):

```
nPos := 1;
// now parse the unicode data
while nPos < Length (strData) - 2 do
begin
  strSingleLine := ReadToNewLine (strData, nPos);
  nLinePos := 1;
  strNumber := ReadToSemicolon (
    strSingleLine, nLinePos);
  strDescr1 := ReadToSemicolon (
    strSingleLine, nLinePos);
  Skip8Semi (strSingleLine, nLinePos);
  strDescr2 := ReadToSemicolon (
    strSingleLine, nLinePos);

  sUnicodeDescr.Add(strNumber + '=' +
    strDescr1 + ' ' + strDescr2);
end;
```

This code could be executed in the message handler of a `wm_user` message posted to the main form in its `OnCreate` event handler, to let the system start up the main form before doing this lengthy operation. The status bar is updated in the loop above to inform users of the current progress. The loop has some further termination code, to skip parsing characters above $FFFF.

The information stored in the string list is extracted when you have to display the description of a character, with this additional code of the `StringGrid1MouseMove` method:

```
if Assigned (sUnicodeDescr) then
begin
  strChar := IntToHex (nChar, 4);
  nIndex := sUnicodeDescr.IndexOfName(strChar);
  if nIndex >= 0 then
    StatusBar1.SimpleText := StatusBar1.SimpleText +
      ' -- ' + sUnicodeDescr.ValueFromIndex [nIndex];
end;
```

Having information about the code points, the program could also create a more logical element tree. This is not too difficult for the various alphabets, but most symbols have a generic name with no indication that they are part of a given group. Coming out with a proper grouping of all Unicode code points is possible from reading the various documents[15], but not parsing the `UnicodeData.txt` file.

Byte Order Mark

Files storing Unicode characters often use an initial header, called Byte Order Mark (BOM) as a signature indicating the Unicode format being used and the byte order form (BE or LE). The following table provides a summary of the various BOM, which can be 2, 3, or 4 bytes long:

00 00 FE FF	UTF-32, big-endian
FF FE 00 00	UTF-32, little-endian
FE FF	UTF-16, big-endian
FF FE	UTF-16, little-endian
EF BB BF	UTF-8

We'll see in the next chapter how Delphi manages the BOM within its streaming classes. The BOM appears at the very beginning of a file with the actual Unicode data immediately following it. So a UTF-8 file with the content *AB* contains five hexadecimal values (3 for the BOM, 2 for the letters):

```
EF BB BF 41 42
```

Unicode in Win32

Since the early days, the Win32 API (which dates back to Windows NT) has included support for Unicode characters. Most Windows API functions have two versions available, an Ansi version marked with the letter A and a widestring version marked with the letter W.

---

15 As we'll see in the next chapter, the new Character unit includes methods for checking whether a Unicode code point is a symbol, a punctuation mark, a space...

As an example, see the following lines from Windows.pas of Delphi 2007:

```
function GetWindowText(hWnd: HWND; lpString: PChar;
  nMaxCount: Integer): Integer; stdcall;
function GetWindowTextA(hWnd: HWND; lpString: PAnsiChar;
  nMaxCount: Integer): Integer; stdcall;
function GetWindowTextW(hWnd: HWND; lpString: PWideChar;
  nMaxCount: Integer): Integer; stdcall;

function GetWindowText; external user32
  name 'GetWindowTextA';
function GetWindowTextA; external user32
  name 'GetWindowTextA';
function GetWindowTextW; external user32
  name 'GetWindowTextW';
```

The declarations are identical but use either `PAnsiChar` or `PWideChar` to refer to strings. Notice that the plain version with no string format indication is just a placeholder for one of them, invariably the 'A' version in past versions of Delphi (where this code is taken from), while in Delphi 2009 (as we'll see) the default becomes the 'W' version. Basically, each API function that takes strings as parameters has two separate versions, while all of the functions that do not refer to strings have a single one, of course.

Windows 95 (and following versions Windows 98 and ME) implemented the A functions and provided the W functions as aliases that do Wide to Ansi conversion. This means those functions generally don't support Unicode, with some exceptions like `TextOutW` (which is implemented as a real Unicode function on Windows 95/98/ME). On the other hand, Windows NT and following versions based on it (Windows 2000, XP, and Vista) implement the W functions, and provide the A functions as aliases doing the Ansi to Wide conversion (at times, slowing down operations).

Even in past versions of Delphi you could pass a WideString value to a 'W' API, by calling it explicitly. For example, the UnicodeWinApi program (which can be compiled both in Delphi2007 and Delphi 2009), has the code:

```
procedure TForm30.btnMessageAClick(Sender: TObject);
begin
  MessageBoxA (Handle, 'देविनाड          की       ','Caption ',   MB_OK);
end;

procedure TForm30.btnMessageWClick(Sender: TObject);
var
  देन : WideString;
begin
  देन := 'देविक      न ';
  MessageBoxW (Handle, PWChar (देन ), 'Caption',   MB_OK);
end;
```

The first call to the ANSI version of `MessageBox` displays a message made of a sequence of question mark symbols, while the second (displayed here) has the correct output[16]:

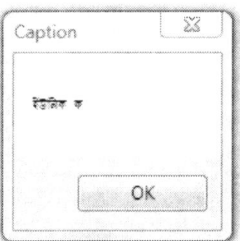

Notice the use of Unicode characters in strings within the source code and also to name a local variable. This was already supported in Delphi 2006 and 2007 provided you saved the source code file in a Unicode format (UTF-16 or UTF-8). A further call paints some text in an uncommon alphabet on the form, with the output displayed below. This is the source code, taken from the editor:

```
procedure TForm30.btnTextOutClick(Sender: TObject);
var
  ws: WideString;
begin
  ws := 'ইউনিক ক';
  Canvas.Font.Size := 20;
  TextOutW(Canvas.Handle, 104, 224, PWChar(ws), Length (ws));
end;
```

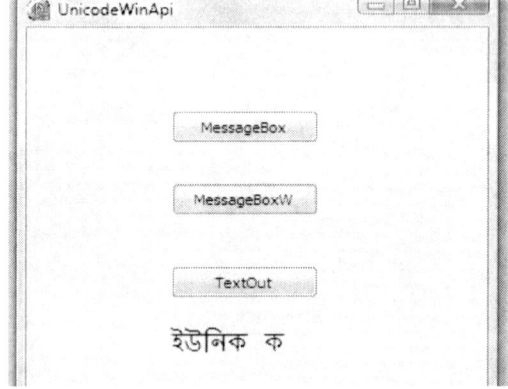

---

16   The sentence is written in Bangla and means "What is Unicode", at least according to http://www.unicode.org/standard/translations/bangla.html. For the variable name I used part of the sentence... which probably (or hopefully) means nothing!

There are two more important facts to keep in mind about strings in the Win32 API. The first is that some of the older operating systems (like Windows 95) offer only a partial implementation of the Wide API functions. The second is that COM used a different approach, with strings in the BSTR format, mapped in Delphi to the non-reference-counted WideString type[17].

Unicode API Call Speed

You might wonder if using Unicode when calling the Windows API would be slower or faster than using the plain "A" API. Needless to say I had the same doubt, with Unicode causing some extra memory load, I was wondering if this move really made sense for programs that don't need Unicode.

In theory, as the only real implementation of the Windows API for Vista and XP is the Unicode-based one, we should expect a faster execution, as the code will skip a string conversion during the call. So I tried to see with the following code, which is part of the UniApiSpeed example:

```
procedure TForm30.btnUserNameClick(Sender: TObject);
var
  I:Integer;
  nSize: DWORD;
  t1: TDateTime;
  str: string;
  pch: PChar;
begin
  nSize := 100;
  SetLength (str, nSize);
  pch := PChar (str);
  t1 := Now;
  for I := 1 to 10000 do
  begin
    GetUserName (pch, nSize);
  end;
  t1 := Now - t1;
  Memo1.Lines.Add ((Sender as TButton).Caption + ' ' +
    FormatDateTime ('ss.zzz', t1));
```

---

17 Some more information about the WideString type and its relationship with COM is available in the section "Unicode Before Delphi 2009" at the end of this chapter. COM support still relies on the WideString type in Delphi 2009, so little has changed in that area of the product.

I compiled the same program in Delphi 7 and in Delphi 2009 and I noticed that the results were almost identical. I tried a similar loop based on the SetWindowText API call, and in this case I noticed a very odd effect. If I run the application in the debugger, it takes a 15% less time than the Delphi 7 counterpart, if I run it stand alone it becomes much slower. The problem, though is that if the program spends any time painting the caption over and over, its results will be totally obscured.

These two tests are probably not very pertinent. I should have tried with many more other API calls to be able to make a definitive statement, but this indicates that by moving to Unicode you can have a similar or slightly improved speed in the API calls. You don't gain a lot (at least while using non-Unicode characters), but you don't incur any extra overhead either[18].

UnicodeString Parameters in API calls

Although most Windows API functions taking a string as parameter are declared in the Windows unit with a PChar parameter, there are some exceptions to this rule.

The GetTextExtentPoint32, ExtTextOut, LoadKeyboardLayout, DrawText, SetWindowText, LoadCursor, WinHelp, and HtmlHelp API declaration have overloaded (and inlined) versions taking a UnicodeString parameter. I guess this might help to apply the proper conversion in case you are passing a string, any string, to them (as you'll better understand after reading about the different string types in Delphi 2009, in the next chapter).

It is not clear why these functions have this special treatment compared with the dozens of other Windows API functions that have PChar parameters. One of the reasons might be the increased compatibility between VCL for Win32 and VCL for .NET if the string type is used rather than a PChar.

---

18 As we'll see in the next chapter there is indeed a potential major overhead related with implicit string conversions done by the Delphi compiler. This is one of the topics covered in the section "Conversions Slow Down the Code" of Chapter 2.
Also notice that some of the Ansi-related string functions were implemented in Delphi 2007 by calling Windows API routines that required conversions to and then back from Unicode. Calls to these routines in Delphi 2009 should be much faster, as detailed by Jan Goyvaerts on this blog at: http://www.micro-isv.asia/2008/09/speed-benefits-of-using-the-native-win32-string-type.

Unicode and Fonts and APIs

Another important fact to keep in mind is that whilst Windows does indeed support Unicode, it does so in different ways in different versions. The Windows 9x (an acronym meaning 95, 98, or ME – Millennium Edition) series has limited support for Unicode. If you have Windows 2000, Windows XP, or some of the server operating system versions, you can take advantage of the Supplemental Language Support. This can be installed in the Regional and Language options of the Control Panel. This extra support comes mostly in the form of extended (or Unicode-enabled) fonts. Vista has extended Unicode support by default.

When Windows XP and Vista need to display a Unicode code point, and this code point is not available in the current font, at times they perform "font substitution", that is they display the code point in a different font[19]. This depends on the text display API being called (DrawText, TextOut, ExtTextOut behave differently), on the font you are using, and on the given code points. That's why using a complete Unicode font is a good idea[20].

If you are interested in more details, you can have a look at the UniFontSubst example, that basically draws a set of strings with different fonts and different API calls on its form. The program uses three standard fonts (Times New Roman, Tahoma, and Arial) displayed top to bottom, and the three API calls mentioned above displayed left to right. This is one of the three portions (there is one for each font) of the painting code:

```
Canvas.Font.Name := 'Times New Roman';
aRect := Rect(10, 60, 250, 100);
DrawText(Canvas.Handle, PChar (str1), Length (str1),
   aRect, DT_LEFT or DT_SINGLELINE or DT_EXPANDTABS
   or DT_NOPREFIX);
TextOut (Canvas.Handle, 260, 60, PChar (str1),
   Length (str1));
aRect := Rect(510, 60, 750, 100);
ExtTextOut (Canvas.Handle, 510, 60, 0, aRect,
   PChar (str1), Length (str1), nil);
```

---

19 You can find a lot of detailed information about font substitution done by different API calls in this Microsoft article:
http://www.microsoft.com/globaldev/getwr/steps/wrg_font.mspx

20 For information and availability of Unicode fonts for Windows, you can refer to Alan Wood's Unicode Resources (which dates a few years back, but is kept up to date) at:
http://www.alanwood.net/unicode/fonts.html.

40 - Chapter 1: What is Unicode?

The string is defined using a sequence of consecutive Unicode code points starting from a random position:

```
var
  str1: string;
  nPoint: Word;
  I: Integer;
begin
  nPoint := 32 + random (1024*64 - 32 - numberOfChars);
  if (nPoint >= $D800 - numberOfChars) and
    (nPoint <= $DFFF) then
  begin
    // retry and skip
    PaintFonts;
    Exit;
  end;

  str1 := ConvertFromUtf32(UCS4Char (nPoint));
  for I := 1 to numberOfChars do
    str1 := str1 + ConvertFromUtf32(
      UCS4Char (nPoint + I));
```

When running the program you can paint the form once or turn on a timer for automatic consecutive redraws. In most cases, you'll see the same string displayed 9 times. Quite often, though, you'll see that the text is not displayed properly when using some fonts (most commonly Tahoma) but is replaced by square blocks. In other cases, you'll see that some of the API calls (`DrawText` in particular) can display the code points anyway, but by replacing the font with another one. Below is a screen shot in which you can see both cases at once:

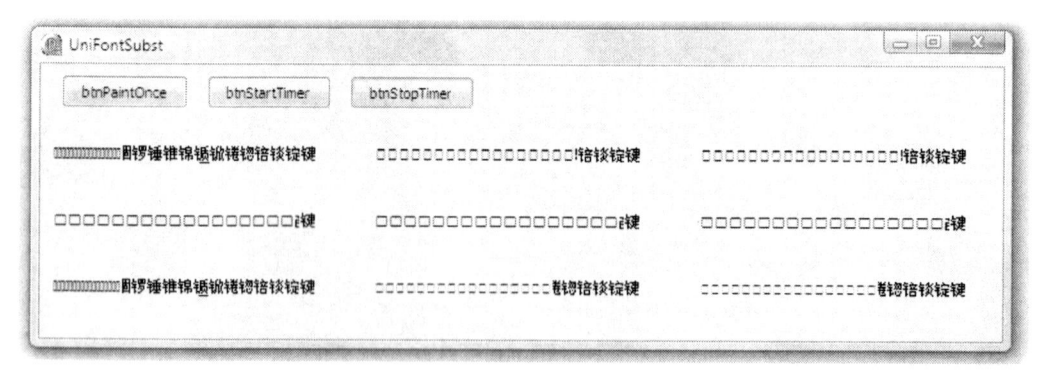

Unicode Before Delphi 2009

If Unicode support in the core of the language (for the string type) and throughout the runtime library and visual component library (VCL) is certainly a brand new feature in Delphi 2009, partial support for Unicode has been part of Delphi for many years now.

For many versions, mostly to support COM, Delphi had a WideChar data type (16-bit characters) and a WideString data type (strings made of WideChar characters). However, the WideString type was not (and still is not) reference counted and is far less efficient than regular Delphi strings. It is merely an encapsulation of the COM BSTR data type[21].

There are also several units and classes with specific support for WideStrings, including the feature-rich WideStrUtils unit (which also includes a good amount of UTF-8-related functions), the `TWideStringList` class, and extensive WideString support in the `TDataSet` and `TField` classes.

What's Next

I don't want to delve into the details of features that change considerably in Delphi 2009 here and we'll have time to cover them later in the book. Now it is time to start looking at the actual implementation for Unicode strings, the new UnicodeString type. There are many changes in using strings in Delphi 2009, that's why the next chapter is one of the longest in the book.

---

21 WideString is a COM BSTR that uses UTF-16 in Windows 2000 and above, while it is based on UCS-2 in Win9x and NT. Some more details are available at: http://msdn.microsoft.com/en-us/library/ms221069.aspx

Chapter 2: The Unicode String Type

As you certainly know, one of the most far-reaching new features of Delphi 2009 is the introduction of a new string type, UnicodeString, which is also the type aliased by the string type. Every time you write "string" in your code, you are now in fact referring to UnicodeString, whilst in past versions of Delphi (except Delphi 1) you were referring to AnsiString.

Along with Char being an alias of WideChar, this is a significant change, affecting your entire code base. That's why a single chapter won't be enough to explain everything you need to know. I'll cover all of the new string type features here, but leave the many and unavoidable issues related with porting existing Delphi code to a Unicode-enabled version of the CodeGear compiler to the next chapter.

Marco Cantù, Delphi 2009 Handbook

From AnsiChar to WideChar

For some time, Delphi included two separate data types representing characters:

- **AnsiChar**, with an 8-bit representation (accounting for 256 different symbols), interpreted depending on your code page;
- **WideChar**, with a 16-bit representation (accounting for 64K different symbols)[22].

In this respect, nothing has changed in Delphi 2009. What is different is that the Char type used to be an alias of AnsiChar and is now an alias of WideChar. Every time the compiler sees Char in your code, it reads WideChar. Notice that there is no way to change this new compiler default[23].

This is quite a change, impacting a lot of source code and with many ramifications. For example, the `PChar` pointer is now an alias of `PWideChar`, rather than `PAnsiChar`, as it used to be. We'll see how this affects the calls to Windows API functions in a later section in this chapter.

Char as an Ordinal Type

The new *large* Char type is still an ordinal type, so you can use `Inc` and `Dec` on it, write `for` loops with a Char counter, and the like.

```
var
   ch: Char;
begin
   ch := 'a';
   Inc (ch, 100);
   ...
   for ch := #32 to High(Char) do
      str := str + ch;
```

---

22 WideChar is simply a 16-bit unsigned integer without any specific character encoding scheme attached. When used in a UnicodeString, though, a WideChar can be interpreted as a surrogate, so that two WideChar can be bound together to represent a single Unicode code point. More about this in the section "UnicodeString and Unicode".

These code snippets are part of different methods of the TestChar example. The only thing that might get you into some (limited) trouble is when you are declaring a set based on the entire Char type:

```
var
  CharSet = set of Char;
begin
  CharSet := ['a', 'b', 'c'];
  if 'a' in charSet then
    ...
```

In this case the compiler will assume you are porting existing code to Delphi 2009, decide to consider that Char as an AnsiChar (as a set can only have 256 elements at most[24]) and issue a warning message:

```
W1050 WideChar reduced to byte char in set expressions.
Consider using 'CharInSet' function in 'SysUtils' unit.
```

The code will probably work as expected, but not all existing code will easily map, as it is not possible to obtain a set of all the characters any more. If this is what you need, you'll have to change your algorithm (possibly following what's suggested by the warning, but I'll get to that in ample detail in the section "Watch Out for Set of Char" of the next chapter, focused on porting existing code to Delphi 2009).

If what you are looking for, instead, is to suppress the warnings (compiling the five lines of code above causes two of them) you can write:

```
var
  charSet: set of AnsiChar; // suppress warning
begin
  charSet := ['a', 'b', 'c'];
  if AnsiChar('a') in charSet then // suppress warning
    ...
```

---

23 As with the string type, the Char type is mapped to a specific data type in a fixed and hard-coded way. Developers have asked for a compiler directive to be able to switch, but this would cause a nightmare in terms of QA, support, package compatibility, and much more. You still have a choice, as you can convert your code to use a specific type, such as AnsiChar.

24 If you try declaring a large set of, say, a range of Integers (like I did in some commented code of the CharTest example) you'll get the error:
    E2028 Sets may have at most 256 elements.

Converting with Chr

Also notice that you can not only convert a numeric value to a character using a type cast to AnsiChar or WideChar but also rely on the classic Pascal technique, the use of the Chr *compiler magic* function (which can be considered as the opposite of Ord). This standard magic function has been expanded to take a word as parameter, rather than a byte.

Notice, though, that unlike character literals (covered in the section "String and Character Literals" later in this chapter), calls to Chr are now always interpreted in the Unicode realm. So if you port code like:

```
Chr (128)
```

from Delphi 2007 to Delphi 2009 you might be in for a surprise. If you use #128, instead, you might get a different result or not depending on your code page.

32-bit Characters

Although the default Char type is now mapped to WideChar, it is worth noticing that Delphi also defines a 4-byte character type, UCS4Char, defined in the System unit as:

```
type
  UCS4Char = type LongWord;
```

While this type definition and the corresponding one for UCS4String (defined as an array of UCS4Char) were already in Delphi 2007, the relevance of the UCS4Char data type in Delphi 2009 comes from the fact it is now used significantly in several RTL routines, including those of the new Character unit discussed next.

The New Character Unit

To better support the new Unicode characters (and also Unicode strings, of course) Delphi 2009 introduces a brand new RTL unit, called Character[25]. The unit defines the `TCharacter` sealed class, which is basically a collection of static class functions[26], plus a number of global routines mapped to the public (and some of the private) functions of the class.

The unit also defines two interesting enumerated types. The first is called `TUnicodeCategory` and maps the various characters in broad categories like control, space, uppercase or lowercase letter, decimal number, punctuation, math symbol, and many more. The second enumeration is called `TUnicodeBreak` and defines the family of the various spaces, hyphen, and breaks.

The `TCharacter` sealed class has over 40 methods that either work on a stand-alone character or one within a string for:

- Getting the numeric representation of the character (`GetNumericValue`).
- Asking for the category (`GetUnicodeCategory`) or checking it against one of the various categories (`IsLetterOrDigit`, `IsLetter`, `IsDigit`, `IsNumber`, `IsControl`, `IsWhiteSpace`, `IsPunctuation`, `IsSymbol`, and `IsSeparator`)
- Checking if it is lowercase or uppercase (`IsLower` and `IsUpper`) or converting it (`ToLower` and `ToUpper`)
- Verifying if it is part of a UTF-16 surrogate pair (`IsSurrogatePair`, `IsSurrogate`, `IsLowSurrogate`, and `IsHighSurrogate`)
- Converting it to and from UTF32 (`ConvertFromUtf32` and `ConvertToUtf32`)

The global functions are almost an exact match of these static class methods, some of which correspond to existing Delphi RTL functions even if generally with different names. There are overloads of some of the basic RTL func-

---

[25] The "Character" name for a unit seems somewhat out of sync with the general naming rules adopted by Delphi's RTL, where "Utils" is often the at the end of collection of functions. It maps to the fact that there is indeed a class inside the unit, called `TCharacter`, although it is a quite a strange class.

[26] For the definition of static class methods and sealed classes see, among other sources, my Delphi 2007 Handbook.

Marco Cantù, Delphi 2009 Handbook

48 - Chapter 2: The Unicode String Type

tions working on characters, with extended versions that call the proper Unicode-enabled code. For example, in the CharTest program I've added the following snippet that tries to convert an accented letter to uppercase:

```
var
   ch1: Char;
   ch2: AnsiChar;
begin
   ch1 := 'ù';
   Memo1.Lines.Add ('WideChar');
   Memo1.Lines.Add ('UpCase ù: ' + UpCase(ch1));
   Memo1.Lines.Add ('ToUpper ù: ' + ToUpper (ch1));

   ch2 := 'ù';
   Memo1.Lines.Add ('AnsiChar');
   Memo1.Lines.Add ('UpCase ù: ' + UpCase(ch2));
   Memo1.Lines.Add ('ToUpper ù: ' + ToUpper (ch2));
```

The traditional Delphi code (the UpCase on the AnsiChar version) handles ASCII characters only, so it won't convert the character[27]. The same is still true (probably for backward compatibility reasons) if you pass a WideChar to it. The ToUpper function works properly (it ends up calling the CharUpper function of the Windows API):

```
WideChar
UpCase ù: ù
ToUpper ù: Ù
AnsiChar
UpCase ù: ù
ToUpper ù: Ù
```

Notice you can keep your existing Delphi code, with the UpCase call on a Char, and it will keep the standard Delphi behavior.

For a better demo of the specific Unicode-related features introduced by the Character unit, you can see the btnUTF16Click method of the CharTest example, which defines a string as[28]:

```
var
   str1: string;
begin
   str1 := '1.' + #9 + ConvertFromUtf32 (128) +
      ConvertFromUtf32($1D11E);
```

---

[27] The same is true for the UpperCase function, which handles only ASCII, while AnsiUpperCase handles everything in Unicode, despite the name.

[28] Unicode code point $1D11E is *musical symbol G clef*.

The program then makes the following tests (all returning True) on the various characters of the string:

```
TCharacter.IsNumber(str1, 1)
TCharacter.IsPunctuation (str1, 2)
TCharacter.IsWhiteSpace (str1, 3)
TCharacter.IsControl(str1, 4)
TCharacter.IsSurrogate(str1, 5)
```

Finally notice that the IsLeadChar function of SysUtils has been modified to handle Unicode surrogate pairs, as well as other related functions used to move to the next character of a string and the like. I'll use some of these functions while working with a string with a surrogate pair in the section "UnicodeString and Unicode."

Of String and UnicodeString

The change in the definition of the Char type is important because it is tied to the change in the definition of the string type. Unlike characters, though, string is mapped to a brand new data type that didn't exist before, called UnicodeString. As we'll see, its internal representation is also quite different from that of the *classic AnsiString*[29] type.

As there was already a WideString type in the language, representing strings based on the WideChar type, why bother defining a new data type? WideString was (and still is) not reference counted and is extremely poor in terms of performance and flexibility (for example, it uses the Windows global memory allocator rather than the native FastMM4).

Like AnsiString, UnicodeString is reference counted, uses copy-on-write semantics and performs quite well. Unlike AnsiString, UnicodeString uses two-bytes per character[30] and is based on UTF-16.

---

29 I'm using the specific terms *classic AnsiString* type, to refer to the string type as it used to work from Delphi 2 until Delphi 2007. AnsiString type is still part of Delphi 2009, but it has a modified behavior, so when referring to its past structure I'll use the term *classic AnsiString*.

30 Actually UTF-16 is a variable length encoding, and at times UnicodeString uses two WideChar surrogate elements (that is, four bytes) to represent a single Unicode code point.

The string type is now mapped to UnicodeString in a hard-coded way as is the Char type and for the same reasons. There is no compiler directive or other trick to change that. If you have code that needs to continue to use the old string type, just replace it with an explicit declaration of the AnsiString type.

The Internal Structure of Strings

One of the key changes related to the new UnicodeString type is its internal representation. This new representation, however, is shared by all reference-counted string types, UnicodeString and AnsiString, but not by the non-reference counted string types, including the ShortString[31] and WideString types.

The representation of the *classic AnsiString* type was the following:

-8	-4	String reference address
Ref count	length	First char of string

The first element (counting backwards from the beginning of the string itself) is the Pascal string length, the second element is the reference count. In Delphi 2009 the representation for reference-counted strings becomes:

-12	-10	-8	-4	String reference address
Code page	Elem size	Ref count	length	First char of string

Beside the length and reference count, the new fields represent the element size and the code page. While the element size is used to discriminate between AnsiString and UnicodeString, the code page makes sense in particular for the AnsiString type (as it works in Delphi 2009), as the UnicodeString type has the fixed code page 1200.

---

31 ShortString is the name of the traditional Pascal string type, a string of AnsiChar limited to 255 characters because it uses a length byte as first element. The ShortString type was the original string definition in Delphi 1. Since Delphi 2 introduced reference-counted long strings, the use of ShortString has declined, but there are specific cases in which they are nice to use and perform better.

A corresponding supporting data structure is declared in the implementation[32] section of System unit as:

```
type
  PStrRec = ^StrRec;
  StrRec = packed record
    codePage: Word;
    elemSize: Word;
    refCnt: Longint;
    length: Longint;
  end;
```

With the overhead of a string going from 8 bytes to 12 bytes, one might wonder if a more compact representation wouldn't be more effective, although the newer fields are more compact than the traditional ones (that could be changed only at the expense of compatibility).

This is a classic trade-off between memory and speed: by storing data in different memory locations (and not using portions of a single location) you gain extra runtime speed, although this is costing extra memory for each and every string you create.

While in the past you had to use low-level pointer-based code to access to the reference count, the Delphi 2009 RTL adds some handy functions to access the various string metadata:

```
function StringElementSize(const S: UnicodeString): Word;
function StringCodePage(const S: UnicodeString): Word;
function StringRefCount(const S: UnicodeString): Longint;
```

There is also a new helper function in the SysUtils unit, called ByteLength, that returns the size of a UnicodeString in bytes ignoring the StringElementSize attributes (so, oddly enough, it won't work with string types other than UnicodeString).

As an example, you can create a string and ask for some information about it, as I did in the StringTest example:

```
var
  str1: string;
begin
  str1 := 'foo';
  Memo1.Lines.Add ('SizeOf: ' + IntToStr (SizeOf (str1)));
```

---

32 As it is in the implementation section you cannot use it in your code, which is understandable for an internal data structure that's implementation specific and subject to change. There are helper functions to access the information you'll generally need to use.

52 - Chapter 2: The Unicode String Type

```
    Memo1.Lines.Add ('Length: ' + IntToStr (Length (str1)));
    Memo1.Lines.Add ('StringElementSize: ' +
      IntToStr (StringElementSize (str1)));
    Memo1.Lines.Add ('StringRefCount: ' +
      IntToStr (StringRefCount (str1)));
    Memo1.Lines.Add ('StringCodePage: ' +
      IntToStr (StringCodePage (str1)));
    if StringCodePage (str1) = DefaultUnicodeCodePage then
      Memo1.Lines.Add ('Is Unicode');
    Memo1.Lines.Add ('Size in bytes: ' +
      IntToStr (Length (str1) * StringElementSize (str1)));
    Memo1.Lines.Add ('ByteLength: ' +
      IntToStr (ByteLength (str1)));
```

This program produced output similar to the following:

```
SizeOf: 4
Length: 3
StringElementSize: 2
StringRefCount: -1
StringCodePage: 1200
Is Unicode
Size in bytes: 6
ByteLength: 6
```

The code page returned by a UnicodeString is 1200, a number stored in the global variable `DefaultUnicodeCodePage`. In the code above (and its output) you can clearly notice that there isn't a direct call to determine the length of a string in bytes, since `Length` returns the number of characters.

Of course, you can (in general) multiply this by the size in bytes of each character, using the expression:

```
Length (str1) * StringElementSize (str1)
```

Not only can you ask for information about a string, but you can also change some of it. A low-level way to convert a string is to call the `SetCodePage` procedure (an operation applicable only to a `RawByteString` type, as we'll see), which can either simply adjust the code page to the real one or perform a full string conversion. I'll use this procedure in the section "String Conversions".

Marco Cantù, Delphi 2009 Handbook

UnicodeString and Unicode

Needless to say the new string type (or new UnicodeString type, to be more precise) maps to the Unicode character set. If you've read the previous chapter, the question becomes, "which flavor of Unicode?"

It should not be surprising to learn that the new string type uses, as I've already mentioned, UTF-16[33]. This makes a lot of sense for many reasons, the most significant being that this is the native string type managed by the Windows API in recent versions of the operating system.

As we've seen in the section covering the WideChar type in Delphi 2009, the new `TCharacter` support class (not only used for WideChar but also for UnicodeString processing) has full support for UTF-16 and surrogate pairs. What I didn't mention in that section is that this has the noticeable side effect of making the number of WideChar elements of a string different from the number of Unicode code points it contains, as a single Unicode code point can be represented by a surrogate pair (that is, two WideChar).

A way to create a string with surrogate pairs is to use the `ConvertFromUtf32`[34] function that returns a string with the surrogate pair (two WideChar) in the proper circumstances, like the following:

```
var
   str1: string;
begin
   str1 := 'Surr. ' + ConvertFromUtf32($1D11E);
```

Now if you ask for the string length, you'll get 8, which is the number of WideChar, but not the number of logical Unicode code points in the string. If you print the string you get the proper effect (well, at least Windows will generally show one square block as placeholder of the surrogate pair, rather than two).

As demonstrated by the `btnSurrogateClick` method of the main form of the StringTest example, computing the number of logical Unicode code points might be more complex than you'd expect:

---

33 More precisely, the UnicodeString type is stored in memory as a UTF-16 string with a little endian representation, or UTF-16 LE.

34 In the code of `ConvertFromUtf32` (or more precisely in the `ConvertFromUtf32` class method of the `TCharacter` class it calls) you can see the actual algorithm used for mapping Unicode code points into surrogate pairs. Interesting reading if you are interested in the details.

54 - Chapter 2: The Unicode String Type

```
n := CharToByteLen (str1, Length (str1) - 1 );
CountChars (str1, Length (str1), cChar, cByte);
n := cChar - 1;
```

A related issue is what happens when looping on each character of the string. A standard `for` loop or a `for-in` cycle will just let you work on each WideChar element of the string, not each logical Unicode code point. So you might have to use a while loop based on the `NextCharIndex` function or adapt the `for` loop checking for surrogates:

```
if TCharacter.IsHighSurrogate (str1 [I]) then
  Memo1.Lines.Add (str1 [I] + str1 [I+1])
```

The complete listing for both cases is available in the same StringTest example, and not listed here as in most cases you can assume to work with the BMP (Basic Multilingual Plane) that treats each WideChar of a Unicode string as a single code point[35].

The UCS4String type

There is also another string type that you can use to handle a series of Unicode code points, the UCS4String type. This data type represents a dynamic array of 4-bytes characters (the UCS4Char type). As such, it has no reference counting or copy-on-write support, and very little RTL support.

Although this data type (that was already available in Delphi 2007) can be used in specific situations, it is not particularly suited for general circumstances. It certainly can be a memory waster, as not only strings use 4 bytes per character, but you can end up with multiple copies in memory.

The Many String Types

Along with the introduction of the new UnicodeString type, the updated internal representation shared by all string types (including the AnsiString

---

[35] The fact that two Unicode code points can be displayed as a single grapheme (see the section "Unicode Code Points and Graphemes" in Chapter 1) makes it even harder to map the number of WideChar in a Unicode string to the number of display characters.

type) makes room for some extra improvements in string management. The Delphi R&D team took advantage of this new internal representation (and all the work they did at the compiler level to enhance string management) to actually provide you with multiple data types and even a brand new string type definition mechanism.

The predefined reference counted[36] string types, in addition to UnicodeString, are:

- **AnsiString** is a single-byte-per-character string type based on the current code page of the operating system, closely matching the *classic AnsiString* of past versions of Delphi;
- **UTF8String** is a string based on the variable character length UTF-8 format;
- **RawByteString** is an array of characters with no code page set, on which no character conversion is accomplished by the system (thus partially resembling the *classic AnsiString*, when used as a pure character array).[37]

The type definition mechanism is revealed when you look at the definition of these new string types:

```
type
  UTF8String = type AnsiString(65001);
  RawByteString = type AnsiString($FFFF);
```

In this section I'll cover the AnsiString and custom string types and then the UTF8String type. I'll focus on RawByteString in the following section covering string conversions, as you'll generally use this string type to avoid conversions.

The New AnsiString Type

Differently from the past, the new AnsiString type string carries one further piece of information, the code page of the characters in the string. The `DefaultSystemCodePage` variable defaults to `CP_ACP`, the current Win-

---

36 This excludes the non-reference counted string types, which include the ShortString, WideString, and UCS4String types.

37 With byte arrays available (as covered in the next chapter) you should try to move to the more specific construct, although a RawByteString might let you migrate your existing code with less effort.

dows code page, but it could be modified by calling the special procedure `SetMultiByteConversionCodePage`. You can do this to force an entire program to work (by default) with characters in a given code page (that the operating system installation must support, of course).

In general, instead, you'd either stick to the current code page or change it for individual strings, calling the `SetCodePage` procedure (introduced earlier while talking about characters and code pages). This procedure can be called in two different ways. In the first case, you change the code page of a string (maybe loaded by a separate file or socket) because you know its format. In the second case, you can call it to convert a given string (something that happens automatically when assigning a string to one of a different code page, as discussed later).

Although you can keep using the AnsiString type to have a more compact in-memory representation of strings, in most cases you'd really want to convert your code to using the new UnicodeString type. That is, keep your strings declared with the generic string type. Still, there are circumstances in which using a specific string type is necessary. For example, when loading or saving files, moving data from and to a database, using Internet protocols where the code must remain in an 8-bit per character format. In all those cases convert your code to use AnsiString[38].

Creating a Custom String Type

Beside using the new AnsiString type, which is tied to the default code page used when compiling the application, you can use the same mechanism to define your own custom string type. For example, you can define a Latin-1 string type (as I've done in the LatinTest example) by writing:

```
type
  Latin1String = type AnsiString(28591);

procedure TFormLatinTest.btnNewTypeClick(
  Sender: TObject);
var
  str1: Latin1String;
begin
  str1 := 'a string with an accent: Cantù';
  Log ('String: ' + str1);
```

---

[38] More porting techniques will be covered in the Chapter 3.

You can use this string type as any other one, but it will be tied to a specific code page. So if you use this string type, when you convert a `Latin1String` to a UnicodeString (for example, to display it in a call to `Log` above), the Delphi compiler will add a conversion call. The last line of the code snippet above has a *hidden* call to `_UStrFromLStr`, which ends up calling more internal functions of the System unit, up to the real conversion operation performed by the `MultiByteToWideChar` Windows API. This is the sequence of calls[39]:

```
procedure _UStrFromLStr(var Dest: UnicodeString;
  const Source: AnsiString);
procedure InternalUStrFromPCharLen(
  var Dest: UnicodeString; Source: PAnsiChar;
  Length: Integer; CodePage: Integer);
function WCharFromChar(WCharDest: PWideChar;
  DestChars: Integer; const CharSource: PAnsiChar;
  SrcBytes: Integer; CodePage: Integer): Integer;
function MultiByteToWideChar(CodePage, Flags: Integer;
  MBStr: PAnsiChar; MBCount: Integer;
  WCStr: PWideChar; WCCount: Integer): Integer; stdcall;
  external kernel name 'MultiByteToWideChar';
```

The Windows API can perform the proper conversions, but these are potentially lossy conversions, as even some characters available in the various Windows code pages cannot be represented in Latin1. An example would be the Euro currency symbol, another smart quotes.

The btnNewTypeClick method above continues showing some more details of the string:

```
Log ('Last char: ' + IntToStr (
  Ord (str1[Length(str1)])));
Log('ElemSize: ' + IntToStr (StringElementSize (str1)));
Log('Length: ' + IntToStr (Length (str1)));
Log ('CodePage: ' + IntToStr (StringCodePage (str1)));
```

Running this code produces the following output:

```
Last char: 249
ElemSize: 1
Length: 30
CodePage: 28591
```

---

[39] As we'll see later in the section "Converting Strings" these conversions can considerably slow down string operations. That's why the compiler will emit warnings for similar implicit conversion operations.

58 - Chapter 2: The Unicode String Type

To prove that my new custom string type is treated differently than the standard AnsiString type (at least on my computer and with my locale), I've written a test method in the LatinTest project that adds the same upper end characters (from #128 to #255) to both an AnsiString and a Latin1String, showing them on a Memo in groups:

```
procedure TFormLatinTest.btnCompareCharSetClick(
  Sender: TObject);
var
  str1: Latin1String;
  str2: AnsiString;
  I: Integer;
begin
  for I := 128 to 255 do
  begin
    str1 := str1 + AnsiChar (I);
    str2 := str2 + AnsiChar (I);
  end;

  for I := 0 to 15 do
  begin
    Log (IntToStr (128 + I*8) + ' - ' +
      IntToStr (128 + I*8 + 7));
    Log ('Lati: ' + Copy (str1, 1 + i*8, 8));
    Log ('Ansi: ' + Copy (str2, 1 + i*8, 8));
  end;
end;
```

The initial part of the output highlights the differences among the two sets (again, the result you'll see might vary depending on your own locale):

```
128 - 135
Lati: ?,f".??
Ansi: €,ƒ„…†‡
136 - 143
Lati: ^?S<OZ
Ansi: ˆ‰Š‹ŒŽ
144 - 151
Lati: ''"".--
Ansi: ''""•--
152 - 159
Lati: ~Ts>ozY
Ansi: ˜™š›œžŸ
```

Having said this, at least at my latitude, a far more interesting example would be to use the code page of a non Latin alphabet, like Cyrillic. As an example, I defined a second custom string type in the LatinTest project:

```
type
  CyrillicString = type Ansistring(1251);
```

Chapter 2: The Unicode String Type - 59

You can use this string in a very similar fashion to the previous code snippet, but the interesting part is to use the high-order characters, those with a numeric value over 127. I've picked a few with a `for` loop:

```
procedure TFormLatinTest.btnCyrillicClick(
  Sender: TObject);
var
  str1: CyrillicString;
  I: Integer;
begin
  str1 := 'a string with an accent: Cantù';
  Log ('String: ' + str1);
  Log ('Last char: ' + IntToStr (
    Ord (str1[Length(str1)])));
  Log('ElemSize: ' + IntToStr (StringElementSize (str1)));
  Log('Length: ' + IntToStr (Length (str1)));
  Log ('CodePage: ' + IntToStr (StringCodePage (str1)));

  str1 := '';
  for I := 150 to 250 do
    str1 := str1 + CyrillicString(AnsiChar (I));
  Log ('High end chars: ' + str1);
end;
```

The output of this method looks like this:

```
String: a string with an accent: Cantu
Last char: 117
ElemSize: 1
Length: 30
CodePage: 1251
High end chars: ––™љ›њќћџ ўџЈ¤Ґ¦§Ё©Є«¬-
®Ї°±Іїґµ¶·ёљЄ»јЅѕїАБВГДЕЖЗИЙКЛМНОПРСТУФХЦЧШЩЪЫЬЭЮЯабвгдежз
ийклмнопрстуфхцчшщъ
```

You can notice that the accented letter has been *converted* to the corresponding non-accented version, as the original value was not available[40]. The string constant is a Unicode string and the assignment to `str1` performs an implicit conversion. In fact, the numeric value of the last character is different.

Also this time the high-end characters are completely different. To obtain the desired effect, consider you have to write the double cast:

```
CyrillicString(AnsiChar (I))
```

---

40 The `WideCharToMultiByte` behind the conversion tries to fail gracefully in certain situations. For example, smart quotes degrade into straight quotes instead of question marks and the accented letter of the sample code lost its accent.

Marco Cantù, Delphi 2009 Handbook

60 - Chapter 2: The Unicode String Type

If you simply concatenate the characters in the string and convert it afterwards, they'll be treated as Unicode characters.

Managing UTF-8 Strings

One of the side effect of the new internal structure for string types, is that we can now also manage strings in the UTF-8 format in a more native way. Unlike the past, when UTF8String was simply an alias of the string type, the new type is now fully recognized: conversions are automatic and all of the existing UTF-8 string manipulation routines have been ported to use the new specific types.

Consider this trivial code (part of the Utf8Test example):

```
var
  str8: Utf8String;
  str16: string;
begin
  str8 := 'Cantù';
  Memo1.Lines.Add( 'UTF-8');
  Memo1.Lines.Add( 'Length: ' + IntToStr (Length (str8)));
  Memo1.Lines.Add( '5: ' + IntToStr (Ord (str8[5])));
  Memo1.Lines.Add( '6: ' + IntToStr (Ord (str8[6])));

  str16 := str8;
  Memo1.Lines.Add( 'UTF-16');
  Memo1.Lines.Add( 'Length: ' + IntToStr (Length (str16)));
  Memo1.Lines.Add( '5: ' + IntToStr (Ord (str16[5])));
```

As you might expect, the `str8` string has a length of 6 (meaning 6 bytes), while the `str16` string has a length of 5 (meaning 10 bytes, though). Notice that Length invariably returns the number of string elements, which in case of variable-length representations doesn't match the number of Unicode code points represented by the string. This is the output of the program:

```
UTF-8
Length: 6
5: 195
6: 185

UTF-16
Length: 5
5: 249
```

The reason is that, as we saw in the last chapter, UTF-8 strings use a variable length implementation, so that characters outside the initial 7-bit ANSI space take at least two characters. This is the case with the *accented u* above. Assigning the same UTF-8 string to an AnsiString variable, and running similar code (again in the Utf8Test example), gives the following:

```
ANSI
Length: 5
5: 249
```

However this time the string length of 5 really means 5 bytes and not just 5 characters.

The support for the UTF-8 format might not be as complete as that for UTF-16, the native string implementation for Delphi 2009, but has been enhanced in very significant ways. There are specific routines for UTF-8 manipulation in the WideStrUtils unit, but also full support for streaming text files in this format[41]. What's core, though, is the fact you can work on such a string and show it in any control without having to perform an explicit conversion (and having to remember if and when to perform one); that certainly helps a lot.

Even if some operations on UTF-8 strings might be slow, because of extra conversions to and from the UnicodeString type, having a specific data type rather than an alias type not enforced by the compiler makes a lot of difference to any Delphi developer who has to deal with this encoding.

You are also free to write overloaded versions of existing routines (or new ones) using this specific string type to avoid any extra conversions.

Converting Strings

We've seen you can assign a UnicodeString value to an AnsiString or a UTF8String and the proper conversions will take place. Similarly, when you assign an AnsiString with a given code page to another one based on a different code page a conversion happens. You can also convert a string by assigning to it a different code page, asking for a conversion to take place:

```
type
   Latin1String = type AnsiString(28591);
```

---

41 I'll cover the TEncoding class and text file conversions later in this chapter, in the section "Streams and Encodings".

62 - Chapter 2: The Unicode String Type

```
procedure TFormStringConvert.btnLatin1Click(
    Sender: TObject);
var
  str1: AnsiString;
  str2: Latin1String;
  rbs: RawByteString;
begin
  str1 := 'any string with a €';
  str2 := str1;

  Memo1.Lines.Add (str1);
  Memo1.Lines.Add (IntToStr (Ord (str1[19])));

  Memo1.Lines.Add (str2);
  Memo1.Lines.Add (IntToStr (Ord (str2[19])));
  rbs := str1;
  SetCodePage(rbs, 28591, True);
  Memo1.Lines.Add (rbs);
  Memo1.Lines.Add (IntToStr (Ord (rbs[19])));
end;
```

In both cases above, the conversion is a lossy conversion, because the Euro symbol cannot be represented in the Latin-1 code page. Notice the use of the `SetCodePage` routine, that can be applied only to a `RawByteString` parameter, hence the assignment. This is the output you'll get:

```
any string with a €
128
any string with a ?
63
any string with a ?
63
```

Conversions Slow Down the Code

The automatic conversions happening behind the scenes are extremely handy, as the system does a lot of work for you, but if you don't carefully consider what you are doing you might end up with some extremely slow code, because of continuous conversions and string copy operations. Consider the following code (part of the StringConvert example):

```
str1 := 'Marco ';
str2 := 'Cantù ';
for I := 1 to 10000 do
  str1 := str1 + str2;
```

Depending on the actual string type of the two strings, the algorithm can be extremely fast or excruciatingly slow. The demo uses string (that is UnicodeString) in a first run and a combination of AnsiString and UTF8String (the worse possible case, as they'll have to be converted back and forth to the UnicodeString type for each assignment) in a second. This is the result of 10,000 iterations:

```
plain: 00.001
mixed: 01.717
```

Yes, you are reading the right numbers, that's about 1,000 times or three orders of magnitude! If this wasn't bad enough, consider what happens with 50,000 concatenations:

```
plain: 00:00.003
mixed: 00:42.879
```

That's another order of magnitude[42]! In other words, an occasional implicit conversion is fine, but never ever let them happen within a loop or recursive routine!

What is important to know, is that you can compile your program with string conversion warnings enabled (which is actually the default), and see where the compiler adds conversion code. On that single line of code used for concatenating strings of different types you'll get the following warnings:

```
W1057 Implicit string cast from 'UTF8String' to 'string'
W1057 Implicit string cast from 'AnsiString' to 'string'
W1058 Implicit string cast with potential data loss from 'string' to 'UTF8String'
```

The "potential data loss" problem arises because not all strings can be expressed in all formats. For example, if you assign a UnicodeString to an AnsiString there are chances that the operation won't be possible. As string conversion operations are quite common, the corresponding two warnings (Implicit string cast and Implicit string cast with potential data loss) are turned off by default.

With these warnings on you'll see many potential pitfalls, but an average program can have many and even an explicit typecast won't remove them but simply change them to a different set of warnings (Explicit string cast

---

42 The increase is exponential due to the fact than larger and larger strings need to be re-allocated in memory many times. What slows down the code is only partially the conversion, but mostly the need to create new large temporary strings rather than keep increasing the size of the current one.

64 - Chapter 2: The Unicode String Type

and Explicit string cast with potential data loss). Turn these warnings off when you are done checking![43]

A fifth similar warning is issued when assigning a string constant to a string, in case some of the characters cannot be converted. The warning in this case is slightly different:

```
[DCC Warning] StringConvertForm.pas(63): W2455 Narrowing given wide string constant lost information
```

This is a warning you should get rid of, as the operation won't make a lot of sense.

As another example of an implicit (and somewhat hidden) conversion slowing down the program execution, consider the following code snippet:

```
str1 := 'Marco Cantù';
for I := 1 to MaxLoop2 do
  str1 := AnsiUpperCase (str1);
```

In cases where the `str1` variable is a UnicodeString all is fine, but in cases where it is an AnsiString, it will cause two conversions. This is not as bad as in the previous case (because the string here is short and a copy of the string is required anyway) but shows a little overhead (for one million iterations):

```
AnsiUpperCase (string):    00:00.289
AnsiUpperCase (AnsiString): 00:00.540
```

The Ensure Calls

Another set of "hidden" operations added by the compiler is the *Ensure String* family of calls, added to check the code page of a string parameter, eventually triggering a conversion if it doesn't match. The most relevant of these calls is `EnsureUnicodeString`.

As it is very hard to achieve an incorrect situation in Delphi (short of a direct cast to the wrong string type), you might wonder why these were added. The reason is that when a UnicodeString is managed by C++Builder code, things can go wrong.

---

[43] These "diagnostic warnings", like the pointer and type safety ones introduced to check for .NET compatibility, can be kept off by default. Even though I'm a proponent of the rule "keep all warnings on and try to compile programs with no hints and warnings" I agree that "diagnostic warnings" should be treated differently.

To make things safe, the compiler adds these extra checks in many different places, particularly when working on a string passed as parameter. While this is the default behavior, you can compile specific code (and libraries) disabling this setting, using the `--string-checks` compiler options or the `$STRINGCHECKS` directive. Given that you have to use them at your own risk, these switches are not documented and not officially supported (although, oddly enough, they are directly available in the project options). Still as potential issues are very limited when using Delphi (and not C++Builder), you can probably turn them off as a regular speedup technique.

For example, if you write the following one liner:

```
function DoubleLengthUpperOn(
   const S: UnicodeString): Integer;
begin
   Result := Length(AnsiUppercase(S));
end;
```

and compile this and an identical version with a different name, with the string checks on and off, and later call them within a loop of 10 million iterations, you'll see the following timing:

```
UpperOn:  00:02.202
UpperOff: 00:02.159
```

This seems very modest, and quite irrelevant. However, if you make the actual code of the functions blazingly fast (for example by removing the `AnsiUpperCase` call), the results for 10 times more iterations becomes:

```
On:  00:03.556
Off: 00:00.310
```

In this case the difference is significant (ten times as much) and seems linear with the number of iterations of the loop. Even if similar cases will be marginal, this is probably a good reason to keep this setting turned off.

For more information on this setting and its effect in terms of generated assembly code, you can refer to the following blog entry by Jan Goyvaerts:

```
http://www.micro-isv.asia/2008/10/needless-string-
   checks-with-ensureunicodestring
```

Watch Out for Literals in Concatenation

Speaking of string concatenation, you have to watch out for concatenations involving string literals. For example consider the following apparently trivial lines of code:

```
Log ('String: ' + str1);
Log (str1 + ' is a string');
```

Now if `str1` is a UnicodeString, there should be no problem at all. If `str1` is an AnsiString, in one of its variations, the concatenation with a Unicode string literal might force different conversions depending whether the string literal comes before or after the string variable. In most mixed string cases involving literals, my suggestion is to add an explicit type cast for the string, like in:

```
Log ('String: ' + UnicodeString(str1));
Log (UnicodeString(str1) + ' is a string');
```

Using RawByteString

What if you need to pass an AnsiString as a parameter to a routine? When the parameter is assigned to a specific string type with an encoding, it will be converted to the proper type, with the potential for data loss. That's why Delphi 2009 introduces yet another custom string type, called RawByteString and defined as:

```
type
   RawByteString = type AnsiString($ffff);
```

This definition creates a string type with no encoding or, to be more precise, with the placeholder `$ffff` indicating *"no encoding"*. A RawByteString can be considered as a string of bytes, which ignores the attached encoding in case of an automatic conversion when assigning to an AnsiString. In other words, when passing a 1-byte per character string as a RawByteString parameter, no conversion is performed, unlike any other AnsiString derived type. You can do a specific conversion by calling the `SetCodePage` routine, as demonstrated earlier in the section "Converting Strings".

As such, it can become a handy replacement of the previous string (or AnsiString) type in code that uses strings for generic and custom data processing which you want to keep with a 1-byte per character representation[44].

Declaring variables of type RawByteString for storing an actual string should rarely be done[45]. Given the undefined code page, this can lead to undefined behavior and potential data loss. On the other hand if your goal is saving binary data using a string-like memory allocation and representation, you can use the RawByteString in the same way you used AnsiString in past versions of Delphi. Replacing non-string code that used AnsiString with RawByteString is an interesting migration path (as you'll see in the section "Don't Move String Data" of Chapter 3).

For now, let's focus on a typical example in which you can use the RawByteString type as a parameter. If you want to display some information about an 8-bit string, you could write either of the following two declarations (these are methods of the main form of the RawTest demo):

```
procedure DisplayStringData (str: AnsiString);
procedure DisplayRawData (str: RawByteString);
```

The code of the two methods is identical (here I've listed only one of the two):

```
procedure TFormRawTest.DisplayRawData(
  str: RawByteString);
begin
  Log ('DisplayRawData(str: RawByteString)');
  Log ('String: ' + UnicodeString(str));
  Log ('CodePage: ' + IntToStr (StringCodePage (str)));
  Log ('Address: ' + IntToStr (Integer (Pointer (str))));
end;
```

Notice the cast to UnicodeString used to display the proper string, which is necessary to avoid the data being treated like a plain AnsiString because of the concatenation of a string literal with a string whose code page is not defined at compile time[46].

---

44 Don't be confused by this extended support for 1-byte per character Ansi-compatible strings: the preferred solution is by far to migrate your string processing code to the UnicodeString type. Don't be too tempted by these new extra string types.

45 For some interesting considerations on RawByteString see Jan Goyvaerts blog post at http://www.micro-isv.asia/2008/08/using-rawbytestring-effectively/

46 Using Log (str) directly would work, as there is no concatenation involved.

68 - Chapter 2: The Unicode String Type

The reason I show the string memory address (beside its content and code page) is that this will let us determine if the string has been converted (and copied) or if it is the exact same string that was passed as a parameter.

Now we can use an AnsiString variable (not simply assigning a string constant but doing some processing, or the result would be different) and pass it as parameter to the two methods, after logging some string data:

```
procedure TFormRawTest.btnRawAnsiClick(Sender: TObject);
var
  strAnsi: AnsiString;
begin
  strAnsi := 'Some text ';
  strAnsi := strAnsi + AnsiChar (210) + AnsiChar (128);

  Log ('String: ' + strAnsi);
  Log ('CodePage: ' + IntToStr (
    StringCodePage (strAnsi)));
  Log ('Address: ' + IntToStr (
   Integer (Pointer (strAnsi))));

  DisplayStringData (strAnsi);
  DisplayRawData (strAnsi);
end;
```

The result will be as expected, since when calling the `DisplayStringData` and the `DisplayRawData` methods no conversions will be performed and all operations will take place in the exact same string:

```
String: Some text Ò€
CodePage: 1252
Address: 28149532

DisplayStringData(str: AnsiString)
String: Some text Ò€
CodePage: 1252
Address: 28149532

DisplayRawData(str: RawByteString)
String: Some text Ò€
CodePage: 1252
Address: 28149532
```

If this looks obvious, it might not be so clear what happens when we pass a UTF8String as an actual parameter to the methods. The calling code is quite similar, although I convert each single character treating it as a UTF-8 value:

```
var
  strUtf8: UTF8String;
```

```
  nChar: Integer;
begin
  strUtf8 := 'Some text ';
  nChar := 210;
  strUtf8 := strUtf8 + UTF8String (AnsiChar (nChar));
  nChar := 128;
  strUtf8 := strUtf8 + UTF8String (AnsiChar (nChar));

  Log ('String: ' + strUtf8);
  Log ('CodePage: ' + IntToStr (
    StringCodePage (strUtf8)));
  Log ('Address: ' + IntToStr (
    Integer (Pointer (strUtf8))));

  DisplayStringData (strUtf8);
  DisplayRawData (strUtf8);
end;
```

This time passing the string as an AnsiString performs an actual conversion (which is a lossy conversion, as the characters cannot be represented by a AnsiChar), while the RawByteString operations process the original string directly and produce the correct output:

```
UTF-8 string
String: Some text Ç
CodePage: 65001
Address: 28804892

DisplayStringData(str: AnsiString)
String: Some text ?
CodePage: 0
Address: 28804732

DisplayRawData(str: RawByteString)
String: Some text Ç
CodePage: 65001
Address: 28804892
```

In the program you can see more tests done with custom-defined string types. Like with the UTF8String test, each time you pass a custom string as an AnsiString a conversion takes place, which is potentially lossy, while using the RawByteString parameter you can keep the string in its original value and display it correctly. Here is a selection of the output lines:

```
Latin string
String: Some text Ò

DisplayStringData(str: AnsiString)
String: Some text Ò?
```

```
DisplayRawData(str: RawByteString)
String: Some text Ò

Cyrillic string
String: Some text TФ

DisplayStringData(str: AnsiString)
String: Some text ??

DisplayRawData(str: RawByteString)
String: Some text TФ
```

New UTF-8 Conversion Functions

Beside many automatic string transformations there are also several new direct string conversion functions you can use. For example, there is a large number of new conversions functions to and from UTF-8 encoding, overloaded for the different string types:

```
function UTF8Encode(...): RawByteString;
function UTF8EncodeToShortString(...): ShortString;
function UTF8ToWideString(...): WideString;
function UTF8ToUnicodeString(...): UnicodeString;
function UTF8ToString(...): string;
```

String and Character Literals

We have seen in several examples that you can assign an individual character literal or a string literal to any of the string types, with the proper conversion taking place behind the scenes.

String literals are invariably considered of the UnicodeString type. Notice that this could cause issues with overloading resolution when passing a constant string to a function like `Pos`, that now has multiple versions. In general, though, the management of string literals is quite direct. As we saw in the last chapter, you can add any Unicode character to a constant string in the editor, and everything will work smoothly.

Character literals cause some more issues though, particularly for backward compatibility reasons. Plain character literals are converted depending on their context. It is more difficult for the compiler to determine what to do with hexadecimal (or decimal) character literals, as in the following code taken from the HighCharTest example:

```
var
   str1: string;
begin
   str1 := #$80;
```

For backward compatibility reasons, all 2-digit string literals are parsed as AnsiChar by default, so that a developer like me living in Europe (or, more technically, having the same code page setting as me) will see the Euro currency symbol displayed in the string. Actually, by executing the statement:

```
   Log (str1 + ' - ' + IntToStr (Ord (str1[1])));
```

I'll get the output:

```
€ - 8364
```

In other words, the literal is treated like an AnsiChar and converted to the proper Unicode code point. If you want to fully move to Unicode, though you might not like this behavior, as you'll never know how a given literal is going to be interpreted. That's why CodeGear introduced in Delphi 2009 a new compiler directive:

```
{$HIGHCHARUNICODE <ON|OFF>}
```

This directive determines how literal values between #$80 and #$FF are treated by the compiler. What I discussed earlier is the effect of the default option (OFF). If you turn it on, the same program will produce this output:

```
 - 128
```

The number is interpreted as an actual Unicode code point and the output will contain a non-printable control character. Another option to express that specific code point (or any Unicode code point below #$FFFF) is to use the four-digits notation:

```
   str1 := #$0080;
```

This is not interpreted as the Euro currency symbol regardless of the setting of the $HIGHCHARUNICODE directive.

What is nice is that you can use the four digits notation to express far eastern characters, like the following two Japanese characters:

```
   str1 := #$3042#$3044;
```

displayed[47] as (along with their Integer representation):

```
あい - 12354 - 12356
```

You can also use literal elements over #$FFFF that will be converted to the proper surrogate pair.

Finally notice that for string literals, the code page is taken from the compiler options, which you can modify for a specific project, and not from the system code page of the computer on which you are compiling or executing the program.

Streams and Encodings

If moving all your strings to Unicode within your application, when working with the RTL and VCL, and while invoking the Windows API isn't that hard, things can become a little more complicated as you read and write your strings to and from files. What happens with the TStrings file operations for example?

Delphi 2009 introduces another brand new class to handle file encodings, called TEncoding and somewhat mimicking the System.Text.Encoding class of the .NET framework. The TEncoding class, defined in the SysUtils unit, has several subclasses representing the encodings automatically supported by Delphi (these are *standard encodings* to which you can add your own):

```
type
  TEncoding = class
    TMBCSEncoding = class(TEncoding)
      TUTF7Encoding = class(TMBCSEncoding)
        TUTF8Encoding = class(TUTF7Encoding)
    TUnicodeEncoding = class(TEncoding)
      TBigEndianUnicodeEncoding = class(TUnicodeEncoding)
```

The TUnicodeEncoding class uses the same UTF-16 LE (Little Endian) format used by the UnicodeString type. One object of each of these classes is available within the TEncoding class, as class data, and has a corresponding getter function and class property:

---

47 あい translates to "meeting" according to BabelFish, but I'm not 100% sure where I originally found it.

```
type
  TEncoding = class
  ...
  public
    class property ASCII: TEncoding read GetASCII;
    class property BigEndianUnicode: TEncoding
      read GetBigEndianUnicode;
    class property Default: TEncoding read GetDefault;
    class property Unicode: TEncoding read GetUnicode;
    class property UTF7: TEncoding read GetUTF7;
    class property UTF8: TEncoding read GetUTF8;
```

The `TEncoding` class has methods for reading and writing characters to byte streams, to perform conversions, plus a special function to handle the BOM called `GetPreamble`. So you can write (anywhere in the code):

```
TEncoding.UTF8.GetPreamble
```

Streaming Strings Lists

The `ReadFromFile` and `WriteToFile` methods of the `TStrings` class can be called with an encoding. If you write a string list to text file without providing a specific encoding, the class will use `TEncoding.Default`, which uses the internal `DefaultEncoding` in turn extracted at the first occurrence by the current Windows code page. In other words, if you save a file you'll get the same ANSI file as before.

Of course, you can also easily force the file to a different format, for example the UTF-16 format:

```
Memo1.Lines.SaveToFile('test.txt', TEncoding.Unicode);
```

This saves the file with a Unicode BOM or preamble. As you do the corresponding `LoadFromFile` operation, if you don't specify an encoding, the loading method will end up calling the `GetBufferEncoding` method of the `TEncoding` class that will determine the encoding depending on the presence of a BOM (or its absence, in which case it will use the default ANSI encoding).

What if you specify an encoding in `LoadFromFile`? The encoding you provide will be used for reading the file, regardless of the actual BOM in the file, often producing an error. I'd rather expect an exception in case of such a discrepancy, saving a file with one code page and forcing to upload it with a different one is certainly a developer error. Not having an exception can

74 - Chapter 2: The Unicode String Type

help in case the encoded file was saved without a BOM, and still should not be considered as an ASCII file, but a UTF one.

But let us focus on the file saving operation. If you don't change the existing Delphi code, your programs will save files as ANSI. If your existing programs don't handle Unicode data, your program and its files will be fully backwards compatible.

But what if a program does handle Unicode data? Let's suppose we have a string list with lines written in different languages[48], like in the following design-time form of the StreamEncoding project:

If we have existing Delphi code that saves the string list to a file and reloads it, it would probably look like:

```
procedure TFormStreamEncoding.btnPlainClick(
  Sender: TObject);
var
  strFileName: string;
begin
  strFileName := 'PlainText.txt';
  ListBox1.Items.SaveToFile(strFileName);
```

---

48 These lines have been extracted from the "What is Unicode?" page of the Unicode Consortium web site, which has its text translated in many different languages using a variety of alphabets.

```
  ListBox1.Clear;
  ListBox1.Items.LoadFromFile(strFileName);
end;
```

Needless to say that the effect would be a total disaster, as only a fraction of the characters used have an ANSI representation, so you'll end with lots of question marks in the list box.

A simple alternative would be to change the code as in the event handler of the second button of the project:

```
  strFileName := 'Utf8Text.txt';
  ListBox1.Items.SaveToFile(strFileName, TEncoding.UTF8);
```

Again, we don't have to specify an encoding when loading the string list, as Delphi will automatically pick it up from the BOM.

If you prefer to save the data as ANSI unless necessary, you could check for the string list content to determine whether to save as ANSI or UTF-8:

```
procedure TFormStreamEncoding.btnAsNeededClick(
  Sender: TObject);
var
  strFileName: string;
  encoding1: TEncoding;
begin
  strFileName := 'AsNeededText.txt';
  encoding1 := TEncoding.Default;

  if ListBox1.Items.Text <>
      UnicodeString (AnsiString(ListBox1.Items.Text)) then
    encoding1 := TEncoding.UTF8;

  ListBox1.Items.SaveToFile(strFileName, Encoding1);
```

This code checks whether you can convert a string to an AnsiString and back to a UnicodeString without losing any content. For a very long string, this double conversion plus comparison would be quite expensive, so you could use the following alternative code instead (which is not as precise, as it relies on a specific code page[49], but comes close):

```
var
   ch: Char;
begin
   ...
   for ch in ListBox1.Items.Text do
```

---

[49] Checking if ch >= 256 does not work if the default code page is something other than Windows 1252. For example "*Cantù*" does not have any characters >= 256, but it cannot be represented in code page 1251.

```
if Ord (ch) >= 256 then
begin
  encoding1 := TEncoding.UTF8;
  break;
end;
```

Using similar code you could decide which format to use, depending on the situation. It might be a better idea, though, to move all of your files to Unicode encoding (UTF-8 or UTF-16), regardless of the actual data. Using UTF-16 will make the files bigger, but will also reduce the conversions when saving and loading.

However, since there is no way to specify a default conversion, going for Unicode encoding of your files would mean the need to change each and every file save operation... unless we use a trick, changing the standard behavior of the class. Such a *hack* could come in the form of a class helper[50]. Consider the following code:

```
type
  TStringsHelper = class helper for TStrings
    procedure SaveToFile (const strFileName: string);
  end;

procedure TStringsHelper.SaveToFile(
  const strFileName: string);
begin
  inherited SaveToFile (strFileName, TEncoding.UTF8);
end;
```

Notice that inherited here doesn't mean to call a base class but the class helped by the class helper. Now you simply write (or keep your code as):

```
ListBox1.Items.SaveToFile(strFileName);
```

to save it as UTF-8 (or any other encoding of your choice). You'll find this code in the StreamEncoding example.

Defining a Custom Encoding

Even if Delphi 2009 comes with a few predefined encodings, you might end up needing more. An example of a not-so-common encoding you might

---

50 If you are interested to learn about class helpers, a good source is my "Delphi 2007 Handbook", but you can certainly find other references searching the web. The concept of class helper is a little known but extremely powerful feature of recent versions of Delphi.

need is UTF-32 (little-endian). Defining and using a custom encoding is certainly possible, although there are a few rough edges.

First of all, you have to define a class that inherits from either TEncoding or one of its descendants. Since there are no existing encoding classes handling 4-bytes characters, I've gone for inheriting from the base class:

```
type
  TUTF32Encoding = class (TEncoding)
  class var
    UTF32Encoding: TUTF32Encoding;
  strict protected
    function GetByteCount(Chars: PChar;
      CharCount: Integer): Integer; override;
    function GetBytes(Chars: PChar;
      CharCount: Integer; Bytes: PByte;
      ByteCount: Integer): Integer; override;
    function GetCharCount(Bytes: PByte;
      ByteCount: Integer): Integer; override;
    function GetChars(Bytes: PByte;
      ByteCount: Integer; Chars: PChar;
      CharCount: Integer): Integer; override;
  public
    function GetPreamble: TBytes; override;
    class function Encoding: TEncoding;
    function GetMaxByteCount(
      CharCount: Integer): Integer; override;
    function GetMaxCharCount(
      ByteCount: Integer): Integer; override;
  end;
```

There are basically two core conversion methods (GetBytes and GetChars), four characters/bytes counting methods, a method to define the BOM or preamble, and a class function used to return a singleton instance, saved in the class variable. Only the two conversion methods are complex, while for everything else all you have to keep in mind is you take 4 bytes, that is SizeOf(UCS4Char), for each character. Here are the methods except the conversion ones, which are covered later in more detail:

```
class function TUTF32Encoding.Encoding: TEncoding;
begin
  if not Assigned (UTF32Encoding) then
    UTF32Encoding := TUTF32Encoding.Create;
  Result := UTF32Encoding;
end;

function TUTF32Encoding.GetByteCount(
  Chars: PChar; CharCount: Integer): Integer;
begin
```

```
  Result := CharCount * SizeOf(UCS4Char);
end;

function TUTF32Encoding.GetCharCount(
  Bytes: PByte; ByteCount: Integer): Integer;
begin
  Result := ByteCount div SizeOf(UCS4Char);
end;

function TUTF32Encoding.GetMaxByteCount(
  CharCount: Integer): Integer;
begin
  Result := (CharCount + 1) * 4;
end;

function TUTF32Encoding.GetMaxCharCount(
  ByteCount: Integer): Integer;
begin
  Result := (ByteCount div 4) + (ByteCount and 1) + 1;
end;

function TUTF32Encoding.GetPreamble: TBytes;
begin
  // UTF-32, little-endian
  SetLength(Result, 4);
  Result[0] := $FF;
  Result[1] := $FE;
  Result[2] := $00;
  Result[3] := $00;
end;
```

The code mimics somewhat the Delphi RTL classes, resembling in particular the TUnicodeEncoding class. The conversion methods are slightly more complicated. Since I don't want to handle the characters directly, I'm using the UnicodeString to UCS4String conversion functions provided by the Delphi RTL. Extracting the physical bytes to store in the stream is a matter of converting to UCS4String and moving the data at a low level:

```
function TUTF32Encoding.GetBytes(Chars: PChar;
  CharCount: Integer; Bytes: PByte;
  ByteCount: Integer): Integer;
var
  u4String: UCS4String;
begin
  Result := CharCount * SizeOf(UCS4Char);
  u4String := UnicodeStringToUCS4String (
    UnicodeString (Chars));
  Move(u4String[0], Bytes^, Result);
end;
```

For the opposite conversion you need to move the binary data to the UCS4String type, convert it, and copy the result in the output buffer:

```
function TUTF32Encoding.GetChars(Bytes: PByte;
  ByteCount: Integer; Chars: PChar;
  CharCount: Integer): Integer;
var
  u4String: UCS4String;
  uString: UnicodeString;
begin
  Result := CharCount;
  SetLength (u4String, Result);
  Move(Bytes^, u4String[0],
    CharCount * SizeOf(UCS4Char));
  uString := UCS4StringToUnicodeString (u4String);
  Move(uString[1], Chars^,
    CharCount * SizeOf(Char));
end;
```

Now with this custom encoding available you can simply write code like in the CustomEncoding demo:

```
procedure TFormCustomEncoding.btnTestEncoding2Click(
  Sender: TObject);
begin
  Memo1.Lines.LoadFromFile ('Utf8Text.txt');
  Memo1.Lines.SaveToFile ('Utf32.txt',
    TUTF32Encoding.Encoding);
  Memo1.Lines.LoadFromFile ('Utf32.txt',
    TUTF32Encoding.Encoding);
end;
```

The only potential problem is that we cannot simply call the LoadFromFile method with no encoding and ask the Delphi RTL to recognize it, as this simply won't work[51]. In Delphi 2009 there is no way to *install* our custom encoding in the RTL to make its preamble known to the BOM-detection code inside the TEncoding.GetBufferEncoding class function. This is demonstrated by the last button of the example.

---

51 Also note that very few editors out there recognize the UTF-32 BOM and encoding.

Unicode and the VCL

Having Unicode string support in the Delphi language is thrilling, having the Win32 APIs remapped to the Wide version opens up a lot of easy migration, but the fundamental change is that the entire RTL and the Visual Component Library (VCL) are now fully Unicode enabled. All of the string (and string lists) managed by components are declared as string, so they now match the new UnicodeString type.

Some of the low-level, internal areas of the RTL, though, rely on different formats. For example property names are based on UTF-8, and so is part of the RTTI support available in the TypInfo unit. Beside some very specific exceptions, everything else has been migrated to UnicodeString and UTF-16.

The Unicode support is a key element, but not the only feature that helps improving the support for building international applications. Other features relate to the use of BiDiMode and Translation support.

Regarding source code files keep in mind you can save them in any format you like, but it is necessary to use a Unicode format if you are using any code point above 255 in your source code (for identifier names, strings, comments, or just about anything else). The editor will prompt you to use such a format when required, but you can go for Unicode source code files anyway.

A Growing Core RTL?

With all of the extra string processing and management runtime level code, are Delphi 2009 executable files bigger than in the past? I've compared the size of a minimal VCL application compiled with runtime packages (MiniPack) and that of a bare-bones Windows API program[52] (MiniSize), compiled in both Delphi 2007 and Delphi 2009, obtaining the following results:

---

[52] These two programs were part of my Mastering Delphi 2005 and I've not copied the code to the source code base of the current book, as they are rather simple. They can be downloaded from the source code of that book, though, at http://www.marcocantu.com/md2005.

	Delphi 2007	Delphi 2009
MiniPack	15,872	16,896
MiniSize	19,456	20,992

The "extra weight" is about 1 KB, an amount that increases if you do string conversions, but should remain quite minimal compared to the size of any real world application.

Unicode in DFM Files

I've just mentioned how the Delphi IDE can treat Unicode-enabled source code files, but we have not seen what happens to DFM files as you add an extended character to one of the properties. A simple experiment would be to open a brand new program, place a button on it, and paste in the button caption a Unicode character, like the Japanese characters of the "String Literals" section.

Viewing the Form as Text or looking at the actual DFM file you'll see the following:

```
object Button1: TButton
  Left = 176
  Top = 104
  Width = 75
  Height = 25
  Caption = #12354#12356
  TabOrder = 0
end
```

Now add another form to the program (as I did in the DfmTest program, or modify the same one), and this time change the Name of the button adding Unicode characters, like:

What is the effect on the DFM in this case? It will be saved in a UTF-8 format (along with the PAS file). Open it as text and you'll see an odd difference between the component `Name` and its `Caption`, which are matching but use different representations:

82 - Chapter 2: The Unicode String Type

```
object Buttonあい: TButton
  Left = 224
  Top = 112
  Width = 75
  Height = 25
  Caption = 'Button'#12354#12356
  TabOrder = 0
end
```

In this case the DFM file is not backward compatible with Delphi 2007.

Localizing the VCL

With the support for Unicode, Delphi's traditional support for "bi-directional mode", or `BiDiMode`, controls mirroring in a form, and the Translation Manager, which is part of the IDE, become even more relevant.

I won't cover `BiDiMode` in detail, nor provide guidance for the Internal and External Translation Managers, as these tools didn't really change compared to past versions of Delphi. The translation architecture of the VCL these tools are based upon has been in Delphi for many versions, but the tools have certainly been improved (and some of their bugs fixed) because they are now under the spotlight.

What's Next

Now that you have seen how Delphi 2009 treats Unicode strings, we can focus on transitioning existing Object Pascal source code from the ASCII world to the Unicode world. There are many related issues involved, like PChar-based pointer math, a good reason to split off that material in a separate chapter.

Coverage of new string-related features doesn't end here, as in Chapter 7 I'll cover other new RTL features like the `TStringBuilder` class and other enhanced classes for streaming text.

Chapter 3: Porting To Unicode

Having native Unicode support in Delphi is a big step forward, and the fact you can continue to use the String type means you can port existing code simply at the cost of recompiling. This change is a big change. From calls to the Windows API to the use of PChar pointer only for the pointer math support, there are many areas of Delphi for which you can expect the migration not to be so easy and straightforward. This chapter delves into those and other possible problems.

Before we dive into the chapter, be aware that if you need to keep compiling your code in past versions of Delphi you can take advantage of the UNI-CODE compiler directive, which is defined by the Delphi 2009 compiler. So you can write code snippets that won't compile in previous versions of Delphi by writing:

```
{$IFDEF UNICODE}
  // Delphi 2009 specific code
{$ENDIF}
```

Char Operations That Fail

As I just mentioned, most of the string and character based operations recompile and migrate smoothly. However, there are some that don't and will require a fix in the code.

A large amount of Pascal, Turbo Pascal, Object Pascal, and Delphi's Object Pascal code assumes that the size of a character is a byte. All of this code can potentially fail when moving to Delphi 2009. As we'll see in the section about `FillChar` below, to get the actual size in bytes of a string you should always multiply the string length by the `StringElementSize` value, as a character often requires two bytes (but not always).

Watch Out for Set of Char

I've already mentioned that you cannot declare a `set of Char` any more, at least not with the meaning this had in past versions of Delphi, that is having a set including all of the possible characters. As covered in the previous chapter, the compiler will assume you are porting existing code to Delphi 2009 and decide to consider your `set of Char` declaration as though it was a `set of AnsiChar`, issuing a warning. Some of your existing code dealing with this construct will fail though.

You can see an example of this warning (and the explicit cast used to remove it) in the CharTest example of Chapter 2. The real issue in this case is that there is no way to define a set of all characters any more, or to express the inclusion of a character in a set with this way of coding. You really have to change the code completely! Consider for example the simple code of the CharTest demo I've just mentioned:

```
var
  charSet: set of Char;
```

```
begin
   charSet := ['a', 'b', 'c'];
   if 'a' in charSet then ...
```

The alternative approach is to avoid the set of characters altogether and use a different algorithm, like:

```
var
   charSet: string;
begin
   charSet := 'abc';
   if Pos ('a', charSet) > 0 then ...
```

This has the advantage that it also works when the characters are not ASCII, while using sets limits you to 256 values in the comparison. Similarly, rather than testing for the inclusion of a character in a range like:

```
if ch1 in ['0'..'9'] then ...
```

which compiles and works only thanks to the reduction of the ch1 variable to a *byte char* (as hinted by the related warning), you should rather code it like you'd do in most other programming languages like:

```
if (ch1 >= '0') and (ch1 <= '9') then ...
```

All of these techniques have the advantage of being backward compatible. If you need to replace your *is character in set* test specifically for Delphi 2009, I'd certainly recommend using the new specific CharInSet function of the SysUtils unit:

```
if CharInSet ('a', charSet) then ...
if CharInSet ('a', ['a', 'b', 'c']) then ...
```

This code is almost identical to the original test, and it is very easy to replace the older tests with the new ones when porting code to Delphi 2009. The CharInSet function is defined for both AnsiChar and WideChar values, and uses as second parameter the set type defined below:

```
type
   TSysCharSet = set of AnsiChar;

function CharInSet(C: AnsiChar;
   const CharSet: TSysCharSet): Boolean; overload; inline;
function CharInSet(C: WideChar;
   const CharSet: TSysCharSet): Boolean; overload; inline;
```

Another alternative approach that is quite efficient and works across versions, is to replace these tests with a case statement like:

```
case Ch of
   'a'..'c': ...
```

86 - Chapter 3: Porting to Unicode

```
end;
```

This also has the advantage of being much faster than the CharInSet function. A final specific case is the test for inclusion in the LeadBytes set:

```
if str[i] in LeadBytes then ...
```

In this case you should use the new IsLeadChar function to replace the test. In some other cases the new Unicode-related tests provided by the Character unit could help as well.

Avoid FillChar for Characters

Although the FillChar procedure was originally intended to be used for filling a string with the same character many times, it is also (even more commonly) used to fill a generic buffer with data. The most frequent use is probably zeroing a data structure, making it impossible to change the actual definition of the procedure (despite its name):

```
var
  rc: TRect;
begin
  FillChar (rc, SizeOf (rc), 0);
```

With strings changing to a character size of two bytes problems arise. The first is because the string is now twice as big, while the second parameter of FillChar is expressed in bytes, and not in number of logical characters. So the first of the two FillChar operations in this code snippet (from the CharTroubles example) fails, with the subsequent display operation showing a *t*:

```
var
  str1, str2: string;
begin
  str1 := 'here comes a string';
  str2 := 'here comes a string';

  FillChar (str1[1], Length (str1), 0); // nope!
  Memo1.Lines.Add ('15 char is: ' + str1[15]);

  FillChar (str2[1],
    Length (str2) * StringElementSize (str2), 0); // yes!
  Memo1.Lines.Add ('15 char is: ' + str2[15]);
```

What's even worse, though is that filling the string with zeros will do, but filling it with a specific character will cause a complete mess. In fact, if you fill the string with the letter *A*, for example:

```
FillChar (str2[1],
   Length (str2) * StringElementSize (str2), 'A');
Memo1.Lines.Add ('15 char is: ' + str2[15]);
```

what you end up doing is not filling the string with the character $41 but with $4141, so the string will become a sequence of Chinese characters:

```
15 char is: 案
```

In other words, you should absolutely stop using `FillChar` for filling a string with copies of the same character and keep using the procedure only for data structures. For filling a string you can use `StringOfChar` instead:

```
str2 := StringOfChar ('A', 15);
Memo1.Lines.Add (str2);
```

If you need an AnsiString result, notice there is an overloaded version of `StringOfChar`, taking an AnsiChar character. Consider, though, that if you write:

```
var
   S: AnsiString;
begin
   S := StringOfChar('A', 15);
```

the compiler will use the WideChar version of `StringOfChar` and will convert the resulting UnicodeString to an AnsiString. To avoid the conversion you can write:

```
S := StringOfChar(AnsiChar('A'), 15)
```

The simple reason is that the compiler cannot call an overloaded function based on the result type, but only based on input parameters.

String Operations That Fail or Slow Down

When working with strings, and particularly when moving existing string processing code to Delphi 2009, there are two different issues for which you have to watch out. First, you have to check if all operations produce the same result, which at times is not the case. Second, you have to be sure that some operations don't become terribly slow.

The terrible slow down generally happens because of implicit string conversions, and in particular when you want to keep AnsiString variables around. If the original AnsiString declaration was in your code to differentiate from the ShortString type, then moving your code to use the generic string type might be your best option.

Turn on All String Conversion Warnings

If you need to keep different string types around or are porting existing code in general, you should at least for some time turn on all of the implicit string conversion warnings, to have a better understanding of how the compiler interprets your code and of the extra (possibly unneeded) operations it will inject into your code. As we saw in the section "Assigning and Converting Strings" of Chapter 2, this can slow down some code by the order of a thousand times.

Remember there are now several string conversion warnings, some of which are not enabled by default. This is a complete list of string/character related warnings worth turning on at least for the conversion phase:

- Explicit string cast
- Explicit string cast with potential data loss
- Implicit string cast
- Implicit string cast with potential data loss
- Narrowing given wide/Unicode string constant lost information
- Narrowing given WideChar constant to AnsiChar lost information
- WideChar reduced to byte char in set expression
- Widening given AnsiChar constant to WideChar lost information
- Widening given AnsiString constant lost information

Remember that you can also turn *specific* string conversion warnings into errors, at least temporarily, so it will be easier to catch them in case your code is causing too many warnings and hints[53]:

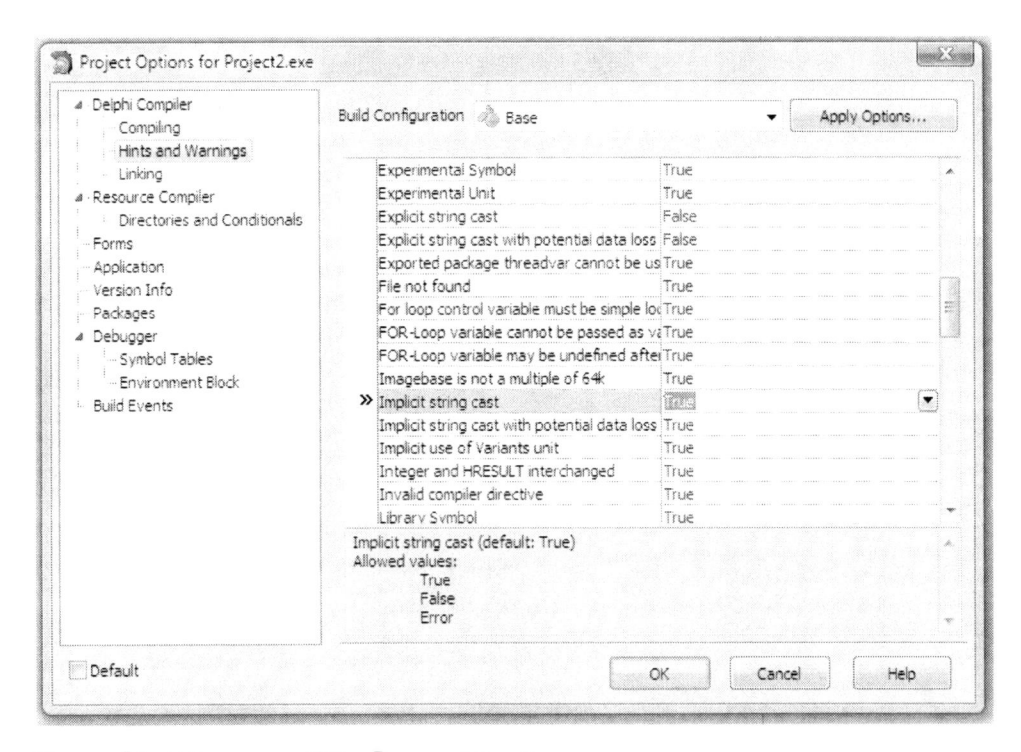

Don't Move String Data

Accessing string data at a low level, for example with a `Move` call, was not a very good idea in the past, as it could defeat reference counting and cause memory overruns and other problems. Calling `Move` for characters is even worse now that we have multiple string representations that are incompatible at the binary level.

As an example, consider the following code (from the MoveStrings demo) that moves data from a string to a buffer and then back to another string:

```
procedure TFormMoveStrings.btnMoveFailureClick(
  Sender: TObject);
```

---

53 More information about the new Project Options dialog box and various settings in Chapter 4, in the section "Project Options Dialog Redesigned".

90 - Chapter 3: Porting to Unicode

```
var
  str1, str2: string;
  buffer: TBytes;
begin
  str1 := 'Hello world';

  SetLength (buffer, Length (str1));
  Move (str1[1], buffer[1], Length (str1));

  SetLength (str2, Length (buffer));
  Move (buffer[1], str2[1], Length (buffer));

  Log (str1 + ' becomes ' + str2);
end;
```

As `Length` returns the number of two-byte characters and `Move` works in bytes, only the first half of the string is copied to the buffer and then to the second string with the trailing part of the target string full of whatever data was in its uninitialized memory:

```
Hello world becomes Hello 圠渾潤 we
```

If you have existing code that uses strings as buffers (like in the example above) and don't want to touch your code, a solution might be to change the string type definition to RawByteString (or, to a lesser extent, AnsiString). The MoveStrings demo also has the same algorithm with the strings declared as:

```
var
  str1, str2: RawByteString;
```

This version of the code produces the proper output, as it would by using AnsiString. Depending on the circumstances (the actual meaning of the data being moved, string or buffer with data), you might prefer one of these types over the other.

Even better, whenever possible, change your code to use a dynamic array of bytes like `TBytes`, the data structure I've used in the code snippet of this section to hold a generic buffer. The `TBytes` type is defined in the SysUtils unit as a dynamic array of bytes:

```
type
  TBytes = array of Byte;
```

Reading and Writing Buffers

When you use pure string operations, your existing code will often port to Delphi 2009 with no major obstacles. When you are saving your string data to files or in-memory buffers, it is much easier to see things go wrong[54].

The following is an example of a misused memory stream, in which data is inserted and extracted using different encodings, which doesn't force a conversion, but makes the system consider the characters of a different type than they actually are and mix them up:

```
var
  memStr: TMemoryStream;
begin
  memStr := TMemoryStream.Create;
  try
    Memo1.Lines.
      LoadFromFile ('StreamTroubles_MainForm.pas');
    Memo1.Lines.SaveToStream(memStr, TEncoding.UTF8);
    memStr.Position := 0; // reset
    Memo2.Lines.LoadFromStream(memStr, TEncoding.Unicode);
  finally
    memStr.Free;
  end;
```

Executing this code results in a totally garbled content for Memo2. Now if in this specific code snippet the error is quite glaring, in most real-world situations you can bump into the same effect in much more subtle ways.

My number one recommendation, whenever saving to a file, is to save the BOM and to make it clear in which format it is encoded[55]. This is no more difficult to achieve when working in memory, because even if you don't remember the actual format, Delphi's streaming code adds the proper BOM even to a memory stream.

---

54 I wish a mismatch of the BOM in the file with the preamble of the requested encoding used for loading would raise an exception, as this would make a little more sense. Of course, you could always read the corresponding bytes, rather than using strings, in case of low-level operations you want to fully control.

55 In the previous chapter, in the section "Streams and Encodings" we saw how to define a class helper for the `TStrings` class to change the default encoding for streaming. Refer to that example as a way to customize the behavior of your existing code without having to update it in many places.

So you could fix the program above by calling the `LoadFromStream` method with no encoding, letting the system check the format declared in the stream itself:

```
var
  memStr: TMemoryStream;
begin
  memStr := TMemoryStream.Create;
  try
    Memo1.Lines.
      LoadFromFile ('StreamTroubles_MainForm.pas');
    Memo1.Lines.SaveToStream(memStr, TEncoding.UTF8);
    memStr.Position := 0; // reset
    Memo2.Lines.LoadFromStream(memStr);
  finally
    memStr.Free;
  end;
```

Appending and Concatenating Strings

Another type of coding you should replace whenever possible is string concatenation code. It is not too hard to look for occurrences of `AppendStr` in your code (also because using it causes a deprecated warning), but it is way more complicated to replace the direct string concatenation performed with the + sign.

Also, the suggestion is to replace direct string concatenation with the use of the `TStringBuilder` class in case you are performing a complex concatenation[56]. For showing a message made of two strings, keeping the + sign is certainly fine.

Again, what you should really look out for is concatenation that causes implicit string conversions, as this means copying the data around many, many times. In other words, appending and concatenating strings works fine when all the string variables (left-value and right-values) are of the same type (all UnicodeString, all AnsiString, all UTF8String, etc.). In that case, the compiler uses the correct code page for string literals.

---

[56] Differently from what has been written, using the `TStringBuilder` class doesn't specifically improve performance, but makes the code more clear (in case of complex conversions and concatenations) and, if you need that, compatible with the .NET counterpart. The `TStringBuilder` class is covered in detail in Chapter 7.

When mixing strings using different code pages, explicit casts should be used to avoid hidden conversions that slow down the code (or cause data loss).

Strings are... Strings (not Bookmarks)

Although you have the new RawByteString type available to represent generic arrays of characters or bytes, my recommendation is to use string types only for processing strings of characters. You might think this is obvious, but it is not.

As an example, the VCL has long used a string type to represent dataset bookmarks. The Bookmark property of the TDataSet class in Delphi 2007 was of type TBookmarkStr, defined as:

```
type
  TBookmarkStr = string;
```

The string was not really there, it was simply an alias of a pointer, but with an odd definition that made available a reference-counting mechanism for bookmarks for free.

This definition has now been changed in Delphi 2009, potentially causing some incompatibilities, as the Bookmark property of the TDataSet class is now of type TBookmark, defined as:

```
type
  TBookmark = TBytes;
```

The older TBookmarkStr type is still defined as an alias but has been deprecated (even if not technically marked with the deprecated directive), so you'll have to change your code to use the TBookmark type rather than the TBookmarkStr type. I'll cover the problems related to moving code that uses bookmarks to Delphi 2009 in Chapter 12. My main point here is, if you ever did anything like this, rewrite your code: there is no better way.

Actual Troublesome "Porting" Cases

While recompiling hundreds of applications from my past books, I bumped into a few specific cases in which porting to Unicode would require some actual fixes and not a simple recompile. Some of these cases are really trivial errors, and you'll easily spot them by looking to the source code, but I think it is important to list them here, as your own code might use similar techniques. I could have built endless examples "on purpose", but I decided to go for real cases, even if possibly less significant.

InliningTest used AnsiString

The following code snippet comes from Mastering Delphi 2005 and was later updated for the Delphi 2007 Handbook[57]. It demonstrates the extra speed gained by inlining the Length function, by providing a similar non-inlined version, written as follows:

```
const
  LoopCount = 100000000;

var
  ssample : string;

function LengthStdcall (const s: AnsiString): Longint;
begin
  Result := Integer(S);
  if Result <> 0 then
    Result := PInteger(Result-4)^;
end;

procedure TForm3.bntLenghtClick(Sender: TObject);
var
  ttt: TTimeTest;
  I, J: Integer;
begin
  ssample:= 'sample string';
  J := 0;
  ttt := TTimeTest.Create;
  try
    for I := 0 to LoopCount do
      Inc (J, LengthStdcall (ssample));
    memo1.Lines.Add ('Length ' +
      ttt.Elapsed + '[' + IntToStr (J) + ']');
  finally
    FreeAndNil (ttt);
  end;
end;
```

The code still works, but the timing you get is certainly suspicious:

---

57 The complete source code is available in the dh2007_InliningTest project folder.

```
Length 15,188[1300000013]
Inline 203[1300000013]
```

The massive extra 15 seconds are required to convert the rather short UnicodeString into an AnsiString one hundred million times. All you have to do to fix this code and get back the expected result is to change the declaration of the LengthStdcall function to:

```
function LengthStdcall (const s: string): Longint;
```

This takes back the timing to (approximately):

```
Length 408[1300000013]
Inline 204[1300000013]
```

Calling Ansi-prefixed Functions

In StrUtils and SysUtils there used to be many functions and procedures with Ansi in their name. What happens to them in the Unicode Delphi? Do you need to remove those, keep them, or what?

There isn't a single answer, but in general you can keep them as they are implemented for the generic string type but it would be even better to move to using the identical routines named without the Ansi prefix.

In some cases, the upgrade is somewhat automatic. Most of the Ansi string functions of the RTL (with or without an Ansi prefix) have been moved to the new AnsiStrings unit and that most of them have an overloaded version based on the UnicodeString type. If you don't include that unit you'll end up binding to the UnicodeString version automatically[58].

In fact there are two different situations:

- Some of the Ansi functions now internally work only on the UnicodeString type. When calling them with an AnsiString parameter, they'll convert the string.

- Some of the Ansi functions have AnsiString and UnicodeString overloads. Depending on the string you pass as parameter, you'll call one version or the other.

---

58 If you want to keep using the AnsiString type, and don't want to add the AnsiStrings unit in too many locations, consider using the unit alias directive, for example redefining SysUtils as SysUtils plus AnsiStrings. On a command line that would be: -ASysUtils=SysUtils;AnsiString

96 - Chapter 3: Porting to Unicode

One function in the first group is `AnsiResemblesText`. You can replace a call to `AnsiResemblesText` with one to `ResemblesText`, as they both work on the UnicodeString type now:

```
function ResemblesText(const AText, AOther: string):
  Boolean; overload;
function AnsiResemblesText(const AText, AOther: string):
  Boolean; overload;
```

Of course if your code needs to use an actual AnsiString, even calling the Ansi version of this function won't save you from the extra implicit string conversions. The overload directive in this case is not effectively used, but let's you add a AnsiString version of the functions in your own units.

One function in the second group is `ReverseString`. In this case the Ansi version of the function takes an AnsiString parameter:

```
function ReverseString(const AText: string):
  string; overload;
function AnsiReverseString(const AText: AnsiString):
  AnsiString;
```

In this situation you might have the opposite problem, that is if you keep the Ansi call and use the UnicodeString type the compiler will inject extra useless and possibly lossy conversions. In such a situation you have to update your code to use the non-Ansi version of the function. In the opposite situation (that is if you use `ReverseString` passing an AnsiString), you can also add a uses statement to refer to the AnsiStrings unit and make this third version of the function available:

```
function ReverseString(const AText: AnsiString):
  AnsiString; overload;
```

To make things even more complicated, there are functions that have a Wide version (again for compatibility with the WideStrUtils unit) and some functions that have only an Ansi version.

In a good number of cases, though, the core units (SysUtils and StrUtils) have only UnicodeString versions with the AnsiString versions now moved to the AnsiStrings unit. A good example might be that of `UpperCase`[59] and related functions:

```
// in SysUtils
function UpperCase(const S: string): string; overload;
function UpperCase(const S: string;
```

---

[59] Though functions such as `UpperCase` now take a UnicodeString parameter, they still operate on ASCII characters only.

```
    LocaleOptions: TLocaleOptions): string;
    overload inline;
function AnsiUpperCase(const S: string):
    string; overload;
function WideUpperCase(const S: WideString): WideString;

// in AnsiStrings
function UpperCase(const S: AnsiString):
    AnsiString; overload;
function UpperCase(const S: AnsiString;
    LocaleOptions: TLocaleOptions): AnsiString;
    overload; inline;
function AnsiUpperCase(const S: AnsiString):
    AnsiString; overload;

// in WideStrUtils
function UTF8UpperCase(const S: UTF8string): UTF8string;
```

Overall three rules apply, from what I can see:

- CodeGear tried to minimize your code changes, so that you might keep at least some Ansi calls as they are without harm.

- You should try to get rid of all Ansi calls (and Wide calls) in your program, at the cost of taking some extra time for the migration.

- In case you want to keep using the AnsiString type (which is not recommended), use the new AnsiStrings unit.

Unicode Strings and Win32

As already mentioned in the previous chapter, the Win32 API has in most cases separate calls for ANSI strings (marked with A) or Unicode strings (marked with W for Wide). To be more precise, these APIs use either a PAnsiChar or a PWideChar. I've already stated that the fact that the Win32 API is so heavily based on UTF-16 makes this format the most obvious choice for a native Windows development tools like Delphi.

In many cases, the ANSI versions of the Windows APIs call the Wide versions performing an extra conversion. In other cases the Wide APIs are indeed slower. Having changed at the same time as the string format, the PChar type alias, and the version of the Windows API mapped means you

98 - Chapter 3: Porting to Unicode

can convert most of your code in a very simple way: You do absolutely nothing! Consider the following example:

```
TextOut (Canvas.Handle, 104, 224,
  PChar(str1), Length (str1));
```

This works equally well in Delphi 2007 and in Delphi 2009, even if the Windows API call ends up being different. This is true for most Win32 API calls with string parameters, that have been remapped from the A (ASCII) to the W (Wide) version, along with a change at the compiler level of `PChar` from `PAnsiChar` to `PWideChar`.

There are some specific APIs, though, that don't have two separate versions and invariably require a `PAnsiChar` pointer. A typical example is given by the `GetProcAddress` function, as exported DLL symbols are limited to Ansi. In those cases you might have both to convert the string and to cast it to a different character pointer type. So a line like:

```
GetProcAddress (hmodule, PChar (strFnName))
```

would become:

```
GetProcAddress (hmodule, PAnsiChar (
  AnsiString(strFnName)));
```

Another particular case is that of the `CreateProcessW` functions. This one exists, but can modify the content of the string with the executable file name and will fail with an exception if you pass a constant string value.

Win32 Console Applications

If you are interested in developing Console applications, keep in mind that all Console Input/Output in Delphi still is and will remain based on Ansi. This is true for routines like `Read`, `Write`, `ReadLn`, and `WriteLn`, among others. The console window displays characters using an ANSI codepage (or even an OEM codepage), and the same operations, when redirected to files, might cause the same problem.

Truly, the Windows Console can be opened in Unicode mode (by running it with the */u* flag: `cmd /u`), but this is rarely done as it works only if your output is sent to a file and not to the screen. Delphi 2009 doesn't support the Unicode mode of the console.

If you want to perform some experiments you can start with the UnicodeConsoleTest demo, in which I use a TTextWriter object[60] with a Unicode encoding, connected with a stream associated with the standard output. Display to the console screen is incorrect, as expected. Redirecting to a file produces a UTF-16 file, but one without the BOM. This is the code:

```
var
  aString: string;
  textWriter1: TTextWriter;
  fileStream1: TFileStream;
begin
  aString := 'My ten Euros (10€)';
  try
    fileStream1 := TFileStream.Create(
      GetStdHandle(STD_OUTPUT_HANDLE));
    textWriter1 := TStreamWriter.Create (
      fileStream1, TEncoding.Unicode);
    try
      textWriter1.Write (aString);
    finally
      textWriter1.Free;
      fileStream1.Free;
    end;
  except
    on E:Exception do
      Writeln(E.Classname, ': ', E.Message);
  end;
end.
```

PChar and Pointer Math

The PChar type in Delphi has traditionally been used in two totally different scenarios. The first is to manage characters and strings in a way compatible with the C language and the Windows API. The second is to replace a generic pointer type, because the PChar was the only pointer type to support pointer math. For example, you can move to the next character of a string writing one of the following two:

```
var
  pCh1: PChar;
```

---

60 The TTextWriter class is covered in Chapter 7.

```
begin
  ...
  pCh1 := PChar1 + 1;
  Inc (PChar1);
```

Not only can you increase a `PChar`, but you can also decrease it, compare it with another pointer, and do many other operations.

The Problem with PChar

This use of `PChar` was so handy that this type was often used instead of other pointers, like `PInteger` in the following code fragment. The code below, extracted from the PointerMath example, reads an array using a pointer (a `PChar` pointer) and moving the pointer from one Integer to the next by adding 4 to it (since an Integer is four bytes). Here is the complete code of the method:

```
procedure TFormPointerMath.Button1Click(Sender: TObject);
var
  TenIntegers: array [1..10] of Integer;
  pOneInteger: PChar;
  I: Integer;
begin
  // write
  for I := 1 to 10 do
    TenIntegers [I] := I;

  // now read using a pointer
  pOneInteger := @TenIntegers;
  for I := 1 to 10 do
  begin
    Memo1.Lines.Add(
      'Address: ' + IntToHex (Integer(pOneInteger), 8) +
      ' - Value: ' + IntToStr (PInteger(pOneInteger)^));
    pOneInteger := pOneInteger + 4;
  end;
end;
```

If you compile this code in any version of Delphi from Delphi 2 to Delphi 2007, you'll get an output like the following:

```
Address: 0012F4A8 - Value: 1
Address: 0012F4AC - Value: 2
Address: 0012F4B0 - Value: 3
Address: 0012F4B4 - Value: 4
Address: 0012F4B8 - Value: 5
Address: 0012F4BC - Value: 6
```

```
Address: 0012F4C0 - Value: 7
Address: 0012F4C4 - Value: 8
Address: 0012F4C8 - Value: 9
Address: 0012F4CC - Value: 10
```

You can see that the address is increased by 4 every time, and the proper value is returned. I have to underline it, because if you now recompile the same exact code in Delphi 2009, you'll get totally different output:

```
Address: 0012F4AC - Value: 1
Address: 0012F4B4 - Value: 3
Address: 0012F4BC - Value: 5
Address: 0012F4C4 - Value: 7
Address: 0012F4CC - Value: 9
Address: 0012F4D4 - Value: 29043072
Address: 0012F4DC - Value: 4476177
Address: 0012F4E4 - Value: 4400843
Address: 0012F4EC - Value: 4403501
Address: 0012F4F4 - Value: 4474789
```

This is not what the code meant, of course, but it is what the code says. Incrementing the pointer by 4 characters in Delphi 2009 means moving 8 bytes ahead, since each character is now two bytes. Not only the output is wrong, but we are also doing an illegal memory access, that could be very dangerous in cases where we were writing to that memory area.

From PChar to PByte

If this problem is potentially troublesome, at least for a lot of low-level code, the solution is at hand. In the code above, you can simply replace the version-specific PChar type with the character-agnostic PByte type[61]. A *pointer to byte*, in fact, remains the same and behaves the same regardless of the size of characters. All you have to do in a method like the one above is to change the pointer variable declaration to:

```
var
  pOneInteger: PByte;
```

Without changing anything else in the code, recompile the program and it should work. The good thing is that (in Delphi 2009) PByte supports the same pointer math that PChar supports. In past versions of Delphi, PByte

---

61 An alternative solution, which is more compatible with past versions of Delphi, is to use PAnsiChar rather than PChar. However, using PByte is generally recommended as it makes your intent more clear and is more readable than using PAnsiChar.

didn't support pointer math, but you could still use it in an algorithm like the one discussed here by changing the *plus one* with an increment call:

```
Inc (pOneInteger, 4);
```

That fact that `Inc` and `Dec` work with most pointer types is little known among Delphi users. Still, having the full pointer math means you can also compare pointers, and do other operations.

PInteger and the POINTERMATH Directive

Still, as we are dealing with Integers, wouldn't it be better to write the code like this (changing the increment to one and skipping one of the casts of the original code)?

```
procedure TFormPointerMath.btnPIntegerClick (
  Sender: TObject);
var
  TenIntegers: array [1..10] of Integer;
  pOneInteger: PInteger;
  I: Integer;
begin
  // write
  for I := 1 to 10 do
    TenIntegers [I] := I;

  // now read using a pointer
  pOneInteger := @TenIntegers;
  for I := 1 to 10 do
  begin
    Memo1.Lines.Add(
      'Address: ' + IntToHex (Integer(pOneInteger), 8) +
      ' - Value: ' + IntToStr (pOneInteger^));
    pOneInteger := POneInteger + 1;
  end;
end;
```

Again, this was possible using an `Inc` call even in Delphi 2007 (and the PointerMathD2007 example, you can open with that version of the IDE, proves it), but in Delphi 2009 you can actually compile the code above by adding to the source code the directive:

```
{$POINTERMATH ON}
```

Don't use PChar for Pointer Math

To summarize this section, stop using `PChar` for anything that isn't character or string related. If you need to be able to keep compiling your code in past versions of Delphi, you can use `Inc` and `Dec` and possibly change some of the other code. If all you need to support is Delphi 2009, convert the code to `PByte` (generally the easier route) or use specific pointer types and the new `POINTERMATH` directive.

In any case, doing a search for `PChar` on your entire code base is generally a good idea!

Variants and Open Arrays Parameters

When you are working with variants, most variant to string conversion code will work as expected, as there is a new variant type:

```
varUString = $0102;
   { Unicode string 258 } {not OLE compatible}
```

All variant-based conversions should work properly, not causing much difference in your variant-related code, unless you have to interact to COM or OLE automation, in which case you still have to use the WideString type (as before, so this is not an actual change).

When working with variant open array parameters, and other untyped data structures, instead, the AnsiString and UnicodeString cases must be handled specifically. For example the `TVarRec` structure has now three distinct string-related entries (it used to have two), among many other types I've omitted:

```
type
  TVarRec = record
    case Byte of
      vtString:        (VString: PShortString);
      vtAnsiString:    (VAnsiString: Pointer);
      vtUnicodeString: (VUnicodeString: Pointer);
      ...
```

If you process an open array parameter with a `case` statement that has specific branches for strings, you have to consider this new alternative.

What's Next

This ends the coverage of Unicode support in Delphi 2009. Next, in Part II I'll take an in-depth look at the changes in the IDE, the compiler and the RTL. In the RTL section we'll get back to further string management features. And further on, in the database part of the book, I'll cover how the changes introduced for Unicode support affect the `TDataSet` class and related classes.

Part II: Delphi 2009 And Its Compiler

Now that I have fully covered the most important new feature of Delphi 2009, Unicode support, it is about time to open up the entire development environment, the compiler, the runtime libraries. This entire section is on core and low-level features, while the user interface and database material will be covered in following parts of the book.

- **Chapter 4: New IDE Features**
- **Chapter 5: Generics**
- **Chapter 6: Anonymous Methods**
- **Chapter 7: More Language and RTL Changes**

Marco Cantù, Delphi 2009 Handbook

Chapter 4: New IDE Features

The 6th incarnation[62] of the Galileo IDE has only a limited set of new capabilities, if you don't take into account the fact that everything has been converted to Unicode, which was probably far from trivial. The most relevant improvements relate with the new extensions to the Project Manager and the ability to share project options among different projects, using the new options files. Windows resource management improves significantly in Delphi 2009, too.

---

62 I'm counting them as follows: 1 was C#Builder, 2 was Delphi 8, 3 was Delphi 2005, 4 was Delphi 2006 (or Borland Developer Studio), 5 was Delphi 2007 (or RAD Studio). The number *6.0* is confirmed also by the name of the folder used by default to install the product.

Installing and Running

Like Delphi 2007, the installation of Delphi 2009 is based on InstallAware. This time around, though, the *installation experience* has been considerably improved, particularly in speed. Delphi 2009 installation can be completed in 20 minutes rather than several hours. The installation of the Update 1 of the product (released at the end of October 2008) is equally smooth.

A noticeable change in this respect is the fact that help is now separately installed, so it can be updated more frequently and separately from the main product (so you don't have to reinstall Delphi to get updated help, or to reinstall help should you want to reinstall the IDE). Installing help can take way more time than installing the actual product and the help install image is bigger than the IDE one.

When installing on Windows Vista, you'll have (by default) the product installed in the following folders:

```
C:\Program Files\CodeGear\RAD Studio\6.0
C:\Users\Public\Documents\RAD Studio\6.0\Demos\
C:\Program Files\Common Files\CodeGear Shared
```

.NET SDK Not Needed

Previously, since Delphi 8 up to and including Delphi 2007, one of the prerequisites for installing the IDE was the presence of the Microsoft .NET SDK (version 1.1 earlier, version 2.0 later)[63]. It is not needed for Delphi 2009. You still have to install the considerably smaller Microsoft .NET runtime, which you might already have as part of the operating system, but don't need the Development Kit, which is much bigger and requires hundreds of MB.

The help engine used by CodeGear is Microsoft's Document Explorer, or *DExplorer*. This was previously available only in the SDK, but now can be

---

63 The .NET SDK was required for the Document Explorer, until Microsoft made available a standalone help installer. Other portions of the .NET architecture used by the Delphi IDE, including the MSBuild engine, are part of the standard runtime, not of the SDK.

deployed as a separate install, which is what CodeGear is using in this version of Delphi.

Delphi help is very large (which is why it takes so much time to install), as it includes both CodeGear documentation and the Microsoft Platform documentation. In this release, however, the team fixed some "ranking" issues so that Delphi-specific topics should always be listed before the generic platform ones. Delphi-specific content was also much improved.

Windows Install Clean Up

At times, when uninstalling Delphi to replace it with an updated version, the installer complains, stops and won't work as expected. In these cases, CodeGear recommends cleaning all of the application folders (including some hidden ones that depend on the operating system). An alternative it to use Microsoft own Windows Install Clean Up utility, that you can find at:

```
http://support.microsoft.com/default.aspx?
   scid=kb;en-us;290301
```

Beware that using such a low-level tool can hamper your system, so proceed with caution (only after reading the instructions and at your own risk).

The -idecaption Flag

You probably know (although this was a well-kept secret for many years[64]) that you can run multiple instances of the IDE, possibly at the same time, with different registry settings using the -R command line flag.

The problem if you run two different versions of the IDE at the same time is that it is hard to tell which is which. Another companion command line parameter for the IDE is -idecaption, that takes a caption as value. Summing the two flags you could run the IDE with the following link:

```
"C:\Program Files\CodeGear\RAD Studio\6.0\bin\bds.exe"
 -pDelphi -rSmall -idecaption="Small Tiburòn"
```

---

64 I documented the -R flag in Chapter 1 of the book "Delphi 2007 Handbook", the section "Running the Delphi IDE".

110 - Chapter 4: New IDE Features

This command runs the Delphi IDE with the Delphi Win32 personality only, activated the "Small" registry settings, and changes the IDE caption to "Small Tiburòn[65]", as shown here:

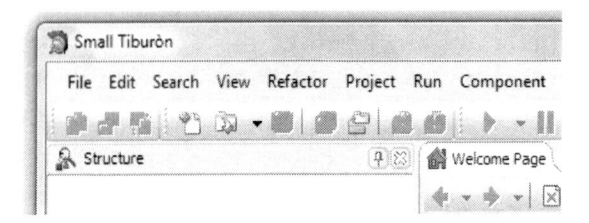

If not specified from the command line, the IDE caption is retrieved from the Registry, in the Personalities section, in which there is a different string for each version (or active personality) of the IDE.

Managing Delphi Projects

Managing projects is a very common operation. If Delphi 2007 added some brand new concepts, like the MSBuild support, the target builds (Debug and Release) and the pre-build and post-build events, the new version makes these features more flexible and much easier to use, starting with a significant revamp of the Project Manager itself. Before we look at the Project Manager, though, we have to look to upgrading project files and the renewed Project Options dialog box.

Upgrading Project Configuration Files

Since the early days of Delphi, the project source code file (with the .DPR extension) contains Object Pascal code and uses one or more separate project configuration files for storing other settings. The format and extension of the project configuration file changed a few times in recent versions, moving from an INI file to an XML file and then to an XML file for MSBuild (the .DPROJ file format).

---

65 As you might have heard, Tiburòn was the field test name for Delphi 2009.

From Delphi 2007 to Delphi 2009 the overall format of this project configuration file doesn't change. But its content is indeed different, and Delphi 2007 doesn't recognize those options added by the newer version of the IDE. When you open an existing Delphi 2007 project, the Delphi 2009 IDE will ask you for the name of a backup file into which it can copy the existing version of the project configuration file:

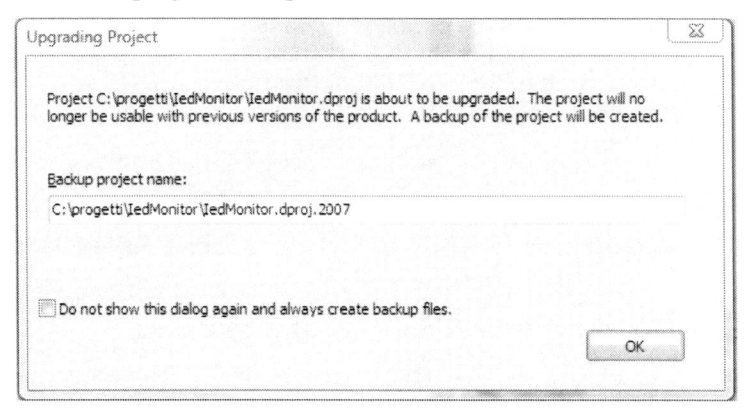

The default name for the project configuration file backup is the project name with the extension `.dproj.2007`. In this specific case, for example, I renamed the project file as `IedMonitor2007.dproj`. After you perform this operation, the IDE will add to the message pane the line:

```
Upgrading project. Backup
C:\progetti\IedMonitor\IedMonitor2007.dproj created.
```

Note though, that an updated Delphi 2009 version of the project configuration file is not created until you actually save it.

The backup version will let you reopen the project in Delphi 2007. If you need backwards compatibility, though, a better idea might be to save the Delphi 2009 version of the project with a different name.

In the new .DPROJ file, Delphi 2009 adds a new project version tag:

```
    <ProjectVersion>11.1</ProjectVersion>
```

The upgrade involved changes in the build configuration (as explained later), and in the resource management. The following sections are new or heavily modified:

```
<PropertyGroup Condition="'$(Config)'=='Release' or
         '$(Cfg_Release)'!=''">
    <Cfg_Release>true</Cfg_Release>
    <CfgParent>Base</CfgParent>
```

```xml
        <Base>true</Base>
    </PropertyGroup>
    <PropertyGroup Condition="'$(Config)'=='Debug' or
            '$(Cfg_Debug)'!=''">
        <Cfg_Debug>true</Cfg_Debug>
        <CfgParent>Base</CfgParent>
        <Base>true</Base>
    </PropertyGroup>
    <PropertyGroup Condition="'$(Base)'!=''">
        <DCC_DependencyCheckOutputName>SimpleApp.exe
        </DCC_DependencyCheckOutputName>
    </PropertyGroup>
    <ItemGroup>
        <DelphiCompile Include="SimpleApp.dpr">
            <MainSource>MainSource</MainSource>
        </DelphiCompile>
        <DCCReference Include="SimpleAppMainForm.pas">
            <Form>Form30</Form>
        </DCCReference>
        <BuildConfiguration Include="Base">
            <Key>Base</Key>
        </BuildConfiguration>
        <BuildConfiguration Include="Release">
            <Key>Cfg_Release</Key>
            <CfgParent>Base</CfgParent>
        </BuildConfiguration>
        <BuildConfiguration Include="Debug">
            <Key>Cfg_Debug</Key>
            <CfgParent>Base</CfgParent>
        </BuildConfiguration>
    </ItemGroup>
```

If you try reopening this project file in Delphi 2007 (the only past version recognizing this format), you'll see the following error:

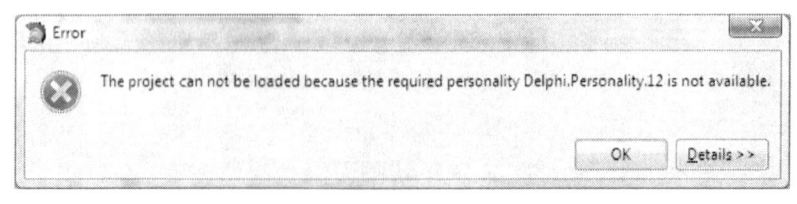

Project Options Dialog Redesigned

The Project Options dialog box is one of the Delphi dialogs I tend to use quite often, and I guess I'm not alone. That's why its extensive redesign in Delphi 2009 at times leaves me puzzled. The redesign involves the pages with options that are part of the build configuration, and (as we'll see later in the section "Build Configurations and Configuration Settings") those pages of the dialog box are in fact used also inside the Project Configuration Manager. Look for example at the differences in the Delphi Compiler Options page between Delphi 2007 (here) and Delphi 2009 (in the next page):

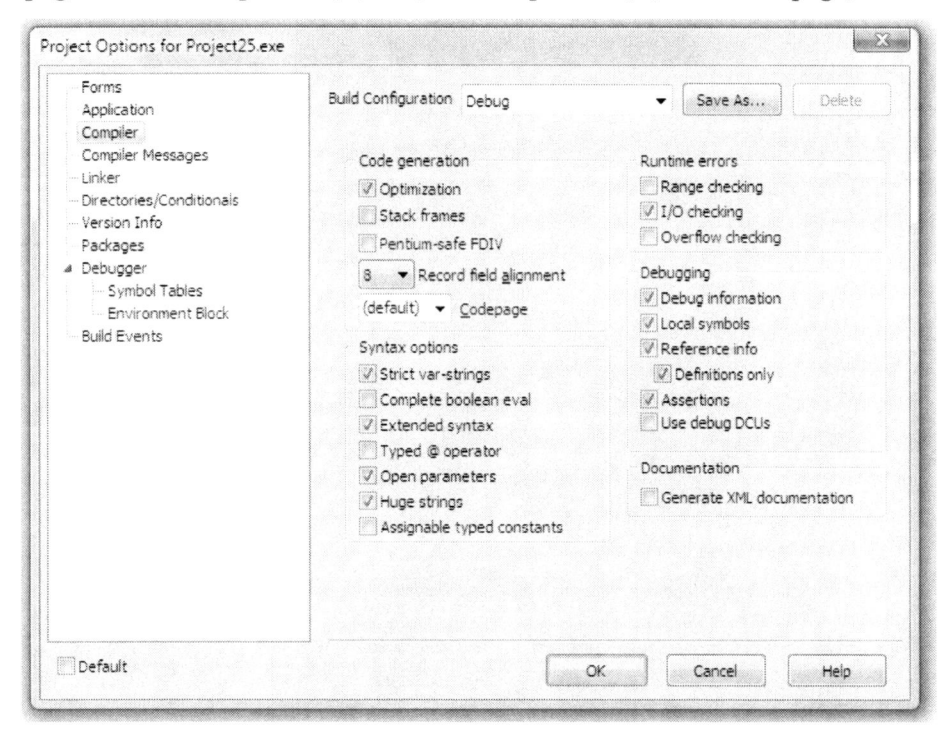

The difference is very significant. In the new design check boxes are replaced by "True/False" and radio buttons by combo boxes with the various options. There is also a help area at the bottom (minimized in the picture above, as I wanted to fit all options of the page in the dialog), providing limited information about the various alternatives. One interesting element the "description" area provides is the default value for the option.

114 - Chapter 4: New IDE Features

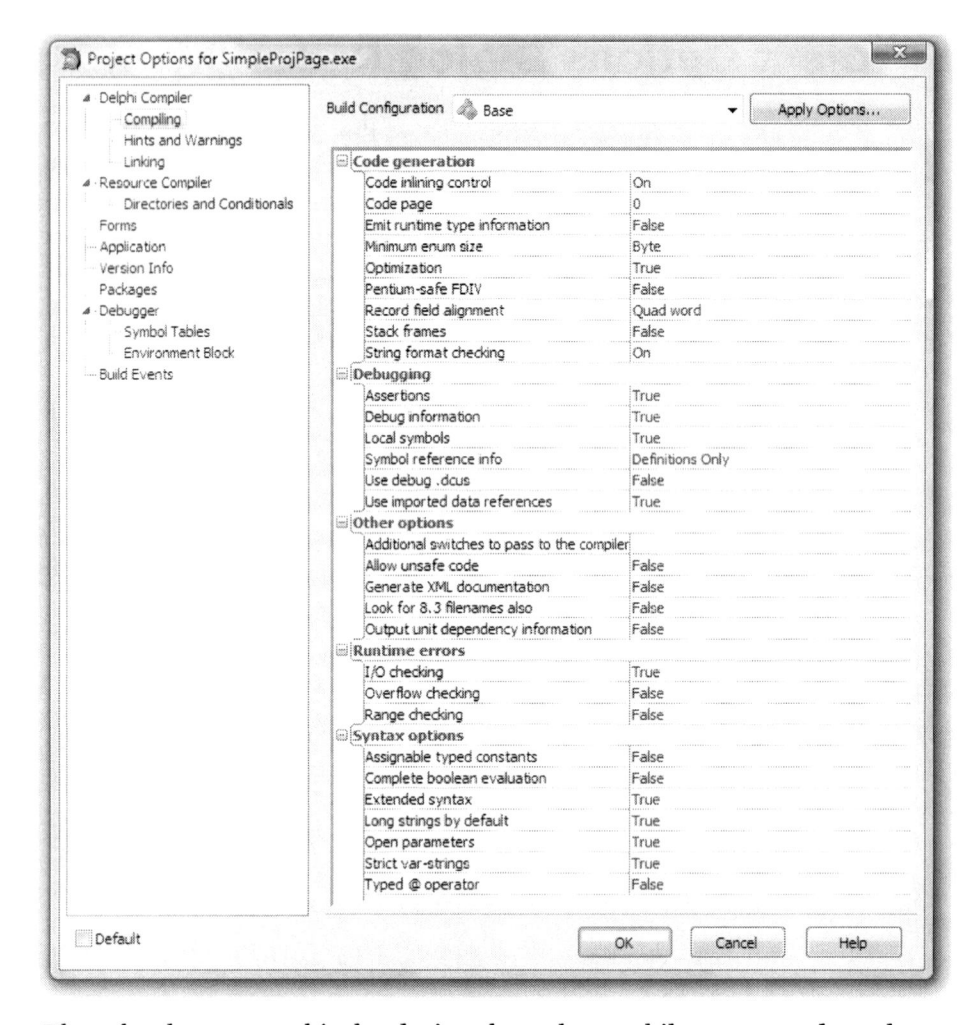

There has been a graphical redesign that takes a while to get used to, also because items within each group are now listed alphabetically, so they are in a different order than before. The directory options have been moved under the main Delphi Compiler node. But beside organizational changes, is there anything missing or new?

New Project Options for the Compiler

In the "Delphi Compiler/Compiling" page, which used to be called compiler, the Code Generation section has the following new options:

- *Code inlining control* corresponds to the $INLINE compiler directive and controls how inlining works.
- *Emit runtime type information* corresponds to -$M flag on the command line or the $M directive, and determines the generation of runtime time information for a given class (or all of the classes of a project).
- *Minimum enum size* corresponds to -$Z flag (or the $Z directive) and determines the minimum size used for values of enumerated types (a Byte, a Word, a Double Word, or a Quad Word).
- *String format checking*, which is on by default, can be disabled to avoid some automatic string format checks[66] and corresponds to the $STRINGCHECKS directive. This compiler option is new to Delphi 2009 and was supposed to remain undocumented and fairly hidden... so it is quite a surprise to see it prominently in the Project Options dialog box.
- *Code page* was already in past versions but is now much more relevant in relationship with how the AnsiString type works, again as covered in Chapter 2.

The Debugging section has the new option *Use imported data references* (mapped to $G), which controls the creation of imported data references (increasing memory efficiency but preventing the access of global variables defined in other runtime packages).

The Runtime errors and Syntax options sections have the same elements (and also the same defaults) as past versions of Delphi. The Other options section sports new options, except the *Generate XML documentation* that was already available:

- *Additional switches to pass to the compiler* can be used to insert directly further command line compiler options not specifically supported by the IDE, although having this feature available now technically means that Delphi 2009 now supports each and every compiler option.

---

66 As we saw in Chapter 2, in many places within the Delphi RTL, there are calls to the EnsureUnicodeString function and other functions of the *Ensure String* family. You can ask the compiler to skip these extra calls by disabling using the --stringchecks compiler options or the $STRINGCHECKS directive. These switches are not documented and not officially supported, but directly available in the Project Options dialog of the IDE, which I find quite odd.

Marco Cantù, Delphi 2009 Handbook

- *Allow unsafe code* will let you compile code deemed unsafe for a managed environment like .NET which makes little (or no) sense with the Win32 compiler.
- *Look for 8.3 filenames also* instructs the compiler to work on very old versions of Windows and corresponds to the -P compiler option.
- *Output unit dependency information* will turn on the `--depends` compiler flag, which is apparently not maintained for now.

Other New Project Options

The Hints and Warnings page corresponds to the old Compiler Messages page. There are, of course, several new hints related with Unicode strings and other new compiler features.

The Linking page, which used to be called Linker, is visually quite different (and much more compact, as there were a few radio buttons) but the only new option is *Set base address for relocatable images*.

The main level Delphi compiler page has exactly the same options as previously found under Directories/Conditionals. What can be quite confusing is that there is another page named Directories and Conditionals which is part of the resource compiler configuration under the Resource Compiler main level page. These pages are brand new and let you control the resource compiler from the Delphi IDE in ways never experienced in the past. There is a specific section later in this chapter, "Managing Resources in the IDE", covering this topic.

Default Projects Location

Since Delphi 2005, the default location for all new projects has been under the user documents folder. Few Delphi developers know this can be modified by setting a value for the Default project edit box in the Environment Options page of the Tools | Options dialog box.

The Project Manager

Along with a redesign of the Project Options dialog box (which I still haven't completely covered when examining the new build configuration features) Delphi 2009 sees a significant update of the Project Manager pane, one of the most commonly used panes of the IDE. Even a cursory glance of its window will reveal some of its new features:

You can see there is a new Build Configurations node, with sub nodes, used to activate a build configuration in a much simpler way than in Delphi 2007. This topic is covered in the later section "Build Configurations and Configuration Settings".

The Project Manager toolbar has several new buttons, up to the point that you'd generally want to remove the Text Labels using the context menu of the toolbar itself. The new Sync button selects the current file in the editor in the Project Manager, only if the file is part of the project, of course. The opposite operation (that is, activate the current selection of the Project Manager in the editor) can be done with a double-click.

The Expand and Collapse buttons will recursively expand and collapse all nodes under the current node. Apply Expand to a project group and you'll see a tree with all configuration and file nodes of all projects in the group. Very handy, I have to say. The fourth new button, Views, is covered in the next section.

Project Manager Views

Another brand new feature is the Project Manager views configuration. On the right side of the toolbar, you can see a new Views button, that let's you change how the Project Manager shows files that have been placed in different folders. There are three options. I tested them by creating a sample program (called ProjManagerTest) with two forms in the main folder and two units in a secondary folder called Shared and placed at the same level in the file system hierarchy:

- **Directory (Nested)** is the default setting (and the only one available in Delphi 8 to Delphi 2007) that shows the files grouped by directory and the directories mimic the actual disk structure with separate nodes you can expand (so you might have have to expand multiple nodes to move down a couple of sub-folders):

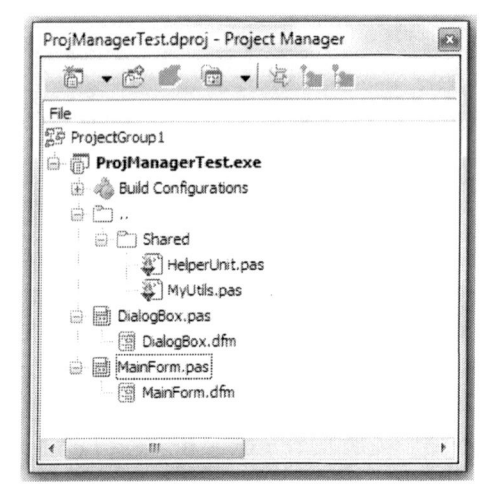

- **Directory (Flat)** is a new view in which the files are still divided by directory but each different directory is part of a list regardless of its position on the file system. In other words, you get a list of folders, each containing files, rather than (possibly) other nested folders:

Chapter 4: New IDE Features - 119

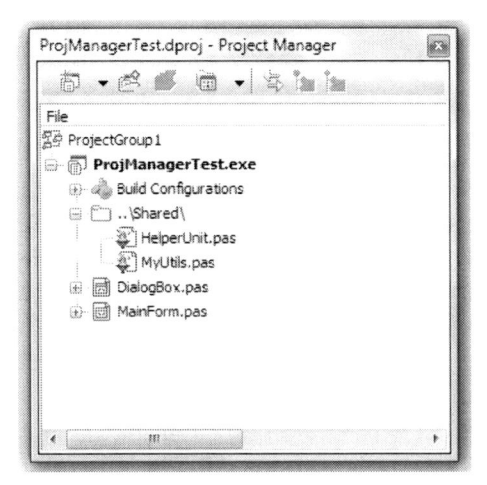

- **List** is a new view corresponding to the traditional Delphi 7 list of files in the project manager. Directories are simply ignored and you get an alphabetic list of files:

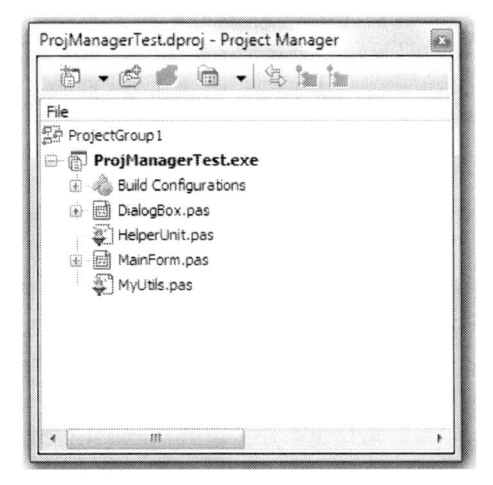

Build Configurations and Configuration Settings

As I mentioned earlier and you can see from the images on the previous pages, the Project Manager has a new Build Configurations node for every project (that is, in cases where you are working with a project group with multiple projects active). This node replaces the rather cumbersome separate window used to manage the build configuration in Delphi 2007. Using the node and its sub-nodes you can change the current build configuration with a double click, and execute an actual build directly on the given node.

By selecting either a specific build configuration or the main node, you can also add a new configuration. Depending on the item selected when you do the operation you'll create a main configuration or a sub-configuration. To be more precise, the node you pick determines the base configuration, since even the predefined configurations inherit their core settings from the Base configuration (which is the core configuration from which Debug and Release inherit). What do I mean by "inherit settings" from a configuration? Delphi 2009 has a new configuration management system, in which you can apply a setting to a specific configuration (like Debug or Release) or set an option that the two configurations don't specify but *inherit* from the Base configuration. In a specific configuration you can see the specific value and the one inherited from a base configuration in two consecutive lines, see if they match and change either one or the other (affecting also the specific configuration). This is achieved by expanding each configuration setting line by selecting the plus sign on the left. This is what you can get by expanding the three Runtime errors lines in the Delphi Compiler/Compiling page:

Runtime errors	
I/O checking	True
Value from "Base"	True
Overflow checking	**False**
Value from "Base"	**True**
Range checking	True
Value from "Base"	**True**

Modifying the setting in the Base configuration will affect also any other configuration which inherits from that setting.

In the Project Manager you can also select a build configuration and export its settings to an "option set" file. This is like saving a configuration *template* or skeleton to an external file, and the configuration will be linked to the file.

This makes it easy to move those same settings to a new or another existing project, as you can use the Project Manager (using the Apply Options Set local menu item while on a build configuration) or the Project Options dialog box (using the Apply Options button) to import a set of configuration options. In both cases Delphi opens up the Apply Option Set dialog box, in which you can pick a file and choose whether to keep the external configuration file linked (so that a change in the file will be reflected in the projects using it) or simply merge the current settings using some *priority* rules:

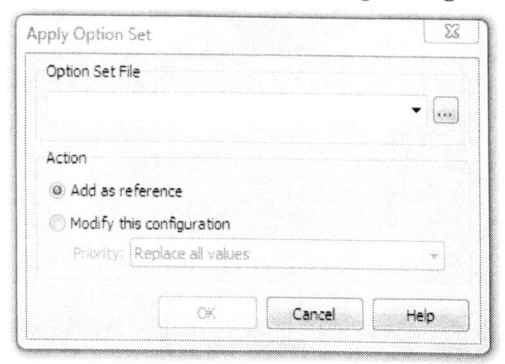

Once you have created an external option set on a file, you can edit it from any project referring to it, using the Edit local menu of the Project Manager pane. This opens up the an editor containing a subset of the pages of the Project Options dialog box, as shown below:

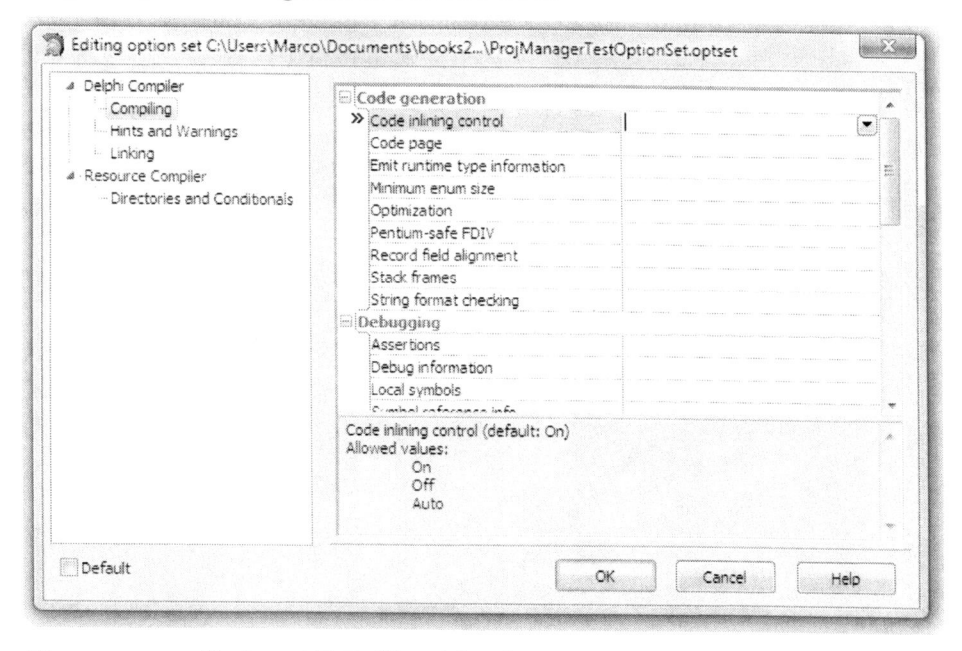

The `.OPTSET` file is an XML file with a format similar to the .DPROJ format, again based on the MSBUILD XML format, and an `OptionSet` project type. In the specific example you can find in the ProjManagerTest folder, the ProjManagerTestOptionsSet.optset file has the following content:

```
<Project xmlns="http://.../msbuild/2003">
  <PropertyGroup>
    <DCC_RunTimeTypeInfo>true</DCC_RunTimeTypeInfo>
  </PropertyGroup>
  <ProjectExtensions>
    <Borland.Personality>Delphi.Personality
      </Borland.Personality>
    <Borland.ProjectType>OptionSet</Borland.ProjectType>
    <BorlandProject><Delphi.Personality/></BorlandProject>
  </ProjectExtensions>
</Project>
```

Project Configuration Manager

With the build options available directly in the Project Manager pane, you don't have to use the Configuration Manager to change the current build configuration. Still, this dialog box was quite handy as it let you change the build configuration for many projects in a project group at the same time. In fact, the Configuration Manager is also available in Delphi 2009, and in a much improved version that let's you manage the various build configuration and option sets for all of the projects of a group at once.

To invoke the Configuration Manager you don't use the local menu of the Project Manager, as in Delphi 2007, but select the corresponding item in the Project menu of the IDE. When you do, you'll get this redesigned user interface:

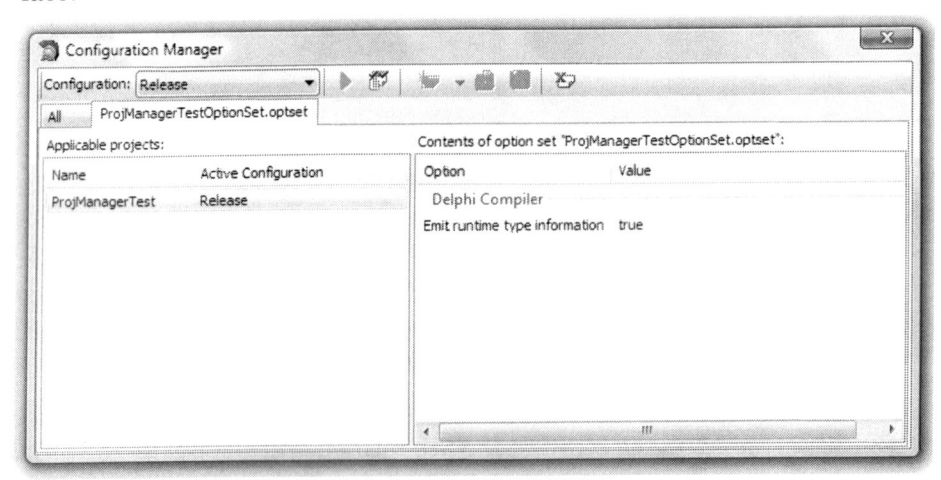

On the left side you can see a list of projects with the active configuration for each of them. On the right side you can see some details for the configuration selected in the tab above it, like the list of the non-default settings (the one in the image is the summary of the option set file listed in the previous section). Using the tab you can also filter the projects on the left side that have the given configuration or option set active.

In Delphi 2009, the Configuration Manager let's you edit the project options for each build configuration, add new configurations, create or edit option sets, modify the active configuration... and perform most of the related operations in a single location, even if it's not trivial to use.

When you are working on multiple projects within a project group, the Configuration Manager has a distinct advantage over browsing in the Project Manager to work on the build configurations. For single projects, the Project Manager now has all you need.

Managing Resources in the IDE

In the most recent versions of Delphi, you could add resource scripts (.RC files) or compiled resource files (.RES files) to the Project Manager to let it compile them along with the project linking them to the executable. In Delphi 2009 managing resources has been simplified by the inclusion of a few more tools.

First, you can now drag individual resource files to the Project Manager to get them included as resources in a project. You can drag icons, bitmaps, and more. Delphi will generate a resource script file for these extra project resources, and compile it directly along with your program, embedding these resources in the executable. You can change any attribute of these resource files (including their internal name) in the Object Inspector:

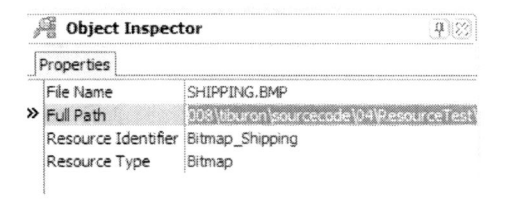

124 - Chapter 4: New IDE Features

Second, under the Project pull-down of the main menu of the IDE there is a new menu item, Resources. Selecting this item brings up the Resources dialog box, which you can use to revise all of the resources of the program, add new resource files, rename them, change the format, and so on:

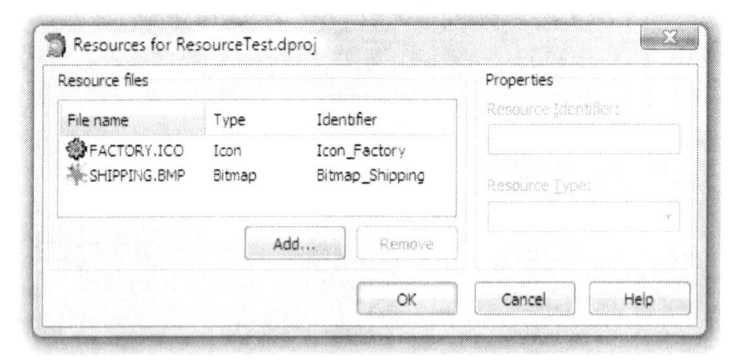

By adding a few resources to a project, at compile time Delphi will generate a proper resource file for you. For the ResourceTest program (with the resources depicted above), Delphi 2009 generates a resource script file listing the project resources called `ResourceTestResource.rc`:

```
Icon_Factory Icon "FACTORY.ICO"
Bitmap_Shipping Bitmap "SHIPPING.BMP"
```

This resource script file is not added to the project (if you do so, you'll see duplicate resource warnings), but it is compiled along with it. In fact, if you make an error, like declaring your bitmap as an icon, the compiler will stop with the error:

```
[BRCC32 Error] ResourceTestResource.rc(2): resource file
SHIPPING.BMP is not in 3.00 format
```

and open the resource script file at the offending line. At compile time, Delphi 2009 generates (or updates) the resource script file, compiles it, and binds it to the executable. The intermediary file is a file with extension DRES that's included in the project with a directive automatically added to the project source code file (along side with the standard RES file including the project icon and string resources):

```
program ResourceTest;

{$R *.dres}

uses
  Forms,
  ResourceTest_MainForm in
```

```
    'ResourceTest_MainForm.pas' {FormResourceTest};
{$R *.res}
begin
  Application.Initialize;
  ...
```

You can see the resource compilation steps in the Output view produced by the compiler since Delphi 2007 introduced MSBuild support. Here is the related output you'll see if you keep the Verbose flag of the resource compiler options on:

```
c:\program files\codegear\rad studio\6.0\bin\cgrc.exe
-c65001 -v ResourceTestResource.rc -foResourceTest.dres

CodeGear Resource Compiler/Binder Version 1.00 Copyright
(c) 2008 Embarcadero Technologies Inc.

Microsoft (R) Windows (R) Resource Compiler Version
6.0.5724.0
Copyright (C) Microsoft Corporation. All rights reserved.

Creating ResourceTest.dres
Using codepage 65001 as default

ResourceTestResource.rc.

Writing ICON:1,                 lang:0x409, size 744
Writing GROUP_ICON:ICON_FACTORY,   lang:0x409, size 20.
Writing BITMAP:BITMAP_SHIPPING,    lang:0x409, size 44264
```

In case you've never used Windows resources directly, the ResourceTest program has a few lines of code to load the icon as the application and main form icon and to load the bitmap in an Image component:

```
procedure TFormResourceTest.btnGifClick(
  Sender: TObject);
begin
  Image1.Picture.Bitmap.LoadFromResourceName(
    hInstance, 'Bitmap_Shipping');
end;

procedure TFormResourceTest.btnIconClick(
  Sender: TObject);
begin
  Icon.LoadFromResourceName(hInstance, 'Icon_Factory');
  Application.Icon.LoadFromResourceName(
    hInstance, 'Icon_Factory');
end;
```

A "New" Resource Compiler

Recent versions of Delphi, up to and including Delphi 2007, used the Borland Resource Compiler (`BRCC32.EXE`) an *outdated* program emitting the following historical copyright notation:

```
Copyright (c) 1990, 1999 Inprise Corporation. All rights reserved.
```

Delphi 2009 ships with a new resource compiler, or (to be more precise) a different resource compiler: the one from the Microsoft Windows SDK. This is certainly beneficial is terms of support for all of new resource formats Windows handles, but causes a few problems due to the fact the the Borland resource compiler from the early days extended the Microsoft one, providing extra features that are now lost.

You can still decide to use the Borland resource compiler, by using the corresponding option[67] in the Resource Compiler page of the Project Options dialog (which let's you also edit other parameters of the resource compiler):

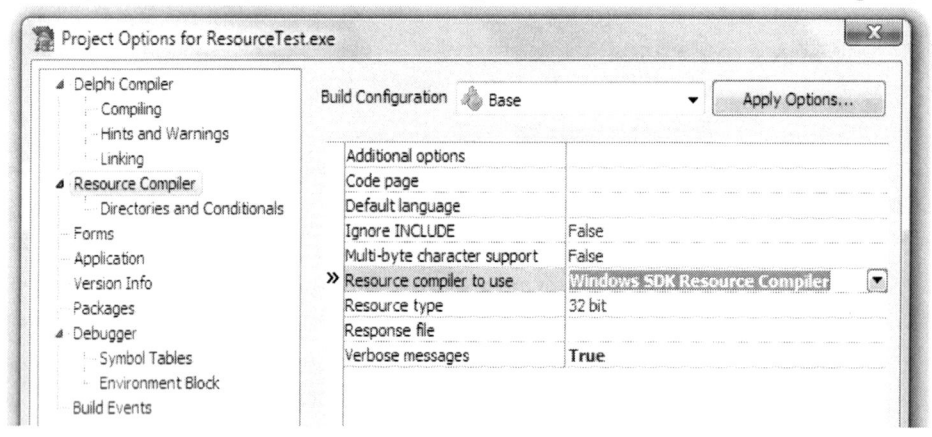

The Windows SDK Resource Compiler is invoked through the new CodeGear Resource Compiler/Binder, which is simply a front end to the SDK compiler. Changes in the resource compiler include the missing ability to handle image (binary) data inline, to support trailing commas after strings

---

[67] During my tests on the final release of Delphi 2009, the option to enable the Borland resource compiler seemed to be ignored by the IDE. Maybe a fix is coming. As these resource compilers are external executable files, you can certainly rename them to redirect the operations, but as the parameters being passed are different, this can lead to errors.

in a string list, the different way to handle strings (now treated as C-language strings, forcing you to escape any \ in a file name with a double backslash), the different way to manage the folders for includes...

Again, if you've never used resource files directly, you can probably ignore any of these changes. Anything managed directly by the Delphi environment, from the embedding of DFM files as resources to the use of the `resourcestring` declaration, is fully backwards compatible. If you did use resources directly, you should revise your resource files with some care.

The Delphi Class Explorer

A brand new pane in Delphi 2009 is the Delphi Class Explorer pane (available from the Delphi Class Explorer item of the View menu). The Delphi Class Explorer offers a project wide representation of the symbols, differently from the Structure View[68], that shows a (somewhat similar) graphical representation of the elements of a single unit.

In the Delphi Class Explorer at the first level, you'll see a list of nodes hosting the global definition of each unit (plus the project file), while the remaining nodes show all of the classes defined in the project:

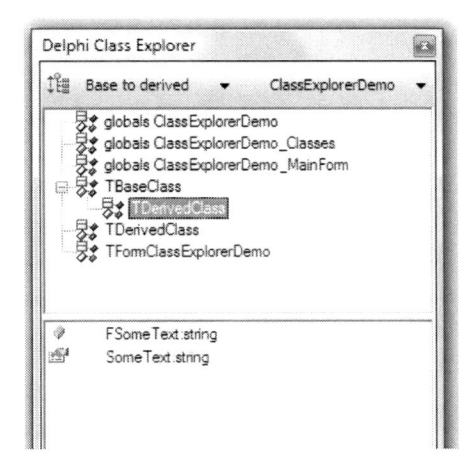

---

68 The Structure View for a source code file was originally called Code Explorer until Delphi 7, not to be confused with the new Delphi Class Explorer.

128 - Chapter 4: New IDE Features

For each class you can see the specific members and the relationship with other classes. This is depicted according to the selection in the first toolbar button: Base to derived (displayed before), Derived to base, or Container (displayed below).

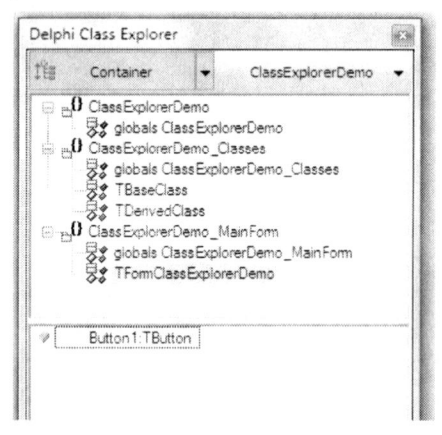

In this last case, classes (and globals) are divided by unit and no inheritance relationship is displayed. The local menu let's you add a new field to a class, a new operation (or a method, including constructors and destructors), or a property, as in the image below:

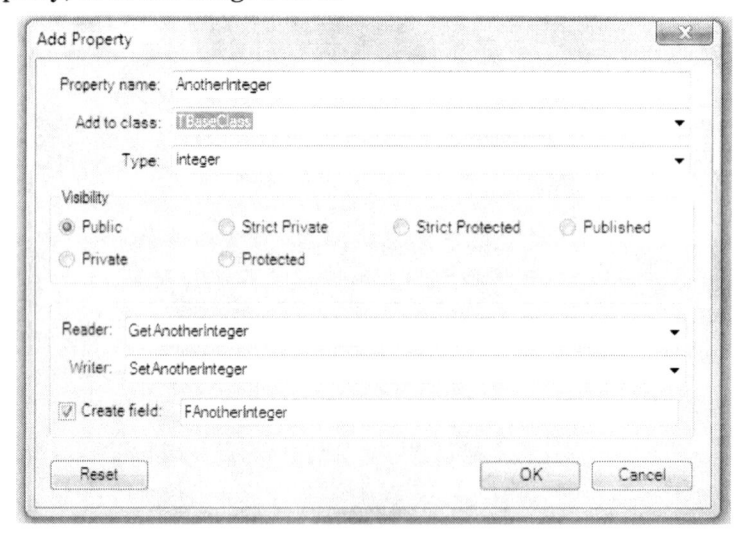

Adding a property works in a proper Delphi way (much more than using UML-based modeling). The tool tends to map to setter and getter methods though you can go for a direct field mapping if you prefer, by adding a property and asking for a corresponding field to be created. The Class Explorer will add the following lines to the class, as in the previous image:

```
type
  TBaseClass = class
  strict private
    function GetAnotherInteger : Integer;
    procedure SetAnotherInteger(val : Integer);
  public
    property AnotherInteger: Integer
      read GetAnotherInteger write SetAnotherInteger;
  strict private
  var
    FAnotherInteger:Integer;
  end;
```

I find the use of a `strict private var` block quite odd, but it is formally correct and probably adding the extra `var` keyword makes code generation easier and less risky. Still, if I were to reformat the code to my liking, I'd take way more time than declaring the property and use Class Completion, which produces cleaner and more standard Delphi code. For me, the Delphi Class Explorer is mostly a tool for navigating the source code of a project, and I'd rather use it than the Model View unless I needed UML diagrams.

Other New Features

The updated Project Options dialog, the new features of the Project Manager and the extended build configurations, the improved support for resources, and the Class Explorer are probably the most significant new features of the IDE in Delphi 2009, if you don't consider the fact that the entire IDE has been Unicode enabled.

There are many other minor features that can help you in the day-by-day work with the Delphi development environment, listed in this section. A noticeable set of improvements, described in a specific chapter, are related to COM. The changes in the IDE related to the large changes in COM support and the Type Library editor, are covered in Chapter 9.

Tool Palette Search Box

In Delphi 2006, you could type while the Tool Palette was selected to filter components starting with those letters (with the exception of the initial T). In Delphi 2007 you could do the same, but also by selecting text inside the component name, so you could pick, say, IdHTTP by typing the more obvious HTTP. In Delphi 2009, the Tool Palette has the same behavior as Delphi 2007, but with a different user interface that makes it more obvious to all users that you can search the components list by typing:

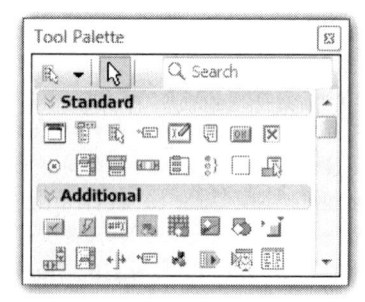

As you select the palette (the handy shortcut is Ctrl+Alt+P), you can start typing in the search box (rather than in the caption of the pane) and the Tool Palette will filter the components being displayed:

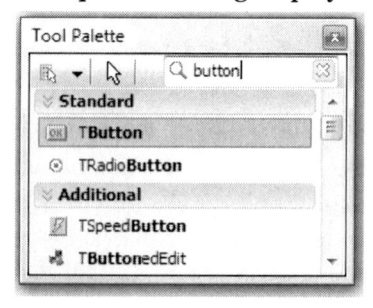

There is another change in the Tool Palette. As many people complained because of the excessive scrolling needed to reach the categories towards the bottom of the list, the auto-collapse of categories is now the default behavior. Another behavior you can fine-tune is whether the current selection of the Search box is kept after selecting a component or not.

Updated Components Wizards

The dialog boxes used to create a new VCL component or import a component (an ActiveX control or a .NET assembly, to be used like a COM control) have been improved and turned into multi-step wizards.

The actual capability to create an empty component skeleton or one wrapping an external control, has not been modified significantly. The only new feature is the ability (for both wizards) to either install the component into an existing package or into a new one which you have to name.

The relevant change is in the user interface of this wizard you can activate from the Components menu of the IDE. For example, the initial page of the New VCL Component wizard has a search box used to filter the base class component to inherit from:

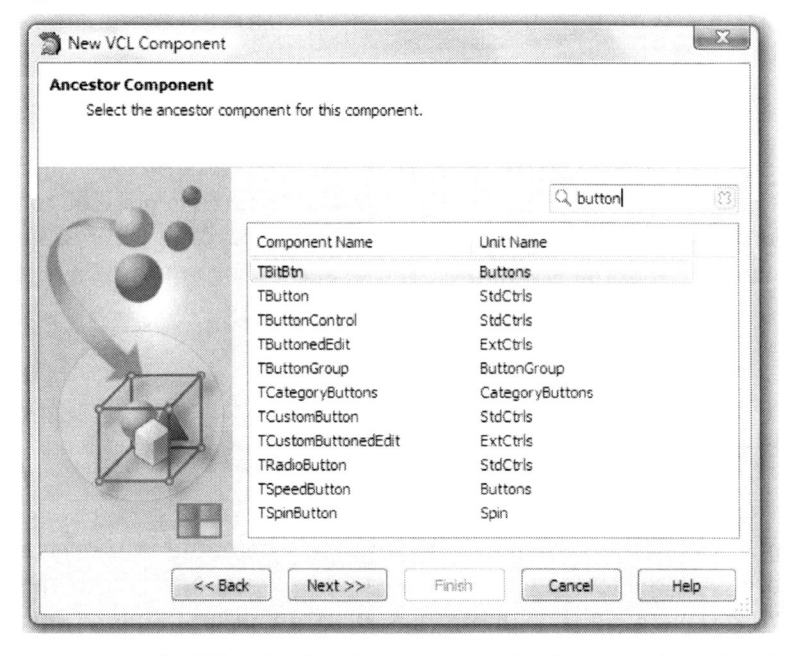

As you proceed, filling in the class name and other standard details, you'll get to the final page, which let's you create a new package or add the new component to an existing one, as shown in the next page.

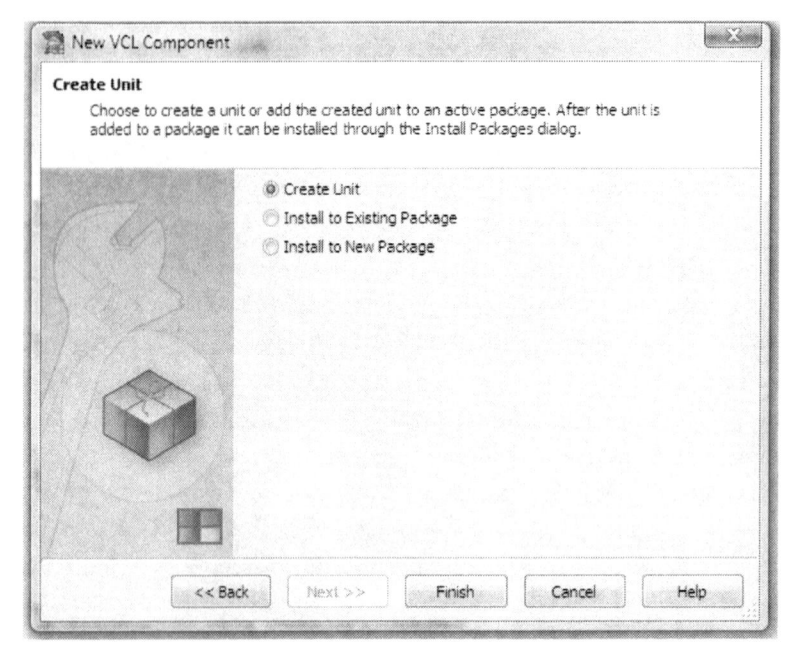

In case you have an active package project, you'll see an extra option to add the new component to it. Similar capabilities have been added to the Import Component wizard. We'll see some of these wizards in practice in Chapter 9, while cover COM programming and in particular importing a type library in Delphi 2009.

Anything New in the Editor?

While the last few versions of Delphi have seen useful improvements in the editor, with the introduction of Block Completion, Live Templates, Refactorings, and many updates in the Code Insight toolset, Delphi 2009 provides updated support for new language features but little more in this area.

What is new is the Auto Invoke option of Code Completion. This is disabled by default and can be enabled in the corresponding section of the Code Insight page of the main Options dialog box of the IDE. What is the effect of Auto Invoke? The editor should keep track of your recent selections and offer to repeat them. How this actually works in practice is hard to tell.

Debugger

Like the rest of the IDE, the debugger has been worked on to fully support Unicode too. This support was partially available in past versions, but Delphi 2009 extends it. For example, if you inspect a string variable with Run | Inspect (or Debug | Inspect in the editor local menu) not only will you get the proper Unicode value but an indication at the bottom will inform you of the actual string type of the variable.

In the next page you can see a comparison between the Inspect pane for an AnsiString and a UnicodeString (reported simply as *string*):

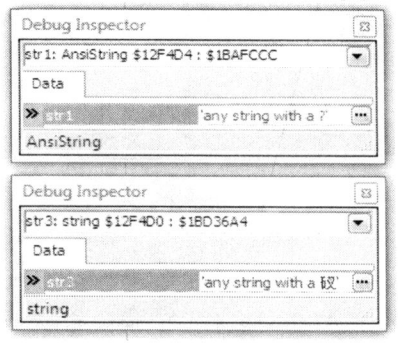

In this case Delphi is actually debugging the btnWarningClick of the main form of the StringConvert example of Chapter 2. The two windows are actually showing the same string, although the first couldn't be converted properly due to the Chinese characters.

There are also other features of the debugger that don't relate to Unicode support. A minor thing is that the CPU view supports the SSE3 and SSE4 instructions (minor at least for somebody who infrequently uses assembly language like me).

A way more interesting, even if still quite low-level, feature is the support of the debugger for the Wait Chain Traversal[69] feature of Vista (and Windows Server 2008). In the Threads Status pane there is now an extra column with information about the various threads that are contributing to a deadlock.

---

69 An MSDN technical article that describes Wait Chain Traversal at the operating system level is available at http://msdn.microsoft.com/en-us/library/ms681622.aspx. Chris Hesik of CodeGear blogged about this new feature of the Delphi debugger at http://blogs.codegear.com/chrishesik/2008/07/21/34833.

This information can be extremely important to understand what happens in your multi-threaded applications.

Debugging and New Language Features

Even if the debugger looks quite similar to the previous version, a lot of effort was devoted to let users debug applications that use generics and anonymous methods. Because of the sophisticated code generation done in the background, the code you are debugging is quite different from that which you originally wrote. Even if with some limited glitches, debugging the new language features generally works well enough.

What's Next

Having looked at the new features of the IDE in Delphi 2009, I can now get back to the language. We have already seen there are many new features related with UnicodeString and AnsiString support, but the compiler has many more improvements.

With generic and anonymous methods (or closures) appearing for the first time in the language, Object Pascal takes its most significant leap forward since Delphi was introduced. That's why there are two full chapters, plus some extra information in a third one, fully devoted to the compiler and the language.

Chapter 5: Generics

The strong type checking provided by Delphi is useful for improving the correctness of the code, a topic I tend to stress in my introductory books. Strong type checking, though, can also be a nuisance, as you might rather have a procedure or a class that can act on different data types. This issue is addressed by a new feature of the Object Pascal language, recently added to similar languages like C# and Java, called *generics*. This is what I wrote in 1994 in a book about C++[70]:

> *Now you can declare a class without specifying the type of one or more data members: this operation can be delayed until an object of that class is actually declared. Similarly, you can define a function without specifying the type of one or more of its parameters until the function is called.*

---

[70] The book is "Borland C++ 4.0 Object-Oriented Programming", written by me with Steve Tendon, with a forward by Philippe Kahn.

136 - Chapter 5: Generics

Now, 14 years later, this feature is getting into Object Pascal. You can guess I'm somewhat excited to have generics (they are called templates in C++) in Delphi, although I have to say I have witnessed distinct overuse of this feature that I didn't fully understand at the time. I doubt generics will be overused in Delphi, quite the contrary: there is the risk that a very significant language upgrade gets almost unnoticed. This chapter will try to delve into the topic, showing you the value of generics in Delphi and how they can be applied even to standard visual programming.

Generic Key-Value Pairs

As a first example of a generic class, I've implemented a key-value pair data structure. The first code snippet below shows the data structure written in a traditional fashion, with an object used to hold the value:

```
type
  TKeyValue = class
  private
    FKey: string;
    FValue: TObject;
    procedure SetKey(const Value: string);
    procedure SetValue(const Value: TObject);
  public
    property Key: string read FKey write SetKey;
    property Value: TObject read FValue write SetValue;
  end;
```

To use this class you can create an object, set its key and value, and use it, as in the following snippets of various methods of the main form of the KeyValueClassic example:

```
// FormCreate
kv := TKeyValue.Create;

// Button1Click
kv.Key := 'mykey';
kv.Value := Sender;

// Button2Click
kv.Value := self; // the form

// Button3Click
ShowMessage('[' + kv.Key + ', ' + kv.Value.ClassName + ']');
```

Generics make it possible to use a much broader definition for the value, but that's not the key point. What's totally different, as we'll see, is that once you've instantiated the key-value generic class, it becomes a specific class, tied to a given data type. This makes your code type safer, but I'm getting ahead of myself. Let's start with the syntax used to define the generic class:

```
type
  TKeyValue<T> = class
  private
    FKey: string;
    FValue: T;
    procedure SetKey(const Value: string);
    procedure SetValue(const Value: T);
  public
    property Key: string read FKey write SetKey;
    property Value: T read FValue write SetValue;
  end;
```

In this class definition, there is one unspecified type, indicated by the placeholder T[71]. The symbol T is frequently used by convention, but as far as the compiler is concerned you can use just any symbol you like. Using T generally makes the code more readable when the generic class uses only one parametric type; in case the class needs multiple parametric types it is common to name them according to their actual role, rather than using a sequence of letters (T, U, V) as it happened in C++ during the early days.

The generic TKeyValue<T> class uses the unspecified type as the type of one of its two fields, the property value, and the setter method parameter. The methods are defined as usual, but notice that regardless of the fact they have to do with the generic type, their definition contains the complete name of the class, including the generic type:

```
procedure TKeyValue<T>.SetKey(const Value: string);
begin
  FKey := Value;
end;

procedure TKeyValue<T>.SetValue(const Value: T);
begin
  FValue := Value;
end;
```

---

71 "T" has been the standard name, or placeholder, for a generic type since the days the C++ language introduced *templates* in the early 1990s. Depending on the authors, the "T" stands for either "Type" or "Template type".

To use the class, instead, you have to fully qualify it, providing the actual value of the generic type. For example, you can now declare a key-value object hosting buttons as value by writing:

```
kv: TKeyValue<TButton>;
```

The full name is required also when creating an instance, because this is the actual type name (while the generic, uninstantiated type name is like a type construction mechanism).

Using a specific type of the value of the key-value pair makes the code much more robust, as you can now only add `TButton` (or derived) objects to the key-value pair and can use the various methods of the extracted object. These are some snippets from the main form of the KeyValueGeneric example:

```
// FormCreate
kv := TKeyValue<TButton>.Create;

// Button1Click
kv.Key := 'mykey';
kv.Value := Sender as TButton;

// Button2Click
kv.Value := Sender as TButton; // was "self"

// Button3Click
ShowMessage ('[' + kv.Key + ',' + kv.Value.Name + ']');
```

When assigning a generic object in the previous version of the code we could add either a button or a form, now we can use only button, a rule enforced by the compiler. Likewise, rather than a generic `kv.Value.ClassName` in the output we can use the component `Name`, or any other property of the `TButton` class.

Of course, we can also mimic the original program by declaring the key-value pair as:

```
kvo: TKeyValue<TObject>;
```

In this version of the generic key-value pair class, we can add any object as value. However, we won't be able to do much on the extracted objects, unless we cast them to a more specific type. To find a good balance, you might want to go for something in between specific buttons and any object, requesting the value to be a component:

```
kvc: TKeyValue<TComponent>;
```

You can see corresponding code snippets in the same KeyValueGeneric demo program. Finally, we can also create an instance of the generic key-value pair class that doesn't store object values, but rather plain integers:

```
var
  kvi: TKeyValue<Integer>;
begin
  kvi := TKeyValue<Integer>.Create;
  try
    kvi.Key := 'object';
    kvi.Value := 100;
    kvi.Value := Left;
    ShowMessage ('[' + kvi.Key + ', ' +
      IntToStr (kvi.Value) + ']');
  finally
    kvi.Free;
  end;
```

Type Rules on Generics

When you declare an instance of a generic type, this type gets a specific version, which is enforced by the compiler in all subsequent operations. So if you have a generic class like:

```
type
  TSimpleGeneric<T> = class
    Value: T;
  end;
```

as you declare a specific object with a given type, you cannot assign a different type to the Value field. Given the following two objects, some of the assignments below (part of the TypeCompRules example) are incorrect:

```
var
  sg1: TSimpleGeneric<string>;
  sg2: TSimpleGeneric<Integer>;
begin
  sg1 := TSimpleGeneric<string>.Create;
  sg2 := TSimpleGeneric<Integer>.Create;

  sg1.Value := 'foo';
  sg1.Value := 10; // Error
  // E2010 Incompatible types: 'string' and 'Integer'

  sg2.Value := 'foo';  // Error
  // E2010 Incompatible types: 'Integer' and 'string'
  sg2.Value := 10;
```

Marco Cantù, Delphi 2009 Handbook

Once you define a specific type in the generic declaration, this is enforced by the compiler, as you should expect from a strongly-typed language like Object Pascal. Type checking is also in place for generic objects as a whole. As you specify the generic parameter for an object, you cannot assign to it a similar generic type based on a different and incompatible type instance. If this seems confusing, an example should help clarifying:

```
sg1 := TSimpleGeneric<Integer>.Create; // Error
// E2010 Incompatible types:
// 'TSimpleGeneric<System.string>'
// and 'TSimpleGeneric<System.Integer>'
```

As we'll see in the section "Generic Types Compatibility Rules" in this peculiar case the type compatibility rule is by structure and not by type name. You cannot assign a different and incompatible type to a generic type once it has been declared.

Generics in Delphi

In the previous example we have seen how you can define and use a generic class in Delphi, one of the most far reaching extensions to the Object Pascal language since Delphi 3 introduced interfaces. I decided to introduce the feature with an example before delving into the technicalities, which are quite complex and very important at the same time. After covering generics from a language perspective we'll get back to more examples, including the use and definition of generic container classes, one of the main reasons this technique was added to the language.

We have seen that when you define a class in Delphi 2009 you can now add an extra "parameter" within angle brackets to hold the place of a type to be provided later:

```
type
   TMyClass<T> = class
     ...
   end;
```

The generic type can be used as the type of a field (as I did in the previous example), as the type of a property, as the type of a parameter or return value of a function, and more. Notice that it is not compulsory to use the type for a local field (or array), as there are cases in which the generic type is used only as a result, a parameter, or is not used in the declaration of the class, but only in the definition of some of its methods.

This form of extended or *generic* type declaration is not only available for classes but also for records (that, in case you didn't notice, in the most recent versions of Delphi can also have methods, properties, and overloaded operators). You cannot declare a generic global function, unlike C++, but you can declare a generic class with a single class method, which is almost the same thing and doesn't clutter the global name space.

A generic class can also have multiple parameterized types, as in following case in which you can specify an input parameter and a return value of a different type for a method:

```
type
  TPWGeneric<TInput,TReturn> = class
  public
    function AnyFunction (Value: TInput): TReturn;
  end;
```

The implementation of generics in Delphi, like in other static languages is not based on a runtime framework. It is handled by the compiler and the linker, leaving almost nothing to the runtime mechanism. Unlike virtual function calls, which are bound at runtime, template methods are generated once for each template type you instantiate, and are generated at compile time! We'll see the possible drawbacks of this approach, but on the positive side it implies that generic classes are as efficient as plain classes, or even more efficient as the need for runtime checks is reduced. Before we look at some of the internals, though, let me focus on some very significant rules which break the traditional Pascal language type compatibility rules.

Generic Types Compatibility Rules

In traditional Pascal and in Delphi's Object Pascal the core type compatibility rules are based on type name equivalence. In other words, two variables are type compatible only if their type name is the same, regardless of the actual data structure to which they refer.

This is a classic example of type incompatibility with arrays (part of the TypeCompRules example):

```
type
  TArrayOf10 = array [1..10] of Integer;
```

142 - Chapter 5: Generics

```
procedure TForm30.Button1Click(Sender: TObject);
var
  array1: TArrayOf10;
  array2: TArrayOf10
  array3, array4: array [1..10] of Integer;
begin
  array1 := array2;
  array2 := array3; // Error
  // E2010 Incompatible types: 'TArrayOf10' and 'Array'

  array3 := array4;
  array4 := array1; // Error
  // E2010 Incompatible types: 'Array' and 'TArrayOf10'
end;
```

As you can see in the code above, all four arrays are structurally identical. However, the compiler will let you assign only those that are type compatible, either because their type has the same explicit name (like TArrayOf10) or because they have the same implicit (or compiler generated, type name, as the two arrays declared in a single statement.

This type compatibility rule has very limited exceptions, like those related to derived classes. A new exception to the rule, and a very significant one, is type compatibility for generic types, which is probably also used internally by the compiler to determine when to *generate* a new type from the generic one, with all of its methods.

The new rule states that generic types are compatible when they share the same generic class definition and instance type, regardless of the type name associated with this definition. In other words, the full name of the generic type instance is a combination of the generic type and the instance type.

In the following example the four variables are all type compatible:

```
type
  TGenericArray<T> = class
    anArray: array [1..10] of T;
  end;

  TIntGenericArray = TGenericArray<Integer>;

procedure TForm30.Button2Click(Sender: TObject);
var
  array1: TIntGenericArray;
  array2: TIntGenericArray;
  array3, array4: TGenericArray<Integer>;
begin
  array1 := TIntGenericArray.Create;
```

```
   array2 := array1;
   array3 := array2;
   array4 := array3;
   array1 := array4;
end;
```

Generic Global Functions (Well, Almost)

As mentioned earlier, you cannot declare a generic global function, but you can have a generic class with a class method, which is very close. This is a sample declaration, taken from the TypeCompRules demo:

```
type
  TGlobalFunction<T> = class
  public
    class function AlmostGlobal: string;
    class function WithParam (t1[72]: T): string;
  end;
```

There isn't much you can do inside a similar class method (at least unless you use constraints, covered later in this chapter), so I wrote some code using special generic type functions (again covered later), which is not relevant to discuss here.

You can call various versions of this "global generic function" as follows:

```
TGlobalFunction<string>.AlmostGlobal;
TGlobalFunction<Int64>.AlmostGlobal;
TGlobalFunction<TButton>.AlmostGlobal;
```

If you call the method with a parameter, however, the parameter's type must match the generic type declaration. So the first two lines below compile, the latter two won't:

```
TGlobalFunction<TButton>.WithParam (btnGlobal);
TGlobalFunction<string>.WithParam ('foo');

TGlobalFunction<Integer>.WithParam (btnGlobal); // [Error]
TGlobalFunction<string>.WithParam (203); // [Error]
```

---

[72] When I first wrote this code, probably with a reminiscence of my C++ days, I wrote the parameter as (t: T). Needless to say in a case insensitive language like Object Pascal, this is not a great idea. The compiler will actually let it go but issue errors every time you refer to the generic type T.

Generic Type Instantiation

With the exception of some optimizations, every time you instantiate a generic type, a new type is generated by the compiler. This new type shares no code with different instances of the same generic type.

Let's look at an example (which is called GenericCodeGen). The program has a generic class defined as:

```
type
  TSampleClass <T> = class
  private
    data: T;
  public
    procedure One;
    function ReadT: T;
    procedure SetT (value: T);
  end;
```

The three methods are implemented as follows (notice that the One method is absolutely independent from the generic type):

```
procedure TSampleClass<T>.One;
begin
  Form30.Log ('OneT');
end;

function TSampleClass<T>.ReadT: T;
begin
  Result := data;
end;

procedure TSampleClass<T>.SetT(value: T);
begin
  data := value;
end;
```

Now the main program uses the generic type mostly to figure out the in-memory address of its methods once an instance is generated (by the compiler). This is the code (which uses a helper Log function to show log strings in a Memo control):

```
procedure TForm30.Button1Click(Sender: TObject);
var
  t1: TSampleClass<Integer>;
  t2: TSampleClass<string>;
begin
  t1 := TSampleClass<Integer>.Create;
  t1.SetT (10);
```

```
    t1.One;

    t2 := TSampleClass<string>.Create;
    t2.SetT ('hello');
    t2.One;

    Log ('t1.SetT: ' +
      IntToHex (PInteger(@TSampleClass<Integer>.SetT)^, 8));
    Log ('t2.SetT: ' +
      IntToHex (PInteger(@TSampleClass<string>.SetT)^, 8));

    Log ('t1.One: ' +
      IntToHex (PInteger(@TSampleClass<Integer>.One)^, 8));
    Log ('t2.One: ' +
      IntToHex (PInteger(@TSampleClass<string>.One)^, 8));
end;
```

The result is something like this (the actual values might vary):

```
t1.SetT: C3045089
t2.SetT: 51EC8B55
t1.One: 4657F0BA
t2.One: 46581CBA
```

As I anticipated, not only does the SetT method get a different version in memory generated by the compiler for each data type used, but even the One method gets a new version, despite the fact they are all identical.

Moreover, if you redeclare an identical generic type, you'll get a new set of implementation functions. Similarly, the same instance of a generic type used in different units forces the compiler to generate the same code over and over, possibly causing significant code bloat. For this reason if you have a generic class with many methods that don't depend on the generic type, it is recommended to define a base non-generic class with those common methods and an inherited generic class with the generic methods: this way the base class methods are only compiled and included in the executable once.

Generic Type Functions

The biggest problem with the generic type definitions we have seen so far is that there is very little you can do with objects of the generic class type. There are two techniques you can use to overcome this limitation. The first is to make use of the few special functions of the runtime library that specifically support generic types; the second (and much more powerful) is to define generic classes with constraints on the types you can use.

I'll focus on the first part in this section and constraints in the next section. As I mentioned, there is a brand new function and two classic ones that have been specifically modified to work on the parametric type (T) of generic type definition:

- `Default` (T) is a brand new function that returns the empty or "zero value" or null value for the current type[73]; this can be zero, an empty string, `nil`, and so on;
- `TypeInfo` (T) returns the pointer to the runtime information for the current version of the generic type;
- `SizeOf` (T) returns memory size of the type in bytes (which in case of a reference type like a string or an object would be the size of the reference, that is 4 bytes).

The GenericTypeFunc example has a generic class showing the three generic type functions in action:

```
type
  TSampleClass <T> = class
  private
    data: T;
  public
    procedure Zero;
    function GetDataSize: Integer;
    function GetDataName: string;
  end;

function TSampleClass<T>.GetDataSize: Integer;
begin
  Result := SizeOf (T);
end;

function TSampleClass<T>.GetDataName: string;
begin
  Result := GetTypeName (TypeInfo (T));
end;

procedure TSampleClass<T>.Zero;
begin
```

---

[73] This zero-initialized memory has the same value of a global variable of the same type. Differently from local variables, in fact, global ones are initialized to "zero" by the compiler.

```
    data := Default (T);
end;
```

In the `GetDataName` method I used the `GetTypeName` function (or the TypInfo unit) rather than directly accessing the data structure because it performs the proper UTF-8 conversion from the encoded ShortString value holding the type name.

Given the declaration above, you can compile the following test code, that repeats itself three times on three different generic type instances. I've omitted the repeated code, but show the statements used to access the `data` field, as they change depending on the actual type:

```
var
  t1: TSampleClass<Integer>;
  t2: TSampleClass<string>;
  t3: TSampleClass<double>;
begin
  t1 := TSampleClass<Integer>.Create;
  t1.Zero;
  Log ('TSampleClass<Integer>');
  Log ('data: ' + IntToStr (t1.data));
  Log ('type: ' + t1.GetDataName);
  Log ('size: ' + IntToStr (t1.GetDataSize));

  t2 := TSampleClass<string>.Create;
  ...
  Log ('data: ' + t2.data);

  t3 := TSampleClass<double>.Create;
  ...
  Log ('data: ' + FloatToStr (t3.data));
```

Running this code (from the GenericTypeFunc program) produces the following output:

```
TSampleClass<Integer>
data: 0
type: Integer
size: 4
TSampleClass<string>
data:
type: string
size: 4
TSampleClass<double>
data: 0
type: Double
size: 8
```

148 - Chapter 5: Generics

Notice that you can use the generic type functions also on specific types, outside of the context of generic classes. For example, you can write:

```
var
  I: Integer;
  s: string;
begin
  I := Default (Integer);
  Log ('Default Integer': + IntToStr (I));

  s := Default (string);
  Log ('Default String': + s);

  Log ('TypeInfo String': +
    GetTypeName (TypeInfo (string));
```

While the calls to Default are brand new in Delphi 2009 (although not terribly useful outside of generics), the call to TypeInfo[74] at the end was already possible in past versions of Delphi. This is the trivial output:

```
Default Integer: 0
Default String:
TypeInfo String: string
```

Generic Constraints

As we have seen, there is very little you can do in the methods of your generic class over the generic type value. You can pass it around (that is, assign it) and perform the limited operations allowed by the generic type functions I've just covered.

To be able to perform some actual operations of the generic type of class, you generally place a constraint on it. For example, if you limit the generic type to be a class, the compiler will let you call all of the TObject methods on it. You can also further constrain the class to be part of a given hierarchy or to implement a specific interface, making it possible to call the class or interface method on an instance of the generic type.

---

[74] You cannot apply the TypeInfo call to a variable, like TypeInfo(s) in the code above, but only to a type.

Marco Cantù, Delphi 2009 Handbook

Class Constraints

The simplest constraint you can adopt is a class constraint. To use it, you can declare generic type as:

```
type
  TSampleClass <T: class> = class
```

By specifying a class constraint you indicate that you can use only object types as generic types. With the following declaration (taken from the ClassContraint project):

```
type
  TSampleClass <T: class> = class
  private
    data: T;
  public
    procedure One;
    function ReadT: T;
    procedure SetT (t: T);
  end;
```

you can create the first two instances but not the third:

```
sample1: TSampleClass<TButton>;
sample2: TSampleClass<TStrings>;
sample3: TSampleClass<Integer>; // Error
```

The compiler error caused by this last declaration would be:

```
E2511 Type parameter 'T' must be a class type
```

What's the advantage of indicating this constraint? In the generic class methods you can now call any TObject method, including virtual ones! This is the One method of the TSampleClass generic class[75]:

```
procedure TSampleClass<T>.One;
begin
  if Assigned (data) then
  begin
    Form30.Log('ClassName: ' + data.ClassName);
    Form30.Log('Size: ' + IntToStr (data.InstanceSize));
    Form30.Log('ToString: ' + data.ToString);
  end;
```

---

75 Two comments here. The first is that InstanceSize returns the actual size of the object, unlike the generic SizeOf function we used earlier, which returns the size of the reference type. Second, the ToString method is a new (relevant) Delphi 2009 method of TObject that I'll cover in details in Chapter 7, in the section "TObjects's New Methods".

150 - Chapter 5: Generics

```
end;
```

You can play with the program to see its actual effect, as it defines and uses a few instances of the generic type, as in the following code snippet:

```
var
  sample1: TSampleClass<TButton>;
begin
  sample1 := TSampleClass<TButton>.Create;
  try
    sample1.SetT (Sender as TButton);
    sample1.One;
  finally
    sample1.Free;
  end;
```

Notice that by declaring a class with a customized ToString method, this custom version will get called when the data object is of the specific type, regardless of the actual type provided to the generic type. In other words, if you have a TButton descendant like:

```
type
  TMyButton = class (TButton)
  public
    function ToString: string; override;
  end;
```

You can pass this object as value of a TSampleClass<TButton> or define a specific instance of the generic type, and in both cases calling One ends up executing the specific version of ToString:

```
var
  sample1: TSampleClass<TButton>;
  sample2: TSampleClass<TMyButton>;
  mb: TMyButton;
begin
  ...
  sample1.SetT (mb);
  sample1.One;
  sample2.SetT (mb);
  sample2.One;
```

Similarly to a class constraint, you can have a record constraint, declared as:

```
type
  TSampleRec <T: record> = class
```

However, there is very little that different records have in common (there is no common ancestor), so this declaration is somewhat limited.

Specific Class Constraints

If your generic class needs to work with a specific subset of classes (a specific hierarchy), you might want to resort to specifying a constraint based on a given base class. For example, if you declare:

```
type
  TCompClass <T: TComponent> = class
```

instances of this generic class can be applied only to component classes, that is, any TComponent descendant class. This let's you have a very specific generic type (yes, it sounds odd, but that's what it really is) and the compiler will let you use all of the methods of the TComponent class while working on the generic type.

If this seems extremely powerful, think twice. If you consider what you can achieve with inheritance and type compatibly rules, you might be able to address the same problem using traditional object-oriented techniques rather than having to use generic classes. I'm not saying that a specific class constraint is never useful, but it is certainly not as powerful as a higher-level class constraint or (something I find very interesting) an interface-based constraint.

Interface Constraints

Rather than constraining a generic class to a given class, it is generally more flexible to accept as type parameter only classes implementing a given interface. This makes it possible to call the interface on instances of the generic type. This use of interface constraints for generics is also very common in the .NET framework. Let me start by showing you an example (called IntfConstraint). First, we need to declare an interface:

```
type
  IGetValue = interface
    ['{60700EC4-2CDA-4CD1-A1A2-07973D9D2444}']
    function GetValue: Integer;
    procedure SetValue (Value: Integer);
    property Value: Integer
      read GetValue write SetValue;
  end;
```

Next, we can define a class implementing it:

```
type
```

```
  TGetValue = class (TSingletonImplementation, IGetValue)
  private
    fValue: Integer;
  public
    constructor Create (Value: Integer = 0);
    function GetValue: Integer;
    procedure SetValue (Value: Integer);
  end;
```

Things start to get interesting in the definition of a generic class limited to types that implement the given interface:

```
type
  TInftClass <T: IGetValue> = class
  private
    val1, val2: T; // or IGetValue
  public
    procedure Set1 (val: T);
    procedure Set2 (val: T);
    function GetMin: Integer;
    function GetAverage: Integer;
    procedure IncreaseByTen;
  end;
```

Notice that in the code of the generic methods of this class we can write, for example:

```
function TInftClass<T>.GetMin: Integer;
begin
  Result := min (val1.GetValue, val2.GetValue);
end;

procedure TInftClass<T>.IncreaseByTen;
begin
  val1.SetValue (val1.GetValue + 10);
  val2.Value := val2.Value + 10;
end;
```

With all these definitions, we can now use the generic class as follows:

```
procedure TFormIntfConstraint.btnValueClick(
  Sender: TObject);
var
  iClass: TInftClass<TGetValue>;
begin
  iClass := TInftClass<TGetValue>.Create;
  try
    iClass.Set1 (TGetValue.Create (5));
    iClass.Set2 (TGetValue.Create (25));
    Log ('Average: ' + IntToStr (iClass.GetAverage));
    iClass.IncreaseByTen;
    Log ('Min: ' + IntToStr (iClass.GetMin));
```

```delphi
    finally
      iClass.val1.Free;
      iClass.val2.Free;
      iClass.Free;
    end;
end;
```

To show the flexibility of this generic class, I've created another totally different implementation for the interface:

```delphi
    TButtonValue = class (TButton, IGetValue)
    public
      function GetValue: Integer;
      procedure SetValue (Value: Integer);
      class function MakeTButtonValue (Owner: TComponent;
        Parent: TWinControl): TButtonValue;
    end;

function TButtonValue.GetValue: Integer;
begin
  Result := Left;
end;

procedure TButtonValue.SetValue(Value: Integer);
begin
  Left := Value;
end;
```

The class function (not listed in the book) creates a button within a Parent control in a random position and is used in the following sample code:

```delphi
procedure TFormIntfConstraint.btnValueButtonClick(
  Sender: TObject);
var
  iClass: TInftClass<TButtonValue>;
begin
  iClass := TInftClass<TButtonValue>.Create;
  try
    iClass.Set1 (TButtonValue.MakeTButtonValue (
      self, ScrollBox1));
    iClass.Set2 (TButtonValue.MakeTButtonValue (
      self, ScrollBox1));
    Log ('Average: ' + IntToStr (iClass.GetAverage));
    Log ('Min: ' + IntToStr (iClass.GetMin));
    iClass.IncreaseByTen;
    Log ('New Average: ' + IntToStr (iClass.GetAverage));
  finally
    iClass.Free;
  end;
end;
```

Interface References vs. Generic Interface Constraints

In the last example I have defined a generic class that works with any object implementing a given interface. I could have obtained a similar effect by creating a standard (non-generic) class based on interface references. In fact, I could have defined a class like (again part of the IntfConstraint project):

```
type
  TPlainInftClass = class
  private
    val1, val2: IGetValue;
  public
    procedure Set1 (val: IGetValue);
    procedure Set2 (val: IGetValue);
    function GetMin: Integer;
    function GetAverage: Integer;
    procedure IncreaseByTen;
  end;
```

What is different between these two approaches? A first difference is that in the class above you can pass two objects of different types to the setter methods, provided their classes both implement the given interface, while in the generic version you can pass only objects of the given type (to any given instance of the generic class). So the generic version is more *conservative* and strict in terms of type checking.

In my opinion, the key difference is that using the interface-based version means having Delphi's reference counting mechanism in action, while using the generic version the class is dealing with plain objects of a given type and reference counting is not involved. Moreover, the generic version could have multiple constraints, like a constructor constraint and lets you use the various generic-functions (like asking for the actual type of the generic type), something you cannot do when using an interface. (When you are working with an interface, in fact, you have no access to the base TObject methods).

In other words, using a generic class with an interface constraint makes it possible to have the benefits of interfaces without their nuisances. Still, it is worth noticing that in most cases the two approaches would be equivalent, and in others the interface-based solution would be more flexible.

Default Constructor Constraint

There is another possible generic type constraint, called default constructor or parameterless constructor. If you need to invoke the default constructor to create a new object of the generic type (for example for filling a list) you can use this constraint. In theory (and according to the documentation), the compiler should let you use it only for those types with a default constructor. In practice, if a default constructor doesn't exist, the compiler will let it go and call the default constructor of TObject.

A generic class with a constructor constraint can be written as follows[76] (this one is extracted by the IntfConstraint example):

```
type
  TConstrClass <T: class, constructor> = class
  private
    val: T;
  public
    constructor Create;
    function Get: T;
  end;
```

Given this declaration, you can use the constructor to create a generic internal object, without knowing its actual type up front, and write:

```
constructor TConstrClass<T>.Create;
begin
  val := T.Create;
end;
```

How can we use this generic class and what are the actual rules? In the next example I have defined two classes, one with a default (parameterless) constructor, the second with a single constructor having one parameter:

```
type
  TSimpleConst = class
  public
    Value: Integer;
    constructor Create;   // set Value to 10
  end;

  TParamConst = class
  public
```

---

[76] You can also specify the constructor constraint without the class constraint, as the former probably implies the latter. Listing both of them makes the code more readable.

156 - Chapter 5: Generics

```
    Value: Integer;
    constructor Create (I: Integer); // set Value to I
  end;
```

As I mentioned earlier, in theory you should be able to use only the first class, while in practice you can use both:

```
var
  constructObj: TConstrClass<TSimpleCost>;
  paramCostObj: TConstrClass<TParamCost>;
begin
  constructObj := TConstrClass<TSimpleCost>.Create;
  Log ('Value 1: ' + IntToStr (constructObj.Get.Value));

  paramCostObj := TConstrClass<TParamCost>.Create;
  Log ('Value 2: ' + IntToStr (paramCostObj.Get.Value));
```

The output of this code is:

```
Value 1: 10
Value 2: 0
```

In fact, the second object is never initialized. If you debug the application trace into the code you'll see a call to TObject.Create (which I consider wrong). Notice that if you try calling directly:

```
  with TParamConst.Create do
```

the compiler will (correctly) raise the error[77]:

```
[DCC Error] E2035 Not enough actual parameters
```

Generic Constraints Summary and Combining Them

As there are so many different constraints you can put on a generic type, let me provide a short summary here, in code terms:

```
type
  TSampleClass <T: class> = class
  TSampleRec   <T: record> = class
  TCompClass   <T: TButton> = class
  TInftClass   <T: IGetValue> = class
  TConstrClass <T: constructor> = class
```

---

[77] Even if a direct call to TParamConst.Create will fail at compile time (as explained here), a similar call using a class reference or any other form of indirection will succeed, which probably explains the behavior of the effect of the constructor constraint.

Marco Cantù, Delphi 2009 Handbook

What you might not immediately realize after looking at constraints (and this certainly took me some time to get used to) is that you can combine them. For example, you can define a generic class limited to a sub-hierarchy and requiring also a given interface, like in:

```
type
   TInftComp <T: TComponent, IGetValue> = class
   ...
   end;
```

Not all combinations make sense: for example you cannot specify both a class and a record, while using a class constraint combined with a specific class constraint would be redundant. Finally, notice that there is nothing like a method constraint, something that can be achieved with a single-method interface constraint (much more complex to express, though).

Predefined Generic Containers

Since the early days of templates in the C++ Language, one of the most obvious uses of generic classes has been the definition of generic containers or lists. When you define a list of objects, like Delphi's own TObjectList, in fact, you have a list that can potentially hold objects of any kind. Using either inheritance or composition you can indeed define custom containers for specific a type, but this is a tedious (and potentially error-prone) approach[78].

Delphi 2009 defines a small set of generic container classes you can find in the new Generics.Collections unit. The four core container classes are all implemented in an independent way (the is no inheritance among these classes), all implemented in a similar fashion (using a dynamic array), and are all mapped to the corresponding non-generic container class of the Contnrs unit:

```
type
   TList<T> = class
   TQueue<T> = class
```

---

78 Here I don't want to cover the difference between the various approaches you could use in Delphi to define specialized container before generics were available, because we do have generics now. You can find material along these lines in my Mastering Delphi 7 book (Sybex) and other editions of that series.

158 - Chapter 5: Generics

```
TStack<T> = class
TDictionary<TKey,TValue> = class
```

The logical difference among these classes should be quite obvious considering their names. A good way to test them, is to figure out how many changes you have to perform on existing code that uses a non-generic container class. As an example, I've taken an actual sample program of the Mastering Delphi 2005 book and converted it to use generics[79].

Using TList<T>

The program, called ListDemoMd2005, has a unit defining a TDate class, and the main form used to refer to a TList of dates. As a starting point, I added a uses clause referring to Generics.Collections, then I changed the declaration of the main form field to:

```
private
   ListDate: TList <TDate>;
```

Of course, the main form OnCreate event handler that does create the list needed to be updated as well, becoming:

```
procedure TForm1.FormCreate(Sender: TObject);
begin
   ListDate := TList<TDate>.Create;
end;
```

Now we can try to compile the rest of the code as it is. The program has a "wanted" bug, trying to add a TButton object to the list. The corresponding code used to compile and now fails:

```
procedure TForm1.ButtonWrongClick(Sender: TObject);
begin
   // add a button to the list
   ListDate.Add (Sender);   // Error:
      // E2010 Incompatible types: 'TDate' and 'TObject'
end;
```

The new list of dates is more robust in terms of type-checking than the original generic list pointers. Having removed that line, the program compiles and works. Still, it can be improved.

---

79 The program uses only a few methods, so it is not a great test for interface compatibility between generic and non-generic lists, but I decided it was worth taking an existing program rather than fabricating one.

This is the original code used to display all of the dates of the list in a List-Box control:

```
var
  I: Integer;
begin
  ListBox1.Clear;
  for I := 0 to ListDate.Count - 1 do
    Listbox1.Items.Add (
      (TObject(ListDate [I]) as TDate).Text);
```

Notice the rather ugly type cast, due to the fact that the program was using a list of pointers (TList), and not a list of objects (TObjectList). The reason might well be that the original demo predates the TObjectList class! We can easily improve the program by writing:

```
  for I := 0 to ListDate.Count - 1 do
    Listbox1.Items.Add (ListDate [I].Text);
```

Another improvement to this snippet can come from using an enumeration (something the predefined generic lists fully support) rather than a plain for loop:

```
var
  aDate: TDate;
begin
  for aDate in ListDate do
  begin
    Listbox1.Items.Add (aDate.Text);
  end;
```

Finally, the program can be improved by using a generic TObjectList owning the TDate objects, but that's a topic for the next section.

As I mentioned earlier, the TList<T> generic class has a high degree of compatibility. It has all the classic methods, like Add, Insert, Remove, and IndexOf. The Capacity and Count properties are there as well. Oddly, Items become Item, but being the default property you seldom explicitly refer to it anyway.

Sorting a TList<T>

What is interesting to understand is how sorting works (my goal here is to add sorting support to the ListDemoMd2005 example). The Sort method is defined as:

```
procedure Sort; overload;
```

```
procedure Sort(const AComparer: IComparer<T>); overload;
```

where the IComparer<T> interface is declared in the Generics.Defaults unit. If you call the first version the program will use the default comparer, initialized by the default constructor of TList<T>. In our case this will be useless.

What we need to do, instead is to define a proper implementation of the IComparer<T> interface. For type compatibility, we need to define an implementation that works on the specific TDate class. There are multiple ways to accomplish this, including using anonymous methods (covered in the next section even though that's a topic introduced in the next chapter). An interesting technique, also because it gives me the opportunity to show several usage patterns of generics, is to take advantage of a *structural*[80] class that is part of the unit Generics.Defaults and is called TComparer. The class is defined as an abstract and generic implementation of the interface, as follows:

```
type
  TComparer<T> = class(TInterfacedObject, IComparer<T>)
  public
    class function Default: IComparer<T>;
    class function Construct(
      const Comparison: TComparison<T>): IComparer<T>;
    function Compare(
      const Left, Right: T): Integer; virtual; abstract;
  end;
```

What we have to do is instantiate this generic class for the specific data type (TDate, in the example) and also inherit a concrete class that implements the Compare method for the specific type. The two operations can be done at once, using a coding idiom that may take a while to digest:

```
type
  TDateComparer = class (TComparer<TDate>)
    function Compare(
      const Left, Right: TDate): Integer; override;
  end;
```

---

80 I'm calling this class *structural* because it helps defining the structure of the code, but doesn't add a lot in terms of actual implementation. There might be a better name, though.

If you think this code looks very unusual, you're not alone. The new class inherits from a specific instance of the generic class, something you could express in two separate steps[81] as:

```
type
  TAnyDateComparer = TComparer<TDate>;
  TMyDateComparer = class (TAnyDateComparer)
    function Compare(
      const Left, Right: TDate): Integer; override;
  end;
```

You can find the actual implementation of the Compare function in the source code, as that's not the key point I want to stress here. Keep in mind, though, that even if you sort the list its IndexOf method won't take advantage of it (unlike the TStringList class).

Sorting with an Anonymous Method

The sorting code presented in the previous section looks quite complicated and it really is. It would be much easier and cleaner to pass the sorting function to the Sort method directly. In the past this was generally achieved by passing a function pointer. In Delphi 2009 this can be done by passing an anonymous method (a kind of method pointer, with several extra features, covered in detail in the next chapter[82]).

The IComparer<T> parameter of the Sort method of the TList<T> class, in fact, can be used by calling the Construct method of TComparer<T>, passing an anonymous method as a parameter defined as:

```
type
  TComparison<T> = reference to function(
    const Left, Right: T): Integer;
```

In practice you can write a type-compatible function and pass it as parameter[83]:

```
function DoCompare (const Left, Right: TDate): Integer;
var
  ldate, rDate: TDateTime;
begin
```

---

81 Having the two separate declarations might help reducing the generated code where you are reusing the base TAnyDateComparer type in the same unit.

82 I suggest you have a look at this section even if you don't know much about anonymous methods, and then read it again after delving into the next chapter.

162 - Chapter 5: Generics

```
    lDate := EncodeDate(Left.Year, Left.Month, Left.Day);
    rDate := EncodeDate(Right.Year, Right.Month, Right.Day);
    if lDate = rDate then
      Result := 0
    else if lDate < rDate then
      Result := -1
    else
      Result := 1;
end;

procedure TForm1.ButtonAnonSortClick(Sender: TObject);
begin
  ListDate.Sort (TComparer<TDate>.Construct (DoCompare));
end;
```

If this looks quite traditional, consider you could have avoided the declaration of a separate function and pass it (its source code) as parameter to the Construct method, as follows:

```
procedure TForm1.ButtonAnonSortClick(Sender: TObject);
begin
  ListDate.Sort (TComparer<TDate>.Construct (
    function (const Left, Right: TDate): Integer
    var
      ldate, rDate: TDateTime;
    begin
      lDate := EncodeDate(Left.Year,
        Left.Month, Left.Day);
      rDate := EncodeDate(Right.Year,
        Right.Month, Right.Day);
      if lDate = rDate then
        Result := 0
      else if lDate < rDate then
        Result := -1
      else
        Result := 1;
    end));
end;
```

This example should have whet your appetite for learning more about anonymous methods! For sure, this last version is much simpler to write than the original comparison covered in the previous section, although for

---

83 The DoCompare method above works like an anonymous method even if it does have a name. We'll see in a later code snippet that this is not required, though. Have patience until the next chapter for more information about this new Delphi 2009 language construct. Notice also that with a TDate record I could have defined less than and greater then operators, making this code simpler, but even with a class I could have placed the comparison code in a method of the class.

many Delphi developers having a derived class might look cleaner and be easier to understand (the inherited version separates the logic better, making potential code reuse easier, but many times you won't make use of it anyway).

Object Containers

Beside the generic classes covered at the beginning of this section, there are also four inherited generic classes that are derived from the base classes defined in the Generics.Collections unit, mimicking existing classes of the Contnrs unit:

```
type
  TObjectList<T: class> = class(TList<T>)
  TObjectQueue<T: class> = class(TQueue<T>)
  TObjectStack<T: class> = class(TStack<T>)
```

Compared to their base classes, there are two key differences. One is that these generic types can be used only for objects; the second is that they define a customized Notification method, that in the case when an object is removed from the list (beside optionally calling the OnNotify event handler), will Free the object.

In other words, the TObjectList<T> class behaves like its non-generic counterpart when the OwnsObjects property is set. If you are wondering why this is not an option any more, consider that TList<T> can now be used directly to work with object types, unlike its non-generic counterpart.

There is also a fourth class, again, called TObjectDictionary<TKey, TValue>, which is defined in a different way, as it can own the key object, the value objects, or both of them. See the TDictionaryOwnerships set and the class constructor for more details.

Using a Generic Dictionary

Of all the predefined generic container classes, the one probably worth more detailed study is the generic dictionary[84], TObjectDictionary<TKey, TValue>. Other classes are just as important, but they seem to be easier to use and understand. As an example of using a dictionary, I've written an application that fetches data from a database table, creates an object for each record, and uses a composite index with an customer ID and a description as key. The reason for this separation is that a similar architecture can easily be used to create a proxy, in which the key takes the place of a light version of the actual object *loaded* from the database.

These are the two classes used by the CustomerDictionary example for the key and the actual value. The first has only two relevant fields of the corresponding database table, while the second has the complete data structure (I've omitted the private fields, getter methods, and setter methods):

```
type
  TCustomerKey = class
  private
    ...
  published
    property CustNo: Double
      read FCustNo write SetCustNo;
    property Company: string
      read FCompany write SetCompany;
  end;

  TCustomer = class
  private
    ..
    procedure Init;
    procedure EnforceInit;
  public
    constructor Create (aCustKey: TCustomerKey);
    property CustKey: TCustomerKey
      read FCustKey write SetCustKey;
  published
    property CustNo: Double
      read GetCustNo write SetCustNo;
    property Company: string
```

---

84 *Dictionary* in this case means a collection of elements each with a (unique) key value referring to it. (It is also known as an associative array.) In a classic dictionary you have words acting as keys for their definitions, but in programming terms the key doesn't have to be a string (even if this is a rather frequent case).

```
    read GetCompany write SetCompany;
  property Addr1: string
    read GetAddr1 write SetAddr1;
  property City: string
    read GetCity write SetCity;
  property State: string
    read GetState write SetState;
  property Zip: string
    read GetZip write SetZip;
  property Country: string
    read GetCountry write SetCountry;
  property Phone: string
    read GetPhone write SetPhone;
  property FAX: string
    read GetFAX write SetFAX;
  property Contact: string
    read GetContact write SetContact;
class var
  RefDataSet: TDataSet;
end;
```

While the first class is very simple (each object is initialized when it is created), the TCustomer class uses a *lazy initialization* (or *proxy*) model and keeps around a reference to the source database shared (class var) by all objects. When an object is created it is assigned a reference to the corresponding TCustomerKey, while a class data field refers to the source dataset. In each getter method, the class checks if the object has indeed been initialized before returning the data, as in the following case:

```
function TCustomer.GetCompany: string;
begin
  EnforceInit;
  Result := FCompany;
end;
```

The EnforceInit method checks a local flag, eventually calling Init to load data from the database to the in-memory object:

```
procedure TCustomer.EnforceInit;
begin
  if not fInitDone then
    Init;
end;

procedure TCustomer.Init;
begin
  RefDataSet.Locate('custno', CustKey.CustNo, []);

  // could also load each published field via RTTI
```

166 - Chapter 5: Generics

```
    FCustNo := RefDataSet.FieldByName ('CustNo').AsFloat;
    FCompany := RefDataSet.FieldByName ('Company').AsString;
    FCountry := RefDataSet.FieldByName ('Country').AsString;
    ...
    fInitDone := True;
end;
```

Given these two classes, I've added a special purpose dictionary to the application. This custom dictionary class inherits from a generic class instantiated with the proper types and adds to it a specific method:

```
type
  TCustomerDictionary = class (
    TObjectDictionary <TCustomerKey, TCustomer>)
  public
    procedure LoadFromDataSet (dataset: TDataSet);
  end;
```

The loading method populates the dictionary, copying data in memory for only the key objects:

```
procedure TCustomerDictionary.LoadFromDataSet(
  dataset: TDataSet);
var
  custKey: TCustomerKey;
begin
  TCustomer.RefDataSet := dataset;
  dataset.First;
  while not dataset.EOF do
  begin
    custKey := TCustomerKey.Create;
    custKey.CustNo := dataset ['CustNo'];
    custKey.Company := dataset ['Company'];
    self.Add(custKey, TCustomer.Create (custKey));
    dataset.Next;
  end;
end;
```

The demo program has a main form and a data module hosting a Client-DataSet[85]. The main form has a ListView control that is filled when a user presses the only button.

After loading the data in the dictionary, the btnPopulateClick method uses an enumerator on the dictionary's keys:

---

85 You might want to replace the ClientDataSet component with a real dataset, expanding the example considerably in terms of usefulness, as you could run a query for the keys and a separate one for the actual data of each single TCustomer object. I have similar code, but adding it here would have distracted us too much from the goal of the example, which is experimenting with a generic dictionary class.

```
procedure TFormCustomerDictionary.btnPopulateClick(
  Sender: TObject);
var
  custkey: TCustomerKey;
  listItem: TListItem;
begin
  DataModule1.ClientDataSet1.Active := True;
  CustDict.LoadFromDataSet(DataModule1.ClientDataSet1);

  for custkey in CustDict.Keys do
  begin
    listItem := ListView1.Items.Add;
    listItem.Caption := custkey.Company;
    listItem.SubItems.Add(FloatToStr (custkey.CustNo));
    listItem.Data := custkey;
  end;
end;
```

This fills the first two columns of the ListView control, with the data available in the key objects. Whenever a user selects an item of the ListView control, though, the program will fill a third column:

```
procedure TFormCustomerDictionary.ListView1SelectItem(
  Sender: TObject; Item: TListItem; Selected: Boolean);
var
  aCustomer: TCustomer;
begin
  aCustomer := CustDict.Items [Item.data];
  Item.SubItems.Add(IfThen (aCustomer.State <> '',
    aCustomer.State + ', ' + aCustomer.Country,
    aCustomer.Country));
end;
```

The method above gets the object mapped to the given key, and uses its data. Behind the scenes, the first time a specific object is used, the property access method triggers the loading of the entire data for the TCustomer object.

Generic Interfaces

In the section "Sorting a TList<T>" you might have noticed a rather strange use of a predefined interface, which had a generic declaration. It is worth looking into this technique in detail, as it opens up significant opportunities and changes (even if modestly) the way interfaces work in the language.

168 - Chapter 5: Generics

The first technical element to notice is that it is perfectly legal to define a generic interface[86], like I've done in the GenericInterface example:

```
type
  IGetValue<T> = interface
    function GetValue: T;
    procedure SetValue (Value: T);
  end;
```

Notice that differently from a standard interface, in case of a generic interface you don't need to specify a GUID to be used as Interface ID (or IID). The compiler will generate an IID for you for each instance of the generic interface, even if implicitly declared. In fact, you don't have to create a specific instance of the generic interface to implement it, but can define a generic class that implements the generic interface:

```
type
  TGetValue<T> = class (TInterfacedObject, IGetValue<T>)
  private
    fValue: T;
  public
    constructor Create (Value: T);
    destructor Destroy; override;
    function GetValue: T;
    procedure SetValue (Value: T);
  end;
```

While the constructor assigns the initial value of the object, the destructor's only purpose is to log that an object was destroyed. We can create an instance of this generic class (thus generating a specific instance of the interface type behind the scenes) by writing:

```
procedure TFormGenericInterface.btnValueClick(
  Sender: TObject);
var
  aVal: TGetValue<string>;
begin
  aVal := TGetValue<string>.Create (Caption);
  try
    Log ('TGetValue value: ' + aVal.GetValue);
  finally
    aVal.Free;
  end;
end;
```

---

86 This is the generic version of the IGetValue interface of the IntfConstraints example, covered in the earlier section "Interface Constraints" of this chapter. In that case the interface had an Integer value, now it has a generic one.

An alternative approach, as we saw in the past for the IntfConstraint example, is to use an interface variable of the corresponding type, making the specific interface type definition explicit (and not implicit as in the previous code snippet):

```
procedure TFormGenericInterface.btnIValueClick(
  Sender: TObject);
var
  aVal: IGetValue<string>;
begin
  aVal := TGetValue<string>.Create (Caption);
  Log ('IGetValue value: ' + aVal.GetValue);
  // freed automatically, as it is reference counted
end;
```

Of course, we can also define a specific class that implements the generic interface, as in the following scenario (from the GenericInterface example):

```
type
  TButtonValue = class (TButton, IGetValue<Integer>)
  public
    function GetValue: Integer;
    procedure SetValue (Value: Integer);
    class function MakeTButtonValue (Owner: TComponent;
      Parent: TWinControl): TButtonValue;
  end;
```

Notice that while the TGetValue<T> generic class implements the generic IGetValue<T> interface, the TButtonValue specific class implements the IGetValue<Integer> specific interface. Specifically, as in a previous example, the interface is remapped to the Left property of the control:

```
function TButtonValue.GetValue: Integer;
begin
  Result := Left;
end;
```

In the class above, the MakeTButtonValue class function is a ready-to-use method to create an object of the class. This method is used by the third button of the main form, as follows:

```
procedure TFormGenericInterface.btnValueButtonClick(
  Sender: TObject);
var
  iVal: IGetValue<Integer>;
begin
  iVal := TButtonValue.MakeTButtonValue (
    self, ScrollBox1);
  Log ('Button value: ' + IntToStr (iVal.GetValue));
end;
```

170 - Chapter 5: Generics

Although it is totally unrelated to generic classes, here is the implementation of the `MakeTButtonValue` class function:

```
class function TButtonValue.MakeTButtonValue(
  Owner: TComponent; Parent: TWinControl): TButtonValue;
begin
  Result := TButtonValue.Create(Owner);
  Result.Parent := Parent;
  Result.SetBounds(Random (Parent.Width),
    Random (Parent.Height), Result.Width, Result.Height);
  Result.Caption := 'btnv';
end;
```

Predefined Generic Interfaces

Now that we have explored how to define generic interfaces and combine them with the use of generic and specific classes, we can get back to having a second look to the Generics.Default unit. This unit defines two generic comparison interfaces:

- `IComparer<T>` has a `Compare` method
- `IEqualityComparer<T>` has `Equals` and `GetHashCode` methods

These classes are implemented by some generic and specific classes, listed below (with no implementation details):

```
type
  TComparer<T> = class(TInterfacedObject, IComparer<T>)
  TEqualityComparer<T> = class(
    TInterfacedObject, IEqualityComparer<T>)
  TCustomComparer<T> = class(TSingletonImplementation,
    IComparer<T>, IEqualityComparer<T>)
  TStringComparer = class(TCustomComparer<string>)
```

In the listing above you can see that the base class used by the generic implementations of the interfaces is either the classic reference-counted `TInterfacedObject` class or the new `TSingletonImplementation` class. This is an oddly named[87] class that provides a basic implementation of `IInterface` with no reference counting.

As we have already seen in the "Sorting a TList<T>" section earlier in this chapter, these comparison classes are used by the generic containers. To

---

[87] The term singleton is generally used to define a class of which you can create only one instance, and not one with no reference counting. I consider this quite a misnomer.

make things more complicated, though, the Generics.Default unit relies quite heavily on anonymous methods, so you should probably look at it only after reading the next chapter.

Smart Pointers in Delphi

When approaching generics, you might get the wrong first impression that this language construct is mostly used for collections. While this is the simplest case for using generic classes, and very often the first example in books and docs, generics are useful well beyond the realm of collection (or container) classes. In the last example of this chapter I'm going to show you a *non-collection* generic type, that is the definition of a smart pointer.

If you come from a Delphi background, you might not have heard of smart pointers, an idea that comes from the C++ language. In C++ you can have pointers to objects, for which you have to manage memory directly and manually, and local object variables that are managed automatically but have many other limitations (including the lack of polymorphism[88]). The idea of a smart pointer is to use a locally managed object to take care of the lifetime of the pointer to the real object you want to use. If this sounds too complicated, I hope the Delphi version (and its code) will help clarify it.

In Delphi objects are managed by reference, but records have a lifetime bound to the method in which they are declared. When the method ends, the memory area for the record is cleaned up. So what we can do is to use a record to manage the lifetime of a Delphi object. Of course, we want to write the code only once, so we can use a generic record. Here is a first version:

```
type
  TSmartPointer<T: class> = record
  strict private
    FValue: T;
    function GetValue: T;
  public
    constructor Create(AValue: T);
```

---

[88] The term polymorphisms in OOP languages is used to denote the situation in which you assign to a variable of a base class an object of a derived class and call one of the base class virtual methods, potentially ending up calling the version of the virtual method of the specific subclass.

```
    property Value: T read GetValue;
end;
```

The `Create` and `GetValue` methods of the record could simply assign and read back the value. Using this code you can create an object, create a smart pointer wrapping it, and refer from one to the other:

```
var
  sl: TStringList;
  smartP: TSmartPointer<TStringList>;
begin
  sl := TStringList.Create;
  smartP.Create (sl);
  sl.Add('foo');
  smartP.Value.Add ('foo2');
```

As you may have worked out, this code causes a memory leak in the exact same way as without the smart pointer! In fact the record is destroyed as it goes out of scope, but it has no way of freeing the internal object. Considering a record has no destructor, how can we manage the object disposal? A trick is to use an interface inside the record itself, as the record will automatically free the interfaced object. Should we add an interface to the object we are wrapping? Probably not, as this imposes a significant limitation on the objects we'll be able to pass to the smart pointer.

A better alternative[89] is probably to write a specific wrapper class, tied to an interface, and use the interface reference counting mechanism to the wrapped object. The internal class might look like the following:

```
type
  TFreeTheValue = class (TInterfacedObject)
  private
    fObjectToFree: TObject;
  public
    constructor Create(anObjectToFree: TObject);
    destructor Destroy; override;
  end;

constructor TFreeTheValue.Create(
  anObjectToFree: TObject);
begin
```

---

[89] Barry Kelly (of the Delphi R&D team) implemented a similar architecture with a interfaced class that uses an anonymous method to free the target object, but I haven't covered anonymous methods yet and the code is more complicated anyway. His code is at: http://barrkel.blogspot.com/2008/09/smart-pointers-in-delphi.html. An updated version uses another anonymous method to simplify the access code: http://barrkel.blogspot.com/2008/11/reference-counted-pointers-revisited.html.

```
    fObjectToFree := anObjectToFree;
end;

destructor TFreeTheValue.Destroy;
begin
   fObjectToFree.Free;
   inherited;
end;
```

Even better, in the actual example I've declared this as a nested type of the generic smart pointer type. All we have to do in the smart pointer generic type, to enable this feature, is to add an interface reference and initialize it with a TFreeTheValue object referring to the contained object:

```
type
   TSmartPointer<T: class> = record
   strict private
      FValue: T;
      FFreeTheValue: IInterface;
      function GetValue: T;
   public
      constructor Create(AValue: T); overload;
      property Value: T read GetValue;
   end;
```

The pseudo-constructor (records don't have real constructors) becomes:

```
constructor TSmartPointer<T>.Create(AValue: T);
begin
   FValue := AValue;
   FFreeTheValue := TFreeTheValue.Create(FValue);
end;
```

With this code in place, we can now write the following code in a program without causing a memory leak:

```
procedure TFormSmartPointers.btnSmartClick(
   Sender: TObject);
var
   sl: TStringList;
   smartP: TSmartPointer<TStringList>;
begin
   sl := TStringList.Create;
   smartP.Create (sl);
   sl.Add('foo');
   Log ('Count: ' + IntToStr (sl.Count));
end;
```

At the end of the method the smartP record is disposed, which causes its internal interfaced object to be destroyed, freeing the TStringList object.

Notice that this disposal takes place even when an exception is raised, so we don't need to protect our code with a `try-finally` block[90].

In the program, I verify that all objects are actually destroyed and there is no memory leak by setting the global `ReportMemoryLeaksOnShutdown` to True in the initialization code. As a counter test, there is a button in the program that causes a leak, which is caught as the program terminates.

So using the smart pointer record we have been able to remove the need for the `Free` call, and hence the need for a `try-finally` block, but there is still quite some code to write (and to remember writing). An extension to the smart pointer class is the inclusion of an `Implicit` conversion operator, providing the capability to assign the target object to the smart pointer:

```
class operator TSmartPointer<T>.
   Implicit(AValue: T): TSmartPointer<T>;
begin
   Result := TSmartPointer<T>.Create(AValue);
end;
```

With this code (and taking advantage of the `Value` field) we can now write a more compact version of the code, like:

```
var
   smartP: TSmartPointer<TStringList>;
begin
   smartP := TStringList.Create;
   smartP.Value.Add('foo');
   Log ('Count: ' + IntToStr (smartP.Value.Count));
```

As an alternative, we can use a `TStringList` variable and use a complicated constructor to initialize the smart pointer record even without an explicit reference to it:

```
var
   sl: TStringList;
begin
   sl := TSmartPointer<TStringList>.
      Create(TStringList.Create).Value;
   sl.Add('foo');
   Log ('Count: ' + IntToStr (sl.Count));
```

As we've started down this road, we can also define the opposite conversion, and use the cast notation rather than the `Value` property:

---

90 In practice, implicit `try-finally` blocks are being added all over the places by the compiler to handle the interface within the record, but we don't have to write them (and the compiler is less likely to forget one).

```
class operator TSmartPointer<T>.
  Implicit(AValue: T): TSmartPointer<T>;
begin
  Result := TSmartPointer<T>.Create(AValue);
end;

var
  smartP: TSmartPointer<TStringList>;
begin
  smartP := TStringList.Create;
  TStringList(smartP).Add('foo2');
```

Now, you might also notice that I've always used a pseudo-constructor in the code above, but this is not needed on a record. All we need is a way to initialize the internal object, possibly calling its constructor, the first time we use it. We cannot test if the internal object is `Assigned`, because records (unlike classes) are not initialized to zero. However we can perform that test on the interface variable, which is initialized.

The extra code of the smart pointer record type is an overloaded `Create` procedure (it cannot be a constructor, as parameterless constructors are not legal for records) and a lazy initialization of the `Value` property:

```
procedure TSmartPointer<T>.Create;
begin
  Create (T.Create);
end;

function TSmartPointer<T>.GetValue: T;
begin
  if not Assigned(FFreeTheValue) then
    Create;
  Result := FValue;
end;
```

With this code we now have many ways to use the smart pointer, including not freeing and not even creating it explicitly:

```
var
  smartP: TSmartPointer<TStringList>;
begin
  smartP.Value.Add('foo');
  Log ('Count: ' + IntToStr (smartP.Value.Count));
end;
```

The fact that the method above creates a string list and frees it at the end sounds certainly a big departure from the standard coding model Delphi developers are used to. And this is only a specific case of using generics for non collections code. To end this section, though. Let me list the complete source code of the smart pointer generic record I've build in several iterations:

```
type
  TSmartPointer<T: class, constructor> = record
  strict private
    FValue: T;
    FFreeTheValue: IInterface;
    function GetValue: T;
  private
    type
      TFreeTheValue = class (TInterfacedObject)
      private
        fObjectToFree: TObject;
      public
        constructor Create(anObjectToFree: TObject);
        destructor Destroy; override;
      end;
  public
    constructor Create(AValue: T); overload;
    procedure Create; overload;
    class operator Implicit(AValue: T): TSmartPointer<T>;
    class operator Implicit(smart: TSmartPointer <T>): T;
    property Value: T read GetValue;
  end;
```

The complete code and some of the usage patterns mentioned in this section are in the SmartPointers project.

What's Next

After covering the changes to the string type, in this chapter we've started exploring another significant new feature of the compiler in Delphi 2009, the support for generic types. Even if the chapter is quite long, we've just started scratching the surface of what can be considered a new programming paradigm for Delphi developers.

But there is more: anonymous methods, covered in the next chapter, provide yet another paradigm shift, and can be used together with generics as I've already anticipated in this chapter. They have a very useful role in multi-threaded applications and many other cases, as you'll see in the next chapter. Certainly Delphi 2009 is not a dull update for those who are, like me, passionate for programming languages in general and the Object Pascal language in particular.

Chapter 6: Anonymous Methods

The Delphi language has had procedural types (that is, types declaring pointers to procedures and functions[91]) and method pointers (that is, types declaring pointers to methods) for a long time. Although you might seldom use them directly, these are key features of Delphi that every developer works with. In fact, method pointers types are the foundation for event handlers in the VCL: every time you declare an event handler, even a pure

---

91 In case you want to learn more, procedural types are covered in Chapter 6 of Essential Pascal, 4th edition; method pointer types are describe in the books of my Mastering Delphi series.

178 - Chapter 6: Anonymous Methods

`Button1Click` you are in fact declaring a method that will be connected to an event (the `OnClick` event, in this case) using a method pointer.

Anonymous methods extend this feature by letting you pass the actual code of a method as a parameter, rather than the name of a method defined elsewhere. This is not the only difference, though. What makes anonymous methods very different from other techniques is the way they manage the lifetime of local variables.

The definition above matches with a feature called closures in many other languages, for example JavaScript. If Delphi anonymous methods are in fact closures, how come CodeGear refers to them using a different term? The reason is that C++Builder has been using the term closures for what we in Delphi call event handlers, so having a different feature with the same name would have been confusing. Moreover, the C# language uses the term anonymous methods for a similar mechanism as Delphi has, so it makes sense to use a similar moniker.

If anonymous methods are a brand new feature for Delphi, they've been around in different forms and with different names for many years in other programming languages, most notably dynamic languages. I've had extensive experience with closures in JavaScript, particularly with the jQuery[92] libraries and AJAX calls. The corresponding feature in C# is called an anonymous delegate.

But I don't want to devote time comparing closures and related techniques in the various programming languages, but rather describe in detail how they work in Delphi 2009.

Syntax and Semantics of Anonymous Methods

An anonymous method in Delphi is a mechanism to *create a method value in an expression context*[93]. A rather cryptic definition, but one encapsulating

---

92 More information about the jQuery JavaScript library at http://jQuery.org.

93 In the words of anonymous methods implementer Barry Kelly of CodeGear R&D, http://barrkel.blogspot.com.

Marco Cantù, Delphi 2009 Handbook

it with a lot of precision and underlining the key difference from method pointers, the *expression context*. Before we get to this, though, let me start from the beginning with a very simple code example (included in the AnonymFirst project along with most others in this section).

This is the declaration of an anonymous method type, something you need as Delphi is and remains a strongly typed language:

```
type
   TIntProc = reference to procedure (n: Integer);
```

This is different from a method reference type only in the keywords being used for the declaration:

```
type
   TIntMethod = procedure (n: Integer) of object;
```

An Anonymous Method Variable

Once you have an anonymous method type you can, in the simplest cases, declare a variable of this type, assign a type-compatible anonymous method, and call the method through the variable:

```
procedure TFormAnonymFirst.btnSimpleVarClick(
   Sender: TObject);
var
   anIntProc: TIntProc;
begin
   anIntProc :=
      procedure (n: Integer)
      begin
         Memo1.Lines.Add (IntToStr (n));
      end;
   anIntProc (22);
end;
```

Notice the syntax used to assign an actual procedure, with in-place code, to the variable. This is something never seen in Pascal in the past.

An Anonymous Method Parameter

As a more interesting example (with even more surprising syntax), we can pass an anonymous method as parameter to a function. Suppose you have a function taking an anonymous method parameter:

180 - Chapter 6: Anonymous Methods

```
procedure CallTwice (value: Integer;
  anIntProc: TIntProc);
begin
  anIntProc (value);
  Inc (value);
  anIntProc (value);
end;
```

The function calls the method passed as parameter twice with two consecutive integers values, the one passed as parameter and the following one. You call the function by passing an actual anonymous method to it, with directly in-place code that looks surprising:

```
procedure TFormAnonymFirst.btnProcParamClick(
  Sender: TObject);
begin
  CallTwice (48,
    procedure (n: Integer)
    begin
      Memo1.Lines.Add (IntToHex (n, 4));
    end);
  CallTwice (100,
    procedure (n: Integer)
    begin
      Memo1.Lines.Add (FloatToStr(Sqrt(n)));
    end);
end;
```

From the syntax point of view notice the procedure passed as parameter within parentheses and not terminated by a semicolon. The actual effect of the code is to call the IntToHex with 48 and 49 and the FloatToStr on the square root of 100 and 101, producing the following output:

```
0030
0031
10
10.0498756211209
```

Using Local Variables

We could have achieved the same effect using method pointers albeit with a different and less readable syntax. What makes anonymous method clearly different is the way they can refer to local variables of the calling method. Consider the following code:

```
procedure TFormAnonymFirst.btnLocalValClick(
  Sender: TObject);
var
  aNumber: Integer;
begin
  aNumber := 0;
  CallTwice (10,
    procedure (n: Integer)
    begin
      Inc (aNumber, n);
    end);
  Memo1.Lines.Add (IntToStr (aNumber));
end;
```

Here the method, still passed to the CallTwice procedure, uses the local parameter n, but also a local variable from the context from which it was called, aNumber. What's the effect? The two calls of the anonymous method will modify the local variable, adding the parameter to it, 10 the first time and 11 the second. The final value of aNumber will be 21.

Extending the Lifetime of Local Variables

The previous example shows an interesting effect, but with a sequence of nested function calls, the fact you can use the local variable isn't that surprising. The power of anonymous methods, however, lies in the fact they can use a local variable and also extend its lifetime until needed[94]. An example will prove the point more than a lengthly explanation.

I've added (using class completion) to the TFormAnonymFirst form class of the AnonymFirst example a property of an anonymous method pointer type (well, actually the same anonymous method pointer type I've used in all of the code of the project):

```
private
  FAnonMeth: TIntProc;
  procedure SetAnonMeth(const Value: TIntProc);
public
  property AnonMeth: TIntProc
    read FAnonMeth write SetAnonMeth;
```

---

94 In slightly more technical details, anonymous methods copy the variables and parameters they use to the heap when they are created, and keep them alive as long as the specific instance of the anonymous method.

182 - Chapter 6: Anonymous Methods

Then I've added two more buttons to the form of the program. The first saves the property an anonymous method that uses a local variable (more or less like in the previous btnLocalValClick method):

```
procedure TFormAnonymFirst.btnStoreClick(
  Sender: TObject);
var
  aNumber: Integer;
begin
  aNumber := 3;
  AnonMeth :=
    procedure (n: Integer)
    begin
      Inc (aNumber, n);
      Memo1.Lines.Add (IntToStr (aNumber));
    end;
end;
```

When this method executes the anonymous method is not executed, only stored. The local variable aNumber is initialized to three, is not modified, goes out of local scope (as the method terminates), and is displaced. At least, that is what you'd expect from a standard Delphi code.

The second button I added to the form for this specific step calls the anonymous method stored in the AnonMeth property:

```
procedure TFormAnonymFirst.btnCallClick(Sender: TObject);
begin
  if Assigned (AnonMeth) then
  begin
    CallTwice (2, AnonMeth);
  end;
end;
```

When this code is executed, it calls an anonymous method that uses the local variable aNumber of a method that's not on the stack any more. However, since anonymous methods *capture* their execution context the variable is still there and can be used as long as that given instance of the anonymous method (that is, a reference to the method) is around.

As a further proof, do the following. Press the Store button once, the Call button two times and you'll see that the same *captured* variable is being used[95]:

---

95 The reason for this sequence is that the value starts at 3, each call to CallTwice passed its parameter to the anonymous methods a first time (that is 2) and then a second time after incrementing it (that is, the second time it passes 3).

```
5
8
10
13
```

Now press Store once more and press Call again. What happens, why is the value of the local variable reset? By assigning a new anonymous method instance, the old anonymous method is deleted (along with its own execution context) and a new execution context is capture, including a new instance of the local variable. The full sequence *Store – Call – Call – Store – Call* produces:

```
5
8
10
13
5
8
```

It is the implication of this behavior, resembling what some other languages do, that makes anonymous methods an extremely powerful language feature, which you can use to implement something that simply wasn't possible in the past.

More on Anonymous Methods

If the variable capture feature is one of the most relevant for anonymous methods, there are a few more techniques that are worth looking at, before we focus on some real world examples.

The (Potentially) Missing Parenthesis

Notice that in the code above I used the `AnonMeth` symbol to refer to the anonymous method, not to invoke it. For invoking it, I should have typed:

```
AnonMeth (2)
```

The difference is clear; I need to pass a proper parameter to invoke the method. Things are slightly more confusing with parameterless anonymous methods. If you declare:

184 - Chapter 6: Anonymous Methods

```
type
  TAnyProc = reference to procedure;
var
  AnyProc: TAnyProc;
```

The call to `AnyProc` must be followed by the empty parentheses, otherwise the compiler thinks you are trying to get the method (its address) rather than call it:

```
AnyProc ();
```

Something similar happens when you call a function that returns an anonymous method, as in the following case taken from the usual Anonym-First example:

```
function GetShowMethod: TIntProc;
var
  x: Integer;
begin
  x := Random (100);
  ShowMessage ('New x is ' + IntToStr (x));
  Result :=
    procedure (n: Integer)
    begin
      x := x + n;
      ShowMessage (IntToStr (x));
    end;
end;
```

Now the question is, how do you call it? If you simply call

```
GetShowMethod;
```

It compiles and executes, but all it does is call the anonymous method assignment code, throwing away the anonymous method returned by the function.

How do you call the actual anonymous method passing a parameter to it? One option is to use a temporary anonymous method variable:

```
var
  ip: TIntProc;
begin
  ip := GetShowMethod();
  ip (3);
```

Notice in this case the parentheses after the `GetShowMethod` call. If you omit them (a standard Pascal practice) you'll get the following error:

```
E2010 Incompatible types: 'TIntProc' and 'Procedure'
```

Without the parentheses the compiler thinks you want to assign the
`GetShowMethod` function itself, and not its result to the `ip` method pointer.
Still, using a temporary variable might not be the best option in this case, as
is makes the code unnaturally complex. A simple call

```
GetShowMethod(3);
```

won't compile, as you cannot pass a parameter to the method. You need to
add the empty parenthesis to the first call, and the Integer parameter to the
resulting anonymous method. Oddly enough, you can write:

```
GetShowMethod()(3);
```

An alternative solution is to use the internal implementation of anonymous
methods, and call the low-level Invoke method that gets added by the compiler (in which case you can omit the empty parenthesis):

```
GetShowMethod.Invoke (3);
```

Behind Anonymous Methods

What is this `Invoke` method? What happens behind the scenes in the implementation of anonymous methods? The actual code generated by the
compiler for anonymous methods is based on interfaces, with a single invocation method called `Invoke`, plus the usual reference counting support
(that's useful to determine the lifetime of anonymous methods and the context they capture).

You can see those interface methods in the editor if you use code completion, in the following way:

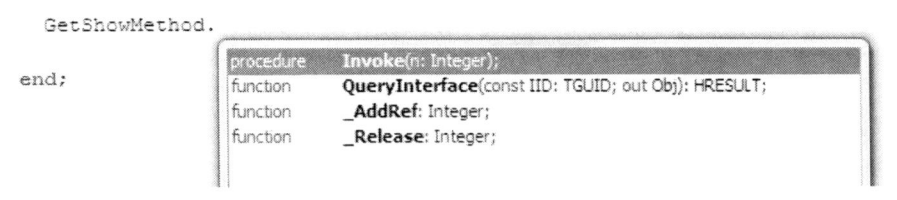

```
GetShowMethod.

end;
```

procedure	**Invoke**(n: Integer);
function	**QueryInterface**(const IID: TGUID; out Obj): HRESULT;
function	**_AddRef**: Integer;
function	**_Release**: Integer;

Getting details of the internals is probably very complicated and of limited
worth. Suffice to say that the implementation is very efficient, in terms of
speed, and requires about 500 extra bytes for each anonymous method.

186 - Chapter 6: Anonymous Methods

In other words, a method reference in Delphi is implemented with a *special*[96] single method interface, with a compiler-generated method having the same signature as the method reference it is implementing. The interface uses all COM rules and takes advantage of reference counting for its automatic disposal. Beside this hidden interface, for each invocation of an anonymous method the compiler creates a hidden object that has the method implementation and the data required to *capture* the invocation context. That's how you get a new set of captured variables for each call of the method.

Ready To Use Reference Types

Every time you use an anonymous method as a parameter you need to define a corresponding reference pointer data type. To avoid the proliferation of local types, Delphi provides a number of ready-to-use reference pointer types in the SysUtils unit. As you can see in the code snippet below, most of these type definitions use parameterized types, so that with a single generic declaration you have a different reference pointer type for each possible data type:

```
type
  TProc = reference to procedure;
  TProc<T> = reference to procedure (Arg1: T);
  TProc<T1,T2> = reference to procedure (
    Arg1: T1; Arg2: T2);
  TProc<T1,T2,T3> = reference to procedure (
    Arg1: T1; Arg2: T2; Arg3: T3);
  TProc<T1,T2,T3,T4> = reference to procedure (
    Arg1: T1; Arg2: T2; Arg3: T3; Arg4: T4);
```

Using these declarations, you can define procedures that take anonymous method parameters like in the following:

```
procedure UseCode (proc: TProc);
function DoThis (proc: TProc): string;
function DoThat (procInt: TProc<Integer>): string;
```

In the first and second case you pass a parameterless anonymous method, in the third you pass a method with a single Integer parameter:

---

96 Although practically the interface used for an anonymous method looks like any other interface, the compiler distinguishes between these *special* interfaces so you cannot mix them in code.

```
UseCode (
  procedure
  begin
    ...
  end);
strRes := DoThat (
  procedure (I: Integer)
  begin
    ...
  end);
```

Similarly the SysUtils unit defines a set of anonymous method types with a generic return value:

```
type
  TFunc<TResult> = reference to function: TResult;
  TFunc<T,TResult> = reference to function (
    Arg1: T): TResult;
  TFunc<T1,T2,TResult> = reference to function (
    Arg1: T1; Arg2: T2): TResult;
  TFunc<T1,T2,T3,TResult> = reference to function (
    Arg1: T1; Arg2: T2; Arg3: T3): TResult;
  TFunc<T1,T2,T3,T4,TResult> = reference to function (
    Arg1: T1; Arg2: T2; Arg3: T3; Arg4: T4): TResult;
  TPredicate<T> = reference to function (
    Arg1: T): Boolean;
```

These definitions are very broad, as you can use countless combinations of data types for up to four parameters and a return type. The last definition is very similar to the second, but corresponds to a specific case that is very frequent, a function taking a generic parameter and returning a Boolean.

Anonymous Methods in the Real World

At first sight, it is not easy to fully understand the power of anonymous methods and the scenarios that can benefit from using them. That's why rather than coming out with more convoluted examples covering the language, I decided to focus on some that have a practical impact and provide starting points for further exploration.

Anonymous Event Handlers

Since the early days, one of the distinguishing features of Delphi has been its implementation of event handlers using method pointers. Now with the advent of anonymous methods, it might be interesting to use this feature to attach a new behavior to an event without having to declare a separate method and capturing the method's execution context, thus avoiding adding extra fields to a form to pass parameters from one method to another.

As an example, I've added an *anonymous click* event to a button, declaring a proper method pointer type and adding a new event handler to a custom button class (defined using an interceptor class[97]):

```
type
  TAnonNotif = reference to procedure (Sender: TObject);

  // interceptor class
  TButton = class (StdCtrls.TButton)
  private
    FAnonClick: TAnonNotif;
    procedure SetAnonClick(const Value: TAnonNotif);
  public
    procedure Click; override;
  public
    property AnonClick: TAnonNotif
      read FAnonClick write SetAnonClick;
  end;
```

The code of this class is fairly simple, as the setter method saves the new pointer and the Click method calls it before doing the standard processing (that is, calling the OnClick event handler if available):

```
procedure TButton.SetAnonClick(const Value: TAnonNotif);
begin
  FAnonClick := Value;
end;
```

---

[97] An interceptor class is a derived class having the same name as its base class. Having two classes with the same name is possible because the two classes are in different units, so their full name (*unitname.classname*) is different. Declaring an interceptor class can be handy as you can simply place a Button control on the form and attach extra behavior to it, without having to install a new component in the IDE and replace the controls on your form with the new type. The only trick you have to remember is that if the definition of the interceptor class is in a separate unit (not the form unit as in this simple example), that unit has to be listed in the uses statement after the unit defining the base class.

```
procedure TButton.Click;
begin
  if Assigned (FAnonClick) then
    FAnonClick (self)
  inherited;
end;
```

How can you use this new event handler? Basically you can assign an anonymous method to it

```
procedure TFormAnonButton.btnAssignClick(
  Sender: TObject);
begin
  btnInvoke.AnonClick :=
    procedure (Sender: TObject)
    begin
      ShowMessage ((Sender as TButton).Caption);
    end;
end;
```

Now this looks rather pointless, as the same effect could easily be achieved using a standard event handler method. The following, instead, starts making a difference, as the anonymous method captures a reference to the component that assigned the event handler, by referencing the Sender parameter.

This can be done after temporarily assigning it to a local variable, as the Sender parameter of the anonymous method hides the btnKeepRefClick method's Sender parameter:

```
procedure TFormAnonButton.btnKeepRefClick(
  Sender: TObject);
var
  aCompRef: TComponent;
begin
  aCompRef := Sender as TComponent;
  btnInvoke.AnonClick :=
    procedure (Sender: TObject)
    begin
      ShowMessage ((Sender as TButton).Caption +
        ' assigned by ' + aCompRef.Name);
    end;
end;
```

As you press the btnInvoke button, you'll see its caption along with the name of the component that assigned the anonymous method handler:

Marco Cantù, Delphi 2009 Handbook

An even more complicated situation is demonstrated by two further buttons, that receive an anonymous method handler by clicking on the form with the left or right mouse button, capturing the mouse click position:

```
procedure TFormAnonButton.FormMouseDown(
  Sender: TObject; Button: TMouseButton;
  Shift: TShiftState; X, Y: Integer);
begin
  if Button = mbLeft then
    btnLeftInvokeForm.AnonClick :=
      procedure (Sender: TObject)
      begin
        (Sender as TButton).Caption :=
          'Last left on [' + IntToStr (X) +
          ',' + IntToStr (Y) + ']';
      end
  else
    btnRightInvokeForm.AnonClick :=
      procedure (Sender: TObject)
      begin
        (Sender as TButton).Caption :=
          'Last right on [' + IntToStr (X) +
          ',' + IntToStr (Y) + ']';
      end;
end;
```

This is another example of capturing the execution context, but this time there can be two capture operations at the same time (each with its own data kept in memory), and there could be even more than two. To implement the same operation with method pointers you'd have to keep an array of mouse clicks tied to each target component or use the components Tag property to store a pointer to this information.

Timing Anonymous Methods

Developers frequently add timing code to existing routines to compare their relative speed. I did the same a few times in examples in Part I of the book, to figure out the speed of Unicode strings. Supposing you have two code fragments and you want to compare their speed by executing them a few million times, you could write the following (which is taken from the String-Convert example of Chapter 2 and discussed in the section "Converting Strings):

```
procedure TFormAnonTiming.btnClassicClick(
  Sender: TObject);
var
  str1: string;
  str2: AnsiString;
  I: Integer;
  t1: TDateTime;
begin
  str1 := 'Marco Cantù';
  t1 := Now;
  for I := 1 to MaxLoop2 do
    str1 := AnsiUpperCase (str1);
  t1 := now - t1;
  Memo1.Lines.Add ('AnsiUpperCase (string): ' +
    FormatDateTime('nn:ss.zzz', t1));

  str2 := 'Marco Cantù';
  t1 := Now;
  for I := 1 to MaxLoop2 do
    str2 := AnsiUpperCase (str2);
  t1 := now - t1;
  Memo1.Lines.Add ('AnsiUpperCase (AnsiString): ' +
    FormatDateTime('nn:ss.zzz', t1));
end;
```

Rather than repeating the timing code over and over, you can write a function with the timing code that would invoke the code snippet through a parameterless anonymous method:

```
function TimeCode (nLoops: Integer; proc: TProc): string;
var
  t1: TDateTime;
  I: Integer;
begin
  t1 := Now;
  for I := 1 to nLoops do
    proc;
  t1 := now - t1;
  Result := FormatDateTime('nn:ss.zzz', t1);
end;

procedure TFormAnonTiming.btnAnonClick(Sender: TObject);
var
  str1: string;
  str2: AnsiString;
```

192 - Chapter 6: Anonymous Methods

```
begin
  str1 := 'Marco Cantù';
  Memo1.Lines.Add ('AnsiUpperCase (string): ' +
    TimeCode (MaxLoop2,
      procedure ()
      begin
        str1 := AnsiUpperCase (str1);
      end));

  str2 := 'Marco Cantù';
  Memo1.Lines.Add ('AnsiUpperCase (AnsiString): ' +
    TimeCode (MaxLoop2,
      procedure ()
      begin
        str2 := AnsiUpperCase (str2);
      end));
end;
```

In the example code you'll also find a slightly better (and more precise) version that uses `GetTickCount` rather then the current time (`Now`), although if you are looking for really precise timing you would be better off using the specific timing service offered by the `QueryPerformanceCounter` Windows API.

Notice, though that if you execute the standard version and the one based on anonymous methods you'll get output like the following:

```
Classic
AnsiUpperCase (string): 00:00.588
AnsiUpperCase (AnsiString): 00:01.087
Anonymous
AnsiUpperCase (string): 00:00.644
AnsiUpperCase (AnsiString): 00:01.153
```

As you can see, the anonymous method version sees a penalty of roughly 8%. The reason is that rather than directly executing the local code, the program has to make a virtual call to the anonymous method implementation. As this difference is consistent, the testing code makes perfect sense anyway. However, if you need to squeeze performance from your code, using anonymous methods won't be as fast as directly writing the code, with using a direct function. Using a method pointer would probably be somewhere in between the two in terms of performance.

Thread Synchronization with the VCL

In multi-threaded applications that need to update the user interface, you cannot access properties of visual components (or in memory-objects) that are part of the global thread without a synchronization mechanism. The VCL, in fact, isn't thread-safe (as is true for most user-interface libraries). Two threads accessing an object at the same time could compromise its state.

The classic solution offered by the TThread class in Delphi is to call a special method, Synchronize, passing as a parameter the reference to another method, the one to be executed safely. This second method cannot have parameters, so it is common practice to add extra fields to the thread class to pass the information from one method to another.

As a practical example, in the book Mastering Delphi 2005 I wrote a WebFind example (a program that runs searches on Google via HTTP and extracts the resulting links from the HTML of the page), with the following thread class:

```
type
  TFindWebThread = class(TThread)
  protected
    Addr, Text, Status: string;
    procedure Execute; override;
    procedure AddToList;
    procedure ShowStatus;
    procedure GrabHtml;
    procedure HtmlToList;
    procedure HttpWork (Sender: TObject;
      AWorkMode: TWorkMode; AWorkCount: Int64);
  public
    strUrl: string;
    strRead: string;
  end;
```

The three protected string fields and some of the extra methods have been introduced to support synchronization with the user interface. For example, the HttpWork event handler hooked to an event of an internal IdHttp object (an Indy component supporting the client side of the HTTP protocol), used to have the the following code, that called the ShowStatus method:

```
procedure TFindWebThread.HttpWork(Sender: TObject;
  AWorkMode: TWorkMode; AWorkCount: Int64);
begin
  Status := 'Received ' + IntToStr (AWorkCount) +
```

194 - Chapter 6: Anonymous Methods

```delphi
    ' for ' + strUrl;
  Synchronize (ShowStatus);
end;

procedure TFindWebThread.ShowStatus;
begin
  Form1.StatusBar1.SimpleText := Status;
end;
```

In Delphi 2009, the Synchronize method has two different overloaded definitions:

```delphi
type
  TThreadMethod = procedure of object;
  TThreadProcedure = reference to procedure;

  TThread = class
    ...
    procedure Synchronize(
      AMethod: TThreadMethod); overload;
    procedure Synchronize(
      AThreadProc: TThreadProcedure); overload;
```

For this reason we can remove the Status text field and the ShowStatus function, and rewrite the HttpWork event handler using the new version of Synchronize and an anonymous method:

```delphi
procedure TFindWebThreadAnon.HttpWork(Sender: TObject;
  AWorkMode: TWorkMode; AWorkCount: Int64);
begin
  Synchronize (
    procedure
    begin
      Form1.StatusBar1.SimpleText :=
        'Received ' + IntToStr (AWorkCount) +
        ' for ' + strUrl;
    end);
end;
```

Using the same approach throughout the code of the class, the thread class becomes the following (you can find both thread classes in the version of the WebFind example that comes with the source code of this book):

```delphi
type
  TFindWebThreadAnon = class(TThread)
  protected
    procedure Execute; override;
    procedure GrabHtml;
    procedure HtmlToList;
    procedure HttpWork (Sender: TObject;
      AWorkMode: TWorkMode; AWorkCount: Int64);
```

```
  public
    strUrl: string;
    strRead: string;
end;
```

Here is another method in its updated version, the part that does the HTML parsing and outputs the URLs and the descriptions of the links in a ListBox:

```
procedure TFindWebThreadAnon.HtmlToList;
var
  strAddr, strText: string;
  nText: integer;
  nBegin, nEnd: Integer;
begin
  Synchronize (
    procedure
    begin
      Form1.StatusBar1.SimpleText :=
        'Extracting data for: ' + StrUrl;
    end);

  strRead := LowerCase (strRead);
  nBegin := 1;
  repeat
    // find the initial part HTTP reference
    nBegin := PosEx ('href="http', strRead, nBegin);
    if nBegin <> 0 then
    begin
      // find the end of the href tag (closing quotes)
      nBegin := nBegin + 6;
      nEnd := PosEx ('"', strRead, nBegin);
      strAddr := Copy (strRead, nBegin, nEnd - nBegin);

      // move on
      nBegin := PosEx ('>', strRead, nEnd) + 1;
      // add the URL if 'google' is not in it
      if Pos ('google', strAddr) = 0 then
      begin
        nText := PosEx ('</a>', strRead, nBegin);
        strText := copy (strRead, nBegin, nText - nBegin);
        // remove cached references and duplicates
        if (Pos ('cache', strText) = 0) then
        begin
          Synchronize (
            procedure
            begin
              if Form1.ListBox1.Items.IndexOf (
                strAddr) < 0 then
              begin
                Form1.ListBox1.Items.Add (strAddr);
```

196 - Chapter 6: Anonymous Methods

```
                    Form1.DetailsList.Add (strText);
                end;
              end);
          end;
        end;
      end;
    until nBegin = 0;
end;
```

I think this demonstrates how using anonymous methods simplifies the code needed for thread synchronization.

Parallel For Loop

One of the core reasons behind the introduction of anonymous methods in Delphi 2009 is the desire to create a *parallel library*, a collection of techniques to allow applications to take advantage of the multi-core CPUs any modern computer has these days. Rather than having to manually code multi-threaded applications, such a library would let you write almost standard code that creates threads behind the scenes.

This library is the subject of many blog posts by Delphi's chief architect Allen Bauer and other members of the R&D team. It is listed among the features expected in the next version of Delphi in the current product roadmap. Meanwhile, anonymous methods let you start experimenting in this direction. Here I'll present a simplified version of a parallel `for` loop (this version works but is not general enough and not completely free of small glitches). I've seen more complete solutions, but their code was too complex to discuss here.

What is a *parallel for*? It is a `for` loop processed in parallel by multiple threads, each taking care of a portion of the loop iterations. Let's start by looking at the original source code, that uses a terribly slow implementation[98] of a function for computing if a number is a prime number:

```
const
  Max = 50000;

procedure TFormParallelFor.btnPlainClick(
```

---

[98] This is done on purpose, to slow down the code. The function becomes slower as the number it is testing increases. This is why splitting the range of numbers to process in two, half for each thread, wont' work: The thread working on higher numbers would take way more time than the other.

```
    Sender: TObject);
var
  I, Tot: Integer;
  Ticks: Integer;
begin
  // counts the prime numbers below a given value
  Tot := 0;
  Ticks := GetTickCount;
  for I := 1 to Max do
  begin
    if IsPrime (I) then
      Inc (Tot);
    Application.ProcessMessages;
  end;
  Ticks := GetTickCount - Ticks;
  Memo1.Lines.Add (Format (
    'No threads: %d - %d', [Ticks, Tot]));
end;
```

Now it would be nice to wrap the core method of the loop (and the final output of the total and time) into separate anonymous methods to be passed to a `ParallelFor` function:

```
procedure TFormParallelFor.btnParallel2Click(
  Sender: TObject);
var
  Tot: Integer;
  Ticks: Cardinal;
begin
  Tot := 0;
  Ticks := GetTickCount;
  ParallelFor (1, Max, 2,
    procedure (I: Integer)
    begin
      if IsPrime (I) then
        InterlockedIncrement (Tot);
    end);
  Ticks := GetTickCount - Ticks;
  Memo1.Lines.Add (Format (
    '2 threads: %d - %d', [Ticks, Tot]));
end;
```

The call is almost identical. I've replaced the for loop with the `ParallelFor` call, removed the `Application.ProcessMessages` call (not needed by a thread), and replaced `Inc` with `InterlockedIncrement` as multiple threads could access the global value (the value captured by the anonymous method) at the exact same time.

The call to `ParallelFor` passes the lower and upper bound of the loop, the number of threads to use, and the actual code to execute. In this case, the program will use two threads, but there are other buttons in the example asking for a single thread or four for them. The final code at the end of the method is executed when the loop is finished, because `ParallelFor` waits for the threads it spawns.

Before looking at the actual implementation of my simple `ParallelFor`, let's see if if helps in any way. I've executed the program on my dual-core laptop, in the classic version, and with 1, 2 or 4 threads, computing the number of primes below 50,000. Here you can see the version, the number of ticks / milliseconds, and the actual result:

```
No threads: 1514 - 5134
1 thread: 1544 - 5134
2 threads: 889 - 5134
4 threads: 1029 - 5134
```

As expected, the threaded version has a small overhead, but running two threads take almost half of the time, while increasing the number of threads adds extra overhead and resource contention, making the result worse (but still better than the original version). In other words, this is quite an effort but it makes sense, because the `ParallelFor` in the optimal case lets us save over 40% of the 1.5 seconds of the original version.

Here is the code of the `ParallelFor` function:

```
procedure ParallelFor (nMin, nMax, nThreads: Integer;
  aProc: TProc<Integer>);
var
  threads: array of TParallel;
  I: Integer;
begin
  // inizialize TParallel class data
  TParallel.CurrPos := nMin;
  TParallel.MaxPos := nMax;
  TParallel.cs := TCriticalSection.Create;
  TParallel.ThCount := 0;

  // create the threads
  SetLength (threads, nThreads);
  for I := 0 to Length (threads) - 1 do
  begin
    threads[I] := TParallel.Create; // suspended
    threads[I].Proc := aProc;
    threads[I].Resume;
  end;
```

```
    while TParallel.ThCount > 0 do
    begin
      Application.ProcessMessages;
      Sleep (100);
    end;
end;
```

This global function sets up the requested number of threads, activates them, and then waits for all threads to finish. The ThCount class data of the TParallel class, in fact, is incremented by each thread on startup and decremented by the class destructor (automatically triggered by setting the FreeOnTerminate property within the thread class constructor).

The core of the work is performed by the thread class which has a critical section that is used when asking for the next value to process:

```
type
  TParallel = class(TThread)
  private
    FProc: TProc<Integer>;
  protected
    procedure Execute; override;
    function GetNextValue: Integer;
  public
    constructor Create;
    destructor Destroy; override;

    property Proc: TProc<Integer>
      read FProc write FProc;
    class var
      CurrPos: Integer;
      MaxPos: Integer;
      cs: TCriticalSection;
      ThCount: Integer;
  end;
```

The most interesting methods are those used to grab the next value and to do the actual processing on it. Their code should be self-explanatory:

```
procedure TParallel.Execute;
var
  nCurrent: Integer;
begin
  nCurrent := GetNextValue;
  while nCurrent <= MaxPos do
  begin
    Proc (nCurrent);
    nCurrent := GetNextValue;
  end;
end;
```

200 - Chapter 6: Anonymous Methods

```
function TParallel.GetNextValue: Integer;
begin
  cs.Acquire;
  try
    Result := CurrPos;
    Inc(CurrPos);
  finally
    cs.Release;
  end;
end;
```

I hope this example demonstrates the possibilities opened up by the introduction of anonymous methods.

AJAX in Delphi

The last example in this section, called AnonAjax, is one of my favorites, for the simple reason that I learned using closures (or anonymous methods) in JavaScript, while writing AJAX applications with the jQuery library.

The `AjaxCall` global function is not unlike the `ParallelFor` function of the previous example, as it also spawns a thread. This time, however, the function terminates without waiting for the thread to complete, but passes the thread an anonymous method to execute on completion. The function is just a wrapper around the thread constructor:

```
type
  TAjaxCallback = reference to procedure (
    ResponseContent: TStringStream);

procedure AjaxCall (const strUrl: string;
    ajaxCallback: TAjaxCallback);
begin
  TAjaxThread.Create (strUrl, ajaxCallback);
end;
```

All of the code is in the `TAjaxThread` class, a thread class with an internal Indy HTTP client component used to access to a given URL, asynchronously:

```
type
  TAjaxThread = class (TThread)
    private
      fIdHttp: TIdHttp;
      fURL: string;
      fAjaxCallback: TAjaxCallback;
    protected
```

```
    procedure Execute; override;
  public
    constructor Create (const strUrl: string;
      ajaxCallback: TAjaxCallback);
    destructor Destroy; override;
  end;
```

The constructor does some initialization, copying its parameters to the corresponding local fields of the thread class and creating the fIdHttp object. The real meat of the class is in its Execute method, which does the HTTP request, saving the result in a stream that is later reset and passed to the callback function – the anonymous method:

```
procedure TAjaxThread.Execute;
var
  aResponseContent: TStringStream;
begin
  aResponseContent := TStringStream.Create;
  try
    fIdHttp.Get (fURL, aResponseContent);
    aResponseContent.Position := 0;
    fAjaxCallback (aResponseContent);
  finally
    aResponseContent.Free;
  end;
end;
```

As an example of its usage, the AnonAjax example has a button used to copy the content of a Web page to a Memo control (adding the requested URL at the beginning):

```
procedure TFormAnonAjax.btnReadClick(Sender: TObject);
begin
  AjaxCall (edUrl.Text,
    procedure (aResponseContent: TStringStream)
    begin
      Memo1.Lines.Text := aResponseContent.DataString;
      Memo1.Lines.Insert (
        0, 'From URL: ' + edUrl.Text);
    end);
end;
```

After the HTTP request has finished, you can do any sort of processing you want on it.

Another example would be to extract links from the HTML file (in a way that resembles the WebFind example covered earlier). Again, to make this function flexible, it takes as a parameter the anonymous method to execute for each link:

202 - Chapter 6: Anonymous Methods

```
type
  TLinkCallback = reference to procedure (
    const strLink: string);

procedure ExtractLinks (strData: string;
  procLink: TLinkCallback);
var
  strAddr: string;
  nBegin, nEnd: Integer;
begin
  strData := LowerCase (strData);
  nBegin := 1;
  repeat
    nBegin := PosEx ('href="http', strData, nBegin);
    if nBegin <> 0 then
    begin
      // find the end of the HTTP reference
      nBegin := nBegin + 6;
      nEnd := PosEx ('"', strData, nBegin);
      strAddr := Copy (strData, nBegin, nEnd - nBegin);
      // move on
      nBegin := nEnd + 1;
      // execute anon method
      procLink (strAddr)
    end;
  until nBegin = 0;
end;
```

If you apply this function to the result of an AJAX call and provide a further method for processing, you end up with two nested anonymous method calls, like in the second button of the AnonAjax example:

```
procedure TFormAnonAjax.btnLinksClick(Sender: TObject);
begin
  AjaxCall (edUrl.Text,
    procedure (aResponseContent: TStringStream)
    begin
      ExtractLinks(aResponseContent.DataString,
        procedure (const aUrl: string)
        begin
          Memo1.Lines.Add (aUrl + ' in ' + edUrl.Text);
        end);
    end);
end;
```

In this case the Memo control will receive a collection of links, instead of the HTML of the returned page. A variation to the link extraction routine above would be an image extraction routine. The `ExtractImages` function grabs the source (`src`) of the `img` tags of the HTML file returned, and calls another `TLinkCallback`-compatible anonymous method (see the source code for the function details).

Now you can envision opening an HTML page (with the `AjaxCall` function), extract the image links, and use `AjaxCall` again to grab the actual images. This means using a triple-nested closure, in a coding structure that some Delphi programmers might find unreadable[99] (it takes a while to get used to it!), but is certainly very powerful and expressive:

```
procedure TFormAnonAjax.btnImagesClick(Sender: TObject);
var
  nHit: Integer;
begin
  nHit := 0;
  AjaxCall (edUrl.Text,
    procedure (aResponseContent: TStringStream)
    begin
      ExtractImages(aResponseContent.DataString,
        procedure (const aUrl: string)
        begin
          Inc (nHit);
          Memo1.Lines.Add (IntToStr (nHit) + '.' +
            aUrl + ' in ' + edUrl.Text);
          if nHit = 1 then // load the first
          begin
            AjaxCall (aUrl,
              procedure (aResponseContent: TStringStream)
              begin
                // load image of the current type only
                Image1.Picture.Graphic.
                  LoadFromStream(aResponseContent);
              end);
          end;
        end);
    end);
end;
```

Beside the fact that the graphic only works in the case where you are loading a file with the same format as the one already in the Image component, the code and its result are both impressive. Here is the effect of pressing the `btnImages` button with the URL of my blog:

---

[99] This code snippet was the topic of a blog post of mine, "Anonymous, Anonymous, Anonymous" of September 2008, which attracted some comments, as you can see on: http://blog.marcocantu.com/blog/anonymous_3.html.

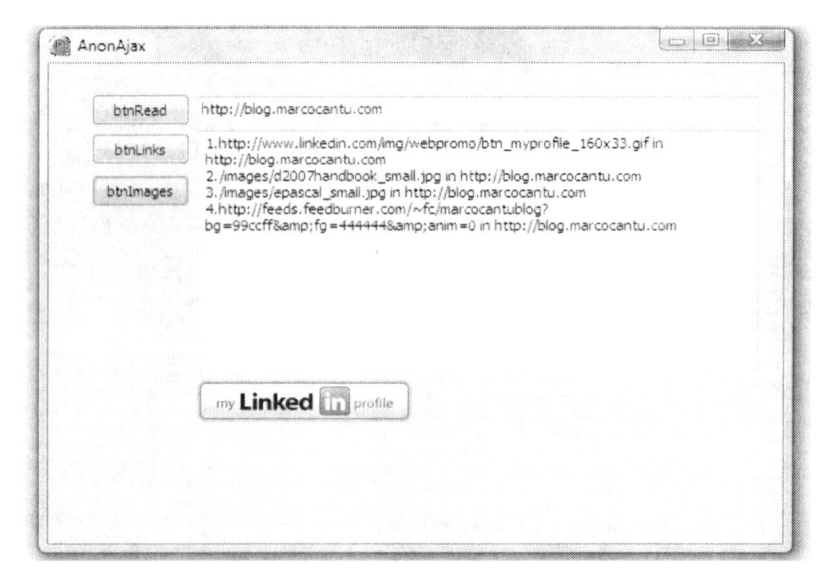

Notice in particular the numbering sequence, based on the capture of the nHit local variable. What happens if you press the button twice, in a fast sequence? Each of the anonymous methods will get a different copy of the nHit counter, and they might potentially be displayed out of sequence in the list, with the second thread starting to produce its output before the first.

Debating the AJAX Demo

After I blogged about this example, there was some debate about the readability and the usefulness of anonymous methods. I replied to these critical voices (some of which do have a point) with another blog post in which I tried to clarify the situation. As it adds some extra information to the use of anonymous methods (and some other alternatives) I think it is worth reporting it, in an slightly edited version:

> *The post I made yesterday on anonymous methods, a new feature in Delphi 2009, stirred controversy. I agree on the readability comments, but you should also consider that using three nested anonymous methods was quite a stretch, not a common usage scenario.*
>
> *Let's start from the beginning and examine only one step. I want to make an HTTP call and process the result. This has to be done in a*

thread, since I don't want it to be blocking. So whether you use anonymous methods or not you need to define a custom *TThread* class. Now suppose you want to use the same thread class (or its HTTP support code) for slightly different situations. You have two traditional options:

1. Inherit a class for each usage scenario and use the template pattern: the thread *Execute* method will call a virtual function each specific class can override. Nice, but in case the specific code is limited, creating many similar classes, mostly used only for a single object in a specific situation is far from a nice architecture.

2. Delphi classic alternative to inheritance is to use events. In fact, you don't inherit from *TButton* to override the *Click* method, but assign an external procedure to the event, using method pointers. Each customization is in a separate method you assign.

Method pointers and anonymous methods are not that different. In one case you can write the procedure in-place, but that is an option. For readability, you can write the method's code as a series of separate functions, each assigned to an anonymous method pointer to be called later on. Will this be more readable? Possibly, even if (from JavaScript experience) I think it is mostly a matter of getting used to one style or another. In other words, syntax aside, the concept of an anonymous method is not far from that of a method pointer, but the fact they introduce a new lifetime model for variables can help.

This brings me to another point, why not keep using method pointers? Having to allocate memory for every invocation of an event (in the case of parallel code execution) would be far from trivial in many cases in which anonymous methods just "magically" work. As a commenter noted about the code, if you hit the button many times the *nHit* stack-based variable gets duplicated and captured for each anonymous method invocation, so not only does it live beyond its original stack location, but you can have multiple instances at the same time.

Would this mean each and every Delphi code would benefit from this new technology? Of course not, I think it is useful in only a fraction of cases. I remain convinced that an Ajax-like call is a nice *scenario and that it will take some time for the Delphi community at large to master this new language feature.*

What's Next

Now that I've covered the two major new language features of Delphi 2009, generics and anonymous methods, it is time to start looking at many other minor (but still relevant) changes. This will be the topic of the first part of the next chapter, that also covers RTL changes since Delphi 2007.

Chapter 7: More Language And RTL Changes

In the initial Unicode chapters and in the last two chapters on language features, I've covered most of the new compiler changes and also introduced a large number of new RTL classes, from `TCharacter` and `TEncoding` to the new generic containers. You can find a complete list in the section "Summary of New Units and New RTL Classes" at the end of this chapter. Here I'm introducing other new features of the compiler and RTL areas that didn't fit in any of the previous chapters.

Marco Cantù, Delphi 2009 Handbook

Other New Language Features

With so many new important features in the Object Pascal language is it easy to miss some of the minor ones, that would have been significant in other versions with a smaller set of changes.

Compiler Version

The specific define for the Delphi 2009 compiler is VER200. If you need to have specific code for one of the recent versions of Delphi, you can base your $IFDEF statements on the following defines:

D2006	VER180
D2007.Win32	VER185 and VER180
D2007.Net	VER190
Delphi 2009	VER200

As usual, you can also use the internal versioning constants in $IF statements, with the advantage of being able to use >= rather than a specific match. The versioning constants are called CompilerVersion and RTLVersion and in Delphi 2009 they are assigned to the floating-point value 20.00.

Below is a code snippet with the tests based on define and one of the constants, extracted from the MinorLang project:

```
{$IFDEF VER200}
  ShowMessage ('Delphi 2009');
{$ENDIF}

{$IF RTLVersion >= 20}
  ShowMessage ('Delphi 2009 or newer');
{$IFEND}
```

A Commented Deprecated Directive

The deprecated directive, used to indicate a symbol is still available for compatibility reasons only, can now be followed by a string that will be displayed as part of the compiler warning. If you define a procedure and call it as in the following code snippet (from the MinorLang demo):

```
procedure DoNothing;
  deprecated 'use DoSomething instead';
begin
end;

procedure TFormMinorLang.btnDepracatedClick(
  Sender: TObject);
begin
  DoNothing;
end;
```

At the call location (in the btnDepracatedClick method) you'll get the following warning:

```
W1000 Symbol 'DoNothing' is deprecated: 'use DoSomething instead'
```

This is way better than the previous practice of adding a comment to declaration of the deprecated symbol, having to click on the error message to get to the source code line in which this is used, jump to the declaration location, and find the comment.

Needless to say the code above won't compile in Delphi 2007, where you get the error:

```
E2029 Declaration expected but string constant found
```

The new feature of deprecated is used rather heavily in the Delphi 2009 RTL and VCL, while I'm expecting third party vendors having to refrain from using it because of the incompatibility with past versions of the compiler, even if they could now use:

```
{$IF RTLVersion >= 20}
  deprecated 'use DoSomething instead';
{$IFEND}
```

Exit with a Value

Traditionally Pascal functions used to assign a result by using the function name, as in:

```
function ComputeValue: Integer;
begin
  ...
  ComputeValue := 10;
end;
```

Delphi has long provided an alternative coding, using the Result identifier to assign a return value to a function:

```
function ComputeValue: Integer;
begin
  ...
  Result := 10;
end;
```

The two approaches are identical and do not alter the flow of the code. If you need to assign the function result and stop the current execution you can use two separate statements, assign the result and then call Exit. The following code snippet looking for a string containing a given number in a string list (part of the MinorLang example) shows a classic example of this approach:

```
function FindExit (sl: TStringList; n: Integer): string;
var
  I: Integer;
begin
  for I := 0 to sl.Count do
    if Pos (IntToStr (n), sl[I]) > 0 then
    begin
      Result := sl[I];
      Exit;
    end;
end;
```

In Delphi 2009 you can replace the two statements with a new special call to Exit passing to it the return value of the function, in a way resembling the C language return statement. So you can write the code above in a more compact version (also because with a single statement you can avoid the begin/end):

```
function FindExitValue (
  sl: TStringList; n: Integer): string;
var
```

```
    I: Integer;
begin
  for I := 0 to sl.Count do
    if Pos (IntToStr (n), sl[I]) > 0 then
      Exit (sl[I]);
end;
```

Setting Properties by Reference

In the Delphi 6 time frame, the Delphi compiler allowed you to define properties using a setter method that had a reference parameter. This unwanted feature was later removed, as it could lead to errors. Now for the sake of COM programming, "put by ref" properties[100] have been added to the language. Still, you have to ask specifically for this feature using a new compiler directive:

```
{$VARPROPSETTER ON}
```

Without this directive, the following code won't compile and issue the error *"E2282 Property setters cannot take var parameters"*:

```
type
  TMyIntegerClass = class
  private
    fNumber: Integer;
    function GetNumber: Integer;
    procedure SetNumber(var Value: Integer);
  public
    property Number: Integer
      read GetNumber write SetNumber;
  end;
```

This class is part of the VarProp example. Now what is very odd is that you can have side effects within the property setter:

```
procedure TMyIntegerClass.SetNumber(var Value: Integer);
begin
  Inc (Value); // side effect
  fNumber := Value;
end;
```

---

100 This is the name Delphi R&D team member Chris Bensen gave to this feature it its blog post introducing the topic:
http://chrisbensen.blogspot.com/2008/04/delphi-put-by-ref-properties.html

Marco Cantù, Delphi 2009 Handbook

The other very unusual effect is that you cannot assign a constant value to the property, only a variable (which should be expected, as with any call involving a parameter passed by reference):

```
var
  mc: TMyIntegerClass;
begin
  ...
  mc.Count := 10; // Error: E2036 Variable required
  mc.Number := n;
```

Again, this feature was introduced for COM support, and you'll see it at the beginning of type library files. Oddly enough if you define a "put by ref" property of string type, you can pass a string variable to it... but the compiler also lets you assign a string constant, which will cause an error at runtime. This is demonstrated in the VarProp example.

Changes in Overloading

The Delphi 2009 compiler sees quite a number of internal changes in the way the compiler chooses the function to call in the case of multiple overloaded versions where none of them is an exact match. This is particularly so when variants are involved.

There are two different situations you might come across:

- Code that used to compile now issues a compiler error
- Code that used to call one method now ends up calling a different one

Needless to say that while the first might be annoying it is easily fixed by adding an explicit type cast, while the second is much more subtle and dangerous, as you might only know that things go wrong only by running the program.

A complete case-by-case analysis would be extremely time consuming, as the combinations are almost endless. What I've done, instead, is to create a program with a few specific and interesting test cases, and show you what happens in Delphi 2007 and Delphi 2009. That's why in the VariantOver folder you'll find two projects, one for each of these versions of the IDE.

Code That Triggers a Compiler Error

Let me start with an example that won't compile any more. Suppose you have two overloaded methods like:

```
procedure ShowValue(I: Integer); overload;
procedure ShowValue(s: string); overload;
```

Now in Delphi 2007 you could call it in the following way:

```
var
   v: variant;
begin
   v := 3;
   ShowValue (v);
```

However if you wrote:

```
   v := 'foo';
   ShowValue (v);
```

This would cause a runtime error, complaining about a wrong variant to boolean conversion. Delphi 2009 changes this considerably. The two calls to ShowValue with a variant parameter simply refuse to compile, claiming that it cannot determine which of the two versions to call:

```
[DCC Error] E2251 Ambiguous overloaded call to 'ShowValue'
   Related method: procedure
TFormVariantOver.ShowValue(Integer);
   Related method: procedure
TFormVariantOver.ShowValue(string);
```

What's nice is that you see more details than in the past. In the error message pane you'll see an error with a plus sign that can be expanded to get further details:

Again, getting a compiler error (a detailed one in this case) is not that bad, as this gives you an option to recognize the potential issue and fix it by casting the variant to a specific type:

```
ShowValue (Integer(v));
ShowValue (string(v));
```

This code works in Delphi 2009 and works better in Delphi 2007 as well, as you won't get the runtime variant conversion error any more.

Code That Calls a Different Method

Things are not as nice in the situations in which the Delphi 2009 compiler ends up calling a different method than you'd expect from previous versions. This is an extremely rare circumstance, but it is technically possible (even if in some convoluted cases).

Consider the following code (part of the VariantOver example), declaring a record type with an `Implicit` conversion:

```
type
  TMyRecord = record
  private
    X: Integer;
  public
    class operator Implicit (
      const Value: Variant): TMyRecord;
  end;
```

Now suppose you have two overloaded methods taking either a record or an Integer parameter:

```
procedure ShowValue3 (const R: TMyRecord); overload;
procedure ShowValue3 (X: Integer); overload;
```

What happens if you pass a variant? The compiler can either convert the variant to the Integer or use the `Implicit` operation to convert it to a record. This is the call :

```
var
  v: Variant;
begin
  v := 10;
  ShowValue3 (v);
end;
```

What happens is that in Delphi 2007 this code calls the Integer overload, while Delphi 2009 compiler gives precedence to the `Implicit` overload.

New and Aliased Integral Types

Although this is not strictly a compiler change, but rather an addition in the System unit, you can now use a set of easier-to-remember aliases for signed and unsigned integral data types. These are the signed and unsigned predefined types in the compiler:

Signed	Unsigned
ShortInt	Byte
SmallInt	Word
Integer	Cardinal
NativeInt	NativeUInt
Int64	UInt64

These types were already in Delphi 2007 and previous versions, but the 64bit ones date back only a few versions of the compiler. The `NativeInt` and `NativeUInt` types, which should depend on the compiler version (32 bit and future 64 bit) were already in Delphi 2007 but they were not documented and, even worse, they were not correct!

If you need a data type that will match the CPU native integer size, these are the types to use. The Integer type, in fact, is expected to remain unchanged when moving from 32-bit to 64-bit compilers.

The following set of predefined aliases added by System unit is however brand new in Delphi 2009:

```
type
  Int8   = ShortInt;
  Int16  = SmallInt;
  Int32  = Integer;
  UInt8  = Byte;
  UInt16 = Word;
  UInt32 = Cardinal;
```

Although they don't add anything new, they are probably easier to use, as it is generally hard to remember if a ShortInt is smaller than a SmallInt, where it is easy to remember the actual implementation of Int16 or Int8[101].

---

101 The new type aliases are very C-like.

TObject's New Methods

The structure of the TObject class has remained quite stable over the years. Delphi 2009 sees some interesting improvements. Not only has the *mother of all Delphi classes* four new methods, but three of these new methods are virtual methods you are supposed to redefine in your own classes. If you've used the .NET framework (using Delphi for .NET or other languages) you'll immediately recognize these methods are part of the System.Object class of the .NET class library[102].

The ToString Method

The ToString virtual function is a placeholder for returning the textual representation (a description) of a given object. The default implementation of the method in the TObject class returns the class name:

```
function TObject.ToString: string;
begin
   Result := ClassName;
end;
```

Some of the new classes of Delphi 2009 override the ToString virtual function, like TStringBuilder and TStringWriter. Among the existing classes, the method has been redefined in the Exception class, to return the messages in a list of exceptions (as covered in the section "The InnerException Mechanism" later in this chapter).

Overall, I think that having a standard way to return the string representation of any object is quite an interesting one. I wish the VCL could be updated to better support the function in several components and control.

Notice that the ToString method often *overloads* the "parse token String" or toString symbol defined in the Classes unit. For this reason you'll often see that symbol referenced as Classes.toString.

---

[102] Similar method names are used for the base classes available in Java, are commonly used in JavaScript, and in other OO languages. The origin of some of them, like that of toString, can be traced back to Smalltalk.

The Equals Method

The `Equals` virtual function is a placeholder for checking if two objects have the same logical value, a different operation than checking if two variables refer to the same object, something you can achieve with the = sign. However, and this is really confusing, the default implementation does exactly that:

```
function TObject.Equals(Obj: TObject): Boolean;
begin
   Result := Obj = Self;
end;
```

There are some cases in the VCL source code in which the `Equals` call is indeed used as a replacement of the = test. The opposite approach is used, for example, by `TStrings.Equals`, in which the class compares the number of strings and the actual strings one by one.

The only section of the library in which this technique is significantly used (and probably the reason it was added) is the generics support, in particular in the Generics.Default and Generics.Collections units. However, defining an object equivalence mechanism "by value" is common in many Delphi libraries and frameworks, and having a standard way of doing this is certainly a big advantage.

The GetHashCode Method

The `GetHashCode` virtual function is another placeholder borrowed from the .NET Framework to let each class calculate the hash code for its objects. The default code returns a seemingly random value[103], the address of the object itself:

```
function TObject.GetHashCode: Integer;
begin
   Result := Integer(Self);
end;
```

The `GetHashCode` virtual function is currently used in the VCL.NET portions of the VCL, but having the same function on both sides can certainly

---

103 With the address of the objects being created generally taken from a limited set of heap areas, the distribution of these number is not even, and this can adversely affect a hashing algorithm.

218 - Chapter 7: More Language and RTL Changes

help unifying the source code in the near future. Again, some of the units providing Generics support use the `GetHashCode` function.

The UnitName Method

The other (unrelated) method is the class function `UnitName`, which is not a virtual function, and returns the name of the unit in which the class is defined. In the past you had to resort to low-level techniques (accessing the internal representation of a class) to access the same information.

Porting an Example from .NET

To demonstrate the new features of `TObject`, rather than write a brand new demo I've decided to port a Delphi .NET example I wrote for Mastering Delphi 2005, and originally called FclSystemObject as it focused on the `System.Object` class. The new example is called SystemObject even if it covers the plain old `TObject` class.

First of all the example has a class that overrides two of the new virtual methods of `TObject`:

```
type
  TAnyObject = class
  private
    Value: Integer;
    name: string;
  public
    constructor Create (aName: string; aValue: Integer);
    function Equals(obj: TObject): Boolean; override;
    function ToString: string; override;
  end;
```

In the implementation of the three methods I simply had to change a call to GetType with that to ClassType:

```
constructor TAnyObject.Create(aName: string;
    aValue: Integer);
begin
  inherited Create;
  name := aName;
  Value := aValue;
end;
```

Marco Cantù, Delphi 2009 Handbook

```delphi
function TAnyObject.Equals(obj: TObject): Boolean;
begin
  Result := (obj.ClassType = self.ClassType) and
    ((obj as TAnyObject).Value = self.Value);
end;

function TAnyObject.ToString: string;
begin
  Result := Name;
end;
```

Notice that objects are considered equal if they are of the same exact class and their value matches, while their string representation includes only the name field. The program creates some objects of this class as its starts, associating them with the elements of two combo boxes:

```delphi
procedure TFormSystemObject.FormCreate(Sender: TObject);
begin
  ao1 := TAnyObject.Create ('ao1', 10);
  ao2 := TAnyObject.Create ('ao2 or ao3', 20);
  ao3 := ao2;
  ao4 := TAnyObject.Create ('ao4', 20);

  ComboBox1.Items.AddObject (ao1.ToString, ao1);
  ComboBox1.Items.AddObject (ao2.ToString, ao2);
  ComboBox1.Items.AddObject (ao3.ToString, ao3);
  ComboBox1.Items.AddObject (ao4.ToString, ao4);

  ComboBox2.Items.AddObject (ao1.ToString, ao1);
  ComboBox2.Items.AddObject (ao2.ToString, ao2);
  ComboBox2.Items.AddObject (ao3.ToString, ao3);
  ComboBox2.Items.AddObject (ao4.ToString, ao4);
end;
```

Notice that two references (ao2 and ao3) point to the same object in memory, and that the last object (ao4) has the same numerical value. As you select items in both combo boxes, you can compare the objects you have selected, both using equals and doing a direct reference comparison:

```delphi
procedure TFormSystemObject.btnCompareClick(
  Sender: TObject);
begin
  Log ('Comparing ' +
    ComboBox1.Items [ComboBox1.ItemIndex] +
    ' and ' +
    ComboBox2.Items [ComboBox2.ItemIndex]);
  Log ('Equals: ' + BoolToStr (
    ComboBox1.Items.Objects [ComboBox1.ItemIndex].Equals (
      ComboBox2.Items.Objects [ComboBox2.ItemIndex]),
    True));
```

```
    Log ('Reference = ' + BoolToStr (
      ComboBox1.Items.Objects [ComboBox1.ItemIndex] =
        ComboBox2.Items.Objects [ComboBox2.ItemIndex],
      True));
end;
```

Here are some of the results:

```
Comparing ao1 and ao4
Equals: False
Reference = False
Comparing ao2 or ao3 and ao2 or ao3
Equals: True
Reference =: True
Comparing ao2 or ao3 and ao4
Equals: True
Reference =: False
```

The program has another button used to test some of these methods for the button itself:

```
procedure TFormSystemObject.btnTestClick(
  Sender: TObject);
var
  btn2: TButton;
begin
  btn2 := btnTest;
  Log ('Equals: ' +
    BoolToStr (btnTest.Equals (btn2), True));
  Log ('Reference = ' +
    BoolToStr (btnTest = btn2, True));
  Log ('GetHashCode: ' +
    IntToStr (btnTest.GetHashCode));
  Log ('ToString: ' + btnTest.ToString);
end;
```

The output is the following (with a hash value that might change upon execution):

```
Equals: True
Reference = True
GetHashCode: 28253904
ToString: TButton
```

TObject Class Summary

As a summary[104], this is the complete interface of the TObject class in Delphi 2009 (notice the different string data types used):

```
type
  TObject = class
    constructor Create;
    procedure Free;
    class function InitInstance(Instance: Pointer):
      TObject;
    procedure CleanupInstance;
    function ClassType: TClass; inline;
    class function ClassName: string;
    class function ClassNameIs(const Name: string):
      Boolean;
    class function ClassParent: TClass;
    class function ClassInfo: Pointer;
    class function InstanceSize: Longint; inline;
    class function InheritsFrom(AClass: TClass): Boolean;
    class function MethodAddress(
      const Name: ShortString): Pointer; overload;
    class function MethodAddress(const Name: string):
      Pointer; overload;
    class function MethodName(Address: Pointer): string;
    function FieldAddress(const Name: ShortString):
      Pointer; overload;
    function FieldAddress(const Name: string):
      Pointer; overload;
    function GetInterface(const IID: TGUID; out Obj):
      Boolean;
    class function GetInterfaceEntry(const IID: TGUID):
      PInterfaceEntry;
    class function GetInterfaceTable: PInterfaceTable;
    class function UnitName: string;
    function Equals(Obj: TObject): Boolean; virtual;
    function GetHashCode: Integer; virtual;
    function ToString: string; virtual;
    function SafeCallException(ExceptObject: TObject;
      ExceptAddr: Pointer): HResult; virtual;
    procedure AfterConstruction; virtual;
    procedure BeforeDestruction; virtual;
```

---

104 Another set of changes affects the internal layout of the class reference data in Delphi 2009. For example, the vmtParent location was -36 in previous versions, but is -48 in Delphi 2009. If you use the symbolic vmt entries, your code will compile unchanged, but if you used the equivalent numeric locations you'll likely get into trouble.

222 - Chapter 7: More Language and RTL Changes

```
    procedure Dispatch(var Message); virtual;
    procedure DefaultHandler(var Message); virtual;
    class function NewInstance: TObject; virtual;
    procedure FreeInstance; virtual;
    destructor Destroy; virtual;
end;
```

Overloaded methods like `MethodAddress` and `FieldAddress` can take either a UnicodeString (UTF-16, as usual) or a `ShortString` parameter that is treated as a UTF-8 string. In fact, the versions taking a plain Unicode string, convert them by calling the function `UTF8EncodeToShortString`:

```
function TObject.FieldAddress(
  const Name: string): Pointer;
begin
  Result := FieldAddress(UTF8EncodeToShortString(Name));
end;
```

Unicode and Class Names

Internally, the class names in Delphi 2009 use the ShortString type but with an UTF-8 encoding (and not the standard ANSI encoding of the ShortString type), both at the `TObject` and RTTI levels. For example, the `ClassName` method is now implemented as:

```
class function TObject.ClassName: string;
begin
  Result := UTF8ToString (
    PShortString (PPointer (
      Integer(Self) + vmtClassName)^)^);
end;
```

In Delphi 2007 this same method was identical except for the `UTF8ToString` call. Similarly in the TypInfo unit, all the functions accessing class names convert the internal UTF-8 ShortString representations to a UnicodeString. For example:

```
function GetTypeName(TypeInfo: PTypeInfo): string;
begin
  Result := UTF8ToString(TypeInfo^.Name);
end;
```

Something similar happens for property names, with most TypInfo functions calling the new `InternalGetPropInfo` function, declared as:

```
function InternalGetPropInfo(TypeInfo: PTypeInfo;
  const PropName: UTF8String): PPropInfo;
```

Changes in Threading Support

We have already seen in Chapter 6, and in particular in the section "Thread Synchronization with the VCL" that the `TThread` has been extended to take advantage of anonymous methods. The extensions take the form of new overloaded versions of the `Synchronize` and `Queue` methods, so existing Delphi code should work smoothly.

Another new feature of Delphi 2009 is the presence of the `TMonitor` record[105], a data structure defined in the System unit that you can use to provide synchronous access to any object. This *monitor* support, which resembles the corresponding class of the .NET framework, let's you define a thread lock tied to a specific object. Rather than having a global synchronization semaphore, you can set one for each control to which you want to allow concurrent access, letting a thread at a time use it.

In other words, the `TMonitor` record grants a lock for an object to a single thread. However, multiple threads can work on different objects at the same time. To acquire a lock on an object you can call the `Enter` or the `TryEnter` methods, while you release the lock (generally in a finally block) using the `Exit` method. The `TMonitor` record in Delphi supports locks and also conditional variables, though the `Wait`, `Pulse`, and `PulseAll` methods, a complex topic I decided not to cover with an example, but focus only on a simpler scenario.

The ListMonitor example has a form with three list boxes and multiple threads accessing those lists in a random way. Each thread operation is fictitiously slow (thanks to a call to `Sleep`), but other threads interested in using the list box will have to wait.

The thread class used by the program has the core code, which writes a starting and a stopping message to the list, waiting in between. This core code is protected with a `TMonitor` connected to the given list object, to avoid any other thread using the list before the first thread is finished:

---

[105] The `TMonitor` record is defined in the System unit. This is important to know, as it is very easy to have conflicts with the `TMonitor` class, defined in the Forms unit. If your unit refers to Forms, in fact, there is no way you can list System after it, as System is invariably the first unit referenced by any other unit. In other words, you'll often have to write `System.TMonitor` to refer to the record. Even if it was named after its .NET counterpart, I find this choice quite confusing.

224 - Chapter 7: More Language and RTL Changes

```
type
  TAddToListThread = class(TThread)
  protected
    procedure Execute; override;
  end;

procedure TAddToListThread.Execute;
var
  aList: TListBox;
  I: Integer;
begin
  while not Terminated do
  begin
    aList := Application.MainForm.FindComponent (
      'ListBox' + IntToStr (GetTickCount mod 3 + 1))
      as TListBox;
    System.TMonitor.Enter (aList);
    try
      aList.Items.Add(IntToStr (GetCurrentThreadID) +
        ' starting: ' + TimeToStr (Now));
      // wait loop, omitted
      aList.Items.Add(IntToStr (GetCurrentThreadID) +
        ' stopping: ' + TimeToStr (Now));
    finally
      System.TMonitor.Exit (aList);
    end;
  end;
end;
```

As I mentioned earlier, the test program for this thread class has three list boxes, added to a list as the program starts, plus a list of threads (notice I'm using generic collections in both cases):

```
procedure TFormListMonitor.FormCreate(Sender: TObject);
begin
  fThreads := TObjectList<TThread>.Create;
  fListBoxes := TList<TListBox>.Create;
  fListBoxes.Add (ListBox1);
  fListBoxes.Add (ListBox2);
  fListBoxes.Add (ListBox3);
end;
```

The threads are added to the list, three at time, when a button is pressed:

```
procedure TFormListMonitor.btnStartThreadsClick(
  Sender: TObject);
var
  I: Integer;
begin
  for I := 1 to 3 do
    fThreads.Add (TAddToListThread.Create (False));
```

Marco Cantù, Delphi 2009 Handbook

```
end;
```

The other button is used to check the lock on the list objects, using the TryEnter call and bailing out immediately when the object is available:

```
procedure TFormListMonitor.btnStatusClick(
  Sender: TObject);
var
  aListBox: TListBox;
begin
  for aListBox in fListBoxes do
  begin
    if System.TMonitor.TryEnter(aListBox) then
    try
      aListBox.Items.Add('Available');
    finally
      System.TMonitor.Exit(aListBox);
    end;
  end;
end;
```

This is a sample of the output, in which you can notice that the starting and stopping messages are always paired by thread:

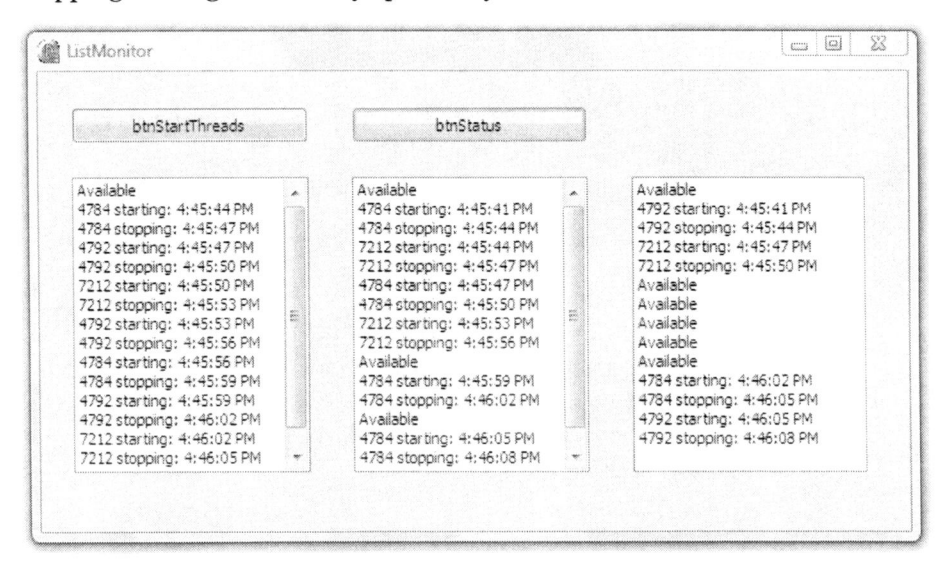

Building Strings

We have seen that the advent of multiple string types causes potential pitfalls in string concatenation (see section "Assigning and Converting Strings" in Chapter 2 and the section "String Operations That Fail or Slow Down" in Chapter 3). Combining these issues with the desire to have unified Win32 and .NET code whenever possible, it is no surprise that CodeGear took an idea from .NET and added it to the native RTL. The idea being a specific class to create a string by adding multiple elements of various data types. Called StringBuilder in .NET, the class has appropriately been renamed TStringBuilder in Delphi.

As a simple example of the use of the TStringBuilder class, consider the following code snippet (taken from the StringBuilder project)

```
var
  sBuilder: TStringBuilder;
  str1: string;
begin
  sBuilder := TStringBuilder.Create;
  try
    sBuilder.Append(12);
    sBuilder.Append('hello');
    str1 := sBuilder.ToString;
  finally
    sBuilder.Free;
  end;
end;
```

Notice in the code the use of a try-finally block, as unlike a reference-counted string you have to remember to dispose of the TStringBuilder object. Another element you can notice above is that there are many different data types that you can pass as parameters to the Append function. A complete list will show up in the editor thanks to Code Completion, as you can see in the following image:

Value: Boolean
const Value: string; StartIndex: Integer; Count: Integer
const Value: TCharArray; StartIndex: Integer; CharCount: Integer
Value: Char; RepeatCount: Integer
Value: Cardinal
Value: Word
const Value: TCharArray
Value: UInt64
const Value: string
Value: Single
Value: ShortInt
Value: TObject
Value: Int64
Value: Integer
Value: SmallInt
Value: Double
Value: Currency
Value: Char
Value: Byte

Other interesting methods of the `TStringBuilder` class include an `AppendFormat` (with an internal call to `Format`) and an `AppendLine` that adds the `sLineBreak` value. Along with `Append`, there is a corresponding series of `Insert` overloaded methods, as well as a `Remove` and a few `Replace` methods.

When you are done, you can use `ToString` to fetch the result of the various operations, but also check the `Length` or access individual `Chars` by index. Notice, though that the semantics of the `Chars` method is different from that of the `string[]` operation. The former uses a 0-based index while the standard Delphi code uses a 1-based index. As a test, consider this method (part of the StringBuilder demo):

```
procedure TFormSBuilder.btnCharPosClick(Sender: TObject);
var
  str1: string;
  sBuilder: TStringBuilder;
begin
  str1 := '1234567890';
  Log ('str1[4]: ' + str1[4]);
  sBuilder := TStringBuilder.Create (str1);
  try
    Log ('sBuilder.Chars[4]: ' + sBuilder.Chars[4]);
  finally
    sBuilder.Free;
  end;
end;
```

In output of this code you'll get the 4th character (using the direct access) and the 5th one (using the Chars property):

```
str1[4]: 4
sBuilder.Chars[4]: 5
```

I understand the desire of making this class compatible with its .NET counterpart, but this difference in character access seems counterintuitive.

Methods Chaining in StringBuilder

A very specific feature of the TStringBuilder class is that most methods are functions that return the current object. This coding idiom opens up the possibility of methods chaining[106], that is calling a method on the object returned by the previous one. Instead of writing:

```
sBuilder.Append(12);
sBuilder.AppendLine;
sBuilder.Append('hello');
```

you can write:

```
sBuilder.Append(12).AppendLine.Append('hello');
```

which can be formatted as:

```
sBuilder.
   Append(12).
   AppendLine.
   Append('hello');
```

I tend to like this syntax better than the original one, but I know it is just syntactic sugar and some people do prefer the original version with the object spelled out on each line. In any case, keep in mind that the various calls to Append don't return new objects (so no potential memory leaks), but the exact same object to which you are applying the methods.

---

[106] On methods chaining (and other techniques helping in writing Domain Specific Languages with Delphi) you can see my blog at:
http://blog.marcocantu.com/blog/static_internal_dsl_delphi.html.

The Speed of Building Strings

Needless to say that most Delphi developers will immediately wonder if using the `TStringBuilder` class would make their code faster or slower than using plain string concatenation or other string operations. The short answer is that performance is similar, with a slight advantage for the classic string concatenation, although real-world situations probably differ from the simple tests I've performed in the StringBuilder example.

I've done three different tests: plain string concatenation, adding Integers to a string, inserting a string within another string (which is much slower and executed a fraction of the times). The complete listing is in the example. Here are the key lines of the 6 methods (excluding the statements used to create and free the `TStringBuilder` objects):

```
// 1a. string concatenation
for I := 1 to MaxLoop do
  str1 := str1 + str2;

// 1b. appending strings
for I := 1 to MaxLoop do
  sBuilder.Append(str2);

// 2a. concatenating numbers
for I := 1 to MaxLoop do
  str1 := str1 + IntToStr (I);

// 2b. appending numbers
for I := 1 to MaxLoop do
  sBuilder.Append(I);

// 3a. inserting in string
for I := 1 to MaxLoop div 100 do
  Insert('hello', str1, 7); // 1-based position

// 3b. inserting in string builder
for I := 1 to MaxLoop div 100 do
  sBuilder.Insert (6, 'hello'); // 0-based position
// 4a. character concatenation
for I := 1 to MaxLoop do
  str1 := str1 + ch;

// 4b. appending a character
for I := 1 to MaxLoop do
  sBuilder.Append(ch);
```

If you execute this program (eventually changing the `MaxLoop` constant to try out with happens with smaller and larger strings), you'll get a result along these lines:

```
1a. Concatenation: 78
1b. TStringBuilder: 109

2a. Concatenation: 265
2b. TStringBuilder: 359

3a. Concatenation: 156
3b. TStringBuilder: 156

4a. Char Concat: 93
4b. TStringBuilder: 31
```

As I mentioned at the beginning, the values are very close, with some advantage for plain string concatenation, with the only exception being the concatenation or appending of individual characters. The reason is that when you add a single character, the overloaded version of `Append` you are executing is specifically optimized, while the generic concatenation code treats the character as a single-character string anyway. The insert operations take almost the same amount of time.

The reason for the difference in case of the string concatenation depends on the fact that the code executed behind the scenes for the plain concatenation is lower level optimized assembly code. On the other hand, the `TStringBuilder` class tends to reduce memory allocations, as it preallocates extra memory: Every time the object needs more memory, its `ExpandCapacity` method doubles the current capacity. This can consume more memory than needed, but reduces the number of allocations (and potential copy operations).

To verify how the allocation works, I've added a `btnCapacityClick` method to the StringBuilder demo, which displays how the `Length` and `Capacity` of a `TStringBuilder` object grow while it is being expanded:

```
for J := 1 to 10 do
begin
  for I := 1 to 200 do
    sBuilder.Append (I);
  Log ('Len/Cap: ' + IntToStr (sBuilder.Length) +
    ':' + IntToStr (sBuilder.Capacity));
end;
```

This is the output, in which you can notice the *doubling* of the capacity whenever extra memory is needed:

```
Len/Cap: 492:512
Len/Cap: 984:1024
Len/Cap: 1476:2048
Len/Cap: 1968:2048
Len/Cap: 2460:4096
Len/Cap: 2952:4096
Len/Cap: 3444:4096
Len/Cap: 3936:4096
Len/Cap: 4428:8192
Len/Cap: 4920:8192
```

Even if speed increments by using TStringBuilder versus plain string concatenation are not always significant, the new class tends to make code more flexible and easier to write, so I recommend switching your existing code to use it whenever possible[107].

Porting a Delphi for .NET Example

As a test of the source code compatibility of Delphi's TStringBuilder class with .NET's StringBuilder class, I've taken another example that I had written in Delphi for .NET for the "Mastering Delphi 2005" book and converted it to a VCL application.

The program had two radio buttons to pick a string of different size, a list box for the output, and two buttons to process the strings with either a TStringBuilder or a plain string. Simply by defining a type alias for TStringBuilder called StringBuilder, the core of the method compiles without a single change:

```
// actual code
strB := StringBuilder.Create;
if rbShort.Checked then
  strB.Append (strSampleShort)
else
  strB.Append (strSampleLong);

for I := 1 to maxCount do
begin
  nPos := I mod strB.Length;
  strB.Remove(nPos, 1);
  strB.Insert(nPos, strB [(I*2) mod strB.Length]);
end;
```

---

[107] For more ideas on this issue, see also my blog post "Not so fast, TStringBuilder" at: http://blog.marcocantu.com/blog/not_so_fast_tstringbuilder.html.

```
    ListBox1.Items.Add (strB.ToString);
    // end of actual code
```

All I had to do was to remember to add a call to Free, as we are not on a reference counted platform like .NET. The string processing code, instead, is totally different between Delphi Win32 and the .NET FCL version, so I had to rewrite it entirely. What is interesting to notice is that in this code which keeps removing and inserting data in the string, the TStringBuilder-based code is noticeably faster:

```
btnSBuilderClick: 00.112
btnStringClick: 00.246
```

Unlike in .NET (where strings are immutable and direct string operations are terribly slow) using a shorter or longer string makes almost no difference, but I've left the radio buttons and the related string constants in the code to keep it as close as possible to the original.

Using Readers and Writers

A totally alternative approach for building large strings or writing to and reading from streams is to use the new reader and writer classes introduced in Delphi 2009, again mapped to their .NET counterparts.

In Delphi there have traditionally been a couple of similar classes (TReader and TWriter) but they are specifically aimed at streaming properties in and out of DFM files. The new classes, instead, are better suited for more general approaches and are focused on reading and writing textual data.

There are four new reading and writing classes, defined in the Classes unit:

- TStringReader and TStringWriter work on a string in memory (directly or using a TStringBuilder)
- TStreamReader and TStreamWriter work on a generic stream (a file stream, a memory stream, and more)

These four classes inherit from the TTextReader and TTextWriter abstract base classes, which provide the interface to a list of operations. Each of the *readers* implements a few basic reading techniques:

```
function Read: Integer; overload;
function Read(const Buffer: TCharArray;
  Index, Count: Integer): Integer; overload;
```

```delphi
function ReadBlock(const Buffer: TCharArray;
  Index, Count: Integer): Integer;
function ReadLine: string;
function ReadToEnd: string;
```

Each of the *writers* has two sets of overloaded operations without (`Write`) and with (`WriteLine`) an end-of-line separator. Here is the first set:

```delphi
procedure Write(Value: Boolean); overload;
procedure Write(Value: Char); overload;
procedure Write(const Value: TCharArray); overload;
procedure Write(Value: Double); overload;
procedure Write(Value: Integer); overload;
procedure Write(Value: Int64); overload;
procedure Write(Value: TObject); overload;
procedure Write(Value: Single); overload;
procedure Write(const Value: string); overload;
procedure Write(Value: Cardinal); overload;
procedure Write(Value: UInt64); overload;
procedure Write(const Format: string;
  Args: array of const); overload;
procedure Write(Value: TCharArray;
  Index, Count: Integer); overload;
```

In the current implementations the write operations transform their content to a string, before writing it (this is different from Delphi's original `TReader` and `TWriter`, which can also work with binary data).

For writing to a stream, the `TStreamWriter` class uses a stream or creates one using the filename and the encoding passed as parameters. So we can write, as I did in the ReaderWriter demo:

```delphi
var
  sw: TStreamWriter;
begin
  sw := TStreamWriter.Create('test.txt',
    False, TEncoding.UTF8);
  try
    sw.WriteLine ('Hello, world');
    sw.WriteLine ('Have a nice day');
    sw.WriteLine (Left);
  finally
    sw.Free;
  end;
```

For reading the `TStreamReader`, you can work again on a stream or a file (in which case it can detect the encoding from the BOM):

```delphi
var
  sr: TStreamReader;
begin
```

```
sr := TStreamReader.Create('test.txt', True);
try
  while not sr.EndOfStream do
    Memo1.Lines.Add (sr.ReadLine);
finally
  sr.Free;
end;
```

Notice how you can check for the EndOfStream status. Compared to the classic Delphi code used for writing and reading a string to and from a text file, passing the first character of the string (str[1], below) as untyped parameter, the readability is much improved. This is a snippet of the classic code as a comparison:

```
var
  fstr: TFileStream;
  str: string;
begin
  fstr := TFileStream.Create (test.txt', fmCreate);
  try
    str := 'Hello, world';
    fstr.Write(str[1], Length (str));
  finally
    fstr.free;
  end;
```

For writing to an in-memory string you can use a specific stream class or use the TStringWriter class, which uses either a TStringBuilder object passed to its constructor or creates an internal one. At the end you can ask for the complete string. The TStringReader works on a string passed as parameter to its only constructor, but it has no easy way to detect the end of the string. The only ready-to-use solution I've found (without extending the class) has been to see if the Peek call returns any value. The following event handler (again from the ReaderWriter application) fills a string in memory with a writer and than reads it back:

```
procedure TFormReaderWriter.btnWriteAndReadClick(
  Sender: TObject);
var
  sw: TStringWriter;
  sr: TStringReader;
  theString: string;
begin
  sw := TStringWriter.Create;
  try
    sw.WriteLine ('Hello, world');
    sw.WriteLine ('Have a nice day');
    sw.WriteLine (Left);
```

```
    theString := sw.ToString;
  finally
    sw.Free;
  end;
  sr := TStringReader.Create(theString);
  try
    while sr.Peek <> -1 do
      Memo1.Lines.Add (sr.ReadLine);
  finally
    sr.Free;
  end;
end;
```

Compared to a direct use of streams (or strings), these classes are particularly handy to use, and provide good performance. When you have to create a very large string with data (say an external XML file) using a stream with a proper writer can provide you with top notch performance.

Another interesting element, is that having a standard interface available, you can write algorithms or classes that work with the two abstract classes, TTextReader and TTextWriter, and can be used for working on strings or in memory streams. As an example of this approach I've written an extremely simplified XML writer class, that doesn't inherit from TTextWriter but rather encapsulates it. This is the class definition, available in the Reader-Writer project:

```
type
  TTrivialXmlWriter = class
  private
    fWriter: TTextWriter;
    fNodes: TStack<string>;
  public
    constructor Create (aWriter: TTextWriter);
    destructor Destroy; override;
    procedure WriteStartElement (const sName: string);
    procedure WriteEndElement;
    procedure WriteString (const sValue: string);
  end;
```

Internally the class uses a stack of strings to keep track of the XML elements that have been opened and not closed yet, providing a semi-automatic close in the WriteEndElement method:

```
procedure TTrivialXmlWriter.WriteStartElement(
  const sName: string);
begin
  fWriter.Write('<' + sName + '>');
  fNodes.Push (sname);
end;
```

```
procedure TTrivialXmlWriter.WriteEndElement;
begin
  fWriter.Write('</' + fNodes.Pop + '>');
end;
```

This is a example of how the class can be used, by populating a TStringWriter (the actual code of the demo is slightly longer):

```
procedure TFormReaderWriter.btnXmlCorrectClick(
  Sender: TObject);
var
  sw: TStringWriter;
  txw: TTrivialXmlWriter;
  theString: string;
begin
  sw := TStringWriter.Create;
  try
    txw := TTrivialXmlWriter.Create (sw);
    try
      txw.WriteStartElement('book');
        txw.WriteStartElement('title');
          txw.WriteString('Delphi 2009 Handbook');
        txw.WriteEndElement;
      txw.WriteEndElement;
    finally
      txw.Free;
    end;
    theString := sw.ToString;
  finally
    sw.Free;
  end;
  Memo1.Lines.Text := theString;
end;
```

To make the class slightly more interesting, the destructor takes care of closing all XML nodes that were left open (although it could as well raise an error, in case such a situation occurs).

Exception(al) Enhancements

Along with TObject, another core Delphi class that has seen a couple of significant improvements in Delphi 2009 is the Exception class. On one side, there is a new virtual function that is called after an exception object has been created, but before it is raised. On another side, there is now support for nested (or inner) exceptions. Finally, but this is not so important, there are some new exception classes in the SysUtils unit.

The InnerException Mechanism

What happens if you raise an exception within an exception handler? The traditional Delphi answer is that the new exception will replace the existing one, which is why it is a common practice to combine at least the error messages, writing code like this (lacking any actual operation, and showing only the exceptions-related statements):

```
procedure TFormExceptions.ClassicReraise;
begin
  try
    // do something...
    raise Exception.Create('Hello');
  except on E: Exception do
    // try some fix...
    raise Exception.Create('Another: ' + E.Message);
  end;
end;
```

This code is part of the ExceptionsTest example. When calling the method and handling the exception, you'll see a single exception with the combined message:

```
procedure TFormExceptions.btnTraditionalClick(
  Sender: TObject);
begin
  try
    ClassicReraise;
  except
    on E: Exception do
      Log ('Message: ' + E.Message);
  end;
end;
```

The (quite obvious) output is:

```
Message: Another: Hello
```

To make exceptions a little more flexible in case of database-related operations, since the early days of the BDE Delphi introduced the idea of a DBError exception with a list of internal error codes, but this is not very flexible. Now in Delphi 2009, to increase .NET compatibility and to improve exception handling in the dbExpress framework[108], there is now system-wide support for nested exceptions.

Within an exception handler, you can create and raise a new exception and still keep the current exception object alive, connecting it to the new exception. To accomplish this, the `Exception` class has a new `InnerException` property, referring to the previous exception, and a `BaseException` property that lets you access the first exception of a series, as exception nesting can be recursive. These are the new elements of the `Exception` class related to the management of nested exceptions, plus a couple of other new methods like the destructor and `ToString`[109]:

```
type
  Exception = class(TObject)
  private
    FInnerException: Exception;
    FAcquireInnerException: Boolean;
  protected
    procedure SetInnerException;
  public
    destructor Destroy; override;
    function GetBaseException: Exception; virtual;
    function ToString: string; override;
    property BaseException: Exception
      read GetBaseException;
    property InnerException: Exception
      read FInnerException;
    class procedure RaiseOuterException(
      E: Exception); static;
    class procedure ThrowOuterException(
      E: Exception); static;
  end;
```

From the perspective of a user, to raise an exception preserving the existing one you should call the `RaiseOuterException` class method (or the identical `ThrowOuterException`, which uses C++-oriented naming). When you handle a similar exception you can use the new properties to access fur-

---

108 The reason I connect this new feature to the dbExpress framework is simple: the DBXCommon and the DBXPlatform units are currently the only two units of the VCL (for Win32) referring to the `InnerException` property.

109 I've omitted from this listing of the `Exception` class other new features compared to Delphi 2007, like the new class data function pointers you can use to hook into exception stack tracing (an advanced topic I won't cover in the book) and the new `RaisingException` method detailed in the next section.

ther information. Notice that you can call `RaiseOuterException` only within an exception handler as the *source code-based* documentation tells:

> *Use this function to raise an exception instance from within an exception handler and you want to "acquire" the active exception and chain it to the new exception and preserve the context. This will cause the FInnerException field to get set with the exception in currently in play.*
>
> *You should only call this procedure from within an except block where this new exception is expected to be handled elsewhere.*

For an actual example you can refer to the ExceptionsTest project. In this project I've added a method that raises a nested exception in the new way (compared to the `ClassicReraise` method listed earlier):

```
procedure TFormExceptions.MethodWithNestedException;
begin
  try
    raise Exception.Create ('Hello');
  except
    Exception.RaiseOuterException (
      Exception.Create ('Another'));
  end;
end;
```

Now in the handler for this outer exception we can access both exception objects (and also see the effect of calling the new `ToString` method):

```
try
  MethodWithNestedException;
except
  on E: Exception do
  begin
    Log ('Message: ' + E.Message);
    Log ('ToString: ' + E.ToString);
    if Assigned (E.BaseException) then
      Log ('BaseException Message: ' +
        E.BaseException.Message);
    if Assigned (E.InnerException) then
      Log ('InnerException Message: ' +
        E.InnerException.Message);
  end;
end;
```

The output of this call is the following:

```
Message: Another
ToString: Another
Hello
```

```
BaseException Message: Hello
InnerException Message: Hello
```

There are two relevant elements to notice. The first is that in the case of a single nested exception the `BaseException` property and the `InnerException` property both refer to the same exception object, the original one. The second is that while the message of the new exception contains only the actual message, by calling `ToString` you get access to the combined messages of all the nested exceptions, separated by an `sLineBreak` (as you can see in the code of the method `Exception.ToString`). The choice of using a line break in this case produces odd looking output, but once you know about it you can format it the way you like, replacing the line breaks with a symbol of your choice or assigning them to the `Text` property of a string list.

As a further example, let me show you what happens when raising two nested exceptions. This is the new method:

```
procedure TFormExceptions.MethodWithTwoNestedExceptions;
begin
  try
    raise Exception.Create ('Hello');
  except
    begin
      try
        Exception.RaiseOuterException (
          Exception.Create ('Another'));
      except
        Exception.RaiseOuterException (
          Exception.Create ('A third'));
      end;
    end;
  end;
end;
```

This called a method that is identical to the one we saw previously and produces the following output:

```
Message: A third
ToString: A third
Another
Hello
BaseException Message: Hello
InnerException Message: Another
```

This time the `BaseException` property and the `InnerException` property refer to different objects and the output of `ToString` spans three lines.

Preprocessing Exceptions

One of the features of the `Exception` class is a new protected virtual function, declared as:

```
procedure RaisingException(P: PExceptionRecord); virtual;
```

According to the documentation (that is, a comment in the source code, not the online help):

> This virtual function will be called right before this exception is about to be raised. In the case of an external non-Delphi exception, this is called soon after the object is created since the "raise" condition is already in progress.

The implementation of the function in the `Exception` class manages the inner exception (by calling the internal `SetInnerException`), which probably explains why it was introduced in the first place, at the same time as the inner exception mechanism.

In any case, now that we have this feature available we can take advantage of it. By overriding this method, in fact, we have a single post-creation function that is invariably called, regardless of the constructor used to create the exception. In other words, you can avoid defining a custom constructor for your exception class and let users call one of the many constructors of the base `Exception` class, and still have custom behavior. As an example, you can log any exception of a given class (or subclass).

This is a custom exception class (defined again in the ExceptionsTest example) that overrides the `RaisingException` method:

```
type
  ECustomException = class (Exception)
  protected
    procedure RaisingException(
      P: PExceptionRecord); override;
  end;

procedure ECustomException.
  RaisingException(P: PExceptionRecord);
begin
  // log exception information (to file would be smarter!)
  FormExceptions.Log('Exception Addr: ' + IntToHex (
    Integer(P.ExceptionAddress), 8));
  FormExceptions.Log('Exception Mess: ' + Message);

  // modify the message
```

```
    Message := Message + ' (filtered)';

    // standard processing
    inherited;
end;
```

What this method implementation does is to log some information about the exception, modify the exception message and then invoke the standard processing of the base classes (needed for the nested exception mechanism to work). The method is invoked after the exception object has been created but before the exception is raised. This can be noticed because the output produced by the `Log` calls is generated before the exception is caught by the debugger! Similarly, if you put a breakpoint in the `RaisingException` method, the debugger will stop there before catching the exception.

New Exception Classes

Another new feature of exceptions is the global availability of a few new specific exception classes (as they are defined in the SysUtils unit):

```
type
  EArgumentException = class(Exception);
    EArgumentOutOfRangeException =
      class(EArgumentException);
  ENoConstructException = class(Exception);
  EMonitor = class(Exception);
    EMonitorLockException = class(EMonitor);
    ENoMonitorSupportException = class(EMonitor);
  EProgrammerNotFound = class(Exception);
```

The last of these new exception classes, `EProgrammerNotFound`, seems more like a joke and is not used once in the VCL source code. I can think of some funny ways[110] of using it, though.

---

110 I have a long tradition in giving talks about the "Fun Side of Delphi", as you can see on my web site at the address http://www.marcocantu.com/funside.

Summary of New Units and New RTL Classes

With all of the classes of the RTL introduced to support Unicode and generics, plus many extra features, it is easy to miss some of the changes. For this reason, at the end of the coverage of the run time library (which was only partially done in this chapter) it is worth having an overall look at the new units and classes of the RTL. I haven't listed global routines, as this would have been a huge task. The following are the new units of the run time library, with the list of the classes they define, if any:

AnsiStrings	(no classes)
Character	TCharacter
Generics.Collection	TArray TEnumerator\<T> TEnumerable\<T> TList\<T> TQueue\<T> TStack\<T> TDictionary\<TKey,TValue> TObjectList\<T> TObjectQueue\<T> TObjectStack\<T> TObjectDictionary\<TKey,TValue>
Generics.Default	TComparer\<T> TEqualityComparer\<T> TSingletonImplementation TDelegatedEqualityComparer\<T> TDelegatedComparer\<T> TCustomComparer\<T> TStringComparer

The following are the new Delphi 2009 classes (or records with methods) that have been added to existing RTL units. Notice in particular that there are now classes in the SysUtils unit (and not only in the Classes unit), while the System unit adds two records with methods. Here is the list:

Classes	TBytesStream TTextReader TTextWriter TStringReader

	`TStringWriter`
	`TStreamWriter`
	`TStreamReader`
SyncObjs	`TSemaphore`
	`TConditionVariableMutex`
	`TConditionVariableCS`
System	`TMonitor`
SysUtils	`TStringBuilder`
	`TEncoding`
	`TMBCSEncoding`
	`TUTF7Encoding`
	`TUTF8Encoding`
	`TUnicodeEncoding`
	`TBigEndianUnicodeEncoding`
ZLib	`TCustomZStream`

More and Less FastCode

Over the last few versions of Delphi, CodeGear has borrowed (in a way that is compliant with the original license) several routines from the FastCode project[111]. Now, although these routines are still in the product, most of them related to string management and are not in the new AnsiStrings unit, and are probably not going to be used as much as the corresponding UnicodeString routines. On the plus side, for FastCode integration, there is a new optimized version of the `RoundTo` in function in the Math unit.

What's Next

This chapter on assorted compiler changes and new features of the Delphi run time library completes the second part of the book, focused on the IDE and the compiler. The third part of the book will be focused on the VCL, including new features in supporting Vista, the Ribbon user interface, translation support, and COM support. After that it will cover database programming and multi-tier database applications.

---

111 See http://www.fastcodeproject.org for more details on the FastCode project and its current status (last time I checked activity was quite low).

Part III: VCL And Databases

Most of the "Delphi experience" relates to its key library, the Visual Component Library, and in particular its subset focused on database development, including client/server and 3-tier architectures. Many visual controls and some of the database access components have received a significant update in Delphi 2009, and are the subject of this third part of the book, which covers also COM, the new Ribbon control, and the new DataSnap 2009 multi tier architecture.

- Chapter 8: VCL Improvements
- Chapter 9: COM Support in Delphi 2009
- Chapter 10: The Ribbon
- Chapter 11: Datasets and dbExpress
- Chapter 12: DataSnap 2009

Marco Cantù, Delphi 2009 Handbook

Chapter 8: VCL Improvements

While maybe not as significant as Unicode support or other compiler changes, the VCL in Delphi 2009 sees a number of small but important improvements (some of which have been requested for a long time by Delphi users). In this chapter I'll focus on some assorted improvements and new controls, while the one after next is dedicated to the new Ribbon component.

The VCL is one of the cornerstones of Delphi and its architecture has significantly contributed to the success of the tool. Even today, looking at user-interface frameworks designed after many years by large IT companies, the VCL stands out considerably[112].

---

[112] If you compare the VCL with the WinForms library of the .NET framework or with leading Java libraries you'll see what I mean. One of the key elements of the VCL, its strict relationship with the Windows API, though, is also one of its weaknesses, as porting it outside of the Windows world has proved hard (as the CLX project and, in part, the VCL for .NET project have demonstrated).

248 - Chapter 8: VCL Improvements

With four brand new components (BalloonHint, ButtonedEdit, CategoryPanelGroup, and LinkLabel) plus Ribbon support and countless small enhancements, the VCL has seen a significant update in Delphi 2009. Some of these updates are specific for Windows XP or Windows Vista and further enhance the support for Vista that's in the VCL since Delphi 2007[113].

VCL Core Improvements

Beside the various changes and fixes to specific components and controls, covered in this chapter, there are some improvements made at the core VCL class level that benefit each and every visual control in the library.

One of these improvements is the addition of the ParentDoubleBuffered property in the TWinControl class, that makes it easier to enable double buffering for an entire form or a group of controls. Double buffering is useful in ensuring correct output where a form has a Vista glass surface (using the GlassFrame property introduced in Delphi 2007) or in other situations in which a program is performing alpha blending of different images.

For the same reason, the corresponding DoubleBuffered property has now been published on most controls (more so than in previous versions).

Custom Hints and Balloon Hints

The TControl class introduces a new property, CustomHint, along with its *parent* property, ParentCustomHint, which lets child objects share the value defined by the parent control:

```
property CustomHint: TCustomHint
  read GetCustomHint write SetCustomHint;
property ParentCustomHint: Boolean
  read FParentCustomHint write SetParentCustomHint
  default True;
```

This new property lets you hook a custom hint object to any visual component, that is an object of any class inheriting from TCustomHint. One such class, introduced in Delphi 2009, is the TBalloonHint class, a very simple

---

113 Vista support in the VCL is covered in detail in my "Delphi 2007 Handbook".

component that adds very little to what the base `TCustomHint` class already provides. The custom hint architecture, though, is more flexible than having only balloon hint support, as you can add your own custom hint classes and use them for any control.

What you can use out-of-the-box is a BalloonHint component. Simply place this non-visual component on a form and hook it to the `CustomHint` property of a control to change the way the hint is displayed. You can see a BalloonHint component below:

Here are the related settings from the DFM file of the HintsDemo example:

```
object btnCustomHint: TButton
  Hint = 'This is a hint for the button'
  CustomHint = BalloonHint1
  ShowHint = True
end
object BalloonHint1: TBalloonHint
  Images = ImageList1
end
```

The BalloonHint component uses the hint provided by the control on to which it is hooked. As a user moves the mouse over the button, the hint will be displayed in a much nicer way than in the past:

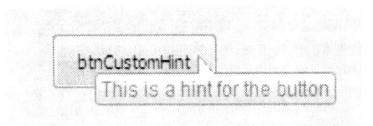

Using the `ParentShowHint` and `ParentCustomHint` properties you can define this setting on a panel and have balloon hints active on each of the controls hosted by the panel. For an example, you can see the `Panel1` control of the HintsDemo project.

You might have noticed in the DFM listing above that the BalloonHint component has an `Images` property, but no image is displayed. One way to set other runtime properties of the BalloonHint component, including the `Title` and the `ImageIndex`, and have a nicer looking hint, is to manually invoke the hint, for example from the `OnMouseEnter` event of a control:

```
procedure TForm30.btnShowHintMouseEnter(Sender: TObject);
begin
  BalloonHint1.Title := 'Hint Title';
```

250 - Chapter 8: VCL Improvements

```
  BalloonHint1.ImageIndex := 1;
  BalloonHint1.Description :=
    'This is a hint suggesting what a user would do';
  BalloonHint1.HideAfter := 5000;
  BalloonHint1.ShowHint;
end;

procedure TForm30.btnShowHintMouseLeave(Sender: TObject);
begin
  BalloonHint1.HideHint;
end;
```

The hint, visible in the image below, will hide after 5 seconds or as soon as the mouse leaves the control:

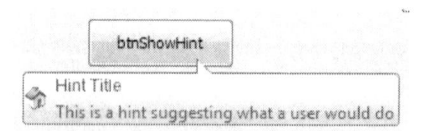

As this would require a lot of work, there is another easier way to set the title and the image index of the custom hint object connected with a control. Since the early days of Delphi, the `Hint` property allowed you to specify a short hint (used as hint) and a longer version (generally for a StatusBar message) separated by the pipe character (|). Using the custom hint association, the `Hint` property is now interpreted as follows:

```
title|message|imageindex
```

So for example, in the HintsDemo project I've customized a button as follows (the value of the hint is a single string):

```
object Button3: TButton
  Hint =
    'This is a button|' +
    'This is a longer description for the button, ' +
    'taking some space|2'
  CustomHint = BalloonHint1
  Caption = 'Button3'
end
```

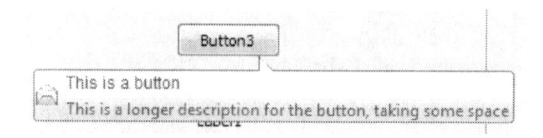

Enhancements to Standard Components

If there are some new features that affect all controls, most of the improvements in the VCL in Delphi 2009 are specific to individual controls. The core standard controls, as well as the common controls, have been extended by Microsoft from one version of Windows to the next, while the VCL has often neglected supporting new these new features of the OS, sometimes for backward compatibility reasons (as similar applications might have problems running on older versions of the operating system, that Delphi has now stopped supporting anyway).

In this section I'll focus on the enhancements of some of the standard core controls of Windows, like buttons and edit boxes. In the following section I'll focus on the (more limited) enhancements of common controls.

Buttons Get New Features

You might think that the classic Windows' push buttons are well established, stable controls. That's actually not true. Since Windows XP, you can hook an image from an image list to a button, and have a graphical bitmap button without having to derive a custom owner-drawn control as Delphi did since the early days with the BitBtn (bitmap button) control. In Delphi 2009 you can now have the same graphical effect with a plain and standard `TButton`. Image list support comes through a series of properties you can use to determine which image to use in each of various states of the button. Here is the list of the new image-related properties of the `TCustomButton` class, listed with only their types:

```
property DisabledImageIndex: TImageIndex ...
property HotImageIndex: TImageIndex ...
property ImageAlignment: TImageAlignment ...
property ImageIndex: TImageIndex ...
property ImageMargins: TImageMargins ...
property Images: TCustomImageList ...
property PressedImageIndex: TImageIndex ...
property SelectedImageIndex: TImageIndex ...
```

252 - Chapter 8: VCL Improvements

Since this feature was introduced in the Win32 API in Windows XP, if your application needs to run on Windows 2000, you should use it with care or avoid using it altogether.

Similarly, if your program is meant to be running on Vista, you can activate more new features, like the command link style used by many standard dialogs of the operating system and split button styles that let you hook a drop down menu to the button, which is activated by pressing the small drop down arrow. The overall layout of the button is determined by the value of the new `Style` property of an enumerated type defined as a nested type[114] of the `TCustomButton` class:

```
type
  TButtonStyle = (bsPushButton, bsCommandLink,
    bsSplitButton);
```

There are further properties you can use depending on the selected style:

- With the split button style (in the API, the `BS_SPLITBUTTON` style value) you can use the `DropDownMenu` property (of type `TPopupMenu`) and customize it in the `OnDropDownClick` event.
- In the case of the command link type (the `BS_COMMANDLINK` style value in the API) you can use the default icon (a green arrow) or a specific image (as mentioned earlier) and provide more information about the action with the new `CommandLinkHint` string property.

Finally, the `ElevationRequired` property, applicable both to a standard button and to a command link one, enables the display of the Windows shield to be used if the button leads to a UAC protected operation. The `ElevationRequired` property sends the `BCM_SETSHIELD` message to the button.

Using all of these new properties can affect the layout of your application quite radically, although you can obtain some of these user interface effects only if the application runs on Windows Vista (or later versions of the operating system). These properties are not very complex to use, so rather than describing the ButtonsDemo example in detail, I'll simply list its key elements, after showing you the design-time form:

---

[114] Nested types, introduced in Delphi 2006, let you define a type within an existing type. A nested type is subject to the visibility rules determined by the class hosting it, and can be private or public. In this case the type `TCustomButton.TButtonStyle` is public. Nested types provide a sort of name space, as the full name includes the outer class. For detailed coverage see, again, the "Delphi 2007 Handbook".

Chapter 8: VCL Improvements - 253

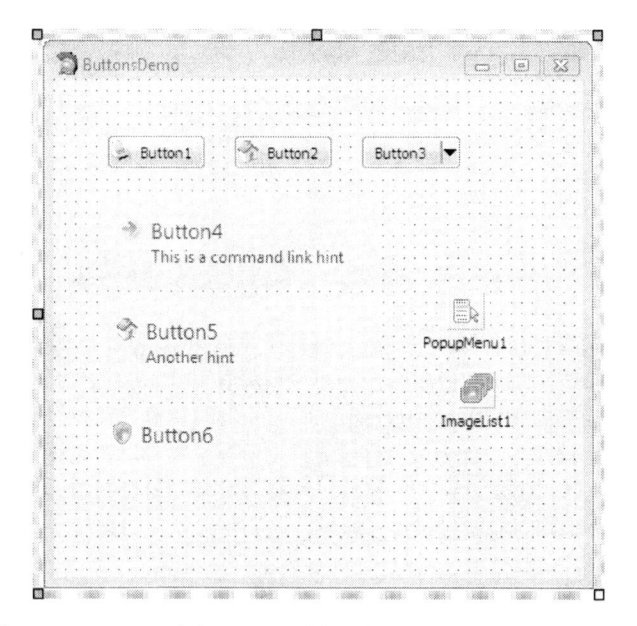

This is the summary of the DFM file of the project:

```
object FormButtonsDemo: TFormButtonsDemo
  object Button1: TButton
    ImageIndex = 0
    Images = ImageList1
    PressedImageIndex = 1
  end
  object Button2: TButton
    ImageIndex = 1
    Images = ImageList1
    PressedImageIndex = 2
  end
  object Button3: TButton
    DropDownMenu = PopupMenu1
    Style = bsSplitButton
  end
  object Button4: TButton
    CommandLinkHint = 'This is a command link hint'
    Style = bsCommandLink
  end
  object Button5: TButton
    CommandLinkHint = 'Another hint'
    ImageIndex = 1
    Images = ImageList1
    Style = bsCommandLink
  end
  object Button6: TButton
```

254 - Chapter 8: VCL Improvements

```
      ElevationRequired = True
      Style = bsCommandLink
    end
    object ImageList1: TImageList...
    object PopupMenu1: TPopupMenu...
end
```

Glowing Labels and LinkLabels

Another classic component that has been extended, mostly with the introduction of a new class representing a modified version of the Microsoft control, is the TLabel component. The extra feature of this component is not something you can use in each and every application, as it let's you add a glow effect on labels painted on a glass frame surface in Windows Vista.

In Delphi this feature is activated using the new GlowSize property of the TLabel class, which is an Integer you basically use like a Boolean value, as setting any value above 0 seems to produce exactly the same effect: painting a one pixel white border around the label[115]. It is very hard to see the difference between a standard and a glowing label in the printed screen shot of the LabelsDemo example (it will be much more clear if you run the demo):

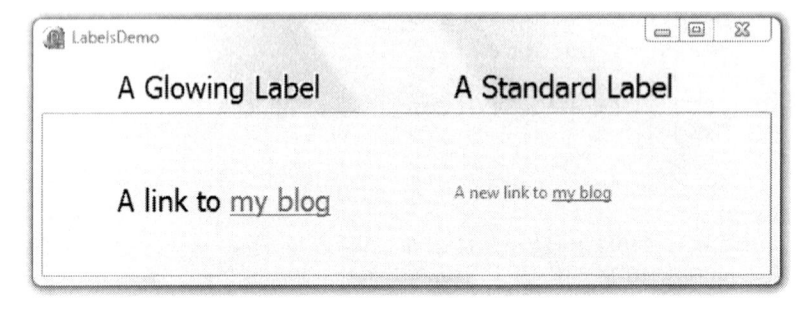

In the bottom area of the form above you can see two instances of the new LinkLabel component, a wrapper of the SysLink Windows class. This is a new control you can use only on Windows XP or later versions (not on Win-

---

115 The Windows API documentation for the corresponding field of the DTTOPS data structure used for painting themed controls claims this is "the size of a glow that will be drawn on the background prior to any text being drawn", but again in this specific case the number seems to have no practical effect. Another element that doesn't correspond to the documentation is that you can actually have a glow even when not painting over the glass surface, even if in this case the visual effect is not as nice.

dows 2000, where it reverts back to a `STATIC` control, that is a plain label, as you can see in `TCustomLinkLabel.CreateParams`).

You can use the `UseVisualStyle` property to move from a standard painting code (like any other label) to a more modern UI, although in the latter case it looks like the control is ignoring the assigned font. In both cases you can use the `Caption` property to specify some text including a hyper link in HTML format (that is an anchor `a` with an `href` attribute: don't try to use other HTML tags, as they'll be displayed in the text):

```
object LinkLabel2: TLinkLabel
  Caption = 'A new link to <a
    href="http://blog.marcocantu.com">my blog</a>'
  UseVisualStyle = True
  OnLinkClick = LinkLabel1LinkClick
end
```

As a user clicks on the link, the control will fire the `OnLinkClick` event passing the URL as parameter:

```
procedure TFormLabelsDemo.LinkLabel1LinkClick(
  Sender: TObject; const Link: string;
  LinkType: TSysLinkType);
begin
  ShowMessage ('Link clicked: ' + Link);
end;
```

You can handle the event and launch the default browser with a `ShellExecute` call, passing the complete URL as parameter.

RadioGroup Text Wrapping

The RadioGroup component (the custom combination of a GroupBox with actual RadioButton controls) gets a single new feature, the support for word wrapping in the radio buttons they contain.

The drawback in this case is that the component won't be able to calculate the vertical spacing of the individual items properly, and if you have (say) an element with three lines of text, it might turn out that the top of the first line or the bottom of the last line won't be visible.

An example of wrapping and one of the problems it can cause are visible in the RadioGroupDemo form:

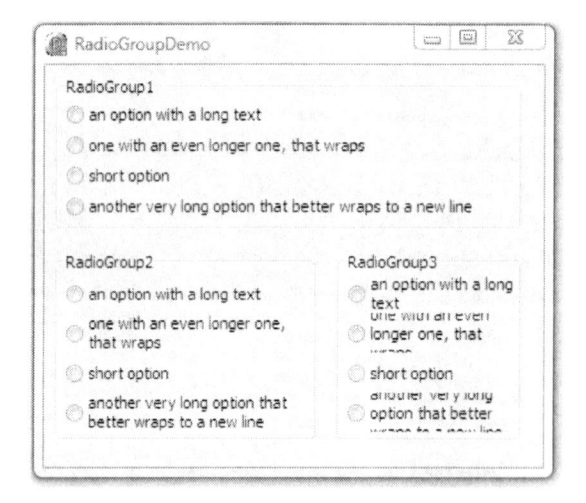

Edits Get Many New Features

The Edit control is another standard and classic control of Windows that over the years got new features (particularly in Windows XP), which the VCL failed to surface, even if Delphi programmers could enable them directly. Now some of these features[116] are easily accessible using new properties of the TEdit class:

- The **Alignment** property enables the alignment of text in an edit control, a feature that was previously available only for DBEdit controls (and implemented in native VCL code, as it wasn't available in early versions of the Win32 API). Setting Alignment activates the ES_LEFT, ES_RIGHT, or ES_CENTER Windows styles, eventually requiring the system to recreate the Edit window (so you should try to avoid changing this property at runtime once the Edit box has been displayed).

- The **NumbersOnly** property sets the ES_NUMBER style of the Edit control, which requires Windows XP or later. This applies an input filter that prevents user from typing non-digit keys, but still let's them paste non-numeric text (and let's the program freely set the Text property).

---

116 For a detailed list of the window styles for an Edit control at the API level, see the SDK documentation at: http://msdn.microsoft.com/en-us/library/bb775464.aspx.

- The **TextHint** property supports in-place text hints displayed when the edit box is empty (again this requires Windows XP or later). The text hint could act as a replacement for a descriptive label, or reinforce one providing a call to action for the user.
- The **PasswordChar** property let's you set a custom password char (replacing the default asterisks, in Windows XP, or round dots, in Windows Vista) with a character or symbol of your own choice. This feature not only requires Windows XP or later but also a themed application.

These properties are also available in components that relate to the Edit control, such as the LabeledEdit (a combination of an Edit and a Label) and the classic MaskEdit control of the VCL. The DBEdit control, instead, doesn't provide the new features of other edit controls. Actually, to be more precise, it inherits the new features from the base **TCustomEdit** class but doesn't expose them in published properties.

In the following runtime form of the EditFamilyDemo example, you can see some of these features (and others I'll explain later) in action:

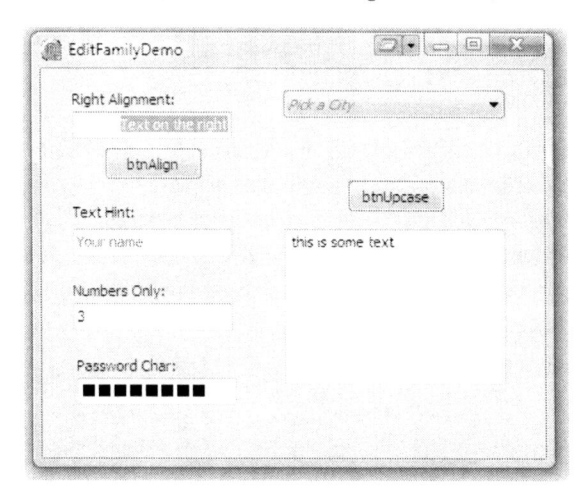

On the left side of the form you can see four edit boxes using some of the new features. The first has its text right aligned, the second displays a text hint, the third allows only numeric input, and the fourth uses Unicode CodePoint 25A0 (Black Square) as its password character. (It is nice that you can use any Unicode symbol for the password character.)

This is the most relevant portion of the DFM file, describing the properties of those four controls:

258 - Chapter 8: VCL Improvements

```
    object edRightAlign: TEdit
      Alignment = taRightJustify
      Text = 'Text on the right'
    end
    object edTextHint: TEdit
      TextHint = 'Your name'
    end
    object edNumber: TEdit
      NumbersOnly = True
      Text = '3'
    end
    object edPassword: TEdit
      PasswordChar = #9632
      Text = 'password'
    end
```

The button close to the first edit let's you switch the alignment property in a round robin fashion, by increasing the value of the enumeration and computing the modulus (the remainder of the division) with the highest possible value:

```
procedure TFormEditFamily.btnAlignClick(Sender: TObject);
begin
  edRightAlign.Alignment := TAlignment (
    (Ord(edRightAlign.Alignment) + 1) mod
    (Ord(High(TAlignment)) + 1));
end;
```

A strictly-related[117] component, the Memo, has a specific new property, CharCase, which lets you force the text to lowercase or uppercase. The text is not just displayed with a given style, but it is actually converted. If you assign mixed case text to the control and later extract that text, you'll retrieve the converted version, as the first two lines of the following event handler demonstrate:

```
procedure TFormEditFamily.btnUpcaseClick(
  Sender: TObject);
begin
  memoLowercase.Lines.Text := 'Mixed Case Text Added';
  ShowMessage (memoLowercase.Lines.Text);

  memoLowercase.CharCase := ecUpperCase;
  memoLowercase.Lines.Text := 'Cantù';
end;
```

---

[117] In the Windows API there is no difference between an Edit and a Memo control, as they are both EDIT controls, initialized with either a single line or a multi line style.

The first time you press the button, the text in the message box will be lowercase. The second time it will be uppercase. Even the accented character at the end of my last name will be converted to an *uppercase accented u*.

ComboBoxes and Text Hints

In the Windows API, ComboBoxes have a strict relationship with Edit boxes, as they got their name (and some of their implementation code) from being a *combination* of an Edit and a ListBox. So you should hardly be surprised to see a TextHint property also added to the TComboBox class, just like the TEdit class. Again, this feature requires Windows XP or a more modern version of Windows[118].

There is a simple combo box with a text hint in the EditFamilyDemo example, as you can see in the last image displayed (a couple of pages back).

The New ButtonedEdit Control

A brand new control that extends the behavior of the Edit control is the ButtonedEdit component, which is a custom VCL control defined in the ExtCtrls unit. This is basically an edit box that can have small buttons on the left or right side, used to interact with the edit box itself. For example, you can add a Cancel button that empties the edit box, and a search or lookup button that validates the input or looks for some related information.

The Delphi IDE uses this component for the Search option of the Tools Palette, as you can see below:

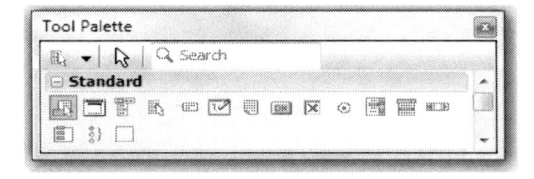

---

[118] The internal code used to set up the text hint for a combo box in Windows XP and Windows Vista is different, but the VCL manages this for you. If you are interested in the details see the two sections of the method TCustomComboBox.DoSetTextHint for Windows version 5.1 (XP) and 6 (Vista).

This component, which requires XP or later versions of Windows, includes all of the new features of the Edit control, like the modern-looking text hint. Setting up the buttons on the sides of the edit box is quite simple. The component has a `LeftButton` and a `RightButton` property, of type `TEditButton`, defined as:

```
type
  TEditButton = class(TPersistent)
  published
    property DisabledImageIndex: TImageIndex;
    property DropDownMenu: TPopupMenu;
    property Enabled: Boolean;
    property HotImageIndex: TImageIndex;
    property ImageIndex: TImageIndex;
    property PressedImageIndex: TImageIndex;
    property Visible: Boolean;
  end;
```

All of the image references are to the ImageList component you can hook to the ButtonedEdit control. You can attach a method to the click on either button using the `OnLeftButtonClick` and `OnRightButtonClick` events of the ButtonedEdit control; you can also attach a Popup menu to the buttons using the `DropDownMenu` property of the `TEditButton` class.

In the ButtonEdits demo I've coded some very simple usage scenarios, just to give an idea of how you can work with this component. At the same time showing some of the other new features introduced for edit boxes. The main form of the example sports three ButtonedEdit controls, two with a single button and one with two buttons. The controls also have text hints and one of them has a drop down menu attached. You can see the form at runtime (with the drop down menu active) in the following image:

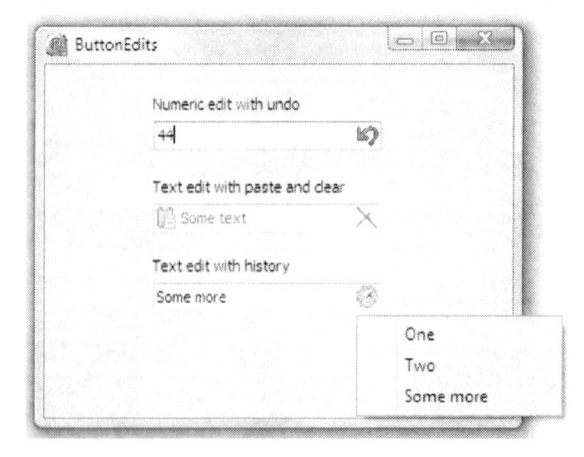

The first control is a numeric edit box with an undo button:

```
object edUndo: TButtonedEdit
  Images = ImageList1
  NumbersOnly = True
  RightButton.ImageIndex = 0
  RightButton.Visible = True
  TextHint = 'A number'
  OnRightButtonClick = edUndoRightButtonClick
end
```

The edUndoRightButtonClick event handler calls the Undo method of the ButtonedEdit control. The second edit control provides two buttons, one for pasting from the clipboard and the second to clear the edit box content (thus restoring the text hint):

```
object edClear: TButtonedEdit
  Images = ImageList1
  LeftButton.ImageIndex = 3
  LeftButton.Visible = True
  RightButton.ImageIndex = 1
  RightButton.Visible = True
  TextHint = 'Some text'
  OnLeftButtonClick = edClearLeftButtonClick
  OnRightButtonClick = edClearRightButtonClick
end
```

The third edit box has a history button, and keeps track of the text that is entered in the window, allowing a user to reselect it:

```
object edHistory: TButtonedEdit
  Images = ImageList1
  RightButton.DropDownMenu = PopupMenu1
  RightButton.ImageIndex = 2
  RightButton.Visible = True
  TextHint = 'Edit or pick'
  OnExit = edHistoryExit
end
```

The component works by adding each new text to the popup menu as the user leaves the edit box, provided this text is not already in the menu:

```
procedure TFormButtonEdits.edHistoryExit(
  Sender: TObject);
begin
  if (edHistory.Text <> '') and
    (PopupMenu1.Items.Find (edHistory.Text) = nil) then
  begin
    PopupMenu1.Items.Add (NewItem (edHistory.Text, 0,
      False, True, RestoreText, 0, ''));
  end;
```

262 - Chapter 8: VCL Improvements

```
end;
```

The predefined menu items and each new menu item added dynamically are connected with the `RestoreText` event handler which takes the caption of the selected menu items, strips any hot key, and copies it to the edit box:

```
procedure TFormButtonEdits.RestoreText(Sender: TObject);
begin
  edHistory.Text := StripHotkey (
    (Sender as TMenuItem).Caption);
end;
```

Updates to Common Controls

The improvements to standard controls in the VCL of Delphi 2009 are extremely important because they are also related with commonly used controls like edits and buttons. The new version of the VCL also includes many enhancements to other controls provided by the Windows API since the move to the 32-bit version of the operating system. Here are some controls that have new features:

- **ImageList**: Although not every single developer will benefit from this, the ImageList component now supports alpha-blended images and lets you set a custom color depth, using a new property with the corresponding name (ColorDepth).
- **TreeView**: Another component with limited updates in the past is the TreeView, which now lets you define an image index for expanded nodes and (on Windows XP or later) support disabled tree nodes.

Grouping in a ListView

One common control worth exploring in some more detail is the ListView, that in Delphi 2009 receives direct support for grouping. This feature requires Windows XP or Vista, with the latter providing extended features.

There are three new properties in the ListView control. The Boolean `GroupView` enables this new kind of display, the `GroupHeaderImages` refers to an ImageList containing the images for the group headers, and the

`Groups` property is a collection of group definitions. Each group can have a main title (`Header`), a related icon (`TitleImage`), a longer description (`Subtitle`), a footer line (`Footer`), plus some more text elements and alignment properties for headers and footer. A set of options let's you set the group as collapsible, remove the header, hide the group, and so on[119].

You can see an example of grouping in a ListView in the main form of the GroupingList application, displayed below at design time:

This is the definition of the groups inside the ListView control (in DFM format), in which I've set a couple of extra descriptions that will show up only if you center the group headers:

```
object ListView1: TListView
  Groups = <
    item
      Header = 'Arrows'
      Footer = 'Footer: You can pick any of the arrows ' +
        'for the caption'
```

---

[119] Some of the extra text elements of the groups are displayed only in specific cases, such as when the group header is centered (in which case several items might end up overlapping). Other features of the ListView, like the subset mode, are far from obvious to activate. I'm not sure how much of this is due to the VCL and how much to the Windows API, but looking at the SDK there is almost no documentation about some of these extended features... which probably makes wrapping them in a component some sort of guess work.

264 - Chapter 8: VCL Improvements

```
        GroupID = 0
        State = [lgsNormal, lgsCollapsible]
        HeaderAlign = taLeftJustify
        FooterAlign = taLeftJustify
        Subtitle = 'Subtitle: Arrow group subtitle'
        TopDescription = 'Top Descr: A group of arrows'
        TitleImage = 0
        SubsetTitle = 'Subset title...'
      end
      item
        Header = 'Houses'
        Footer = 'Which house would you prefer?'
        GroupID = 1
        State = [lgsNormal, lgsCollapsible]
        HeaderAlign = taLeftJustify
        FooterAlign = taLeftJustify
        Subtitle = 'Houses with different colors for ' +
          'the roof...'
        TitleImage = 1
        ExtendedImage = -1
      end>
    GroupHeaderImages = ImgGroups
    GroupView = True
end
```

The only code of the example is used to change the alignment of the header and footer of each group. This is the event handler of one of the three toolbar buttons:

```
procedure TFormGroupingList.tbRightClick(
  Sender: TObject);
var
  aGroup: TCollectionItem;
begin
  for aGroup in ListView1.Groups do
  begin
    (aGroup as TListGroup).HeaderAlign := taRightJustify;
    (aGroup as TListGroup).FooterAlign := taRightJustify;
  end;
end;
```

Beside grouping support, the ListView control has another unrelated new event, OnItemChecked, triggered when a user selects an item of the ListView.

Marquee and More for ProgressBar Controls

The ProgressBar component is another common control that got extended features over the last few years that were not directly supported by the VCL. If you are not using runtime themes you can set a custom color for the bar and its background, using the `BarColor` and `BackgroundColor` properties.

A nice feature, available on Windows XP and Vista, is the marquee style of the progress bar, in which the bar keeps moving to show the program is working without indicating a specific position. This is a good option in situations in which you don't know exactly how much time the operation will take, but still indicate to the user to wait as the requested operation is taking place. To enable this, set the `Style` property to `pbstMarquee` and optionally change the default value for the `MarqueeInterval` property, to make the graphic element move slower or faster. As an example, these are the settings of the first ProgressBar of the SuperProgress demo:

```
object ProgressBar1: TProgressBar
   Style = pbstMarquee
   MarqueeInterval = 20
end
```

On Windows Vista, the ProgressBar control has an extended feature, called smooth reverse. If you are setting a progress position and you are advancing it by a large amount the control will generally move smoothly (with a sort of animation) to the new position. By activating smooth reverse the same happens if you have to (unexpectedly) move the progress Position backwards: rather than jumping back, it will gradually get there.

This effect cannot be captured by a static image, so you should try the SuperProgress demo for yourself. The second and third controls of the demo differ only by the value of the `SmoothReverse` property. There are three buttons below the progress bar that let you loop or move them back and forth, to experiment with the visual effect. The code is fairly trivial, so I've omitted it from the text of the book.

Three radio buttons on the side of the main form of the example let you change the `State` property of the second ProgressBar. This is another new property of the control in Delphi 2009. You can change the default state to a paused or error state, and the green progress bar will change to yellow or red respectively:

266 - Chapter 8: VCL Improvements

```
procedure TFormSuperProgress.RadioGroup1Click(
  Sender: TObject);
begin
  case RadioGroup1.ItemIndex of
    0: ProgressBar2.State := pbsNormal;
    1: ProgressBar2.State := pbsError;
    2: ProgressBar2.State := pbsPaused;
  end;
end;
```

Check Boxes in a Header

Another common control, albeit not very frequently used, is the HeaderControl component. In the VCL of Delphi 2009, this control now supports fixed width header sections (using the `NoSizing` Property), extra non-visible headers if they don't fit (using the `Overflow` property) and, more interestingly, check boxes within the header sections.

To enable this feature you have to turn it on for the control as a whole and then for each individual section, as indicated by the properties of the control (and its `Sections` collection) in the CheckBoxHeader example:

```
object HeaderControl1: THeaderControl
  Sections = <
    item
      AutoSize = True
      CheckBox = True
      Text = 'one'
    end
    item
      AutoSize = True
      CheckBox = True
      Checked = True
      Text = 'two'
    end
    item
      AutoSize = True
      CheckBox = True
      Text = 'three'
    end
    item
      AutoSize = True
      CheckBox = True
      Text = 'four'
    end>
  OnSectionCheck = HeaderControl1SectionCheck
```

```
    CheckBoxes = True
end
```

With these properties for the control, the form of the example (at design time) looks as follows:

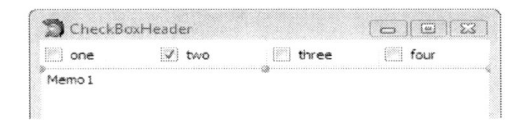

The problem with this new feature, though, is that the new OnSectionCheck event doesn't fire. The internal CNNotify message handler method intercepts the specific message and properly updates the status of the Checked property of the header section, but this property setter fails to trigger the corresponding event[120].

RichEdit 2.0

The RichEdit component in Delphi used to encapsulate the original version of the corresponding common control. To support a newer version of the control, the VCL in Delphi 2009 now uses the version 2 specific DLL hosting this common control:

```
RichEditModuleName = 'RICHED32.DLL'; // Delphi 2007
RichEditModuleName = 'RICHED20.DLL'; // Delphi 2009
```

In practice this means a newer and more robust version, but not a lot of new features. In fact quite the opposite, as the VCL component is basically unchanged. This means most of your existing Delphi code based on this common control will keep working, and the VCL will take care of some internal differences between versions. The only exception is due to the difference in the line separator format[121].

---

[120] This is apparently a bug that was reported to CodeGear, even if quite late in the release cycle.

[121] A possible (negative) side effect of adopting version 2 of the Rich Edit Windows common control is caused by a change in the way line endings are managed. In the past, new lines where represented by the CR LF sequence (#13#10), while in the newer version they are represented as CR (#13). If you have existing code that processes the text of the control or its current selection, it might not work properly any more because of this change.

268 - Chapter 8: VCL Improvements

An interesting element is how the RichEdit handles Unicode text and saving and loading to and from Unicode files. The code added to the control in Delphi 2009 makes it work more or less like any other `TStringList`. You can specify an encoding when saving, and if you don't set one when loading the component will use the BOM to determine the correct format. The default for saving, though, remains the default code page used by the operating system.

In the UniRichEdit example all I wanted to show was saving the current file as UTF-16, so I've added two buttons to the form with the following code:

```
procedure TFormUniRichEdit.Button1Click(Sender: TObject);
begin
  RichEdit1.Lines.SaveToFile('local.rtf',
    TEncoding.Unicode);
end;

procedure TFormUniRichEdit.Button2Click(Sender: TObject);
begin
  RichEdit1.Lines.LoadFromFile('local.rtf');
end;
```

The program uses an ActionList component populated with some of the standard editing actions, that have remained unchanged (as proof that you can easily upgrade existing applications). The various actions are exposed in a toolbar. If you run the program and load the default file I've added to its folder, you should see output like the following:

Native VCL Components

After looking at standard controls and common controls provided by the Windows API, wrapped by corresponding VCL controls, it is now time to focus on new features of native VCL controls and one brand new control, the CategoryPanels component.

In particular I'll start by looking at a few extensions to the Action Manager architecture, devote some time to panels, cover some global VCL components, and have a look at the extended support for graphics, now including PNG images, for both the Image and ImageList components.

The Action Manager Components

One set of native components that have seen some minor improvements are those of the Action Manager architecture[122]. The ActionManager component has three new properties for large images, disabled images, and both large and disabled ones.

The PopupActionBar has support for action bar styles, using the new `Style` property. The entire set of action menus and toolbars has support for themed displays on Windows XP or later. If you set the *platform default-style* for the ActionManager, the associated visual component will pick the look and feel of the current version of the operating system at runtime.

About Panels

Until a few years back, the Panel component was a commonly used component with limited features, even if it did support docking. In Delphi 2006 it got a significant redesign, with the advent of panels that don't use absolute positioning for the controls they contain, but a specific positioning rule. These special panels are the FlowPanel control and the GridPanel control[123]. All controls gain a small new feature, as you can now disable the (almost

---

122 The role of the Action Manager architecture and of the related components is going to increase significantly starting with Delphi 2009 thanks to the connection with the Ribbon components, covered in Chapter 9.

generally useless) panel caption, by triggering the new `ShowCaption` property to False rather than setting the `Caption` property to an empty string.

You might wonder if this was really needed, as we managed to live without this feature for so many years, but the fact is that panels can now be hosted by a new custom VCL control, called CategoryPanelGroup. This panel container uses the hosted panel caption as a title, so the `Caption` is needed to identify the panels even when you don't want it to be visible.

The New CategoryPanelGroup Control

A family of components for which we have probably seen the largest number of VCL controls available over the years has been the so-called *Outlook Sidebar* family, mimicking the well established interface that was originally introduced by the Microsoft email program.

In modern applications, styles have changed a lot from the original collection of large icons used for the various sections of the program, but the usage of a sidebar with options and commands continues. For the first time, Delphi 2009 offers a similar component out of the box.

The CategoryPanelGroup control is a visual container of CategoryPanel controls. You create these category panels using the shortcut menu of the CategoryPanelGroup at design time or calling its `CreatePanel` method at runtime. The individual CategoryPanels refer to the container using the `PanelGroup` property, while the grouping controls has a `Panel` property (a bare-bones `TList` of pointers) or a list of child controls, in the standard `Controls` property.

If you try adding any other control directly to the CategoryPanelGroup the IDE will show the error "*Only CategoryPanels can be inserted into a CategoryPanelGroup.*" Of course, once you've defined a few CategoryPanels you can add virtually any control you like to them. Here is the user interface of this control, taken from the CategoryPanels demo:

---

123 Once more, you can refer to my Delphi 2007 Handbook for more information about these controls. Sorry to keep referring to my previous book, but there is little public information covering these controls... and my previous book really complements this one.

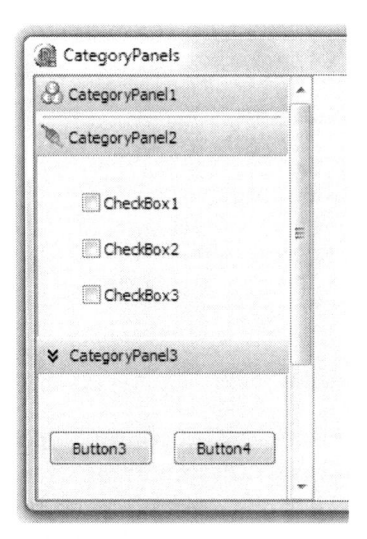

The grouping control and the individual panels have a plethora of properties which you can use to customize the user interface, managing headers with multiple images depending on their collapsed or expanded status, activate gradient backgrounds for the headers, change the font and the *Chevron* colors, and much more.

These are the settings of the panels above (from which I've removed details of the hosted controls):

```
object CategoryPanelGroup1: TCategoryPanelGroup
  VertScrollBar.Tracking = True
  HeaderFont.Color = clWindowText
  HeaderFont.Name = 'Tahoma'
  Images = ImageList1
  object CategoryPanel1: TCategoryPanel
    Caption = 'CategoryPanel1'
    CollapsedImageIndex = 0
    ExpandedImageIndex = 0
    object Button1: TButton...
    object Button2: TButton...
  end
  object CategoryPanel2: TCategoryPanel
    Caption = 'CategoryPanel2'
    Collapsed = True
    CollapsedImageIndex = 2
    ExpandedImageIndex = 1
    object CheckBox1: TCheckBox...
    object CheckBox2: TCheckBox...
    object CheckBox3: TCheckBox...
  end
```

```
    object CategoryPanel3: TCategoryPanel
      Caption = 'CategoryPanel3'
      object GridPanel1: TGridPanel
        Align = alClient
        Caption = 'GridPanel1'
        ControlCollection = <...>
        ShowCaption = False
        object Button3: TButton...
        object Button4: TButton...
        object Button5: TButton...
        object Button6: TButton...
      end
    end
end
```

If we look at the header images, the first panel uses the same one for both states, the second uses two different images for the expanded and collapsed states, while the third has no custom images and uses the default *Chevron* symbol. The third CategoryPanel doesn't host its controls directly, but has a GridPanel (with 4 buttons) aligned to its entire surface. This is an example of how you can combine a CategoryPanel with panels providing custom positioning. The program has a little code as well. A first button is used to add a new dynamic CategoryPanel to the group and place a button over it:

```
procedure TFormCategoryPanels.btnAddCategoryClick(
  Sender: TObject);
var
  newPanel: TCategoryPanel;
begin
  newPanel := CategoryPanelGroup1.CreatePanel(self)
    as TCategoryPanel;
  NewPanel.Caption := 'Dynamic Panel';
  with TButton.Create(self) do
  begin
    Caption := 'New button';
    Parent := NewPanel;
    SetBounds (10, 10, Width, Height);
  end;
end;
```

Notice that the CreatePanel method of the category panel group control returns a generic TCustomCategoryPanel, so I had to cast the type to the specific TCategoryPanel type to refer to the Caption property. The reason for this apparently strange behavior is that the category panel group control creates an object of a class which you can configure in an inherited class by overriding the GetCategoryPanelClass virtual function. Still, this is a little unusual, as most other VCL controls that let you customize the class of an internal object refer to a specific class and not a partially defined base class as in this case. This approach apparently makes the control more customizable, as you can have a different implementation class not exposing some of the base class properties, but it also makes code that assumes the given type (and you have to assume a type to be able to use the individual panels, as in the code above) quite error prone. The code above will fail in case of a different category panel class.

A second button shows the two different ways to list the existing category panels of a group that I mentioned earlier, the generic `Controls` array or the specific (but less type safe) `Panels` property. The former, in fact, is an array of controls, while the latter is a list of pointers[124]:

```
procedure TFormCategoryPanels.btnListPanelsClick(
  Sender: TObject);
var
  I: Integer;
begin
  ListBox1.Clear;
  for I := 0 to CategoryPanelGroup1.ControlCount - 1 do
    ListBox1.Items.Add (
      (CategoryPanelGroup1.Controls[I] as TCategoryPanel).
        Caption);
  for I := 0 to CategoryPanelGroup1.Panels.Count - 1 do
    ListBox1.Items.Add (
      TCategoryPanel(CategoryPanelGroup1.Panels[I]).
        Caption);
end;
```

TrayIcon Update

The TrayIcon component, first introduced in Delphi 2007, has a new `OnBalloonClick` event, used for handling a click on the area of the balloon help when this is visible. To show this in practice I've extended the MyTrayIcon example of Delphi 2007 Handbook into the new MyTrayIconClick example, that has the following DFM definition for its main form:

```
object FormMyTrayIconClick: TFormMyTrayIconClick
  object TrayIcon1: TTrayIcon
    BalloonHint = 'sample balloon hint'
```

---

124 This would have been a nice case for using a generic list or objects list, rather than a plain `TList`, but as this was added in parallel to the new compiler features it is not surprising it doesn't rely on them.

274 - Chapter 8: VCL Improvements

```
        BalloonTitle = 'hi'
        BalloonTimeout = 1000
        BalloonFlags = bfInfo
        Icon.Data = {...}
        PopupMenu = PopupMenu1
        Visible = True
        OnBalloonClick = TrayIcon1BalloonClick
        OnMouseDown = TrayIcon1MouseDown
      end
      object PopupMenu1: TPopupMenu...
    end
```

While the `TrayIcon1MouseDown` event handler shows the Balloon hint, the `TrayIcon1BalloonClick` method displays a simple message box, just to prove the event handler works.

Default Fonts for Application and Screen Global Objects

Delphi applications start with a predefined default font, determined at design time. This is problematic when you might want the same executable to run smoothly on different versions of Windows, like XP and Vista, that use different default fonts.

The `Application` global object in Delphi 2009 can provide a standard font to all forms that have `ParentFont` set to True. To accomplish this you can set the `DefaultFont` property of the `Application`. This can be used, for example, to migrate the look and feel of an application to Vista, by setting the font of each form to *Segoe UI* more easily than in the past. Notice that this property as well as the status of the `ParentFont` setting is checked when the form is created, and produces no effect if you change it at runtime.

That's why in the AppFont example I've added the font definition code in the project source code file (the `CheckWin32Version` function is covered later in the section "Extended Vista Support"):

```
begin
  Application.Initialize;
  if CheckWin32Version(6) then // at least Vista
  begin
    Application.DefaultFont.Name := 'Segoe UI';
    Application.DefaultFont.Size := 9;
  end;
  Application.MainFormOnTaskbar := True;
```

At this point all I had to do was to turn on the `ParentFont` property for each of the two forms at design time. Two buttons, one in each form, display their font name, as a proof that the technique works (although you can probably see the different fonts in those forms). These are the properties of the secondary form:

```
object FormSecondary: TFormSecondary
  Caption = 'Secondary'
  ParentFont = True
  Visible = True
```

Now that the forms have the `ParentFont` property set to True, we can go ahead and dynamically change the font in all forms by writing code like:

```
procedure TFormAppFont.btnChangeFontClick(
  Sender: TObject);
begin
  Application.DefaultFont.Name := 'Times New Roman';
  Application.DefaultFont.Size := 10;
end;
```

Similarly, the `Screen` global object can now be used to customize the font used by default in Delphi native message boxes, thanks to the new `MessageFont` property. After setting this value, you can call routines like `ShowMessage` and `MessageDlg` and get a form that uses the given font. This is the case, however, only if the calls are not redirected to use the new task dialogs provided by Vista. In other words, this `MessageFont` property only has effect if you are not running on Vista or if you are running on Vista and disable the global variable `UseLatestCommonDialogs`.

Both cases are demonstrated by the event handler of the following button, part of the AppFont application:

```
procedure TFormAppFont.btnScreenFontClick(
  Sender: TObject);
begin
  Screen.MessageFont.Name := 'Segoe UI';
  Screen.MessageFont.Size := Screen.MessageFont.Size + 2;
  UseLatestCommonDialogs :=
    cbUseLatestCommonDialogs.Checked;
  ShowMessage ('Hello');
  MessageDlg ('Hello', mtINformation, [mbOK], 0);
end;
```

If you are running this program on Vista, by changing the status of the check box, you can see a custom message box with an increasingly larger font or a standard task dialog, with the default system font. Here is an example of this large font in a dialog:

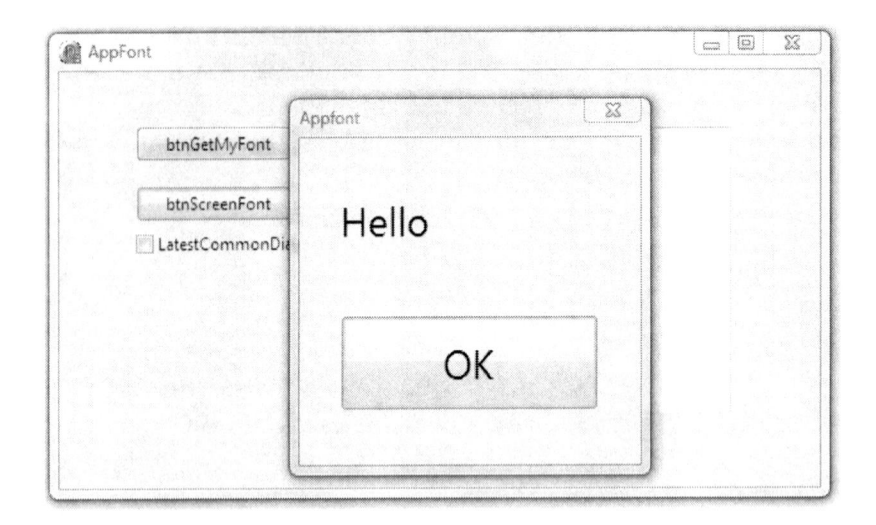

Improved Graphics Support

In the early days, Delphi graphic support was mostly limited to bitmaps. Over the years, there have been extensions to the image formats you could use in the Image component, including JPEG format support[125]. In Delphi 2009 the support for multiple images has been extended to PNG and all formats can now be used with the Image control as well as with the ImageList control.

Moreover, the ImageList control supports setting a specific color depth, although increasing its value will clear all images from the current image list. There have also been enhancements in the ImageList editor and alpha channel support.

The TBitmap class now supports the alpha channel, using the new AlphaFormat property, while TGraphic class has support for transparent images using the SupportsPartialTransparency property.

As there are many changes, I've picked a few worth underlining in the GraphicTest program, starting with the most significant change, that is the native support for multiple formats including PNG (which is new). The support for the formats comes from a set of units that define inherited

---

125 Technically notice that all JPEG-related support (specifically that of the Jpeg.pas unit) has been moved to a new package, called vclimg.bpl. If you had references from other packages you might have to update them manually.

TGraphic classes that you can selectively include in your application. Here are the units and the graphics classes they make available:

Format	Unit	Class
JPEG	jpeg.pas	TJPEGImage
GIF	GIFImg.pas	TGIFImage
PNG[126]	pngimage.pas	TPngImage

Simply by including the corresponding unit you can directly load a file of those formats (plus the standard Bitmap, Icon, and Metafile formats) into an Image component. As the format is determined by the file extension, you can easily load graphic files[127] with different formats with simple code (part of the GraphicsTest example) like:

```
procedure TFormGraphicsTest.btnLoadImageClick(
  Sender: TObject);
var
  strFilename: string;
begin
  case fImgNo of
    0: strFilename := 'adog.jpg';
    1: strFilename := 'Athene.png';
    2: strFilename := 'CodeGear.gif';
  end;
  Image1.Picture.LoadFromFile(strFileName);
  fImgNo := (fImgNo + 1) mod 3
end;
```

The program also has some code to create an empty bitmap in memory. A user can draw on this bitmap by moving the mouse over the image control. The bitmap can then be saved in the three different formats. For example, the code for saving the file in JPEG format looks like this:

```
var
  jpgImg: TJPEGImage;
begin
  jpgImg := TJPEGImage.Create;
  try
```

---

126 The support for PNG images in Delphi 2009 comes from the pngdelphi project by Gustavo Daud, originally available on Source Forge. The GIF support, which has been available for some time, was based on the version by Anders Melander. This goes some way to explaining the inconsistent unit names.

127 The file format is determined by looking at the file extension, according to a set of internal registrations. There is no check of the actual image data to determine its format.

278 - Chapter 8: VCL Improvements

```
    jpgImg.Assign(Image1.Picture.Graphic);
    jpgImg.SaveToFile('test.jpg');
  finally
    jpgImg.Free;
  end;
```

To avoid repeating this code for the PNG and GIF formats, I've written a simple routine to take care of the various differences:

```
procedure SaveWithClass (graph: TGraphic;
  graphClass: TGraphicClass; const strFilename: string);
var
  grapImg: TGraphic;
begin
  grapImg := graphClass.Create;
  try
    grapImg.Assign(graph);
    grapImg.SaveToFile(strFilename);
  finally
    grapImg.Free;
  end;
end;
```

This works only with the default settings, though, as you'll need to work on the specific TGraphic descendant class to to trigger its compression level and other specific options for the given format. In the demo program the routine is called like this:

```
SaveWithClass (Image1.Picture.Graphic,
  TPngImage, 'test.png');
SaveWithClass (Image1.Picture.Graphic,
  TGIFImage, 'test.gif');
```

The support for multiple image formats doesn't relate exclusively to the Image component, but has also been extended to the ImageList component. This means you can now have PNG-based image lists, for example. I've already used an ImageList in other demos of this chapter into which I've loaded PNG images from the GlyFX library licensed by CodeGear and included in Delphi (and installed, by default, in the \Program Files\Common Files\CodeGear Shared\Images\GlyFX folder).

If you are interested in doing so and need to handle the *transparent* color (something the GlyFX library images require if you want to use them for buttons, List Views, Tree Views and most other visual controls) you have to set the ColorDepth property to cd32Bit *before* loading the images. Be wary as setting this property clears the ImageList. As an example in the GraphicsTest program there is an ImageList component with the following settings:

Marco Cantù, Delphi 2009 Handbook

Chapter 8: VCL Improvements - 279

```
object ImageList1: TImageList
  ColorDepth = cd32Bit
  Bitmap = {}
end
```

If you fail to do this step before loading the images, they'll have a black background which is very hard to remove with code (and impossible to remove when hooking the images of the ImageList to other visual components). If you try to do it from program code after loading the images, you will simply clear the image list.

If you want to access the individual elements of the ImageList you can do so by calling, among others, the Draw method, as in:

```
ImageList1.Draw(Image2.Canvas, 10, 10, 0);
ImageList1.Draw(Image2.Canvas, 10, 30, 1);
```

You can pass further parameters to the Draw method, indicating a drawing style (to generate selected and focused images from the standard ones) and choose to draw a mask or an actual image:

```
ImageList1.Draw(Image2.Canvas, 30, 10, 4,
  dsSelected, itImage);
ImageList1.Draw(Image2.Canvas, 30, 30, 4,
  dsTransparent, itImage);
ImageList1.Draw(Image2.Canvas, 30, 50, 4,
  dsFocus, itImage);
ImageList1.Draw(Image2.Canvas, 30, 70, 4,
  TDrawingStyle.dsNormal, itImage);
```

Notice the last call that explicitly refers to the TDrawingStyle enumerated type, as there is a dsNormal value part of the TBandDrawingStyle enumeration of the ExtCtrls unit, included in the project because it defines the Image component.

The previous two code snippets are part of a routine used to paint elements of an ImageList over a Image component, producing the following output:

280 - Chapter 8: VCL Improvements

As an aside while speaking of the Image component, the companion data-aware `TDBImage` component, used for displaying images extracted from database BLOB fields, now supports a *"best fit"* display of the image when setting its `Proportional` property.

The Clipboard and Unicode

The `Clipboard` global object is a rather simple wrapper of the corresponding API, defined in the ClipBrd unit. A notable extension to this component is the way it handles Unicode strings. As you paste text into the clipboard, in fact, the Delphi wrapper will now associate the `CF_UNICODETEXT` clipboard format to the data, rather than the classic `CF_TEXT` format.

This is demonstrated by the simple UniClipboard program, which can add the contents of an edit box to the Clipboard (containing a plain text or two Japanese characters) and paste it after checking which clipboard formats are currently associated with the available Clipboard data (as there can be more than one). Here is the relevant code:

```
procedure TFormUniClipboard.btnCopyClick(
  Sender: TObject);
begin
  Clipboard.Open;
  Clipboard.AsText := Edit1.Text;
  Clipboard.Close;
end;

procedure TFormUniClipboard.btnPasteClick(
  Sender: TObject);
begin
  Clipboard.Open;
  if Clipboard.HasFormat(CF_TEXT) then
    Memo1.Lines.Add('CF_TEXT');
  if Clipboard.HasFormat(CF_UNICODETEXT) then
    Memo1.Lines.Add('CF_UNICODETEXT');
  Memo1.Lines.Add(Clipboard.AsText);
  Clipboard.Close;
end;
```

Extended Vista Support

In this chapter we have seen that quite a number of new properties and features can only be used on the Vista version (or newer) of the Windows operating system. I think it is worth providing a short summary in this final section.

Before I get to that, though, notice that the VCL uses a new special support function, CheckWin32Version, that returns True if the version of the operating system is equal to or greater than the version passed as parameter (using one or two Integers for the major version, and optionally the minor one). This function was already in Delphi 2007, but I had missed it in my book (and didn't see it used too often in the VCL source code).

As an example, look at the following snippet, which I added to the UniClipboard program (even if it is totally unrelated):

```
if CheckWin32Version(6) then
  ShowMessage ('Running on Windows Vista or later');
if CheckWin32Version(5) then
  ShowMessage ('Running on Windows 2000 or later');
```

In Delphi 2007 the VCL introduced Vista support, provided task dialogs (with redirection of standard messages and the TaskDialog component), the GlassFrame property, enhanced common dialogs (again with new components and a partial redirection of the existing ones), improvements in themes support in the management of the minimized main form, with the MainFormOnTaskbar property of the Application global object.

On top of these features, that already make programs integrate smoothly with the latest version of the Windows operating system, Delphi 2009 includes the following Vista-specific features:

- The GlowSize property of the Label component.
- The elevation, command link, and drop down menu support for the Button control.
- Smooth reverse support for the ProgressBar control.
- Text hints for the ComboBox component.
- Some extended grouping features of the ListView control.
- Themed hint windows.

Finally a helpful feature for Vista support is the new `Application` global object setting for the default font to be used by each form of an application. This is significant as Vista has a new default font (*Segoe UI*), compared to Windows XP (and earlier versions).

What's Next

In this section I've explored countless improvements to classic VCL controls in Delphi 2009, partially related with new features provided by the operating system. I also shown an example of one brand new component, the CategoryPanelGroup.

This is not the only new visual component of the VCL, quite the contrary. A notable extension to the native set of VCL controls in Delphi 2009 is the support for the Ribbon user interface. This topic is so significant that I've decided to devote a specific chapter to it, rather than covering it in this all-encompassing VCL updates chapter.

Before we get to the Ribbon control, though, there is another area of the VCL that was significantly modified in Delphi 2009: COM support. As we'll see in the next chapter, there is the introduction of an interface definition language (RIDL), a different role for type library files, a new IDE pane, and updated Wizards. For those who use COM in their architecture, this is positive news.

Chapter 9: COM Support In Delphi 2009

For many years the Component Object Model (COM) technology has been at the foundation of the Windows operating system, both as a way to let applications talk with the OS and to let programs talk to each other. COM is the only object model for Windows that works across languages in a native way. The fact that COM programming was far from easy and that it provided a not-so-robust foundation, was one of the reasons Microsoft mentioned for abandoning it and moving to a managed object model like the one in the Microsoft .NET Framework.

Despite Microsoft calling COM obsolete when .NET was announced, the COM technology is still heavily in use in many Windows applications and is far from dead. COM also provides an easy way to let Win32 applications work alongside .NET ones. In any case, I don't want to delve into a history of COM here or a comparison with .NET. I just want to focus on the fact that even if not growing and not used any more for communication among different computers, COM is still at the heart of many Windows programs. Moreover, Delphi traditionally made it very easy to write COM servers and use existing ones, so many Delphi developers rely on this technology.

Given this introduction, it is relevant to notice that there are significant changes in the COM support provided by Delphi 2009. In particular, the role of type libraries has been significantly downplayed and there is a new type of source code file, Restricted IDL files, that assume a central role for COM development in this version of Delphi.

IDL, Type Libraries, and RIDL

Originally the definition of COM objects was based on an Interface Definition Language (IDL) specified by Microsoft (and not too different from the one in use for CORBA at the time). With the advent of Visual Basic, though, Microsoft need a simpler, higher level, visually-oriented format, so they started using type libraries, a binary resource format compiled into servers you could query to ask for the classes exposed by the server and their methods. Type libraries became a *de-facto* standard, even if their format was never specified in detail. Delphi started relying on type libraries from the early days, both for importing the specification of a server that has a type library and for creating a server. In a server, type libraries are used at runtime to initialize internal registries by the VCL architecture[128].

In Delphi 2009 type libraries have been downplayed, although they are still part of the architecture. When creating a new COM server, you still use the type library editor but end up creating a Restricted IDL (RIDL) source code file. The RIDL file is used both for generating the type library (something you can do manually by invoking the new GenTLB.exe utility; available in the Delphi bin folder) and for generating the corresponding Delphi language interfaces (still stored in a <projectname>_TLB.pas file). When opening

---

128 The part of the VCL that focuses on COM development was originally called the DAX framework, for Direct ActiveX framework. Now this term is seldom used, although internal references to it remain.

an existing project or creating a client that refers to an existing type library, the RIDL is created from the type library (which could be achieved manually using the new -I flag of the `tlibimp.exe` utility).

A Textual RIDL

Again, the RIDL is the base format used as a starting point for Delphi code generation of COM interfaces (both on the client and on the server side).

One of the big advantages of this format, beside avoiding a bug that would occasionally trash the binary TLB file irrevocably, is that using a text file makes it much easier to use a RIDL file with version control, compare different versions, and (a possible extension) support large multi-user projects with multiple partial RIDL files.

The RIDL, like the full blown IDL, uses a syntax vaguely resembling the C++ language syntax and many decorators. For example, an interface with a single method could be described as[129]:

```
interface INumberProp: IUnknown
{
   HRESULT _stdcall Increase(void);
};
```

In C++ the colon after a class introduces a list of base classes, meaning that `INumberProp` inherits from `IUnknown`. The content of the class is within braces (or curly brackets). Each method has the return value, followed by optional modifiers (including the calling convention), the name, and the parameters, if any (`void` means no parameter).

As mentioned, each symbol is generally prefixed by some attributes, including the interface ID (IID), a version number, a description, and other flags:

```
[
   uuid(4D24B32A-DE61-4EBE-AE53-6DF2D3DC80DA),
   version(1.0),
   helpstring("Interface for NumberProp Object"),
]
interface INumberProp: IUnknown
{
   ...
}
```

---

[129] The complete source code from which I took these code snippets is in the next section, "The RIDL Format".

For a more detailed description of the COM IDL you can refer to Microsoft's own documentation. You can find the syntax specification of RIDL files (well hidden) in the Delphi help at:

```
ms-help://embarcadero.rs2009/devwin32/
   wtlusingobjectpascaloridlsyntax_xml.html
```

(Notice that the help page title refers to the previous version of Delphi, as now the Type Library editor uses RIDL syntax exclusively.)

The RIDL Format (COM Servers)

To see what this new RIDL format is all about, let's convert an existing COM project by opening it in Delphi 2009. As an example, I've taken the SimpleServer COM example of Mastering Delphi 2005 and converted it to Delphi 2009. Beside the standard project file format conversion, Delphi warned me of the type library migration:

```
Converting '...\08\SimpleServer\SimpleServer.tlb'
    to .ridl format
  Reading  'SimpleServer.tlb'
  Writing  'SimpleServer.ridl'
  Adding   'SimpleServer.ridl'
  Removing 'SimpleServer.tlb'
```

If we look at the project files in the Project Manager, we can see the new RIDL file:

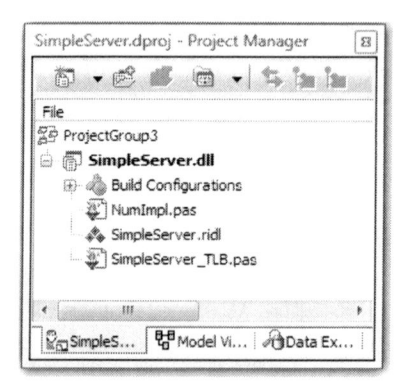

If we look to the project file source code, instead, we can still see the classic reference to the TLB resource file. The type library, in fact, is still included in the executable, after it is compiled from the RIDL file.

How the TLB gets converted and how the RIDL file is generated mostly depends on some Tools Options for the type library. These options are quite different than in the past. In particular, as this is an *in-process* server, to keep the code compatible (and easier from the Delphi perspective) we need to enable `safecall`[130] mapping for any COM interface, using the Environment Options settings below:

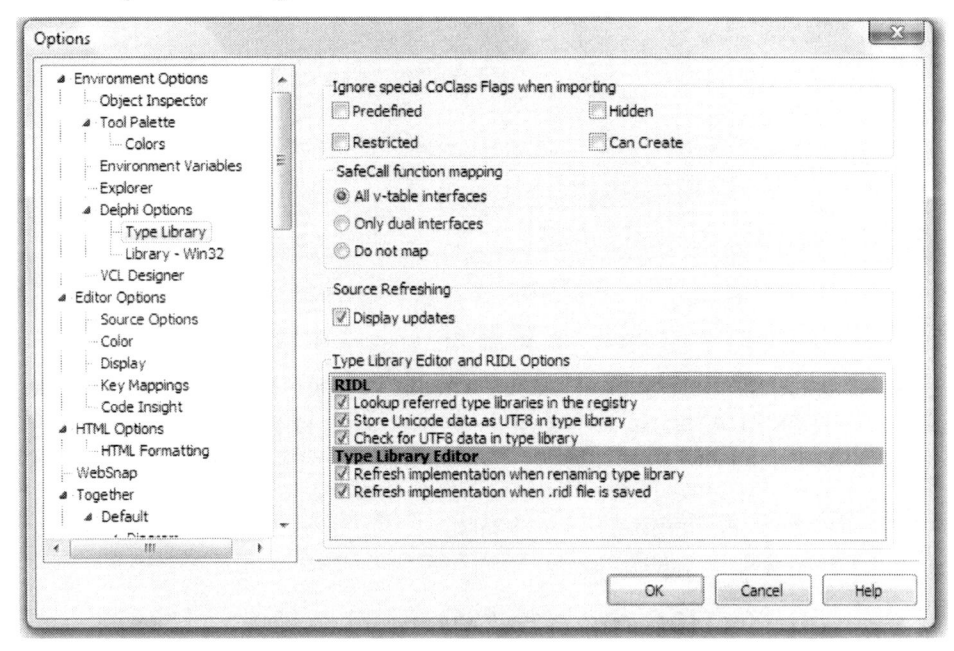

As the default is to have `safecall` mappings only for dual interfaces, you'll generally have to change these settings, and need to do so before opening the project (or reopen the project after changing the settings, as the Delphi

---

[130] Using the `safecall` convention all COM calls are mapped, so the error checking done in terms of HRESULT in the system are remapped to exceptions on the Delphi side. Basically each function or procedure becomes a function with an HRESULT return value, as requested by COM dual interfaces, and an extra out parameter is possibly added for the actual return value. On the server side Delphi wraps the code in a try except block which will eventually trap an exception and return an error code. On the client side, an error code in a call will force Delphi to raise the corresponding exception.

288 - Chapter 9: COM Support in Delphi 2009

IDE will suggest to you, but beware you might have to open the type library editor a couple of times before the code is generated the way you asked).

If you can reopen the type library in the IDE, you'll see a type library editor very similar to the past:

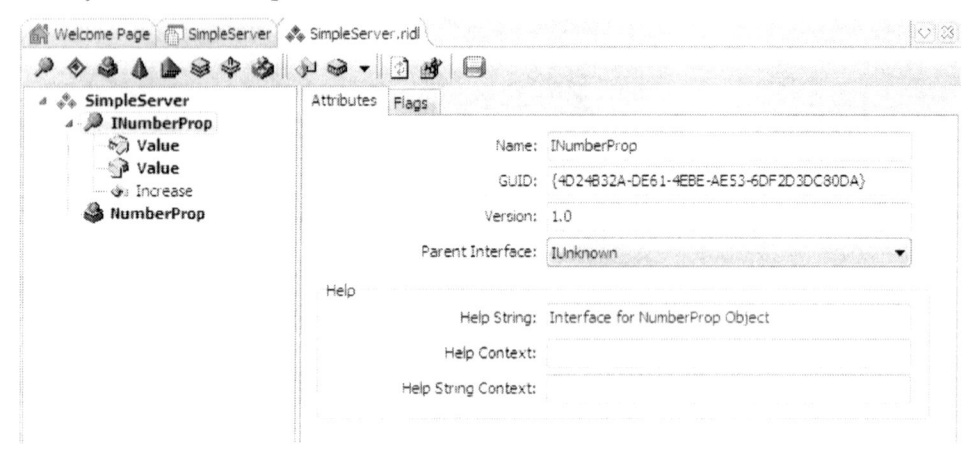

Refresh the type library editor implementation (using the Refresh button of the toolbar of this pane) to generate or update the RIDL file.

For the SimpleServer example, which I've upgraded from an older version of Delphi, I got the following RIDL code, which imports a standard Delphi type library, defines the `INumberProp` interface, with a property and a method, and defines the `NumberProp` *coclass* (construction class) for the server object implementing the interface:

```
library SimpleServer
{
  importlib("stdole2.tlb");
  [
    uuid(4D24B32A-DE61-4EBE-AE53-6DF2D3DC80DA),
    version(1.0),
    helpstring("Interface for NumberProp Object"),
    oleautomation
  ]
  interface INumberProp: IUnknown
  {
    [propget, id(0x00000065)]
    HRESULT _stdcall Value([out, retval] long* New);
    [propput, id(0x00000065)]
    HRESULT _stdcall Value([in] long New);
    [id(0x00000066)]
    HRESULT _stdcall Increase(void);
  };
```

Marco Cantù, Delphi 2009 Handbook

```
    [
      uuid(BDC9A273-A973-4DB4-ADE7-8F0A49004D29),
      version(1.0),
      helpstring("NumberProp")
    ]
    coclass NumberProp
    {
      [default] interface INumberProp;
    };
};
```

This interface is independent from the `safecall` mapping decisions, which are reflected only in the corresponding Delphi code. You can see a first interface, based on `IUnknown`, with a `Value` property defined by a getter and a setter and an `Increase` method. In terms of the corresponding Delphi interface, the code is generated as follows (and remains very similar to the past) and placed in a `SimpleServer_TLB.pas` unit:

```
type
  INumberProp = interface(IUnknown)
    ['{4D24B32A-DE61-4EBE-AE53-6DF2D3DC80DA}']
    function Get_Value: Integer; safecall;
    procedure Set_Value(New: Integer); safecall;
    procedure Increase; safecall;
    property Value: Integer
      read Get_Value write Set_Value;
  end;

  CoNumberProp = class
    class function Create: INumberProp;
    class function CreateRemote(
      const MachineName: string): INumberProp;
  end;
```

Having forced the generation of `safecall` mappings, I didn't have to touch the original source code of the implementation class:

```
type
  TNumberProp = class(TTypedComObject, INumberProp)
  private
    fValue: Integer;
  protected
    procedure Increase; safecall;
    function Get_Value: Integer; safecall;
    procedure Set_Value(New: Integer); safecall;
  public
    procedure Initialize; override;
    destructor Destroy; override;
  end;
```

290 - Chapter 9: COM Support in Delphi 2009

When everything works fine, porting existing code will be smooth. What might happen, though, is that if you set up the wrong calling convention (or the IDE picks the wrong calling convention despite your settings), you'll see both the interface and the implementation class having extra methods with the `stdcall` convention and the HRESULT return value directly visible. If this happens, the extra methods are added to the class, aliased as the class already has similarly names methods, and this can really mess up the code, preventing it from compiling and making it far from trivial to restore it (unless, of course, you got back to the previous version in the file history or simply avoid saving the modified file).

Registering and Calling the Server

Now that I have recompiled the server, I can register it in the system to be able to call it (and also use the new Registered Type Libraries pane of the Delphi IDE). After compiling, you can use the menu command Run | Register ActiveX Server. The first time I did it, it raised the following so-terribly-descriptive error: Unspecified Error. It turns out, if you are running the IDE on Vista with User Account Control (UAC) active, you cannot perform this step as the IDE will not try to elevate the user operation. By running the IDE as administrator, the registration succeeds. Here are the two messages:

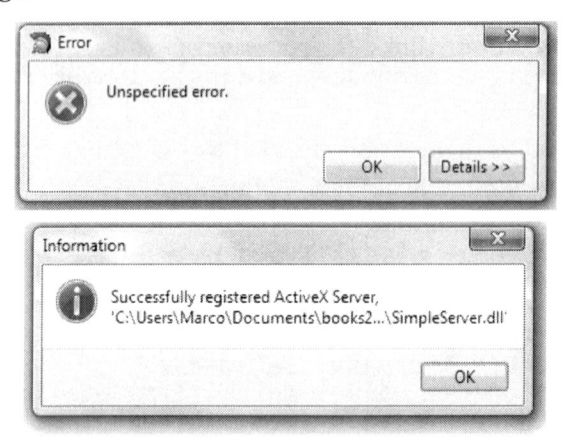

The New Registered Type Libraries Pane

Once the server is registered you can double check it is in the system by opening the new Registered Type Libraries view of the Delphi IDE, using the corresponding command located under the View menu.

This editor pane lists all registered type libraries (or ActiveX controls) on the system, let's you unregister any of them, register new ones, search the list of type libraries. As you can see below, the list should include our newly registered library:

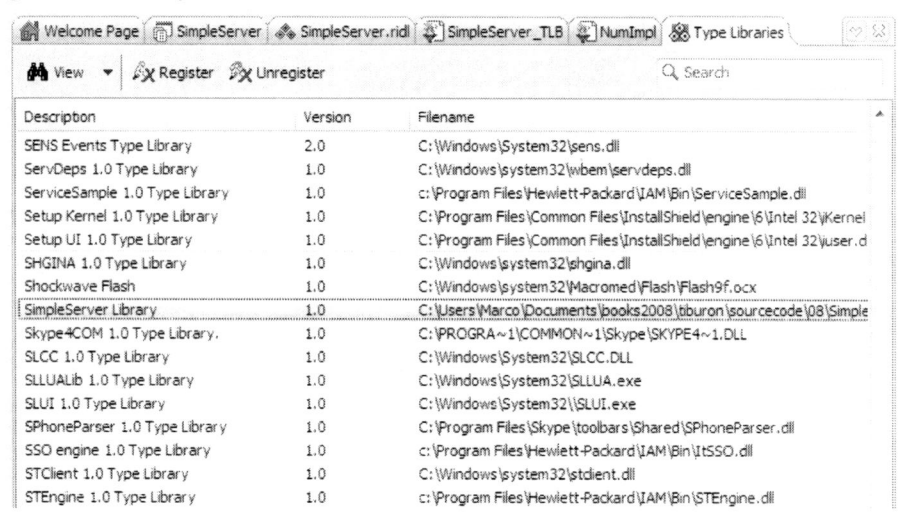

Notice you cannot use this dialog to import a type library or create a client wrapper for it. For this purpose you need to use the revamped type library importer. Select the Component | Import Component menu item, and pick the Type Library option, as shown in the next page:

292 - Chapter 9: COM Support in Delphi 2009

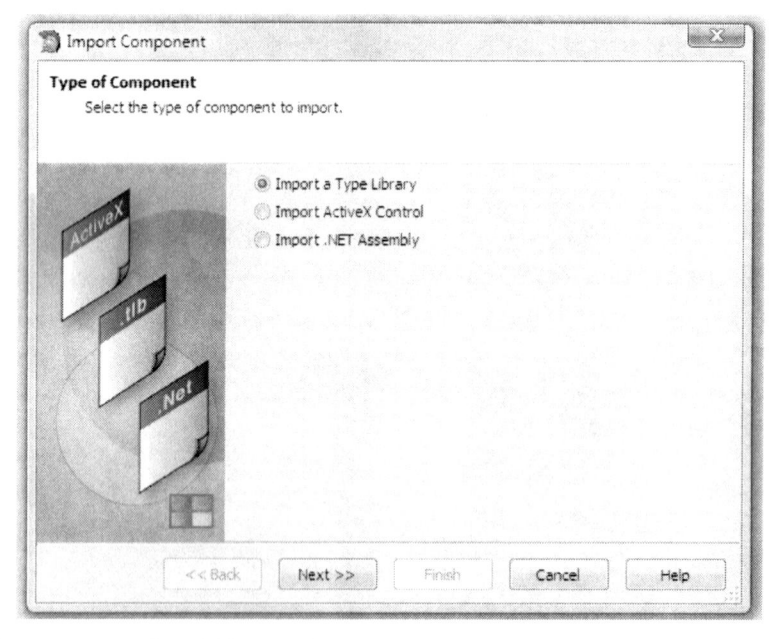

The next step should be to choose one of the registered types libraries or add a new one. As the list is generally very long, the new search box will come quite handy to find the specific type library you are looking for, in this case one of those with the word "simple" in them:

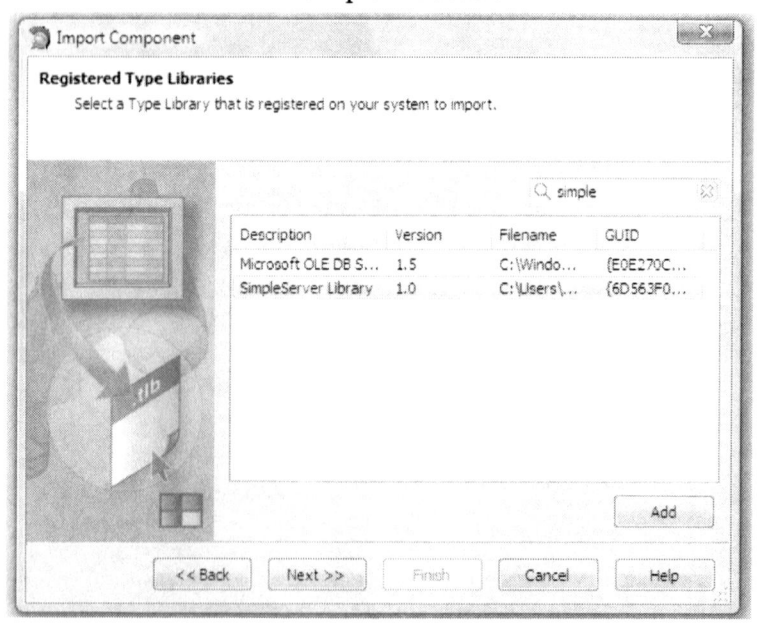

The following step lets you add the component to a package, generate an import unit, or add it directly to the current project. In any case, you'll end up with a type library import file almost identical to the one generated on the server side by the type library editor (or, to be more precise, by processing the RIDL file).

I've performed the steps above in the SimpleClient project, which is the new edition of another project that was part of Mastering Delphi 2005 and previous volumes of the series. The program creates two COM objects from the server at start up, hooks them to buttons and spin edits, and has a third button for dynamically creating a temporary object. (One of the goals of the original project was to showcase COM objects lifetime, which is why whenever an object is destroyed the server will display a message box).

This is the do-it-all code snippet, which used the generated *CoClass*:

```
var
  Num3: INumberProp;
begin
  // create a new temporary COM object
  Num3 := CoNumberProp.Create;
  Num3.Value := 100;
  Num3.Increase;
  ShowMessage ('Num3: ' + IntToStr (Num3.Value));
end;
```

Again, there is very little (if anything) you have to do on the client side of a COM application to move it to Delphi 2009. However, if you are creating a new client project, as I did, you'll probably like the improvements in the type library import wizard.

COM and Unicode

One of the reasons changes in COM support and COM clients in particular, are limited is due to the fact that COM applications generally don't use plain Delphi strings but rely on the native and COM-enabled WideString type (or BSTR in COM terms). As we saw in Part I of the book, the WideString type already used two-bytes per characters and did not change since Delphi 2007. The reason this less-efficient string type is still round is for COM and Automation support, so it should come at no surprise I'm talking about it in the section focused on COM.

294 - Chapter 9: COM Support in Delphi 2009

In slightly more technical terms, one of the advantages of the WideString type is that you can use it in a remote server call as its data can be *marshalled* to a COM Automation server. This won't be the case for UnicodeString, a data type which makes sense only in Delphi and not in other languages (with the notable exception of C++Builder 2009, of course).

Returning Features: Active Forms

Some other features from the Delphi 7 times got back into Delphi 2009 after a long absence. One of them is the ActiveX Control Wizard (including Active Forms). Notice, though, that this wizard doesn't generate the proper HTML deployment files as it did in the past. Actually most of the COM-related wizards have been improved graphically (and partially in their feature set) for Delphi 2009, as you can see in the overview provided by Chris Bensen in his *sneak peek* blog post at:

```
http://chrisbensen.blogspot.com/2008/07/
    tiburn-sneak-peek-com-wizards.html
```

As an example I've created a new ActiveX library, and added to it an Active Form (picking the icon of the ActiveX page of the New Items dialog box):

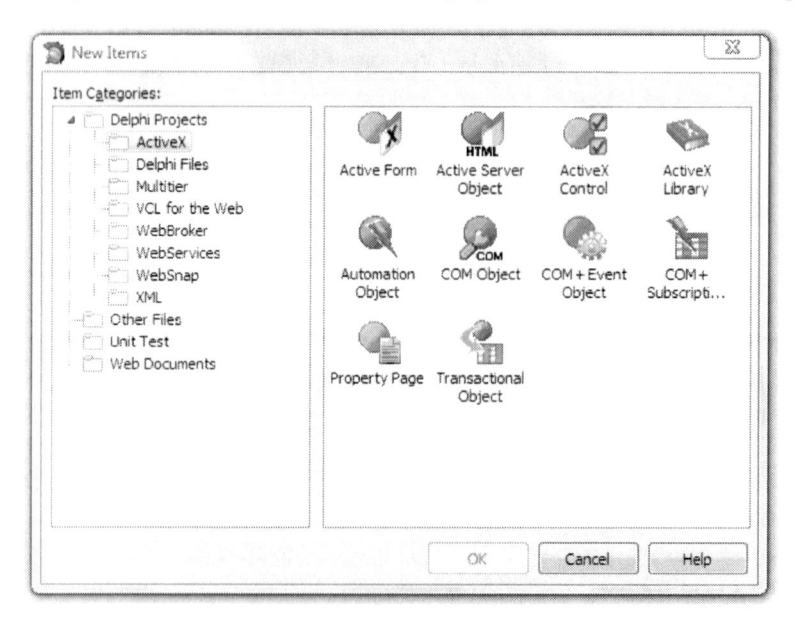

I've then added a standard About box, generated the Active Form, saved everything, and added a button to the Active Form button that displays some versions of the "What is Unicode?" sentence in different languages and alphabets in a Memo control.

Now I can compile and register the ActiveX Library, but how do I get the form to display in Internet Explorer? I opened up a very old Active Form project (a Delphi 5 project, to be precise), grabbed the HTML Delphi generated for it, and replaced the GUID in it with the CoClass GUID and the ActiveX library name with the current one:

```
<html>
  ...
  <object
    classid="clsid:AE64FD40-25C5-4697-B19C-8CE781695B71"
    codebase="./MyActiveForm_Project.ocx"
    width=570
    height=328
    align=center
  >
  </object>
</html>
```

At this point I can open the HTML file (in the same folder as the OCX library) with Internet Explorer, pass a couple of security warnings like:

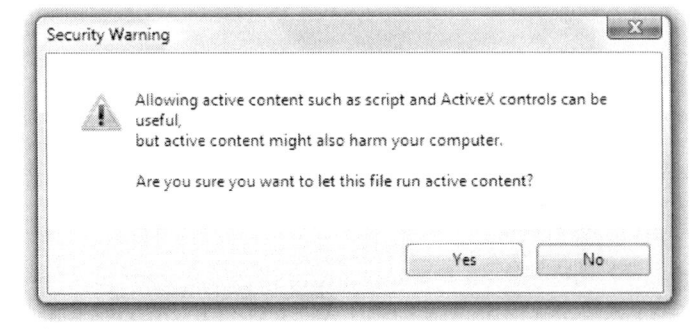

and continue to the HTML page embedding the ActiveX form:

Delphi 2009 ActiveForm Test Page

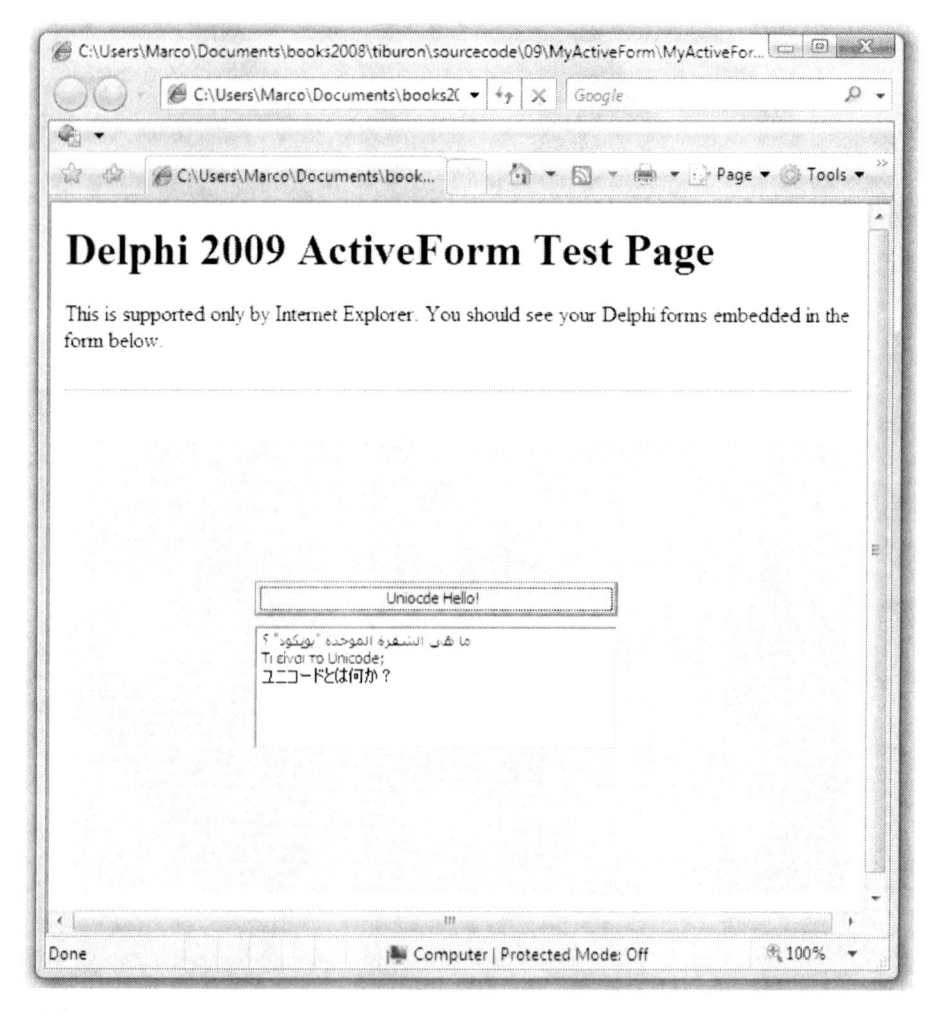

This is supported only by Internet Explorer. You should see your Delphi forms embedded in the form below.

Building an ActiveForm in Delphi 2009 is an interesting exercise to bring back memories of a time Microsoft was trying to impose a proprietary and Windows only model to the web, a tentative initiative that utterly failed. But does it make any technical sense to use it now? As much as I disliked the unsafe ActiveX technology back them, and with all of the extra power (including more open client technologies) you have now at the browser level, I'd generally say no.

Still, there are specific in-house situations for which a simplified deployment would make things easier... or some not-so-smart customers for which a web application is good as it runs in the browser. In these niche situations, if you already have an investment in this technology, it might make sense to go for it... but the sooner you can move away from a vision of a Win32-only, Internet Explorer-only Internet, the better.

What's Next

In this short chapter I've explored some of the most significant changes to COM support in Delphi 2009, including the new RIDL files, the different role of type libraries, and some of the updated Wizards and IDE tools. I didn't have room to describe the COM technology in any detail, as this used to take two large chapters in my Mastering Delphi series.

Now that we've seen all the changes to the core VCL and its COM subsystem, it is time to focus on the single most interesting visual feature of the VCL in Delphi 2009, the brand new Ribbon control.

Chapter 10: The Ribbon

In the early 80s, along with the initial advent of the PC revolution, IBM decided to try standardizing rules for the user interface of (at the time DOS-based) PC applications. This specification was called Common User Access (CUA) and Microsoft championed it for many years in DOS programs and in all early versions of Windows, to the point that it has become a natural way of interacting with most programs. You know that the Copy and Paste commands will be under an Edit menu and you have to look under File for saving or loading a document, so there is one less thing you have to learn for every new program.

Even if there were many additions to CUA, including toolbars, shortcut menus, command bars, and more, its core structure held for about 20 years. Microsoft broke away from this rule for the first time in Office 2007 (and partially in Windows Vista) with the definition of a new user interface paradigm, called Fluent User Interface. This interface is generally known as the Ribbon Interface from its core visual element.

Marco Cantù, Delphi 2009 Handbook

300 - Chapter 10: The Ribbon

I don't want to delve into the debate here as to whether this was really a good move or not (I do have a few doubts), but only focus on the fact that this user interface and its set of stringent rules is not trivial to implement without some ready-to-use visual components. Delphi 2009 has such a set of visual controls, which are the subject of the current chapter. They were developed for CodeGear by Jeremy North[131].

Introducing the Fluent User Interface

As mentioned above, the Fluent User Interface was invented by Microsoft, who are seeking a patent for it[132]. This patent doesn't focus on the code behind the user interface (the ribbon controls used in Office 2007), but on the design of the user interface itself. Microsoft also refers to this user interface as "Microsoft for the Office UI."

This means that the Microsoft patent, if granted, will still apply even if the VCL implementation available in Delphi 2009 is a brand new version of the controls (in no way related with the code that Microsoft uses in Office and other applications, and that Microsoft doesn't license). That's why we have to look at the "legal side" of this component before looking at its use.

Notice that unlike other guidelines, the Office Fluent UI Design Guidelines, describing how applications based on the Ribbon should work, are not public, but are "Microsoft's confidential information".

---

[131] Jeremy North is the author of several Delphi components, IDE extensions, and tools for developers (including the extended Quality Central client). He did also a lot of work to help with the development of Compact Framework programs written in Delphi for .NET. You can find more about Jeremy at his site, http://www.jed-software.com.

[132] Information about this patent request and the related discussion can be found on Wikipedia at: http://en.wikipedia.org/wiki/Ribbon_(computing).

The Legal Side of the Ribbon

When you install Delphi 2009, you'll be presented with a rather strange looking dialog (which was required by Microsoft):

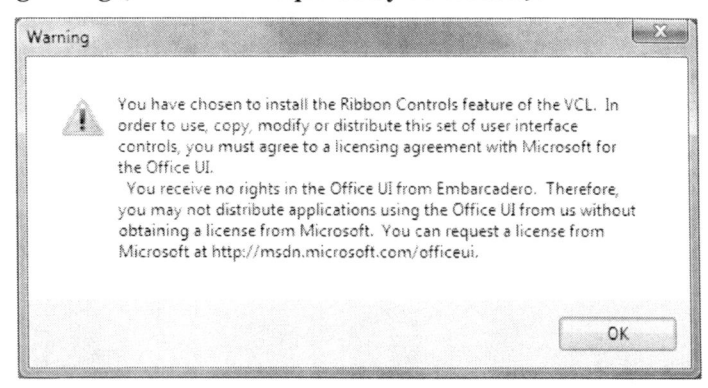

As you can see, Microsoft asks anyone that wants to use their Fluent User to accept the terms of their Office UI license. This license is royalty free, but there are guidelines and limitations related with what you can do. The most significant issue is that you are not allowed to create programs which compete directly with Microsoft Office. There are also UI guidelines you have to follow, as you cannot adapt the Ribbon UI to your desire, but have to make it work in a way that is consistent with Microsoft's own approach. For fuller information, refer to the web site mentioned in the dialog box displayed earlier and to registration site:

```
http://msdn.microsoft.com/officeui
http://msdn.microsoft.com/en-us/office/aa973809.aspx
```

Once you agree with the license and register your application you'll be able to download the 119 page PDF with the Office UI design guidelines.

A First Simple Ribbon

My first Ribbon example is a very bare-bones demo showing how the component works, but actually providing no real user interface. As we'll see in the next section, the only real way to create a complete Ribbon-based user interface is to use the Action Manager architecture along with it. It is possible to use the Ribbon component without Actions, but it is very clumsy and extremely limited... so after a simple example I'll move in that direction.

We can, in fact, start some initial experiments with a plain Ribbon component, creating tabs and groups, and placing a couple of standard components into them. To follow my steps, simply create a new application and place a Ribbon component on its main form. Once you have that component in place you can use its shortcut menu (selecting it in the form or in the Structure pane) to add a new tab. The same menu will let you remove a tab or add the Application menu and Quick Access toolbar, as we'll see later on. You can also work on the Ribbon Tabs by using the `Tabs` collection of the Ribbon component (technically a collection of `TRibbonTabItem` objects, each of which is connected with a `TRibbonPage`, a sort of panel) and the related AddItem command. This is available in the Structure view:

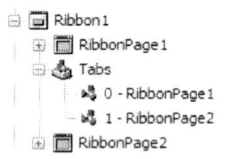

The header of a Ribbon with two tabs and pages looks like this at design time in the Delphi 2009 IDE:

In this case I've kept on the (default) `ShowHelpButton` property that shows the question mark in the top right of the control, I've also kept on the `UseCustomFrame` property (something I'll cover later on).

Here are a few other properties of the Ribbon control of the BareBoneRibbon example:

```
object Ribbon1: TRibbon
  Caption = 'Ribbon Caption'
  DocumentName = 'Document Name'
  Tabs = <
    item
      Caption = 'RibbonPage1'
      Page = RibbonPage1
    end
    item
      Caption = 'RibbonPage2'
      Page = RibbonPage2
    end>
  StyleName = 'Ribbon - Luna'
```

```
    object RibbonPage1...
    object RibbonPage2...
end
```

Once you have one or more Ribbon tabs, you can add Ribbon groups (or boxes) to them. Again, you can work with the shortcut menus of the components right in the form or in the Structure pane. Here is how a Ribbon page with a few (empty) groups can look:

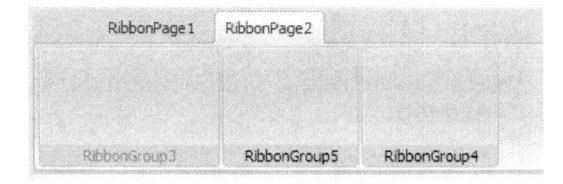

On a Ribbon page, you can add a group, remove a group, or reorder groups, through a simple specific dialog box (which tends to be easier to use, rather than dragging groups around the Ribbon page, hoping they'll stick in place).

What can you place in a group? You generally populate them with elements of various types, from commands to options, that are connected with Actions of an ActionManager component. If you want to hack something together, most certainly diverging from the Ribbon UI specification, you can add plain buttons or special purpose RibbonSpinEdit controls to the groups, as I've done in this demo. Again, this is not the recommended approach, although the RibbonSpinEdit control itself does fit within the Ribbon UI specification.

You can see the first two populated pages of my demo at runtime in the screen shot below:

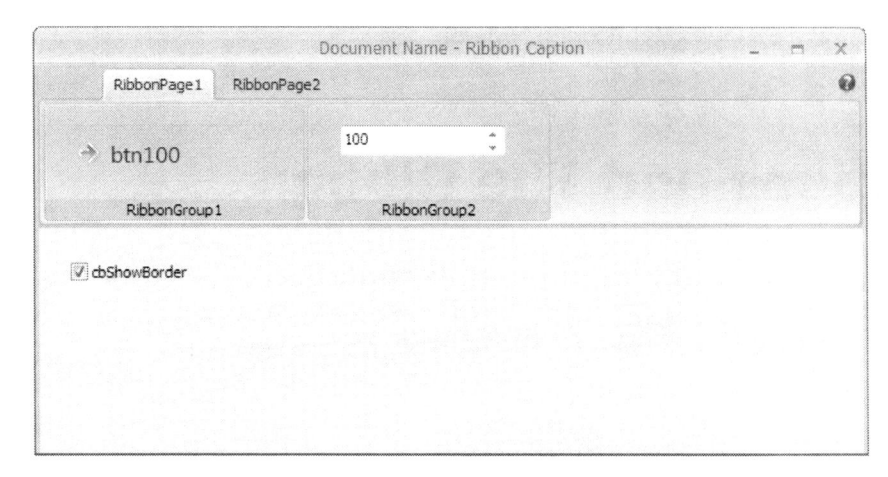

304 - Chapter 10: The Ribbon

This form is different from the usual one, because its caption and standard borders have been replaced by a special custom frame, painted by the Ribbon control itself. This is the default style for the Ribbon UI, with further graphical elements (like the Application menu) added, as we'll see later.

You can indeed disable the `UseCustomFrame` property. I've done that at runtime, when a user unchecks the check box, with this code:

```
procedure TFormBareBoneRibbon.cbShowBorderClick(
  Sender: TObject);
begin
  Ribbon1.UseCustomFrame := cbShowBorder.Checked;
  self.RecreateWnd;
end;
```

Although this works when removing the custom frame, if you re-enable it the forms border won't be repainted properly[133]. I guess it currently makes sense to trigger this property at design time or when the form is created.

Another important setting to keep in mind is that if Ribbon control is reduced below the size of 300x250, it will be displayed in a minimized state (again, according to the Ribbon UI specification). If you want to avoid this, as some users might get confused, you can indicate minimum width and height settings for the form:

```
object FormBareBoneRibbon: TFormBareBoneRibbon
  Caption = 'BareBoneRibbon'
  Constraints.MinHeight = 270
  Constraints.MinWidth = 320
  ...
```

The size is computed by adding some extra space for the borders to the minimum Ribbon size. This is something you have to remember doing in each form that uses the Ribbon control.

Actions and The Ribbon

As I mentioned a few times already, the Ribbon control is based on Delphi's ActionManager architecture. We'll see how to create a Ribbon-based UI with these components in the next example. Before I get to that, however, I need

---

[133] This is a bug that will be fixed. As a workaround you can use the code provided in the bug report at http://qc.codegear.com/wc/qcmain.aspx?d=68955.

to recap the key features of this architecture for those who've never used it[134]. If you used the ActionManager component in the past, you can skip the next two sections and jump to "Actions and Ribbon in Practice."

From Events to Actions

Delphi's event handling architecture is very open: You can write a single event handler and connect it to the OnClick events of a toolbar button and a menu. You can also connect the same event handler to different buttons or menu items, because the event handler can use the Sender parameter to refer to the object that fired the event. It's a little more difficult to synchronize the status of toolbar buttons and menu items. If you have a menu item and a toolbar button that both toggle the same option, then every time the option is toggled, you must both add the check mark to the menu item and change the status of the button to show it pressed.

To overcome this and similar problems, Delphi includes an event-handling architecture based on actions. An *action* (or command) plays two separate roles at the same time:

- It indicates the operation to accomplish when user interface elements (menu item, button) connected to the action are activated, with its OnExecute event handler.
- It determines the status of the user interface elements (or clients) connected to the action, including their textual description, enable status, check status, and so on.

The connection of the action with the user interface of the linked controls is very important and should not be underestimated, because it is where you can get the real advantages of this architecture.

In practice, an action object has properties that will be applied to the linked controls (called *action clients*). These properties include, among others, the Caption, the graphical representation (ImageIndex), the status (Checked, Enabled, and Visible), and user feedback (Hint and HelpContext).

---

[134] This introduction to actions and the ActionList and ActionManager components has been extracted from my book "Mastering Delphi 7" and edited somewhat. The original version has also a few specific examples to explain the concepts I've omitted in this summary.

Marco Cantù, Delphi 2009 Handbook

The base class for all action objects is `TBasicAction`, which introduces the abstract core behavior of an action, without any specific binding or connection (not even to menu items or controls). The derived `TContainedAction` class introduces properties and methods that enable actions to appear in an action list or action manager. The further derived `TCustomAction` class introduces support for the properties and methods of menu items and controls that are linked to action objects. Finally, there is the derived ready-to-use `TAction` class.

Each action object is connected to one or more client objects through an ActionLink object. Multiple controls, possibly of different types, can share the same action object, as indicated by their `Action` property. Technically, the internal ActionLink objects maintain a bidirectional connection between the client object and the action.

The client controls connected to actions are usually menu items and various types of buttons (buttons, check boxes, radio buttons, speed buttons, toolbar buttons, and the like). Remember that you should not set the properties of the client controls you connect with an action, because the action will override the property values of the client controls. For this reason, you should generally write the actions first and then create the menu items and buttons you want to connect with them. When you are using the Ribbon control, that's the only way to proceed, so there is no alternative to the best practice.

The ActionList and ActionManager Components

Action objects exists in memory but are not VCL components. In fact, they are managed by container components, called ActionList and ActionManager. The former is an older and simpler actions container, the latter introduced user interface integration and generation, which are being extended. The ActionList component has a special component editor you can use to create several actions (including many predefined actions) and manage them. Actions are grouped in textual categories:

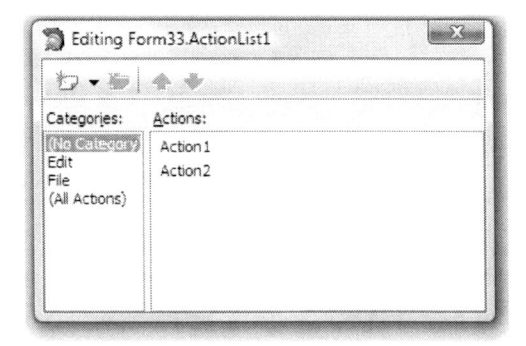

The ActionManager component, originally introduced in Delphi 6, has further options to let you create and manage an user interface for the actions. Beside the collection of actions, the ActionManager has a collection of toolbars and menus tied to them. The development of these toolbars and menus is completely visual: You drag actions from a special component editor of the ActionManager to the toolbars to access the buttons you need. Notice that working with the Ribbon is somewhat similar; you can drag actions to Ribbon groups to have ready-to-use Ribbon command buttons.

Components of this architecture include, beside the ActionManager component itself, an ActionMainMenuBar control, an ActionToolBar control, a PopupActionBarEx component, and a CustomizeDlg component used to let end users customize the user interface. These visual components are not used when you work with a Ribbon, so I don't want to cover them in detail. Instead, let me build a step by step example using the ActionManager and a Ribbon control.

Actions and Ribbon in Practice

After this fast-paced introduction to Delphi's Action Manager architecture, let's start creating an actual demo. The first step, of course is to create a VCL application and add an ActionManager component to its main form. Next you can drop a Ribbon control onto the form. The control should automatically hook itself to the action manager, if not use its `ActionManager` property.

Before adding any action to the ActionManager, add ImageList controls and connect them to it. Adding standard actions, in fact, will automatically populate the image lists. Add one ImageList for the standard `Images` of the

ActionManager (standard images are used for the Ribbon commands) and one for the `LargeImages` property (used by the Ribbon application menu and by large buttons in any Ribbon Group). You should have settings like:

```
object RibbonEditorForm: TRibbonEditorForm
  Caption = 'RibbonEditor'
  Constraints.MinHeight = 300
  Constraints.MinWidth = 400
  object Ribbon1: TRibbon
    ActionManager = ActionManager1
    Caption = 'RibbonEditor'
    StyleName = 'Ribbon - Luna'
  end
  object ActionManager1: TActionManager
    LargeImages = listLarge
    Images = listStandard
    StyleName = 'Ribbon - Luna'
  end
  object listStandard: TImageList...
  object listLarge: TImageList...
end
```

As my goal is to create a simple editor (not a full word processor as I don't mean to infringe the Ribbon license, you know), I basically need to place a RichEdit control aligned to the client area of the form and add most of the standard actions for editing (the 6 standard actions of the Edit category), rich edit support (the 8 standard actions of the Format category), file support (the 8 standard actions of the File category), and a few more (Download action of the Internet category and Font action of the Dialogs category).

Groups And Commands

Now that I have all of these actions in place, I can create a Ribbon user interface for them. After creating two tabs and a few groups, I can drag actions into the groups. Here are a couple of groups:

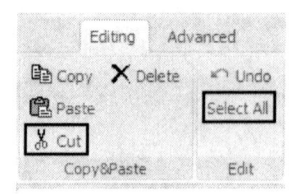

These groups host direct commands, so there is nothing specific to set. Another group has a set of non-exclusive options, like setting the text in bold and italic. For the action items of such a group it is better to pick the `csCheckBox` value for the `CommandStyle` property (rather than the default `csButton`). The effect is to have a set of check boxes you can toggle by either selecting the check area or the icon and the text of the command. This is an example from the demo:

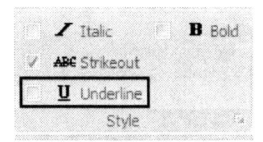

The only exception to dragging actions into groups is represented by the Font Dialog action, that I can hook as dialog action to one of the groups, using its the group `DialogAction` property. This adds a small graphical element in the bottom right corner of the group, as in the previous image.

Another option is to have alternative options, represented by radio buttons, setting the `CommandStyle` property to `csRadioButton`, with this visual effect:

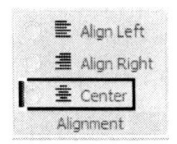

As you select one the items of a Ribbon group, you'll see the various properties for the corresponding `TActionClientItem` object. But how are these objects managed? It turns out that the ActionManager component will have a "toolbar" for each group of the Ribbon, as you can see in the ActionManager component editor.

Even better, you can see the actual internal structure of these objects using the Structure view and expanding the ActionManager component collection, not those of the Ribbon! Here is a small portion of it for the RibbonEditor demo (and the visual elements covered earlier):

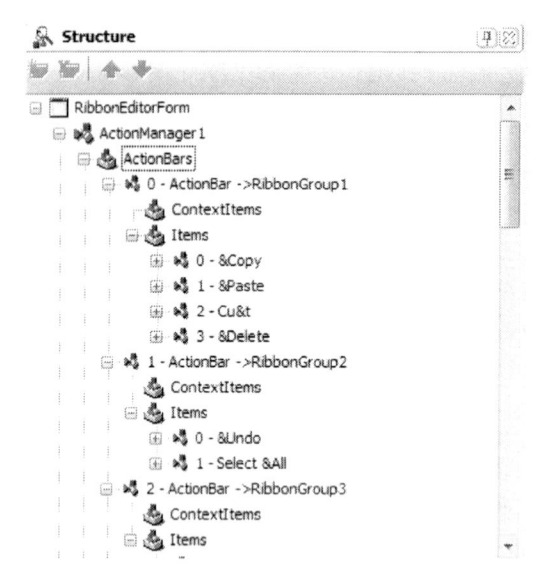

This means you can navigate among the elements in the various Ribbon groups in a less visual but more detailed way, selecting elements that are not visible, picking up small separators, and even adding new ActionClientItem objects. You will be able to configure these new ActionClientItem objects by defining text elements and separators, picking actions, or connecting them to visual controls.

Application Menu

To complete our application, for which we hooked several custom actions but had to write no actual code, we should add two other relevant elements of the Ribbon user interface. Both are added using commands of the Ribbon component editor (the shortcut menu that appears at design time when the component is selected) and can be added only if the `ActionManager` is set.

The first key element is the Application menu, the round control element in the top left corner of the Ribbon replacing the traditional Windows application menu. Here is the component at runtime in the demo:

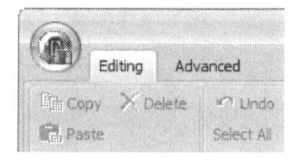

This element features a drop down menu that would be initially empty. The idea is to use it for file-related operations, and you can add the various standard File Open and Save actions to it. Again, it is possible to drag actions to this toolbar, but it is not easy, as it tends to close down. I find it easier to select it in the Structure view, add items, and hook each item to the corresponding action.

If the left of the Application menu is simply a list of file-oriented actions with large icons, the right side should host a list of recently used files. The Ribbon control has specific support for handling this "most recently used" (MRU) list[135]. In this simplified demo I've decided to handle only the Load and Save As operations. Each of them adds an entry to the MRU list by calling a custom method that, in turn, invokes the AddRecentItem method of the Ribbon control. This operation adds a new entry at the top of the Recent Documents list, eventually deleting an existing entry referring to the same file name.

The OnAccept events of the FileOpen1 and FileSaveAs1 actions have the following (similar) code, which calls the custom AddToMru method listed below them:

```
procedure TRibbonEditorForm.FileOpen1Accept(
  Sender: TObject);
begin
  RichEdit1.Lines.Clear;
  RichEdit1.Lines.LoadFromFile(FileOpen1.Dialog.FileName);
  Ribbon1.DocumentName := FileOpen1.Dialog.FileName;
  AddToMru(FileOpen1.Dialog.FileName);
end;

procedure TRibbonEditorForm.FileSaveAs1Accept(
  Sender: TObject);
begin
  RichEdit1.Lines.SaveToFile(FileSaveAs1.Dialog.FileName);
  Ribbon1.DocumentName := FileSaveAs1.Dialog.FileName;
  AddToMru(FileSaveAs1.Dialog.FileName);
end;

procedure TRibbonEditorForm.AddToMru(
```

---

135 In the source code of the demo you'll also find the code I wrote to manually manage the MRU list, using a common action and processing the caption on selection. Considering the good quality of the automatic support, I don't think it is worth exploring the manual approach. The reason I left it in the code is it shows how to dynamically extend the Ribbon user interface and use actions shared among different client elements.

312 - Chapter 10: The Ribbon

```
   const strFilename: string);
begin
  Ribbon1.AddRecentItem(strFilename);
end;
```

When one of the MRU list items is selected, the Ribbon control triggers an `OnRecentItemClick` event handler, which I've coded in a quite naïve way, as it doesn't check if the file is already active in the editor. Also, this information is not saved between sessions. All I wanted to show is how you can manually populate the most recently used list, obtaining an effect like:

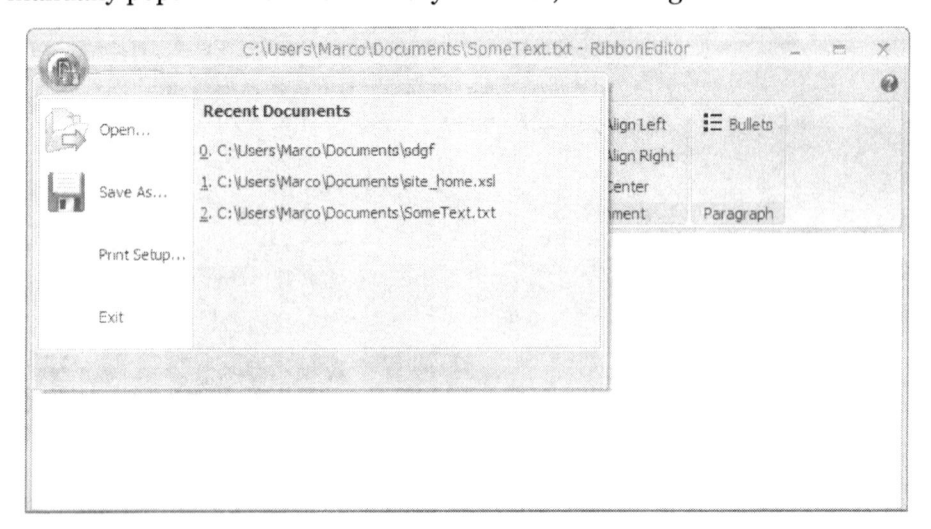

This is the event handler for the MRU list selection:

```
procedure TRibbonEditorForm.Ribbon1RecentItemClick(
  Sender: TObject; FileName: string; Index: Integer);
begin
  RichEdit1.Lines.Clear;
  RichEdit1.Lines.LoadFromFile(FileName);
  Ribbon1.DocumentName := FileName;
end;
```

The right page of the Application Menu can also be used to display buttons, by setting the `CommandType` property of the `ApplicationMenu` object of the Ribbon control to `ctCommands` (rather than the default `ctRecent`). In this case, any item added to the `RecentItems` collection will appear as a button. This is demonstrated by the Application Menu demo that ships with Delphi 2009, an interesting example as it works in a similar way to Office 2007.

Quick Access Toolbar

The second graphical element of the Ribbon is its Quick Access Toolbar, a toolbar with system operations automatically managed by the system. This is added to the right of the round Application menu selector, in this case showing a couple of actions (Save As and Exit):

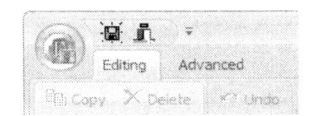

Next to the actions there is also the customize drop down button that lets a user add extra commands to this toolbar, something quite powerful but that you might want to disable[136].

With these steps I have build a very simple but somewhat complete Ribbon-based editor. If you look among the samples that ship with Delphi you'll find one with extra features and a nicer looking user interface, but no management of the most recently used files.

Supporting Key Tips

After all of these steps we have a fully working application with a nice Fluent UI. Users can click on the various visual elements (tab pages, controls) to work with it. But what about using the keyboard? Beside the fact you can still associate shortcut keys to the various actions (like a classic Ctrl-C for Copy), the Ribbon has its own keyboard-enabled interface.

All you have to do it to provide an appropriate value for the KeyTip property of each of the Ribbon user interface elements (tabs, groups, action items), and you'll be able to activate them using the Alt key. For example, in the RibbonEditor I've set the following key tips for pages, groups, and action items:

```
RibbonPage1      'Editing'           KeyTip = 'E'
RibbonPage2      'Advanced'          KeyTip = 'A'
```

---

[136] Letting users customize their toolbars is a feature I find debatable. Power user certainly benefit from it, but you might get a extra support calls from newbies who cannot figure out why their favorite toolbar buttons have disappeared. As 80% of users generally use only 20% of the features, over-customization is not always a good idea.

314 - Chapter 10: The Ribbon

```
RibbonGroup1       'Copy&Paste'         KeyTip = 'C'
RibbonGroup2       'Edit'               KeyTip = 'E'
RibbonGroup3       'Style'              KeyTip = 'S'
RibbonGroup4       'Alignment'          KeyTip = 'A'
RibbonGroup5       'Paragraph'          KeyTip = 'P'

item         Action = EditCopy1         KeyTip = 'C'
item         Action = EditPaste1        KeyTip = 'P'
items        Action = EditCut1          KeyTip = 'T'
items        Action = EditDelete1       KeyTip = 'D'
items        Action = EditUndo1         KeyTip = 'U'
items        Action = EditSelectAll1 KeyTip = 'S'
```

The value of the `KeyTip` should be one or more uppercase letters[137] or numbers, and the effect is to visually display the alternative key tips of the given selection level as the user presses the Alt key (don't hold it, just press it once) and follows with the various selections. By displaying the actual key tips to the user, it teaches the user the proper shortcuts over time. As an actual example, when you press (and release) the Alt key in the RibbonEditor demo, you'll see:

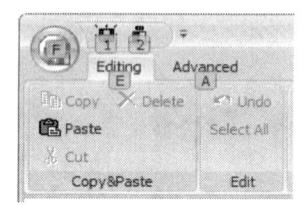

Only the first level key tips are displayed, now if you press the *E* key, activating the Editing tab, the Ribbon will show the keys for the individual action items and the groups, but only if the groups have a group dialog connected (which happens for the Style group):

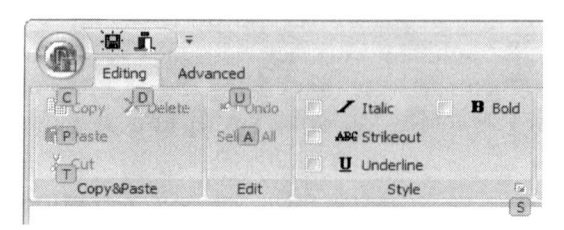

---

[137] Don't use lowercase letters, as they simply don't work. In theory the Ribbon component should convert them to uppercase automatically, but this doesn't seem to work for now (in Delphi 2009 Update 1).

Don't forget to set the key tips for all of your Ribbon user interface elements, or the use of the control will be limited for those preferring the speed of keyboard selection.

The Ribbon Components

We have already seen through a practical example the role of the various Ribbon related components, from the Ribbon control itself to tabs and groups. These provide the overall organization of the user interface, and provide a wide range of options which I certainly cannot explore in detail here. Even without trying for complete coverage, though, I can certainly provide a few more hints.

Let's focus on the Ribbon group object first. One of the most important visual features of a group is its `GroupAlign` property, which can be either vertical or horizontal. Vertical might be better for large buttons, while horizontal is preferred for having rows of related small buttons. You can also use the `Columns` and `Rows` property of a group to change its overall layout. By default, the Ribbon groups have a vertical layout with three rows, as three buttons will fit in a group vertically. Remember that the Ribbon must be at least a given height, and so must its groups (scrollbars are never displayed in a Ribbon control).

Of course, if you set a button to be large, it will fill the entire group. In this case (taken from the standard RibbonDemo that comes with Delphi), the button is large and uses the split button style to show a drop down menu):

You obtain this effect by setting the proper styles of the ActionItem and providing a few sub-items, hooked with other actions:

```
item
  Action = EditPaste1
  CommandProperties.ButtonSize = bsLarge
  CommandProperties.ButtonType = btSplit
  Items = <
    item
```

```
          Action = EditPaste1
        end
        item
          Action = EditPasteSpecial
        end
        item
          Action = EditPasteHyperlink
        end>
    end
end
```

At the opposite, you can have small buttons with no captions using a horizontal layout. Here is an example of a group with two rows of command buttons:

The key properties of this group are:

```
object RibbonGroup8: TRibbonGroup
  Caption = 'Lines'
  GroupAlign = gaHorizontal
  Rows = 2
end
```

But how do you obtain the graphical effect of the grouped buttons? This is not automatic, as you have to modify the `TActionClientItem` objects of the group, removing the caption (turning off the `ShowCaption` property), setting a specific value for their `CommandProperties.GroupPosition` sub-property, and using the `NewRow` property as required:

```
Items = <
  item
    Action = RichEditAlignCenter1
    CommandProperties.GroupPosition = gpStart
  end
  item
    Action = RichEditAlignRight1
    CommandProperties.GroupPosition = gpMiddle
  end
  item
    Action = RichEditAlignLeft1
    CommandProperties.GroupPosition = gpEnd
  end
  item
    Action = RichEditUnderline1
```

```
      NewRow = True
      CommandProperties.GroupPosition = gpStart
    end
    item
      Action = RichEditItalic1
      CommandProperties.GroupPosition = gpMiddle
    end
    item
      Action = RichEditBold1
      CommandProperties.GroupPosition = gpEnd
    end>
  ActionBar = RibbonGroup8
end
```

This might seem a lot of manual work, but it lets you have a lot of control over the exact placement of the elements, rather than trusting some internal algorithm that might not work as you like.

Coming to action items, beside positioning and many other graphical elements, the most important decision you have to make is to pick the core user interface and behavior. If you pick a button, as in most of the cases of this demo, you can still use the `TButtonProperties` structure connected with the `CommandProperties` property I mentioned earlier. This let's you pick a button size, a button type, a group position and a text association using values of the following enumerations (defined as nested types):

```
type
  TButtonSize = (bsSmall, bsLarge);
  TButtonType = (btNone, btDropDown, btSplit,
    btGallery);
  TGroupPosition = (gpNone, gpStart, gpMiddle,
    gpEnd, gpSingle);
  TTextAssociation = (taImage, taDropdown);
```

What is very interesting to notice is that the object connected with the `CommandProperties` property depends on the command type. So if you pick, for example, a text element, you'll see properties like `Alignment`, `EllipsisPosition`, and `Font` rather than those listed earlier for a button command. But which are the available command types for Action Client Items used by the Ribbon[138]?

---

138 In theory these command types could be used by any other visual container of action links, as this is defined as part of the Action Manager architecture and not specifically tied to the Ribbon. At the moment, though, all other action viewers and styles ignore this property.

Here is a list provided by the documentation (that is, the source code of the ActMan unit):

- `csButton` - command is a button
- `csMenu` - command is a menu
- `csSeparator` - command is a separator with a caption
- `csText` - command only displays text (clicking on it does nothing)
- `csGallery` - command displays a gallery (a feature not supported in the current version of the Ribbon control)
- `csComboBox` - command has an office 2007 combo box (notice this is automatically set when using the RibbonComboBox control)
- `csCheckBox` - command appears like an office 2007 check box
- `csRadioButton` - command appears like an office 2007 radio button
- `csControl` - command has a `TControl` associated with it
- `csCustom` - allows further expansion by third parties

An interesting case is the use of the `csControl` style, which lets you place almost any graphical control of the VCL to the Ribbon. For example, in the usual RibbonEditor demo, I've added a group with a ButtonedEdit control with a right button and a `TextHint` and a microscopic TreeView control:

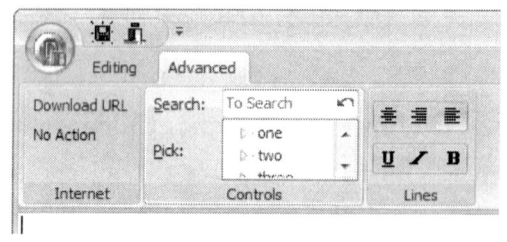

All I had to do was to manually add an ActionToolbar to the ActionManager (using the Structure view), connect this toolbar with a new empty Ribbon group, pick a control in the Tool Palette, and select the Ribbon Group to add an action item connected with the corresponding control. Finally, I set the proper width for the entire action item and its label. Here is the textual definition of one of the ActionToolbar items:

```
item
  Items = <
    item
      Caption = '&Search:'
```

```
      CommandStyle = csControl
      CommandProperties.Width = 150
      CommandProperties.ContainedControl = ButtonedEdit1
      CommandProperties.LabelWidth = 50
    end
    item
      Caption = '&Pick:'
      CommandStyle = csControl
      NewRow = True
      CommandProperties.Width = 150
      CommandProperties.ContainedControl = TreeView1
      CommandProperties.LabelWidth = 50
    end>
  ActionBar = RibbonGroup7
end>
```

Again, the ActionManager architecture and the new Ribbon control with its support classes have so many features, that I could go on for many more pages covering them. Here, in any case, are a few more interesting suggestions (not shown in practice in my demo):

- You can customize the Application menu, for example changing the "Recent Documents" caption or the icon size by using the `ApplicationMenu` property of the Ribbon control.
- Similarly, you can customize the behavior of the Quick Access menu by setting various sub-properties of the `QuickAccessToolbar` property of the Ribbon control
- The reason you don't set a size for the Ribbon groups but let them adapt to the size of the contained items is due to a specific request in the Fluent UI Design Guidelines.
- Users can right-click on Ribbon items to add them to the Quick Access Toolbar and perform related operations.

Ribbons for Database Applications

It is quite obvious to see how the use of the Ribbon controls would apply to a document oriented application, but what about programs doing totally different operations, like working on database data? Considering that we have a set of standard database-related actions available, we might be tempted to use the Ribbon to replace the classic DBNavigator, and this is indeed possible (and also quite simple to achieve). I'm not exactly sure this respects Microsoft usage rules for the Fluent UI, but it certainly doesn't infringe the rule of not cloning Office.

To create the DataRibbon application I had to place a ClientDataSet, with a DataSource, and a DBGrid on a form for the database side; add an ImageList, an ActionManager, and a Ribbon for the user interface side. Now I had to create a few custom actions (basically all of the custom DataSet actions minus the Refresh action, plus the Undo action, and also the FileOpen and FileExit actions), create a Ribbon tab with three groups and drag some of the actions to them. No code was involved so far. Then all I had to do was open the ClientDataSet on start-up, using the ClientDataSet file as Ribbon document name, and do the same when the FileOpen operation is executed:

```
procedure TFormDataRibbon.FileOpen1Accept(
  Sender: TObject);
begin
  ClientDataSet1.Close;
  ClientDataSet1.FileName := FileOpen1.Dialog.FileName;
  Ribbon1.DocumentName := ClientDataSet1.FileName;
  ClientDataSet1.Open;
end;
```

This is almost the complete code of the program, everything else is a collection of settings stored in the DFM file and obtained with visual operations at design time. Want to have a look at this settings? Here is a minimal summary, with tight typesetting (this is out of 788 lines of DFM source code), worth looking at to get the overall picture of the relationship between the Ribbon and the ActionManager:

```
object FormDataRibbon: TFormDataRibbon
  object Ribbon1: TRibbon
    ActionManager = ActionManager1
    Caption = 'DataRibbon'
    Tabs = <item Page = RibbonPage1 end>
    StyleName = 'Ribbon - Luna'
    object RibbonPage1: TRibbonPage
      Caption = 'DBNavigation'
      Index = 0
      object RibbonGroup1: TRibbonGroup
        Caption = 'Browse'
        GroupIndex = 1
      end
      object RibbonGroup2: TRibbonGroup
        Caption = 'Edit'
        GroupIndex = 2
      end
```

```
        object RibbonGroup3: TRibbonGroup
          Caption = 'File'
          GroupIndex = 0
        end
      end
    end
object ImageList1: TImageList...
object ActionManager1: TActionManager
  ActionBars = <
    item
      Items = <
        item Action = DataSetFirst1 end
        item Action = DataSetPrior1 end
        item Action = DataSetNext1 end
        item Action = DataSetLast1 end>
      ActionBar = RibbonGroup1
    end
    item
      Items = <
        item Action = DataSetDelete1 end
        item Action = DataSetEdit1 end
        item Action = DataSetInsert1 end
        item Action = DataSetPost1 end
        item Action = DataSetCancel1 end
        item Action = ClientDataSetUndo1 end>
      ActionBar = RibbonGroup2
    end
    item
      Items = <
        item Action = FileOpen1 end
        item Action = FileExit1 end>
      ActionBar = RibbonGroup3
    end>
  Images = ImageList1
  StyleName = 'Ribbon - Luna'
  object DataSetFirst1: TDataSetFirst...
  object DataSetPrior1: TDataSetPrior...
  object DataSetNext1: TDataSetNext...
  object DataSetLast1: TDataSetLast...
  object DataSetInsert1: TDataSetInsert...
  object DataSetDelete1: TDataSetDelete...
  object DataSetEdit1: TDataSetEdit...
  object DataSetPost1: TDataSetPost...
  object DataSetCancel1: TDataSetCancel...
  object ClientDataSetUndo1: TClientDataSetUndo
    Caption = 'Undo'
    FollowChange = False
  end
  object FileOpen1: TFileOpen
    Caption = '&Open...'
```

322 - Chapter 10: The Ribbon

```
      Dialog.Filter = 'CDS|*.cds|XML|*.xml'
      Dialog.InitialDir = '...\CodeGear Shared\Data'
      OnAccept = FileOpen1Accept
    end
    object FileExit1: TFileExit...
  end
object DBGrid1: TDBGrid
  Align = alClient
  DataSource = DataSource1
end
object DataSource1: TDataSource
  DataSet = ClientDataSet1
end
object ClientDataSet1: TClientDataSet
  FileName = '...\CodeGear Shared\Data\customer.cds'
end
```

I could have extended the example with basic edit operations (like Copy and Paste) and others, but I've basically reached my goal to prove that, even if a little unusual, the Ribbon can be used for a database oriented program as well. This is the program in action:

Using Screen Tips

Another elements of the Ribbon user interface is the use of large and detailed hints, know as screen tips. Screen tips are generally used for the Ribbon by hooking them to the various actions, but can be used also in applications that don't use the Ribbon, and even in applications that don't use actions. Delphi 2009 has specific support for screen tips with two different components:

- The ScreenTipsManager component is the overall screen tips handler. It can handle screen tip details for each of the actions in a related ActionList or ActionManager component, and has its own editor to let you generate a screen tip for each action, as we'll see later.
- The ScreenTipsPopup control provides a specific user interface for screen tips or can be hooked to any visual controls, providing a screen tip for user interface elements not connected with actions. This control still needs to be connected with a ScreenTipsManager component.

Here I'll show you two different examples. The first is the stand-alone and simple use of screen tips in an example that has no Ribbon and no actions. The second will be an extension of a Ribbon demo featuring screen tips.

Screen Tips with No Ribbon

As I mentioned, you can use screen tips in applications that have no Ribbon. To show this technique can be added to any program, I've taken a classic Delphi "hello, world" kind of demo, a program with a list box, an edit, and a button used to add the text of the edit to the list box.

I've added a ScreenTipsManager component (with default settings) and three ScreenTipsPopup controls to this classic demo, one for each visual control. Each ScreenTipsPopup control has a `ScreenTip` property referring to a `TScreenTipItem`: You can customize such items with a `Header`, an `Image`, and a `Description`, among other properties. The ScreenTipsPopup has an `Associate` property you can use to refer to the visual control to which the screen tip is connected (this control must have its `ShowHint` property on).

Finally, if you want to hide the small glyph for the ScreenTipsPopup control, you have to set the Visible property to False. This is what I've done in the demo for two of our three controls. You can, in fact, show the screen tip only when a user moves over this small glyph, only when a user moves over the associated control (by hiding the glyph), or in both cases.

This is the screen tip of the Add button of the PlainTips demo:

Notice the small glyph for the hint connected with the list box on the left side of the control (and to the left of the visible screen tip). Here are the most relevant properties for the screen tips components of this example:

```
object FormPlainTips: TFormPlainTips
  object ScreenTipsPopup1: TScreenTipsPopup
    Associate = ListBox1
    ScreenTip.Description.Strings = (
      'List of text elements that were added')
    ScreenTip.Header = 'List'
    ScreenTip.Image.Data = {...}
    ScreenTip.ShowImage = True
    ScreenTipManager = ScreenTipsManager1
  end
  object ScreenTipsPopup2: TScreenTipsPopup
    Associate = btnAdd
    ScreenTip.Description.Strings = (
      'Add the text to the list box, avoiding...')
    ScreenTip.Header = 'Add Text'
    ScreenTip.Image.Data = {...}
    ScreenTip.ShowImage = True
    ScreenTipManager = ScreenTipsManager1
    Visible = False
```

```
    end
    object ScreenTipsPopup3: TScreenTipsPopup
      Associate = edText
      ScreenTip.Description.Strings = (
        'Text to be added to the listbox')
      ScreenTip.Header = 'Text'
      ScreenTip.Image.Data = {...}
      ScreenTip.ShowFooter = False
      ScreenTip.ShowImage = True
      ScreenTipManager = ScreenTipsManager1
      Visible = False
    end
    object ScreenTipsManager1: TScreenTipsManager
      FooterImage.Data = {...}
    end
  end
end
```

Notice that one of the ScreenTipsPopup controls is visible, while another has no footer. The footer shows some text and an optional image shared by all screen tips and provided by the ScreenTipsManager component.

Screen Tips Manager and Actions

Even if you can use Screen Tips without a Ribbon and an ActionList or Action Manager, the latter is the scenario in which they work best and for which there is specific support. In fact, as you place a ScreenTipsManager component in a form that uses an ActionList or ActionManager (with or without a Ribbon control), you'll be able to use the various features of the component editor, that is the commands of its shortcut menu:

- The Generate Screen Tips command will help you create a basic screen tip for each action and connect them. If you have already defined screen tips for some actions, they'll be preserved.
- The Regenerate Screen Tips command works like the previous command, but will remove all existing tips and let you start from scratch.
- The Edit Screen Tips command will let you view and customize all of the action-related screen tips, with an easy-to-use editor.

As an example, I've used this feature for the RibbonEditor application, creating the RibbonEditorTips version of the program. All I had to do build a first version was to add a ScreenTipsManager component, go to its `LinkedActionList` collection and add an item referring to the ActionManager component of the example, and call its Generate Screen Tips shortcut menu command. This generates a plain screen tip for each action.

To make the screen tips visible, though, you have to take two more steps: In the form, you have to turn on the ShowHints property (as this is not available at the Ribbon control level); in the Ribbon control you have to assign the ScreenTipsManager component to the ScreenTips property. This is enough to have a basic tip showing up as you move the mouse over of the items of the Ribbon user interface, as in the following case:

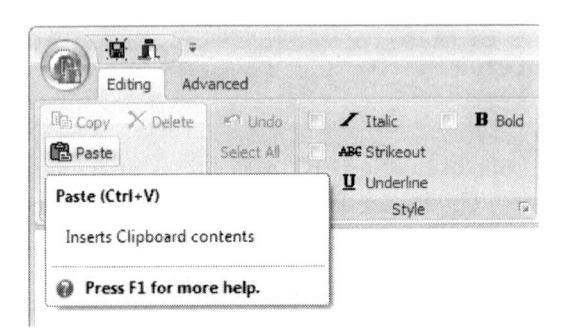

This is a very basic hint. You can customize it by editing the given screen tip item in the ScreenTips collection of the ScreenTipsManager component:

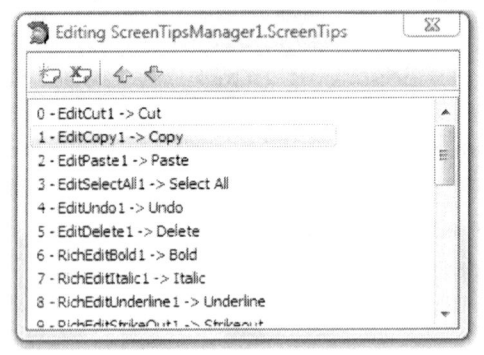

However, to make things much easier, you should use the custom screen tips editor instead by double-clicking on the ScreenTipsManager component. This is how the editor looks for that given screen tip:

Chapter 10: The Ribbon - 327

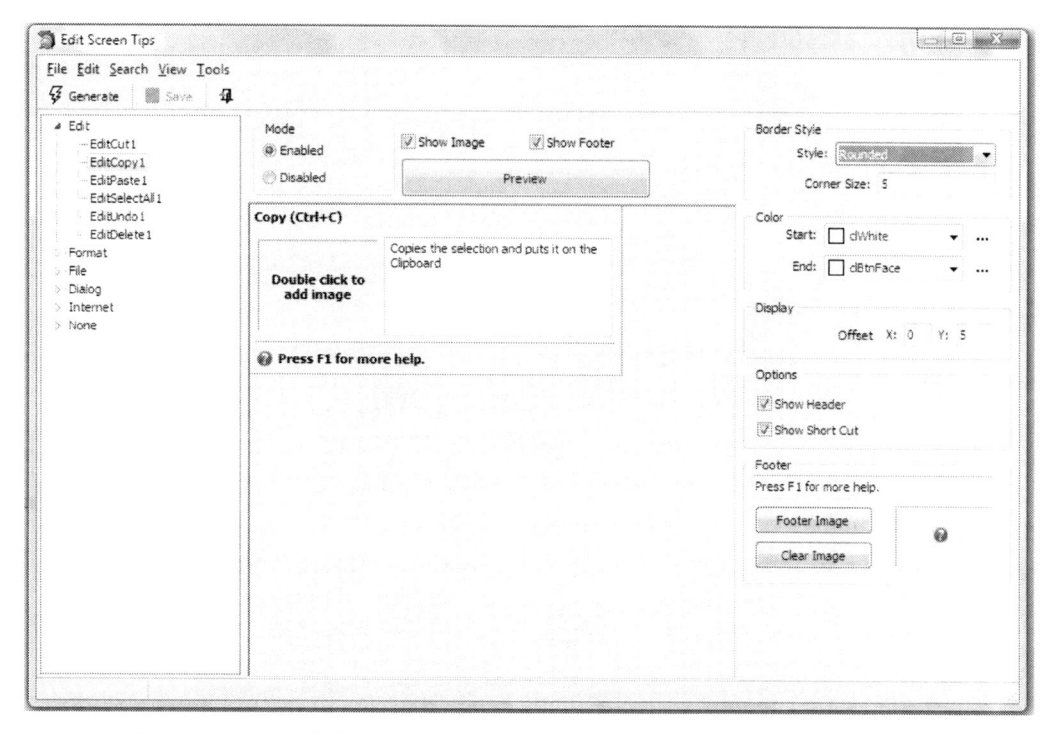

The summary of the properties for the RibbonEditorTips example, considering only differences from the previous version, are listed below:

```
object RibbonEditorForm: TRibbonEditorForm
  ShowHint = True
  object Ribbon1: TRibbon
    ScreenTips = ScreenTipsManager1
  end
  object ScreenTipsManager1: TScreenTipsManager
    FooterImage.Data = {...}
    LinkedActionLists = <
      item
        ActionList = ActionManager1
        Caption = 'ActionManager1'
      end>
    ScreenTips = <
      item
        Action = EditCut1
        Description.Strings = ('Cuts the selection...')
        Header = 'Cut'
      end
      item
        Action = EditCopy1
        Description.Strings = ('Copies the selection...')
```

```
            Header = 'Copy'
            ShowImage = True
        end
        ...
    end
end
```

What's Next

After touching on the RTL at the end of Part II of the book, in the last three chapters I've covered the new features of VCL visual controls (Chapter 8), the changes in COM support (Chapter 9), and the brand new Ribbon component, based on the ActionManager architecture (the current chapter).

Another cornerstone of the VCL is its database support. The core database technology hasn't changed since the last version, if you don't consider the fact that it now supports Unicode. Actually, the `TDataset` class introduced support for Unicode in past versions, but that was based on the WideString type, not on the new UnicodeString type. Changes in the database access architecture, including the dbExpress library, will be covered in the next chapter, while the vastly improved DataSnap multi-tier architecture will be the topic of Chapter 12.

Chapter 11: Datasets And DbExpress

With all the focus on Unicode and new Delphi language features, you might get the impression that there is little new in Delphi 2009 for database developers. This impression would be quite wrong. Not only does database support now fully embrace Unicode, compared to the partial support for metadata in past versions, but there are also several relevant new features in dbExpress, including a brand new version of DataSnap that I'll cover in Chapter 12. Here, instead, I'll focus on the core features of `TDataSet` and related classes, the improved dbExpress, and touch on several associated topics.

A Unicode ClientDataSet

Before we start looking into the changes to the database components in Delphi 2009, I think it is worth first having a look at an example of a Unicode-based database application. To keep things simple, for now, I'll use a ClientDataSet component filled dynamically with strings coming from multiple alphabets. In this example, called UniCds, the ClientDataSet data structure is defined at runtime, in the `OnCreate` event handler of the main form:

```
procedure TFormUniCds.FormCreate(Sender: TObject);
begin
  cds.FieldDefs.Clear;
  cds.FieldDefs.Add ('code', ftInteger, 0, True);
  cds.FieldDefs.Add ('uni', ftWideString, 30, False);
  cds.FieldDefs.Add ('ansi', ftString, 30, False);
  cds.CreateDataSet;
  cds.Open;
end;
```

The ClientDataSet is initially empty. You can type in the associated DBGrid to add data, or press the `btnPopulate` button that fills the dataset with the list of Unicode strings with the text "What is Unicode?" written in many languages, loaded from the UTF-8 text file produced by the StreamEncoding example of Chapter 2.

This is the code used to load the data, doing a behind the scenes conversion from the UTF-8 file encoding to the UTF-16 encoding used by the UnicodeString type and by the wide string field:

```
procedure TFormUniCds.btnPopulateClick(Sender: TObject);
var
  I: Integer;
  sList: TStringList;
  strLine: string;
begin
  sList := TStringList.Create;
  try
    I := 1;
    sList.LoadFromFile('utf8text.txt');
    for strLine in sList do
    begin
      cds.InsertRecord([I, strLine, AnsiString(strLine)]);
      Inc (I);
    end;
  finally
```

```
    sList.Free;
  end;
end;
```

Nothing extraordinary, for sure, but it is nice to have such a simple and straightforward solution for creating a multilingual application with output like this:

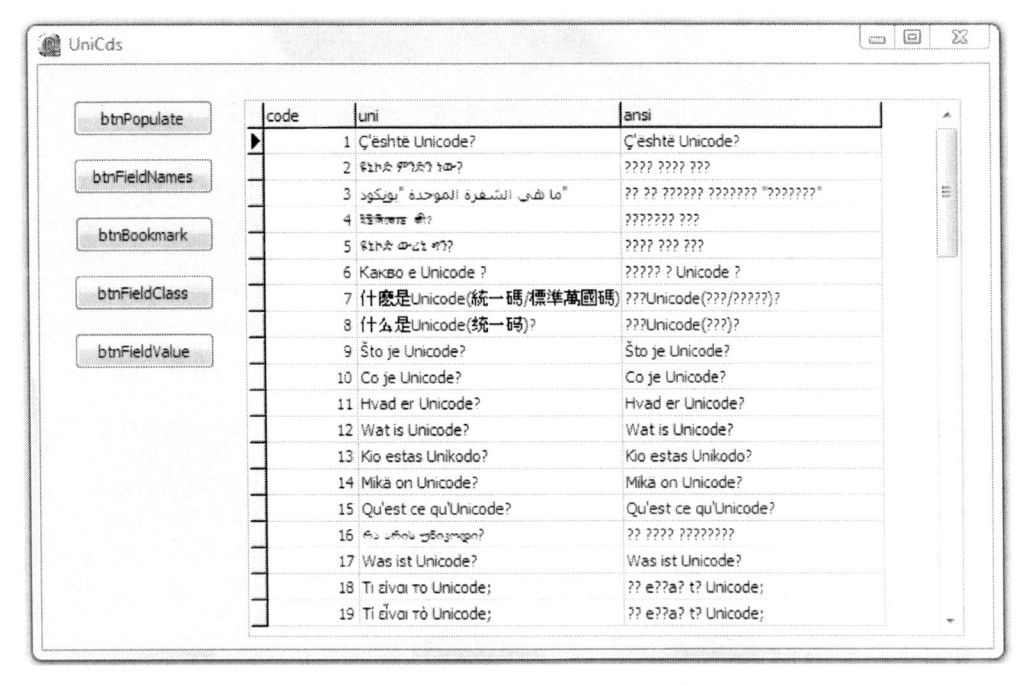

What is different from past versions of Delphi, however, is not the code in the ClientDataSet component. In fact, you could use the `ftWideString` field type even in past version of the CodeGear IDE. Reading the data from the file and adding to the database, would have been only slightly more complicated. What was not easy to achieve was to display this data in a DBGrid or any other visual data-aware (or non data-aware) component of the VCL.

Still, support for Unicode extends beyond the visual representation. The techniques used in the past for supporting database field and table names based on the Unicode character set were not based on the Delphi 2009 UnicodeString type, but on the WideString type, and have been considerably modified in Delphi 2009.

Unicode in Datasets, Take 2

The `TDataSet` and `TField` classes were among the few classes already supporting Unicode since Delphi 2006. That Unicode support, though, was based on the WideString type, which is still available but is not the standard approach used in Delphi 2009 for supporting Unicode. As we saw in Chapter 2, the WideString type represents a less-optimized and non-reference counted type holding wide characters, originally introduced for COM compatibility.

If you compare the source code of the database components of the VCL of Delphi 2006 and Delphi 2009 you'll clearly see that most of the properties declared as WideString have reverted to the predefined string type, up to the point that the source code looks more similar to previous versions, like Delphi 7 and Delphi 2005. For example, if you looked at the source code of the `TField` class, in Delphi 2007 you could see the following properties:

```
type
  TField = class(TComponent)
  public
    property FullName: WideString read GetFullName;
    property DisplayLabel: WideString
      read GetDisplayLabel write SetDisplayLabel
    property FieldName: WideString
      read FFieldName write SetFieldName;
    property LookupKeyFields: WideString
      read FLookupKeyFields write SetLookupKeyFields;
    property LookupResultField: WideString
      read FLookupResultField write SetLookupResultField;
    property KeyFields: WideString
      read FKeyFields write SetKeyFields;
```

Now in Delphi 2009 these are all declared as *string*! In most cases the change was highly compatible when moving to the WideString version, and it remains highly compatible both if you are moving from recent versions of Delphi or older ones. There are specific cases, though, in which you might experience problems. Also, if for any reason you explicitly used the WideString type, you should generally replace it with the UnicodeString type (or even better the core, generic, string type).

Notice, though, that if the `TField` object and related definitions in the DB unit have been converted from WideString to UnicodeString, this is not true throughout the VCL. The data-aware controls, in fact, still reference the field names using the old 2-bytes-per-character string type. As an example, in the `TDBEdit` class you can see:

```
property DataField: WideString
   read GetDataField write SetDataField;
```

This is far from optimal, because this type is not reference counted and is less efficient that the UnicodeString type. Also, as you'll generally use the UnicodeString type in your source code, this implies string type conversions.

Unicode String Lists

A strictly related change is the return to the `TStrings` type for lists of strings, instead of the replacement `TWideStrings` type used in recent versions. In these cases, for compatibility reasons, there is often an overloaded version that is compatible with the WideString implementation. For example, the `GetFieldsList` method of the `TDataSet` class is now defined as:

```
procedure GetFieldNames(List: TStrings);
   overload; virtual;
procedure GetFieldNames(List: TWideStrings);
   overload; virtual;
```

The potential problem with this approach is that if you wrote (or migrated) your code to something like the following code[139], it won't be optimized, as the program will have to convert the string types:

```
var
   WideList: TWideStringList;
begin
   WideList := TWideStringList.Create;
   try
      cds.GetFieldNames (WideList);
      ShowMessage (WideList.Text);
   finally
      WideList.Free;
   end;
end;
```

---

139 This code snippet is taken from the UniCds demo, introduced at the beginning of the chapter.

334 - Chapter 11: Datasets and dbExpress

Such a program, left as it is, should compile and produce correct results (while when moving database related code that used list of fields from Delphi 7 to Delphi 2006 didn't always compile). My suggestion, though, is to rewrite your code, locating any occurrence of the TWideStrings and TWideStringList classes and moving them to the *preferred* TStrings and TStringList types:

```
var
   List: TStringList;
begin
   List := TStringList.Create;
   try
      cds.GetFieldNames (List);
      ShowMessage (List.Text);
   finally
      List.Free;
   end;
```

Of course, if you have code that predates Delphi 2006, you can leave it as it is and it will automatically be *upgraded* to use Unicode string lists.

Bookmarks

The TDataSet class manages bookmarks to keep track of a given record of the dataset and let a program jump back to it. Technically bookmarks are pointers to internal data structures, but (for many versions) they were declared as if they were strings to take advantage of string reference counting:

```
type
   TBookmark = Pointer;
   TBookmarkStr = string;
```

The TBookmarkStr type was used as data type of the Bookmark property of the TDataSet class. As I already mentioned in the section "Strings are... Strings" of Chapter 3, these definitions have been modified in Delphi 2009[140]:

```
type
   TBookmark = TBytes;
```

---

[140] With the new deprecated directive now taking a description as parameter, I'm not really sure why this almost obsolete data type is simply commented as deprecated. Using the proper directive in the case described here, would have issued a very clear warning before the error message.

```
TBookmarkStr = AnsiString;
  // deprecated use TBookmark instead.

// from SysUtils:
TBytes = array of Byte;
```

The data type of the Bookmark property of the TDataset class is now of type TBookmark, that is a (reference counted) array of Byte. This means that existing code that uses the Bookmark property is unlikely to compile any longer.

For example, if you have the following legal code from a past version of Delphi:

```
var
  bookm: TBookmarkStr;
begin
  // save curent position
  bookm := cds.Bookmark;
  // move away
  cds.First;
  // get back
  Cds.Bookmark := bookm;
```

as you compile it you'll see the error:

```
E2010 Incompatible types: 'AnsiString' and 'TBytes'
```

What you should do is change the code to:

```
var
  bookm: TBookmark;
```

A simple search and replace of TBookmarkStr with TBookmark in your entire source code base will generally do.

Field Types and Strings

It is interesting to notice how the different field types are mapped to different native string types. I'm specifically referring to the TStringField and TWideStringField types, of course. The Value property for these field types changed from earlier versions of Delphi, but it was kept the same until Delphi 2007, despite the changes in metadata support (including the field names, mentioned earlier):

	Delphi 7	Delphi 2007	Delphi 2009
`TStringField.Value`	string	string	AnsiString
`TWideStringField.Value`	WideString	WideString	UnicodeString

In case your program uses a `TWideStringField` mapped to a Unicode string field of the database, the data is kept in Unicode format. What happens, instead, when you access the `AsString` property of a `TStringField` object? The implementation of the corresponding getter method remaps the access to the `AsAnsiString` method, that forces the conversion of the string buffer to the AnsiString type.

Notice that a `TWideStringField` object uses the same UTF-16 encoding of a UnicodeString in Delphi 2009, while a `TStringField` object uses the basic AnsiString type. You would need to write extra support code (which won't be trivial to write) for using a different code page or UTF-8 encoding with `TStringField`.

Other Dataset Enhancements

Beside the changes we've see that related to Unicode support and changes in the string and `PChar` types, there are other relevant new features in the `TDataSet` class, some meant for the end users, and some for the component developers.

New Field Types

As we'll see in Chapter 12, the new multi-tier architecture of Delphi 2009 is based on the use of datasets, records, and fields, both for passing parameters and results. This is why Delphi 2009 has many new field types, which are not strictly meant for direct database processing. The new field types are:

```
ftLongWord, ftShortint, ftByte, ftExtended,
ftConnection, ftParams, ftStream
```

While the first four represent language data types, the last three are clearly meant for transferring higher level data structures (database connections, parameters, and streams).

A More Virtual Dataset

When you need to extend an existing class of a library like the VCL, the only way you can change the behavior of existing classes, without rewriting too much code is to use inheritance. However, the problems often lies in the fact that the derived class can modify only what's declared as virtual in the base class.

So for example the fact that the method `MoveBy` is now declared as virtual in the `TDataSet` class means that any `TDataSet` derived class can modify it more easily.

```
function MoveBy(Distance: Integer): Integer; virtual;
```

Another very interesting case is when the base class has to create internal support objects and does so using a virtual function, to let you customize the type of the internal object (by using a derived type instead of the base one). To make this possible, the classes of these internal objects should also have a virtual constructor you can optionally replace and modify.

This is the area in which the dataset architecture has seen a helpful extension in Delphi 2009. Here is a list of support classes that now have virtual constructors:

```
type
  TIndexDef = class(TNamedItem)
    constructor Create(Owner: TIndexDefs;
      const Name, Fields: string; Options:
      TIndexOptions); reintroduce; overload; virtual;

  TIndexDefs = class(TDefCollection)
    constructor Create(ADataSet: TDataSet); virtual;

  TFieldDefList = class(TFlatList)
    // from base class
    constructor Create(ADataSet: TDataSet); virtual;

  TFields = class(TObject)
    constructor Create(ADataSet: TDataSet); virtual;
```

In the TDataSet class for each of these and other data structures, there is now a virtual function that returns the reference of the class to create:

```
type
  TDataSet = class
  protected {indirect creation of internal objects}
    function GetFieldDefsClass:
      TFieldDefsClass; virtual;
    function GetFieldDefListClass:
      TFieldDefListClass; virtual;
    function GetFieldsClass:
      TFieldsClass; virtual;
    function GetFieldListClass:
      TFieldListClass; virtual;
    function GetCheckConstraintsClass:
      TCheckConstraintsClass; virtual;
    function GetAggFieldsClass:
      TFieldsClass; virtual;
    function GetIndexDefsClass:
      TIndexDefsClass; virtual;
    function GetParamsClass:
      TParamsClass; virtual;
```

What these functions do in their implementation is to return the value of a corresponding global variable holding the default class for the given internal object:

```
var
  DefaultFieldDefsClass: TFieldDefsClass = TFieldDefs;
  DefaultFieldDefClass: TFieldDefClass = TFieldDef;
  DefaultLookupListClass: TLookupListClass =
    TDefaultLookupList;
  DefaultIndexDefClass: TIndexDefClass = TIndexDef;
  DefaultCheckConstraintClass: TCheckConstraintClass =
    TCheckConstraint;
  DefaultParamClass: TParamClass = TParam;
  DefaultParamsClass: TParamsClass = TParams;
  DefaultFieldsClass: TFieldsClass = TFields;
  DefaultFieldListClass: TFieldListClass = TFieldList;
  DefaultIndexDefsClass: TIndexDefsClass = TIndexDefs;
  DefaultFieldDefListClass: TFieldDefListClass =
    TFieldDefList;
  DefaultCheckConstraintsClass: TCheckConstraintsClass =
    TCheckConstraints;
```

This means that to globally customize all datasets in your application you can modify these global variables, while if you need a specific dataset to return a different internal object, you should do so by deriving a new class and overriding one of the virtual functions mentioned earlier.

The case of the TLookupList class is slightly different, with the class transformed into an abstract class and the derived class TDefaultLookupList providing the actual implementation.

How can we take advantage of this new feature in practice? To demonstrate how easy it is to customize these standard objects, I've written an example called CustomFields. In the example I customize the field definition class and also map field types to a custom field class, using the public array DefaultFieldClasses.

CustomFields is a simple application with a ClientDataSet component, a DataSource component, a DBGrid, a tool bar with a few buttons, and a Memo control for logging information. The program defines a class for field definitions, in which I've added an extra property, only for the sake of the demo[141]:

```
type
  TMyFieldDef = class (TFieldDef)
  private
    FExtraDescription: string;
    procedure SetExtraDescription(const Value: string);
  public
    function ToString: string; override;
    property ExtraDescription: string
      read FExtraDescription write SetExtraDescription;
  end;

function TMyFieldDef.ToString: string;
begin
  Result := Name + ' - ' + ExtraDescription +
    ' [' + ClassName + ']';
end;
```

This custom class must be installed before the ClientDataSet is created (not before it is opened) so I've added the following line to the initialization section of the main form of the program:

```
initialization
  DefaultFieldDefClass := TMyFieldDef;
```

When clicking on the second toolbar button, the program modifies the ExtraDescription property for the first field definition and the fetches it along with more field definition class information:

---

141 It might be interesting to add into each field definition a reference to metadata information, a data dictionary, a field definition, or anything that would let you have a more flexible and powerful data access layer.

340 - Chapter 11: Datasets and dbExpress

```
procedure TFormCustomFields.btnFieldDefClick(
  Sender: TObject);
begin
  (ClientDataSet1.FieldDefs[0] as TMyFieldDef).
    ExtraDescription := 'This is the first column';
  Log ('ClientDataSet1.FieldDefs[0].ToString: ' +
    ClientDataSet1.FieldDefs[0].ToString);
end;
```

The output of this call is:

```
ClientDataSet1.FieldDefs[0].ToString:
  CustNo - This is the first column [TMyFieldDef]
```

The second customization is based on the definition of a custom string field type derived from the AnsiString type:

```
type
  TMyStringField = class (TStringField)
  protected
    function GetAsString: string; override;
  end;

function TMyStringField.GetAsString: string;
begin
  Result := inherited GetAsString + ' is not Unicode';
end;
```

This class makes a rather odd customization, adding a fixed string to the output of each AnsiString field. The simplest way to connect the custom field class to all fields of a given type (whose internal format must be compatible) is to use the `DefaultFieldClasses` global array:

```
initialization
  DefaultFieldClasses [ftString] := TMyStringField;
```

Again there is a button asking for field class information, but the effect of this code is clearly visible in the DBGrid:

Chapter 11: Datasets and dbExpress - 341

```
CustomFields
Open   Get Field Definition   Get Field Class
CustNo  Company                                              Addr 1
  1221  Kauai Dive Shoppe is not Unicode                     4-976 Sugarloaf Hwy is not Unicode
  1231  Unisco is not Unicode                                PO Box Z-547 is not Unicode
  1351  Sight Diver is not Unicode                           1 Neptune Lane is not Unicode
  1354  Cayman Divers World Unlimited is not Unico           PO Box 541 is not Unicode
  1356  Tom Sawyer Diving Centre is not Unicode              632-1 Third Frydenhoj is not Unicode
  1380  Blue Jack Aqua Center is not Unicode                 23-738 Paddington Lane is not Unicode
  1384  VIP Divers Club is not Unicode                       32 Main St. is not Unicode
  1510  Ocean Paradise is not Unicode                        PO Box 8745 is not Unicode
  1513  Fantastique Aquatica is not Unicode                  Z32 999 #12A-77 A.A. is not Unicode
  1551  Marmot Divers Club is not Unicode                    872 Queen St. is not Unicode
  1560  The Depth Charge is not Unicode                      15243 Underwater Fwy. is not Unicode
  1563  Blue Sports is not Unicode                           203 12th Ave. Box 746 is not Unicode
  1624  Makai SCUBA Club is not Unicode                      PO Box 8534 is not Unicode

ClientDataSet1.Fields[1].ToString: TMyStringField
```

In more complex situations you can override the dataset class and redefine the `GetFieldClass` virtual method[142]. Again, by inheriting from a custom dataset class you can customize the support classes specifically, while the approach I've used triggers the change for each dataset of the current application, which is something you might want or not.

Fields Extensions

Beside the change of some property types from WideString back to string, as mentioned earlier in the section "Unicode in Datasets, Take 2" the `TField` class now has support for some of the new dataset field types (plus it differentiates between `AsString`, which now returns a UnicodeString, and the new `AsAnsiString`):

```
type
  TField = class(TComponent)
  public
```

---

142 It would also have been possible to customize the field definition to field mapping by modifying the `CreateField` method of the `TFieldDef` class, if only the method was virtual in the base class!

Marco Cantù, Delphi 2009 Handbook

```
    property AsExtended: Extended
      read GetAsExtended write SetAsExtended;
    property AsAnsiString: AnsiString
      read GetAsAnsiString write SetAsAnsiString;
    property AsBytes: TBytes
      read GetAsBytes write SetAsBytes;
```

Notice despite the introduction of Unicode, database mapping didn't change, because by default databases consider as *string* an AnsiString text, and not a Unicode-enabled text, for which you need to use a specific field type. That's why the classic ftString type, managed by the TStringField class, is still based on AnsiString. If you want to have Unicode strings in your database you need to use the ftWideString type and the corresponding TWideStringField class, exactly like in past versions of Delphi. I've already highlighted in the section "Field Types and Strings" how the two string field types handle internal values.

There are also a few new TField derived classes, for handling some of the new field types. Here is the first line of the declaration of these new classes, so you can see which is the base class:

```
type
  TLongWordField = class(TNumericField)
  TShortintField = class(TIntegerField)
  TByteField = class(TIntegerField)
  TUnsignedAutoIncField = class(TLongWordField)
  TExtendedField = class(TNumericField)
```

With these new classes, the hierarchy of the TField classes defined in the DB unit becomes even bigger. To help you get a full picture, I've provided a complete class tree below :

```
TField
  TStringField
    TWideStringField
    TGuidField
  TNumericField
    TIntegerField
      TAutoIncField
      TSmallintField
      TShortintField
      TByteField
      TWordField
    TLongWordField
      TUnsignedAutoIncField
    TLargeintField // Int64
    TFloatField
      TCurrencyField
```

```
      TExtendedField
      TBCDField
      TFMTBCDField
   TBooleanField
   TDateTimeField
      TDateField
      TTimeField
   TSQLTimeStampField
   TBinaryField
      TBytesField
         TVarBytesField
   TBlobField
      TMemoField
      TWideMemoField // widestring memo
      TGraphicField
   TObjectField
      TADTField // Abstract Data Type
      TArrayField
      TDataSetField
      TReferenceField
   TVariantField
   TInterfaceField
      TIDispatchField
   TAggregateField
```

BLOB fields Considered ANSI

Most field types are fully compatible with past versions of Delphi. This is particularly true for string types, despite the new UnicodeString support, because fields managing ANSI strings and wide strings were and are still different. Similarly, memo fields holding ANSI or Unicode strings are mapped to the separate `TMemoField` and `TWideMemoField` field classes. The only potential pitfall could arise with generic BLOB field used to store string-based information. When accessing a `TBlobField` object as a string, how should Delphi 2009 consider the data? Once more, the decision was to favor backwards compatibility, so the string data within a BLOB field is considered to be ANSI based as in past versions of Delphi. You should use `TWideMemoField` for Unicode data in a BLOB as suggested by this comment in the `GetAsString` method of the `TBlobField` class:

```
// For backwards compatibility, read untyped data as Ansi.
// Use TWideMemoField for blobs associated with Unicode
// string data.
```

Parameters Extensions

Like fields, parameters have a few new properties, but in this case you can not only see support for the new field types, but also for the new kinds of parameters used for DataSnap:

```
type
  TParam = class(TCollectionItem)
  public
    property AsShortInt: LongInt;
    property AsByte: LongInt;
    property AsLongWord: LongWord;
    property AsLargeInt: LargeInt;
    property AsAnsiString: AnsiString;
    property AsBytes: TBytes;
    // Used by TSQLServerMethod
    property AsDataSet: TDataSet;
    property AsParams: TParams;
    property AsStream: TStream;
```

More on these new kinds of parameters in Chapter 12, where I'll cover the new DataSnap. Notice that the core implementation of these parameters, though, adds support for an IParamImplementation interface, used to assign objects to the Variant value of a TParam object. There are a few pre-defined classes implementing this interface: the TParamObject class (for generic parameters), the TParamDataSetObject class (for dataset parameters), the TParamParamsObject class (for parameters representing parameters, and the TParamStreamObject class (for stream parameters).

DataSet Internals

You probably know that the TDataset class is a base abstract class providing the foundations of Delphi database access. You might not know, though, that this class has a large number of virtual abstract methods requiring a rather low level implementation of buffer-level management, which in the past where all based on PChar pointers.

Needless to say, in Delphi 2009 this isn't true any more. Most low level pointers are now declared either as PByte or TBytes (that is, array of Byte). To clean up code and simplify it, the DB unit introduces and uses the new `TRecordBuffer` type and modifies the list of buffers type (that used to be an array of `PChar`):

```
type
  TRecordBuffer = PByte;
  TBufferList = array of TRecordBuffer;
```

For example, this is the definition of the record buffer management functions in all versions from Delphi 3 to Delphi 2007:

```
function AllocRecordBuffer: PChar; virtual;
procedure FreeRecordBuffer(
  var Buffer: PChar); virtual;
procedure GetBookmarkData(Buffer: PChar;
  Data: Pointer); virtual;
function GetBookmarkFlag(
  Buffer: PChar): TBookmarkFlag; virtual;
```

This is the same set of `TDataSet` methods in Delphi 2009:

```
function AllocRecordBuffer: TRecordBuffer; virtual;
procedure FreeRecordBuffer(
  var Buffer: TRecordBuffer); virtual;
procedure GetBookmarkData(Buffer: TRecordBuffer;
  Data: Pointer); overload; virtual;
function GetBookmarkFlag(
  Buffer: TRecordBuffer): TBookmarkFlag; virtual;
```

I could list dozens of other methods with similar differences. What is important to notice is that many of these are virtual methods, the methods you need to implement to define a custom dataset. Methods of the public interface of `TDataSet`, instead, see very limited changes. In other words, the changes to the `TDataSet` class have little effect on users of dataset classes, but significantly affect those who wrote a custom dataset class.

Porting a (Simple) Custom Dataset

For Mastering Delphi 7 I wrote[143] a custom dataset based on a record-to-stream architecture. So I thought that porting that custom dataset to Delphi 2009 would be a good test of the effort involved in such a process.

---

143 The original code actually dates back to my Delphi Developer Handbook, written for Delphi 3, and was modified for the Delphi 7 book. I have no room here to cover in detail what it takes to write a custom dataset, as that is far from an easy task. If you are interested in learning about the details of how to write a custom dataset you can refer to one of those two old books of mine.

Having done this porting (without going all the length to support Unicode strings in my dataset), I have to say it was simple. The custom dataset is divided in two source code units: the MdDsCustom unit, which defines an abstract high level `TMdCustomDataSet` class, and the MdDsStream unit, which defines the actual implementation class `TMdDataSetStream`.

I opened both units, did a Search/Replace of `PChar` to `TRecordBuffer` finding 19 occurrences in the first unit and 4 in the second, and accepted them all. Most of the references to `PChar` where in the signature of the virtual methods that have been modified, a couple were local temporary variables used to store the current buffer, obtained with the `ActiveBuffer` method of the `TDataSet` class that now returns a `TRecordBuffer`.

At this point the component would compile. In the main program I had to tweak the code for testing bookmarks, by declaring the local variable as:

```
// bm: TBookmarkStr; // old
bm: TBookmark; // new
```

That was it! In a matter of minutes the custom dataset was up and running, and I could even reopen an existing demo file, with some data. The dataset source code files and the demo program are available in the StreamDsDemo folder. Here is the sample output:

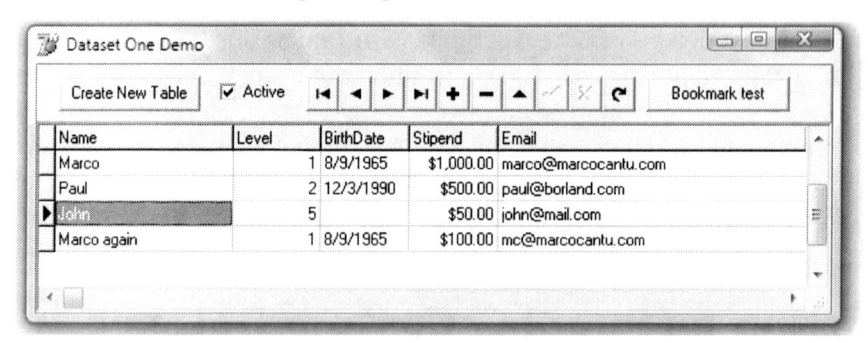

dbExpress in Delphi 2009

Delphi 2007 saw a significant update to the dbExpress architecture, with the release of version dbExpress IV. Delphi 2009 has some improvements, but they can be considered as minor... if you don't keep in the picture the support for multi-tier data that has been dubbed DataSnap 2009, but is technically part of the dbExpress architecture, as least on the client side. DataSnap 2009 is the subject of the next chapter, so I won't cover it here.

Focusing only on client/server applications, what are the changes in dbExpress? Nothing astonishing, but some interesting improvements (and a couple of problems). I'll explore the changes by working on a very simple dbExpress program borrowed from Delphi 2007 Handbook (and originally written for Mastering Delphi 6, I believe). The new version of the program is called DbxMulti2009.

Connection Settings and Connection Strings

As you create a new dbExpress application (or open an existing one), and select the SQLConnection component editor (the shortcut menu of the component) you'll immediately see something different from the past:

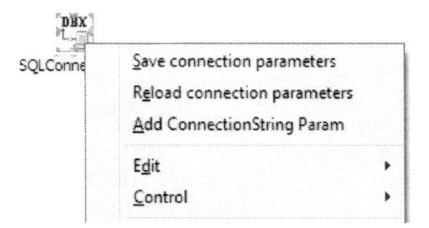

The Connection editor command (*Edit Connection Properties*) and the corresponding dialog box are gone, and so has the dialog box with the list of installed drivers. You now have two choices for modifying the dbExpress configuration: The first is to manually edit the dbxdrivers.ini and dbxconnections.ini files and the second is to use the SQLConnection component, its properties, and its new component editor commands. In particular, after you've selected a connection, you can choose from:

- *Reload connection parameters* will copy the dbxconnections.ini setting to the SQLConnection component for the current configuration. Notice that when the settings have been modified, compared to the original version, the `ConnectionName` property in the Object Inspector will have an asterisk after its name, indicating a modified set of connection data:

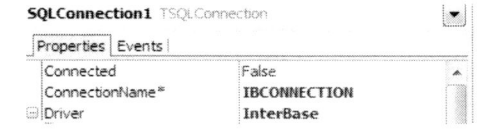

348 - Chapter 11: Datasets and dbExpress

- On the other hand, *Save connection parameters* will update the dbxconnections.ini with the local settings for the current configuration
- *Add ConnectionString Param* will add an extra property to the component, with the complete configuration saved in a single string property, something very handy for configuring the status based on an external INI file or some other configuration settings.
- Once you've added a connection string, this command will replaced with the commands *Refresh ConnectionString Param* and *Remove ConnectionString Param.*

For the specific demo, adding the connection string parameter will add a `ConnectionString` line to the `Params` property, with the following content (which I've split on to multiple lines for readability, while it has to be in a single line because it is part of a `TStringList`):

```
DelegateConnection=dbxpoolconnection,
DriverName=INTERBASE,
DRIVERUNIT=DBXDynalink,
DRIVERPACKAGELOADER=TDBXDynalinkDriverLoader,
DRIVERPACKAGE=DBXCommonDriver110.bpl,
DRIVERASSEMBLYLOADER=
   Borland.Data.TDBXDynalinkDriverLoader,
DRIVERASSEMBLY=Borland.Data.DbxCommonDriver,
Version=11.0.5000.0,
Culture=neutral,
PublicKeyToken=a91a7c5705831a4f,
GETDRIVERFUNC=getSQLDriverINTERBASE,
DATABASE=..\CodeGear Shared\Data\Employee.GDB,
ROLENAME=RoleName,
USER_NAME=sysdba,
PASSWORD=masterkey,
SERVERCHARSET=,
SQLDIALECT=3,
BLOBSIZE=-1,
COMMITRETAIN=False,
WAITONLOCKS=True,
ERRORRESOURCEFILE=,
LOCALECODE=0000,
INTERBASE TRANSISOLATION=ReadCommited,
TRIM CHAR=False
```

Notice that this one-line configuration setting includes standard database settings (in the last part), driver configuration settings, the actual database to connect to, and even delegate driver information.

This new approach is based on a new internal data structure, the `TConnectionData` persistent class, that can be accessed using the new `ConnectionData` read-only property of the SQLConnection component. This class stores all configuration settings in an internal `TBDXProperties` list, can refer to a further `TConnectionData` structure with a delegate connection, and has support methods like:

```
procedure UpdateProperties(NewProperties: TStrings);
procedure AddProperties(NewProperties: TStrings);
procedure ReloadProperties;
procedure RefreshProperties;
```

As an example I've used this property to extract the connection string from the `ConnectionData` (information also available in the connection `Params` property). I've written this code in the `OnExecute` event handler action that I've added to the ActionManager component of the program:

```
procedure TForm1.ActionGetInfoExecute(Sender: TObject);
begin
  ShowMessage (SQLConnection1.ConnectionData.
    Properties ['ConnectionString']);
end;
```

Setting Driver Properties and Delegate Drivers

Another noticeable difference relates to the configuration of drivers and delegate drivers. As you select a value for the `Driver` property in Delphi 2009 at design-time, you'll be able to expand this property and set a few values. Among them there is a reference to the delegate driver, that you can expand as well to configure it. In other words if you need to set a trace file, for example, you can now do so directly in the driver configuration. This is how the Object Inspector looks in a such a case:

350 - Chapter 11: Datasets and dbExpress

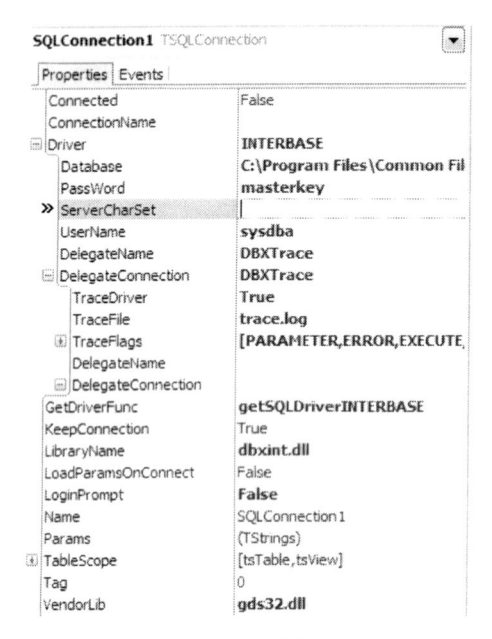

Deployment and INI files

The release version of Delphi 2009 had an unwanted side effect related with the deployment of dbExpress configuration files. This issue has been solved in the Update 2, but you might see it if you are using a trial version or a non-updated version. This is why you can probably ignore this section.

In the release version, if you configured the TSQLConnection component setting a connection and a driver, your application needed to read the dbxdrivers.ini and dbxconnections.ini files at runtime, which was not the case in the past. If the files were not available you'd see an error like[144]:

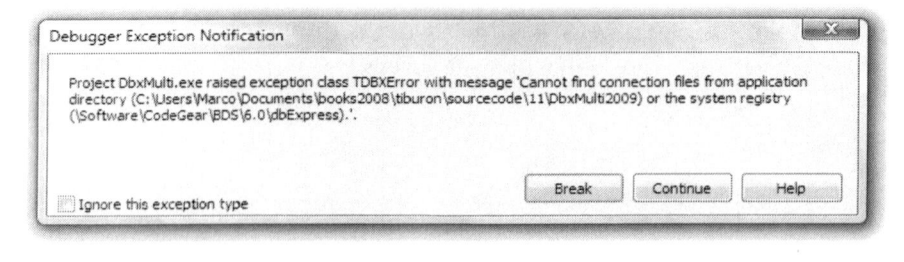

---

144 The error message is a little confusing, as the file are not missing in the system registry, of course, but in the folder referenced by the system registry, which on my system is C:\Users\Public\Documents\RAD Studio\dbExpress.

This was due to the fact that even if the various configuration settings of the driver had been loaded in the proper connection properties (including `LibraryName`, `VendorLib`, and `GetDriverFunc`) and parameters (stored in the `Params` string list), the code would try to refresh them anyway. The line that triggered the error was the following (from the `SetDriverName` method of the `TSQLConnection` class):

```
DriverProperties := TDBXConnectionFactory.
  GetConnectionFactory.GetDriverProperties(FDriverName);
```

A workaround (until this problem was fixed in Update 2, but still quite interesting as a general technique) is to create and install an in-memory connection manager[145] before the property is assigned, that is, before the form is loaded (as I've done this in the dbxMulti2009 example):

```
procedure SetConnectionManager;
var
  ConnFact: TDBXConnectionFactory;
begin
  ConnFact := TDBXMemoryConnectionFactory.Create;
  ConnFact.Open;
  TDBXConnectionFactory.SetConnectionFactory(ConnFact);
end;

initialization
  SetConnectionManager;
```

Again, you won't need this code after applying Update 2 to Delphi 2009.

Drivers in the Executable

Finally, to make the application work you have to add the DbxInterBase unit to your uses clause, which contains the driver and metadata information for the specific database.

This unit is generally added automatically as you set the Driver in the SQL-Connection component, but I've seen situations in which this was not managed properly, leading to the following error:

If you want to handle multiple databases at runtime, changing the configuration dynamically or loading it from configuration files, you should

---

[145] The original code, and the rationale behind it, can be found on the blog of Chau Chee Yang, at the address http://chee-yang.blogspot.com/2008/09/delphi-2009-using-dbx4-framework.html.

352 - Chapter 11: Datasets and dbExpress

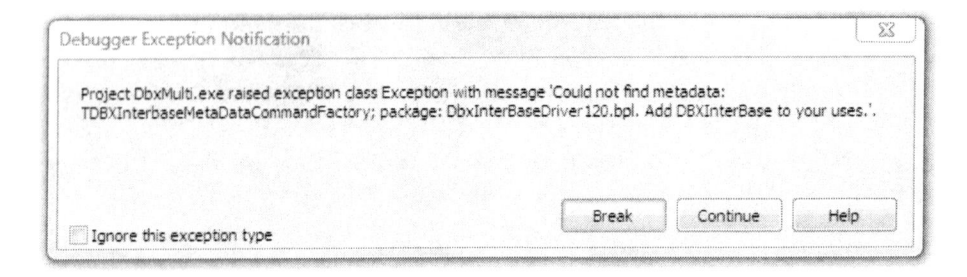

manually add the proper units for the various databases to the application: DbxOracle, DbxMSSQL, DbxMySql, DbxBlackfishSQL, DbxDb2, DbxInformix, the two Sybase drivers, and so on. In the past this driver and metadata information was added to each project, just in case it might need it, while now you can include only the support for the databases you are going to use in the executable.

Notice that these units add driver and metadata access information to the dbExpress configuration, but they don't embed the actual dbExpress driver[146] (in this case dbxint.dll), that you still have to deploy along with your application and the vendor library.

Extended Metadata Support

A recent feature of dbExpress, even if not new to Delphi 2009, is its extended support for metadata. This feature was introduced in the December 2007 Update of Delphi 2007, but was not covered in Delphi 2007 Handbook (which was released before that update).

The new metadata support is used extensively by the Data Explorer pane of the Delphi IDE, but can also be used by any application. In short, you'll not only be able to browse the database structure but also to use classes and objects to modify it, rather than relying directly on the native database SQL commands for creating and modifying data structures. Not only will the code look more object-oriented, but it will be also easier to target different database servers with the same code, as dbExpress abstracts the metadata capabilities of each server.

---

146 This is different than in past versions of Delphi, in which it was possible to include a specially compiled unit containing the driver code, effectively embedding the driver library into the executable file.

I don't want to delve into the details of dbExpress metadata, which is actually quite complex to manage, but only show you a simple example you can use to add new tables to a database. Before doing any operation on metadata in dbExpress, you need to initialize a specific provider and to keep a reference to this object around (in the example in a private field of the form):

```
type
  TFormMetaCreateTable = class (TForm)
  private
    metaProv: TDBXDataExpressMetaDataProvider;

procedure TFormMetaCreateTable.InitMetaProvider;
begin
  if not Assigned (metaProv) then
  begin
    metaProv := TDBXDataExpressMetaDataProvider.Create;
    metaProv.Connection := SqlConnection1.DBXConnection;
    metaProv.Open;
  end;
end;
```

Notice that the metadata is connected with and depends on the actual connection and its configuration, basically the driver you are working on. The unit that defines the metadata provider, which you have to include in your uses clause, is DBXDataExpressMetaDataProvider.

With this configuration available, here is the code used to create the table:

```
procedure TFormMetaCreateTable.btnCreateClick(
  Sender: TObject);
var
  MetaDataTable: TDBXMetaDataTable;
begin
  InitMetaProvider;

  MetaDataTable := TDBXMetaDataTable.Create;
  MetaDataTable.TableName := edTableName.Text;
  MetaDataTable.AddColumn(
    TDBXInt32Column.Create('id'));
  MetaDataTable.AddColumn(
    TDBXDecimalColumn.Create('amount', 10, 2));
  MetaDataTable.AddColumn(
  TDBXUnicodeCharColumn.Create('city', 32));

  metaProv.QuoteIdentifierIfNeeded(' ');
  metaProv.CreateTable(MetaDataTable);
  Log ('Table ' + MetaDataTable.TableName + ' created');
end;
```

Beside creating tables, you can add other settings, from indexes to views to referential integrity constraints. You can use the metadata also to query the database structure. This is the traditional code you can use in dbExpress to access the available tables, using the `GetTableNames` method of the SQL-Connection component:

```
procedure TFormMetaCreateTable.btnTableListOldClick(
  Sender: TObject);
var
  sl: TStringList;
  str: string;
begin
  sl := TStringList.Create;
  try
    SqlConnection1.GetTableNames(sl);
    for str in sl do
    begin
      Log (str);
    end;
  finally
    sl.Free;
  end;
end;
```

Using the metadata provider you can access much more than table names, although this sample snippet basically only does that, filtering out the system tables:

```
procedure TFormMetaCreateTable.btnTableListMetaClick(
  Sender: TObject);
var
  dbxTable: TDBXTablesTableStorage;
begin
  InitMetaProvider;

  dbxTable := metaProv.GetCollection (
    TDBXMetaDataCommands.GetTables)
    as TDBXTablesTableStorage;
  while dbxTable.Next do
    if not (dbxTable.TableType = 'SYSTEM TABLE') then
      Log (dbxTable.TableName);
end;
```

Notice the use of the `TDBXMetaDataCommands` class, that has a collection of public constants used to help write the various metadata commands, which are basically string commands. The output of the previous event handler (after creating a new table with the default name) is displayed below:

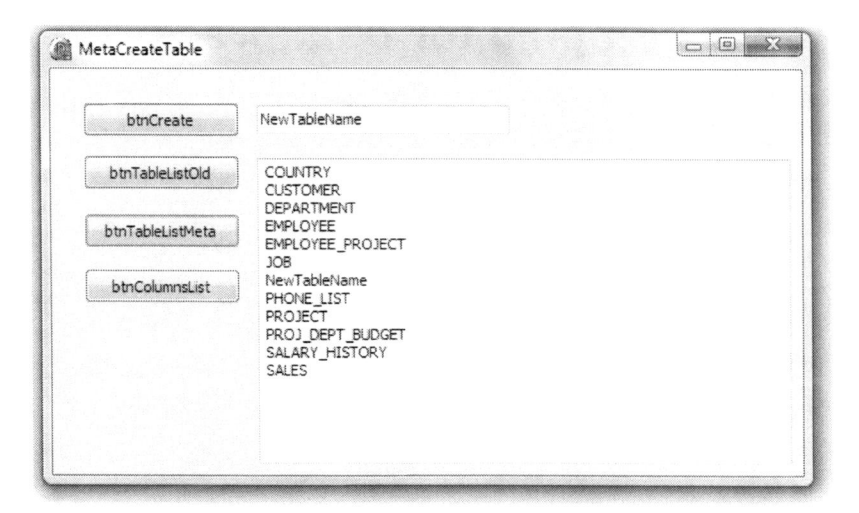

In a very similar way the program reads the names and types of the columns of the new table (or of the table named in the edit box):

```
procedure TFormMetaCreateTable.btnColumnsListClick(
  Sender: TObject);
var
  dbxTable: TDBXColumnsTableStorage;
begin
  InitMetaProvider;

  dbxTable := metaProv.GetCollection (
    TDBXMetaDataCommands.GetColumns + ' ' +
    edTableName.Text) as TDBXColumnsTableStorage;
  while dbxTable.Next do
    Log (dbxTable.ColumnName +
      ' [' + dbxTable.TypeName + ']');
end;
```

In this case you have to combine a command text (`GetColumns`) with specific information about the table you are interested in, which is quite odd. A helper function with a parameter would probably have made more sense.

Notice that the two calls to `GetCollection` of the metadata provider, in the last two code snippets, return objects of different classes that inherit from `TDBXTable` (ultimately a custom `TDBXValueList`). In the last case the class returned is `TDBXColumnsTableStorage`, while in the previous code snippet the class was `TDBXTablesTableStorage`.

Data Pumping for dbExpress

When working with multiple databases it is often necessary to migrate data from one server to another, and with table definitions not exactly identical among different servers this operation can take time. Following approach of the old DataPump available for the BDE, the Internet services team of CodeGear[147] has built a dbExpress data pump application:

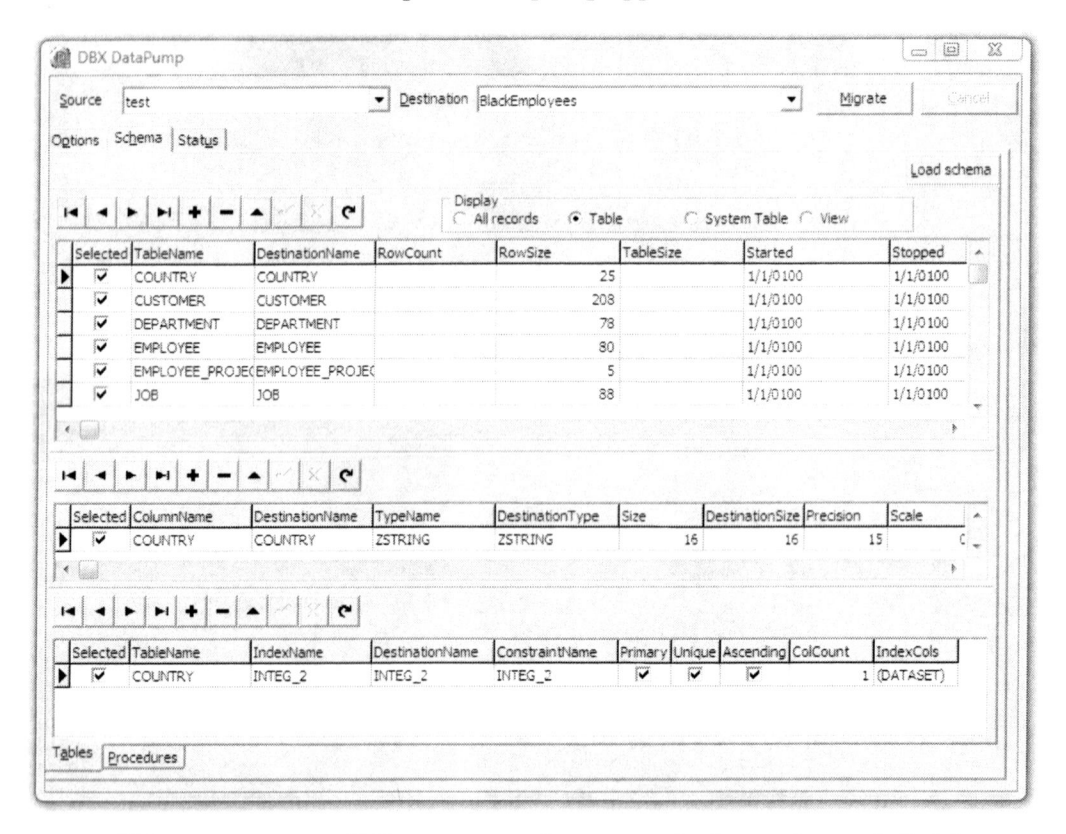

This program uses dbExpress metadata extensively to migrate definitions and actual data between servers for which there is a dbExpress driver with metadata support. The application is not part of Delphi, because it was pro-

---

[147] The tool was developed by Jon Benedicto, Yorai Aminov, and John Kaster, who's the head of the Internet services team at CodeGear. John Kaster is well known to the Delphi community, as he was involved with the product and the MIDAS technology, among other things. John's blog is at: http://blogs.codegear.com/johnk.

duced by a different group within CodeGear, but is available among the Delphi 2009 database examples. In my installation, the project is under:

```
C:\Users\Public\Documents\
   RAD Studio\6.0\Demos\database\projects\dbxdatapump\
```

Using the tool is relatively simple, but what's great is having the entire source code at your disposal.

Data-Aware Controls

At first look, considering the data-aware controls of the VCL you might see very little change. In effect, it is true that they have limited new features, if you don't consider the fact that all data-aware controls are now Unicode enabled.

We also saw in the last chapter how to create a database navigator based on the Ribbon control. Still, it would be nice to have some of the features that were added to other controls of the VCL. For example, the TDBEdit class inherits from TCustomEdit, but it doesn't expose properties like NumbersOnly or TextHint.

Would it be hard to make those extra features available, even without inheriting a custom component from the TDBEdit class? We can do so either by using the protected hack, or (the solution I prefer) with a local interposer class. This is the class I've added to the main form of the DbEditPlus example, to make the two extra properties available:

```
type
  TDbEdit = class (DBCtrls.TDBEdit)
  public
    property NumbersOnly;
    property TextHint;
  end;
```

The program has a simple form with a number of edit boxes (obtained automatically by dragging the fields from the fields editor). Now the first of these edits is connected to a numeric database field, which limits its input to numbers, decimal separators, exponential values, and a few more I'd like to remove.

We can do that easily (and even have the specific Windows error message) by writing in the OnCreate event handler of the form:

358 - Chapter 11: Datasets and dbExpress

```
procedure TFormDbEditPlus.FormCreate(Sender: TObject);
begin
  ClientDataSet1.Open;
  DbEdit1.NumbersOnly := True;
end;
```

Managing the `TextHint` is not that easy, because if all you do is set that property you have to move the focus manually to the given edit box to make it start work. There might be a better way, but I resorted to simulating that behavior in code. As setting the focus won't work until the form is created and visible, I've decided to execute the code when a specific button is pressed, but it wouldn't be difficult to automate:

```
procedure TFormDbEditPlus.btnTextHintClick(
  Sender: TObject);
var
  aControl: TWinControl;
begin
  aControl := ActiveControl;
  DbEdit4.TextHint := 'Enter second address line';
  DbEdit4.SetFocus;
  aControl.SetFocus;
end;
```

The combined effect of the features of this demo (error while entering a letter and text hint when a field is empty) is visible in this screen shot:

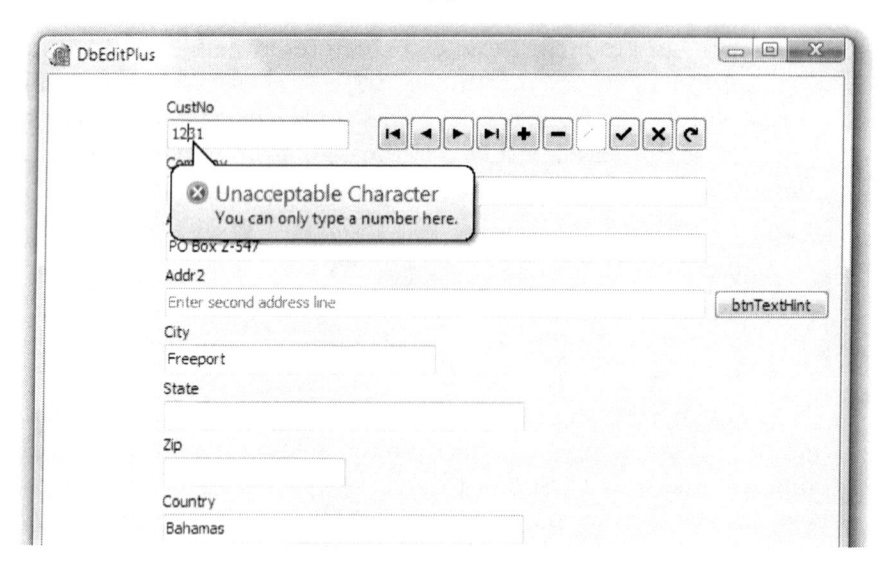

Marco Cantù, Delphi 2009 Handbook

From DBImage to Poor Old DBGrid

A specific new feature of the DBImage control is its new `Proportional` property. What is also relevant is that the DBImage control inherits the ability to handle new file formats, like PNG, from the Image control.

Despite rumors, the DBGrid control hasn't been revamped in Delphi 2009 and remains quite an old control with limited capabilities. What CodeGear has done, instead, is to make one of the third party grid controls available to registered users of Delphi 2009[148], the InfoPower Grid Essentials, by Woll2-Woll Software. This special edition of the control (with limited features compared to the full InfoPower control set) is not part of the Delphi installation but has to be downloaded separately from the Delphi registered users download page, at:

```
http://cc.codegear.com/reg/delphi
```

This is possible only if you bought and registered Delphi 2009, of course. Refer to the Woll2Woll web site, for more information about this extended database grid and their other offerings, at:

```
http://www.woll2woll.com
```

What's Next

This chapter focused on new features of Delphi database architecture a significant part of the VCL, both in terms of size and importance. I've detailed how the Unicode support has been modified and covered some new features of the dbExpress architecture.

The most important change to the Delphi database architecture, though, is in its revamped multi-tier support, called DataSnap and originally introduced in Delphi 5 with the name MIDAS. The new architecture resembles the original one, and uses some of those components, but is not tied to COM any more, uses a different transport layer, and opens up interesting possibilities. That's why there is an entire chapter devoted to DataSnap 2009.

---

148 At least for some time, it is not clear if the offer will last indefinitely.

Chapter 12: DataSnap 2009

For a long time Delphi has included a technology for building multi-tier database applications. Formerly known as MIDAS and later as DataSnap, Delphi's multi-tier technology was based on COM, even if the remote connectivity could be provided by sockets and HTTP, instead of DCOM. For some time, it even supported CORBA. A slightly modified version, provided SOAP connectivity.

Delphi 2009 still includes the classic DataSnap, but provides a brand new remoting and multi-tier technology as well. It is partially based on the dbExpress architecture. This new technology is still called DataSnap, but to avoid confusion is generally referenced as "DataSnap 2009".

Building a First DataSnap 2009 Demo

Before I get into too many details, let me start with a simple three-tier database-oriented demo. This will help clarify a few points and also cover differences from the previous version of the technology.

Building a Server

The first step is building a DataSnap 2009 server application. This can be a standard VCL application, to which you add a server module (found in the Delphi files page of the New Items dialog box).

To the server module (but we could also have used a standard data module) you generally add the dbExpress components to connect to the data base server, plus a dataset provider to expose the given datasets:

```
object IBCONNECTION: TSQLConnection
  ConnectionName = 'IBCONNECTION'
  DriverName = 'Interbase'
  LoginPrompt = False
  Params.Strings = (
    'DriverName=Interbase'
    'Database=C:\Program Files\...\Data\Employee.GDB')
end
object EMPLOYEE: TSQLDataSet
  CommandText = 'EMPLOYEE'
  CommandType = ctTable
  SQLConnection = IBCONNECTION
end
object DataSetProviderEmployee: TDataSetProvider
  DataSet = EMPLOYEE
end
```

This server module is built in a very similar way to how it would have been in the past. What is new is the need to include in the program three new components that provide configuration and connectivity in place of the COM support (which is totally gone). The three components are:

- **DSServer**, the main server configuration component, which is needed to wire all the other DataSnap 2009 components together.

- **DSServerClass**, a component needed for each class you want to expose. This component is not the class you make available, but acts as a class factory to create objects of the class you want to call from a remote client. In other words, the DSServerClass component will refer to the class that has the public interface.
- **DSTCPServerTransport**, a component that defines the transport protocol to be used (this is the only protocol directly available in Delphi 2009) and its configuration, such as which TCP/IP port to use.

In the demo these components are in the main form of the server, configured as follows:

```
object DSServer1: TDSServer
  AutoStart = True
  HideDSAdmin = False
  OnConnect = DSServer1Connect
  OnDisconnect = DSServer1Disconnect
end
object DSTCPServerTransport1: TDSTCPServerTransport
  PoolSize = 0
  Server = DSServer1
  BufferKBSize = 32
end
object DSServerClass1: TDSServerClass
  OnGetClass = DSServerClass1GetClass
  Server = DSServer1
  LifeCycle = 'Session'
end
```

We'll get to some of the details of these properties later on. The reason you don't see the value of the TCP/IP port in the listing above is that I've not modified the default value of 211.

The only Delphi code you need to write is the "class factory" code that is needed to connect the DSServerClass1 component to the server module exposing the providers:

```
procedure TFormFirst3Tier2009Server.
  DSServerClass1GetClass(DSServerClass: TDSServerClass;
  var PersistentClass: TPersistentClass);
begin
  PersistentClass := TDSFirst3TierServerModule;
end;
```

This is all you need for the server. In the actual example I've added a logging statement to the method above, as well as to the event handlers of the OnConnect and OnDisconnect events of the DSServer component.

Again, there is no need to register it in any way. Simply run it, maybe using the *Run | Run Without Debugging* command of the Delphi IDE, so you can build the client and connect it to the server even at design time.

The First Client

Now that we have a server available, we can move on and build a first client. In the DataSnap 2009 client application we need to use an SQLConnection component associated with the new DataSnap dbExpress driver, configured with the proper TCP/IP port.

Next we need a DSProviderConnection component, used to refer to the server class, with the ServerClassName property. This is not the intermediary class factory in the server (DSServerClass1), but the actual target of the class factory, in my example the TDSFirst3TierServerModule class.

Like in a traditional DataSnap application, the provider can be used by the ClientDataSet component to fetch (and update) the remote dataset. First, you have to assign the RemoteServer property of the ClientDataSet, picking the DSProviderConnection1 component from the drop down list. Next, you can select the DataSetProviderEmployee provider from the drop down of the ProviderName property, populated with all exported DataSet-Provider components of the remote data module.

This is a summary of the properties of these components, plus a DataSource used to display the database table in a DBGrid:

```
object SQLConnection1: TSQLConnection
  DriverName = 'Datasnap'
end
object DSProviderConnection1: TDSProviderConnection
  ServerClassName = 'TDSFirst3TierServerModule'
  SQLConnection = SQLConnection1
end
object ClientDataSet1: TClientDataSet
  ProviderName = 'DataSetProviderEmployee'
  RemoteServer = DSProviderConnection1
end
object DataSource1: TDataSource
  DataSet = ClientDataSet1
```

```
end
```
That's all it takes for an introductory demo. Now if you run the server first and the client next, you can press the Open button of the client and see the database data. Also notice the log produced by the server, like in the next screen shot of the combined programs:

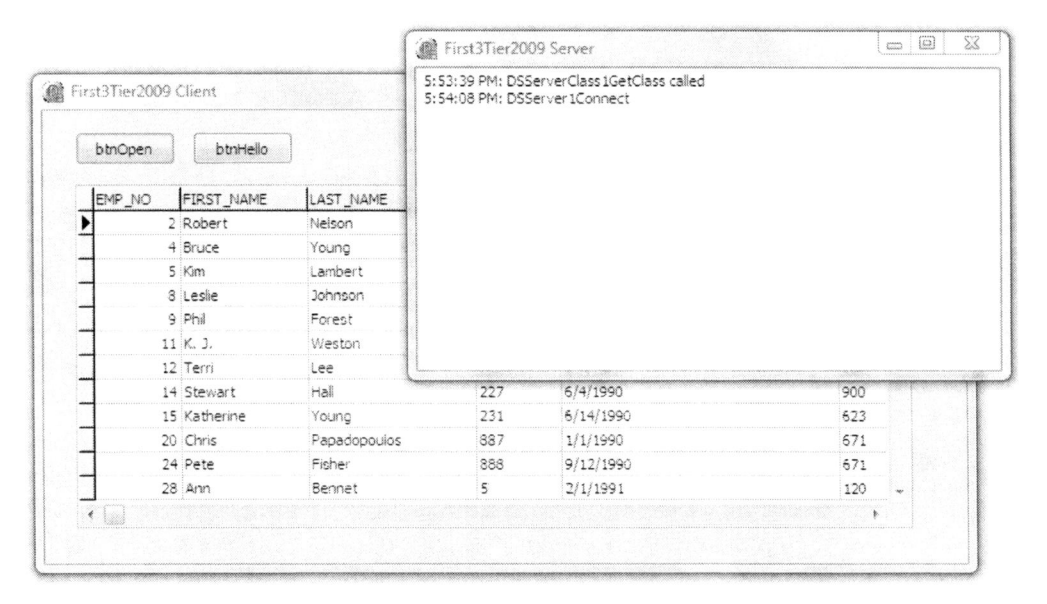

From DataSnap to DataSnap 2009

Compared to traditional DataSnap application, there are a few significant differences, more related to the architecture and deployment than the actual code you have to write:

- There is no COM involved for the development of the server. Even if a client could already use sockets in the past, a socket-to-Com mapping service was required on the server. Now the client and server applications communicate directly over TCP/IP.
- As a side effect, you don't have to register the server, nor run any helper service on it. All the server has to provide to the client is an open TCP/IP port the client can reach
- You must manually run the application on the server, or create a service for it. In the past the COM support implied the server application would be started as needed.

- The server implementation is slightly more complicated in terms of components, but there is very little code behind the scenes, as for the COM counterpart.
- The client implementation is almost identical, as we need a standard SQLConnection component, in place of a specific connection object.
- On the server side, the TDSServerModule class inherits from TDataModule, including the IAppServer interface (the same interface used in the past by a COM-based TRemoteDataModule) and enabling the $MethodInfo compiler directive.
- As the client-side dbExpress driver is a pure 100% Delphi driver, you don't need do deploy any DLL on the client computer, even if you are using dbExpress for the connectivity.
- Pay a lot of attention when closing the server application. Unlike in the COM architecture, which warns you about pending connections, a DataSnap 2009 server will seem to close, but won't until there are no remaining connections to it. However, even after the connections have been closed it will remain running in memory, even if the main form is gone. You'll need to use Task Manager (or Process Explorer) to terminate the server. You might think that closing all existing client applications will be enough, but it is not: The Delphi IDE, in fact, can open a connection to the server even automatically, for browsing its exposed classes and methods. Be sure to close any SQLConnection to the server before stopping it.

Adding Server Methods

As in the past, you can write methods in the server that can be called by the client. In the past, this was based on COM, so you had to add interfaces to the type library and implement then in the server objects, and call the methods using COM dispatch interfaces on the client. In DataSnap 2009 the remote methods calls, or server method calls, are based on Delphi's RTTI. Notice, however, that parameters passing is based on dbExpress parameter types, and not on Delphi language types.

You can have multiple server side classes that expose methods, but to continue with the simple project that I've already built, I added an extra method to the server module class (in the server application), using the following code:

```
type
  TDSFirst3TierServerModule = class(TDSServerModule)
    IBCONNECTION: TSQLConnection;
    EMPLOYEE: TSQLDataSet;
    DataSetProviderEmployee: TDataSetProvider;
  private
    { Private declarations }
  public
    function GetHello: string;
  end;

function TDSFirst3TierServerModule.GetHello: string;
begin
  Result := 'Hello from TDSFirst3TierServerModule at '
    + TimeToStr (Now);
end;
```

To enable remote invocation you have to connect the class for which you want to expose methods to a DSServerClass factory. (In this case, we've already done so in the database portion of the demo). The second requirement is to use a class that is compiled with the $MethodInfo directive turned on, but this already takes place in the declaration of the base TDSServerModule class. This means that, in practice, all we have to do is to add a public method to the server module, and everything else will work.

How do we call this server method from the client application? There are basically two alternatives. One is to use the new SqlServerMethod component and call the server method as if it was a stored procedure. The second is to generate a proxy class in the client application and use this proxy class to make the call.

In the First3Tier2009 client demo I've implemented both approaches. For the first, I've added an SqlServerMethod[149] component to the form of the client, tied it to the connection, picked a value for the ServerMethodName property in the Object Inspector (among the many available, as the standard IAppServer interface methods are listed as well), and checked the value of the Params property. This is a copy of the component settings (which actu-

---

149 Oddly enough the SqlServerMethod component is named with a mixed case "Sql", while all other dbExpress components use uppercase "SQL". Not a big deal, but I though it was worth noticing.

ally include the result of a sample call performed when checking the parameters):

```
object SqlServerMethod1: TSqlServerMethod
  GetMetadata = False
  Params = <
    item
      DataType = ftWideString
      Precision = 2000
      Name = 'ReturnParameter'
      ParamType = ptResult
      Size = 2000
      Value = 'Hello from TDSFirst3TierServerModule...'
    end>
  SQLConnection = SQLConnection1
  ServerMethodName = 'TDSFirst3TierServerModule.GetHello'
end
```

Notice that the native string type is mapped to a string parameter of 2,000 characters. After configuring the SqlServerMethod component, the program can call it using the input parameters (none in this case) and the output parameters (the result) as in a stored procedure or query call:

```
procedure TFormFirst3Tier2009Client.btnHelloClick(
  Sender: TObject);
begin
  SqlServerMethod1.ExecuteMethod;
  ShowMessage (SqlServerMethod1.Params[0].Value);
end;
```

To make it easier to write the calling code we can use the second approach I mentioned earlier, creating a local proxy class in the client application. To accomplish this, we can ask the Delphi IDE to parse the interface of the server class and create local proxy class for it, by clicking on the SQLConnection component and selecting the command *Generate Datasnap client classes*. In the case of this example, Delphi will generate a unit with the following class (from which I've omitted the code of the constructors and the destructor):

```
type
  TDSFirst3TierServerModuleClient = class
  private
    FDBXConnection: TDBXConnection;
    FInstanceOwner: Boolean;
    FGetHelloCommand: TDBXCommand;
  public
    constructor Create(
      ADBXConnection: TDBXConnection); overload;
    constructor Create(
```

```
    ADBXConnection: TDBXConnection;
    AInstanceOwner: Boolean); overload;
  destructor Destroy; override;
  function GetHello: string;
  end;
function TDSFirst3TierServerModuleClient.GetHello: string;
begin
  if FGetHelloCommand = nil then
  begin
    FGetHelloCommand := FDBXConnection.CreateCommand;
    FGetHelloCommand.CommandType :=
      TDBXCommandTypes.DSServerMethod;
    FGetHelloCommand.Text :=
      'TDSFirst3TierServerModule.GetHello';
    FGetHelloCommand.Prepare;
  end;
  FGetHelloCommand.ExecuteUpdate;
  Result := FGetHelloCommand.Parameters[0].
    Value.GetWideString;
end;
```

Notice that the generated code doesn't use the high level SqlServerMethod component, but rather calls directly into the low-level dbExpress implementation objects, like the TDBXCommand class[150].

Having this proxy class available, the client program can now call the server method in a more language-friendly way, although we do need to create an instance of the proxy class (or create one and keep it around). This code does exactly the same as the previous code based on the SqlServerMethod component:

```
procedure TFormFirst3Tier2009Client.btnHelloClick(
  Sender: TObject);
begin
  with TDSFirst3TierServerModuleClient.Create(
    SQLConnection1.DBXConnection) do
  try
    ShowMessage (GetHello);
  finally
    Free;
  end;
end;
```

If the code is actually longer than the previous version, this is because the method we are calling has no parameters, thus making the language binding

---

[150] There is a demo of the low-level dbExpress classes in the section "Using the DBX-Common classes" of Chapter 10 of my Delphi 2007 Handbook.

code less relevant. Still, having a ready-to-use proxy object, we could have written:

```
ShowMessage (ServerProxyObject.GetHello);
```

Sessions and Threading with a Non-Database DataSnap Server

If using the `IAppServer` interface directly is going to be the most common way for using DataSnap 2009, it is equally possible to use this multi-tier technology for remote method invocation outside of the database context. You can also use the same technology to access database data or perform database operations without using the `IAppServer` interface, which is fine if all you want to do is read data from the server. If you want to let the client application modify the data and post it back to the server, using custom methods could become tedious compared to the ready-to-use `IAppServer` interface, implemented by the ClientDataSet and the DataSetProvider components.

In any case, in this second example, I want to create a minimal server exposing a couple of simple classes. In the following sections I'll use this simple server to explore a couple of relevant issues, like server memory management and server (and client) threading.

The first server class (with two methods) I want to publish in the Dsnap-MethodServer project is the following:

```
{$MethodInfo ON}
type
  TSimpleServerClass = class(TPersistent)
  public
    function Echo (const Text: string): string;
    function SlowPrime (MaxValue: Integer): Integer;
  end;
{$MethodInfo OFF}
```

The code of the first method simply echoes the input, repeating its last part, while the second method performs the most classic slow computation of my books (already used in the ParallelFor example of Chapter 6, among others). This is the code of the two methods:

```delphi
function TSimpleServerClass.Echo(
  const Text: string): string;
begin
  Result := Text + '...' +
    Copy (Text, 2, maxint) + '...' +
    Copy (Text, Length (Text) - 1, 2);
end;

function TSimpleServerClass.SlowPrime(
  MaxValue: Integer): Integer;
var
  I: Integer;
begin
  // counts the prime numbers below the given value
  Result := 0;
  for I := 1 to MaxValue do
  begin
    if IsPrime (I) then
      Inc (Result);
  end;
end;
```

I'll use the latter method to discuss some threading issues in practice. I've omitted the extra statements used to log the server operations from the code snippet above.

The server application has only one unit, which defines the main form and two server side classes. The form has the usual DataSnap server components, a DSServer and a DSTCPServerTransport, plus two DSServerClass component, one for each of the classes I want to expose. After compiling the server and starting it, I've let Delphi create a client proxy using the SQLConnection component of a new client application. This is the client proxy class:

```delphi
type
  TSimpleServerClassClient = class
  private
    FDBXConnection: TDBXConnection;
    FInstanceOwner: Boolean;
    FEchoCommand: TDBXCommand;
    FSlowPrimeCommand: TDBXCommand;
  public
    constructor Create(
      ADBXConnection: TDBXConnection); overload;
    constructor Create(
      ADBXConnection: TDBXConnection;
      AInstanceOwner: Boolean); overload;
    destructor Destroy; override;
    function Echo(Text: string): string;
    function SlowPrime(MaxValue: Integer): Integer;
```

```
  end;
```

In the client program, the OnClick event of the button calls the Echo server method, after creating an instance of the proxy, if needed:

```
procedure TFormDsnapMethodsClient.btnEchoClick(
  Sender: TObject);
begin
  if not Assigned (SimpleServer) then
    SimpleServer := TSimpleServerClassClient.Create (
      SQLConnection1.DBXConnection);
  Edit1.Text := SimpleServer.Echo(Edit1.Text);
end;
```

In the example, pressing this button the sample text "Marco" is transformed by the server call into "Marco...arco...co". This is a complete example of how you can create a totally custom server, with no database access involved and no use of the IAppServer interface. This is not the only method invocation technique available in Delphi, as you can use SOAP, socket-based applications, or third-party tools... but having this extra feature on top of the remote database access capability is certainly a plus.

One of the reasons I'm focusing on this example is it can help us clarifying some relevant features of DataSnap 2009. One of them is how server side objects relate to client proxies or server method invocation. This is better demonstrated by a server object that keeps track of its own state, like the following second server class of the demo project:

```
{$MethodInfo ON}
type
  TStorageServerClass = class(TPersistent)
  private
    FValue: Integer;
  public
    procedure SetValue(const Value: Integer);
    function GetValue: Integer;
    function ToString: string; override;
  published
    property Value: Integer read GetValue write SetValue;
  end;
{$MethodInfo OFF}
```

While the getter and setter methods simply read and write the local field, the ToString function returns both the value and an object identifier based on its hash code:

```
function TStorageServerClass.ToString: string;
begin
  Result := 'Value: ' + IntToStr (Value) +
```

```
      ' - Object: ' + IntToHex (GetHashCode, 4);
end;
```

I'll use this method to figure out how the life cycle of server objects work. In this class the property definition only makes sense for the server as it is not exposed to the client. The interface of the corresponding proxy becomes (after removing private fields, standard constructors and destructor):

```
type
  TStorageServerClassClient = class
  public
    procedure SetValue(Value: Integer);
    function GetValue: Integer;
    function ToString: string;
```

Notice that compiling this class produces the following warning, unless you manually mark the method as `override`:

```
Method 'ToString' hides virtual method of base type
'TObject'
```

The goal of this example is to figure out what happens when multiple client applications use the same server. The behavior of a DataSnap 2009 server in such a case depends on the value of the `LifeCycle` string property of the DSServerClass component being used.

Server Objects Life Cycle

The `LifeCycle` property of the DSServerClass component can assume the following three string values[151] (which are read from the DSServerClass component when the DSServer object is opened, ignoring any change at runtime):

- **Session** indicates that the server will create a different object for each client socket connection, that is, a server object for each client. The server objects are released when the connection is closed. Multiple clients will have independent status and separate database access in case of the server object is a data module, maybe with its own database connection component. This is the default setting.
- **Invocation** indicates that a new server object is created (and destroyed) every time the server method is invoked. This is a classic

---

[151] The three string values for this property are the three constants of the TDSLifeCycle class, defined in the DSNames unit.

stateless behavior, making the server extremely scalable, but also subject to fetching the same data over and over.

- **Server** indicates a shared server object, a singleton. Each client will use the same server object instance, the same data, potentially causing synchronization problems (as different client invocations are performed by different server threads). Access to shared server objects must be protected by synchronization techniques (for example using the new `TMonitor` record).

Beside using these default settings, you can customize the creation and destruction of server side objects using the `OnCreateInstance` and `OnDestroyInstance` events of the DSServerClass component. This could be used, for example, to implement server side object pooling.

A Client Starting the Server and Opening Multiple Connections

As a practical example, the DsnapMethods project let's you create multiple client connections from a single instance of a client application (using multiple instances will yield the same result), by creating multiple instances of the form that has the SQLConnection component and stored a local instance of the client proxy, created the first time it is used. Not only can the client create multiple client connections, but it can also start the server program with a given life cycle setting. This is easy to achieve because the client and the server application are on the same computer.

To accomplish this I've added to the unit of the main form of the server a global variable, used to determine the DSServerClass `LifeCycle` property:

```
var
  ParamLifeCycle: string;

procedure TFormDsnapMethodsServer.DSServerClass2GetClass(
  DSServerClass: TDSServerClass;
  var PersistentClass: TPersistentClass);
begin
  DSServerClass2.LifeCycle := ParamLifeCycle;
  Log ('LifeCycle: ' + DSServerClass2.LifeCycle);
  PersistentClass := TStorageServerClass;
end;
```

The value of the `ParamLifeCycle` global variable is initialized using the command line parameters of the server application, which has the following code at the beginning of its project file source code:

```
begin
  if ParamCount > 0 then
    ParamLifeCycle := ParamStr(1);
  Application.Initialize;
```

With this code available on the server, the main form of the client application (which has no connection, as the connection is configured in the secondary forms) has a RadioGroup with the following values:

```
object rgLifeCycle: TRadioGroup
  ItemIndex = 0
  Items.Strings = (
    'Session'
    'Invocation'
    'Server')
end
```

When clicking on a button, the client program reads the current value and passes it as parameter to the server[152] (notice you cannot run the server twice, as you cannot have the same listening socket at the same port opened by two applications at the same time on a computer):

```
procedure TFormDsmcMain.btnStartServerClick(
  Sender: TObject);
var
  aStr: AnsiString;
begin
  Log (rgLifeCycle.Items[rgLifeCycle.ItemIndex]);
  aStr := 'DsnapMethodsServer.exe ' +
    rgLifeCycle.Items[rgLifeCycle.ItemIndex];
  WinExec (PAnsiChar (aStr), CmdShow);
end;
```

Now the main form of the client application also has a button used to create instances of the secondary form, which are destroyed when they are closed (in their `OnClose` event handler), closing the specific connection to the server. Another button is used to log the status of the current client forms:

```
procedure TFormDsmcMain.btnUpdateStatusClick(
  Sender: TObject);
var
```

---

[152] Remember that the `WinExec` API uses a `PAnsiChar` parameter and has no *wide* version, as module names in Windows are not Unicode enabled, like function names exposed by DLLs and referenced by the `GetProcAddress` API.

```
    I: Integer;
begin
  for I := 0 to Screen.FormCount - 1 do
    if Screen.Forms[I].ClassType = TFormDsmcClient then
      Log (IntToStr (I) + ': ' +
        Screen.Forms[I].ToString);
end;
```

When calling `ToString` for one of the secondary forms, this returns the status of the connected server object, calling its public `ToString` method:

```
function TFormDsmcClient.ToString: string;
begin
  InitStorageServer;
  Result := StorageServer.ToString;
end;
```

As a first execution example, I've created the server with the default *Session* life cycle, opened two client forms, set the values to 3 and 4, and asked for the overall status, with this result:

```
Session
1: Value: 3 - Object: 1C38400
2: Value: 4 - Object: 1C384E0
```

In a second execution, I've gone for the the *Invocation* life cycle, and asking for the overall status twice I saw the following output:

```
Invocation
1: Value: 0 - Object: 1D185B0
2: Value: 0 - Object: 1D18490
1: Value: 0 - Object: 1D185C0
2: Value: 0 - Object: 1D185D0
```

Notice that you are getting a new object for each execution, and the object's status is always zero (and any setting will immediately be lost when the object is destroyed immediately after each invocation). Needless to say, this makes sense only for stateless operations.

Finally, I've repeated the same steps (setting values to 3 and 4) with the *Server* life cycle setting, and this time every client form uses the same server object, with the last value set:

```
Server
1: Value: 4 - Object: 1E08490
2: Value: 4 - Object: 1E08490
```

In other words, the practice shows... that the theory is correct! While exploring life cycle configuration in the demo, we've also looked at an example of a client starting the (local) server it needs and of a client with multiple concurrent connections to the server.

Memory Management

The management of server side objects in memory is tied to the client connections and the server objects life cycle setting. Server side objects are generally kept in memory until the connection is closed (*Session*) or until the server is closed (*Server*), regardless of any active connection.

The situation is different for the *Invocation* life cycle, as in this case the server side object (`TStorageServerClass` in the example) is created at every invocation and should be immediately destroyed. What happens, however, is that (in Delphi 2009 with the Update 1 installed) for every invocation of a server method there is a leak of the server side object. For example, using the *Invocation* life cycle in the program, creating a client connection, and calling a server method twice, produces the following error when the server is closed:

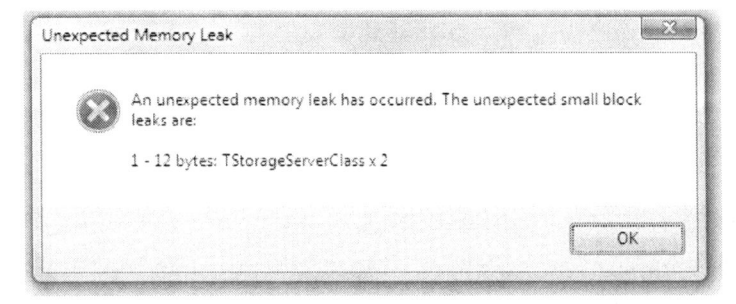

To fix the problem you can manually free the server side object by handling the `OnDestroyInstance` event of the related DSServerClass component (which receives a single parameter, with a very long name and class name, with the server class information and the server class instance attached):

```
procedure TFormDsnapMethodsServer.DSSC2DestroyInstance(
  DSDestroyInstanceEventObject:
    TDSDestroyInstanceEventObject);
begin
  // only if LifeCycle = 'Invocation'?
  DSDestroyInstanceEventObject.ServerClassInstance.Free;
end;
```

Thread Management

Another related issue is the management of threads on the server (and in some cases in the client). The thread manager is the TCP/IP transport component, which can use thread pooling to improve call efficiency. You can configure server thread pooling by using the PoolSize property of the server transport component (and set a thread limit using the MaxThreads property).

According to the documentation (in the source code, not in the help file) the value of the PoolSize property should be 10 by default, but it looks like this remains set to zero by default, thus disabling thread pooling. Set it at a value you like, but not 10, as this would be reset due to an apparent error in the component definition[153].

The threads on the server are created on a per-connection basis, not a per-request basis, and kept around while the connections are open. This means that the thread pooling model and configuration need to be adapted to the server life cycle configuration. Notice also that a client should not make two concurrent calls using the same connection, as this can mess up with the server side thread[154].

As the server is a multi-threaded application, every time a server object referenced a global resource (like the server form used for logging, in some of my examples) it should use a monitor or critical section. The new TMonitor record of Delphi 2009, covered in Chapter 7, should help providing a light-weight and simple to use synchronization mechanism.

As an example of how the threading model works, in the DsnapMethods application I added a very slow operation. We can now try to figure out what is its effect. The slow operation is tuned by passing to the SlowPrime server method call a different number, in the demo extracted from a corresponding UpDown control.

---

153 The PoolSize property, in fact, has a declared default value of 10, but as this is not set in the constructor, the effect is that a value of 10 won't be saved in the DFM file and will get lost.

154 Well, the fact that client cannot make multiple concurrent calls using a single connection is the theory, as reported by the limited documentation available. In practice, if you try to call the server using threads, and making a second request before the first is done, the server will queue the requests, at least when using the *Session* life cycle. We'll see this in an example later in this section.

Activating two client connections (in two separate client applications), making them slow (by using a large value like 100,000), and calling then rapidly, you'll see the following log on the server:

```
Client connected
Client connected
Starting SlowPrime for 1BA8490
Starting SlowPrime for 1BA84E0
Done SlowPrime for 1BA84E0
Done SlowPrime for 1BA8490
```

The methods on the server are effectively executed in parallel threads, and it might happen (as in the log above) that the second thread started ends before the first. Notice that things could be dangerous in case of a server object with shared state among connections, and even the unprotected logging I'm using in the project could cause harm.

If you try out this application, you'll immediately notice that while it is waiting for the server to respond the client application is blocked, not responding to user requests. In this case the culprit is the time required by the server to do the requested processing, but it might as well be a very large data packet to return or a terribly slow network connection.

Unless you have everything under strict control (a fast local network, a server performing relatively short operations, the ClientDataSet asking for a limited number of records in each packet...), it might be the case of adding some extra support on the client side to make the application more responsive. Lacking an option to generate a thread-based client proxy, for the DsnapMethodsClient project I've created a thread manually. The thread class of the project needs references to the client proxy, the value of the parameter, and the form where to display the output:

```
type
  TPrimesClientThread = class (TThread)
  private
    FMaxValue: Integer;
    FSimpleServer: TSimpleServerClassClient;
    FCallingForm: TFormDsmcClient;
  protected
    procedure Execute; override;
  public
    constructor Create (MaxValue: Integer;
      SimpleServer: TSimpleServerClassClient;
      CallingForm: TFormDsmcClient);
  end;
```

380 - Chapter 12: DataSnap 2009

While the constructor simply stores its parameter, the `Execute` method does the actual work (using an anonymous method):

```
procedure TPrimesClientThread.Execute;
var
  nResult: Integer;
begin
  nResult := FSimpleServer.SlowPrime(FMaxValue);
  Synchronize (procedure ()
    begin
      FCallingForm.lblPrimesTh.Caption :=
        IntToStr (nResult);
      // FCallingForm.btnPrimesTh.Enabled := True;
    end);
end;
```

This is invoked by a new button added to the client form:

```
procedure TFormDsmcClient.btnPrimesThClick(
  Sender: TObject);
begin
  // btnPrimesTh.Enabled := False;
  if not Assigned (SimpleServer) then
    SimpleServer := TSimpleServerClassClient.Create (
      SQLConnection1.DBXConnection);
  TPrimesClientThread.Create(
    SpinEdit2.Value, SimpleServer, self);
end;
```

The two commented lines in the two code snippets above (used to disable and enable the button) can be used to avoid concurrent calls from the same client connection (as you can now create two client side forms and call the slow operation in each of them), but as I mentioned in an earlier note even if you leave them commented and try executing a request before the previous one terminated, they'll be queued on the server, as the server log demonstrates. However, I did notice that when queuing requests it is very likely there will be server side memory leaks, so I'm not really recommending to stretch DataSnap server with this approach, but rather try to avoid making multiple simultaneous requests on a single connection from a multi-threaded client.

Porting an Old DataSnap Demo

Having explored some of the alternatives in using DataSnap 2009, let me get back to the most classic usage scenario, that is multi-tier database applications. As we've already seen the steps for creating a brand new DataSnap database application, let now focus on a equally relevant issue: porting an existing DataSnap (or MIDAS) application to this new architecture.

As a practical example, I've decided to port the ThinPlus[155] application of Mastering Delphi 2005, which showcases a few capabilities of DataSnap, and will let me cover a more complete example, besides focusing on what needs to be done to port a COM server invoked from a client using a socket to a pure socket-based architecture. The new example (with server and client projects) is in the ThinPlus2009 folder.

Notice that porting DataSnap applications to the new architecture is an interesting option, but not a compulsory one. Traditional DataSnap servers and clients can still compile and work properly in Delphi 2009.

Porting the Server

For porting the server project, I followed these steps:

- I removed the initialization section of the remote data module unit, called AppsRDM. The code removed was the call to the constructor of the `TComponentFactory` class.
- I also removed the `UpdateRegistry` class method of the `TAppServerPlus` class from the same remote data module unit.
- At that point I could eliminate from the uses clause of the remote data module the COM and ActiveX related units: ComServ, ComObj, VCLCom, and StdVcl.

---

[155] The program is described in detail in the book Mastering Delphi 2005, but also in previous editions like Mastering Delphi 7. Here I'll provide only an overview of some of its features. Those books can certainly give you a broader picture of the original features of DataSnap (and previously MIDAS), which are mostly still available in the Delphi 2009 version.

- Next I had to remove the reference to the custom `IAppServerPlus` interface that was used by the project to provide custom server methods (the interface was defined in the project type library).
- I deleted the type library and RIDL file (just created when the project was opened in Delphi 2009) from the project and the disk. I also had to remove a uses statement referring to the type library unit.
- I moved the only server method (`Login`) from the protected section to the public section of the remote data module class, removing from it the `safecall` modifier. As the `TRemoteDataModule` class is already compiled with `$MethodInfo` turned on, there is no need to add this declaration to the project unit.
- Finally, I added to the main form of the program the usual trio of components (server, server class, and server transport), wired them together, and returned the `TAppServerPlus` in the `OnGetClass` event handler of the server class component.

That was all it took to upgrade an old DataSnap server to the Delphi 2009 version. It might seem a lot, but it was actually quite fast. Now it was time to look into the client application, one that does a few custom operations.

Upgrading the Client

Porting the client application to DataSnap 2009 is generally easier than porting the server. The core step is to remove the connection components (my demo had three, as it let users experiment with the various connectivity options) and replace it with an SQLConnection and a DSProviderConnection, and make the ClientDataSet component refer to this new remote connection component.

The only specific code I had to change was the call to the `Login` server method. This took place in the `OnAfterConnection` of the connection component, and I've now moved it to the corresponding event of the SQLConnection component:

```
procedure TClientForm.SQLConnection1AfterConnect(
  Sender: TObject);
begin
  // was: ConnectionBroker1.AppServer.
  //        Login (Edit2.Text, Edit3.Text);
  SqlServerMethod1.ParamByName('Name').AsString :=
```

```
    Edit2.Text;
  SqlServerMethod1.ParamByName('Password').AsString :=
    Edit3.Text;
  SqlServerMethod1.ExecuteMethod;
end;
```

What this call does is to pass client login information to the server. The server validates the information and, only if it succeeds, will it let the provider expose its data. The password check is trivial, but the approach could be interesting. This is the Login method on the server:

```
procedure TAppServerPlus.Login(
  const Name, Password: WideString);
begin
  if Password <> Name then
    raise Exception.Create (
      'Wrong name/password combination received');
  ProviderDepartments.Exported := True;
  ServerForm.Add ('Login:' + Name + '/' + Password);
end;
```

Notice that in case the server returns an exception this will be clearly displayed (indicating where it comes from, *Remote error*) on the client side:

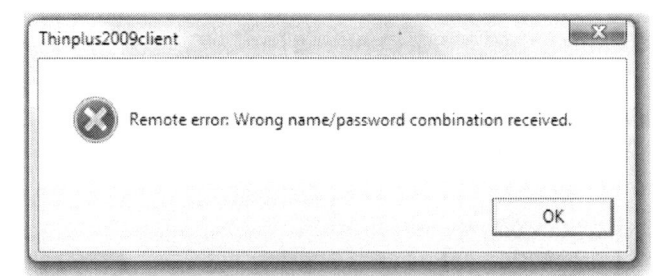

Advanced Features of ThinPlus2009

I upgraded the ThinPlus client and server applications to DataSnap 2009 following the steps mentioned earlier, even if these are some rather complex DataSnap programs, with several customizations. These include fetching data packets manually, using a master/details structure, executing a parametric query, transferring extra data along with the data packets, and the custom remote login I've just covered.

It is worth having a look at these features, even if briefly, as they should help those of you that have not used DataSnap (or not a lot) to appreciate its power. Those who have used it already, instead, will figure out how easily the code can be ported to the new architecture. The server application defined a master/details structure, based on the following settings of the (respectively) provider, the master data set, the data source used to refer to it, and the details dataset that refers to the data source:

```
object ProviderDepartments: TDataSetProvider
  DataSet = SQLDepartments
end
object SQLDepartments: TSQLDataSet
  CommandText = 'select * from DEPARTMENT'
  SQLConnection = SQLConnection1
end
object DataSourceDept: TDataSource
  DataSet = SQLDepartments
end
object SQLEmployees: TSQLDataSet
  CommandText =
    'select * from EMPLOYEE where dept_no = :dept_no'
  DataSource = DataSourceDept
  Params = <
    item
      Name = 'dept_no'
      ParamType = ptInput
    end>
  SQLConnection = SQLConnection1
end
```

On the client side, the program uses a first ClientDataSet connected with the provider and a second ClientDataSet that refers to a special *data set field* of the first one:

```
object cds: TClientDataSet
  FetchOnDemand = False
  PacketRecords = 5
  ProviderName = 'ProviderDepartments'
  RemoteServer = DSProviderConnection1
  object cdsDEPT_NO: TStringField...
  object cdsDEPARTMENT: TStringField...
  ...
  object cdsSQLEmployees: TDataSetField
    FieldName = 'SQLEmployees'
  end
end
object cdsDet: TClientDataSet
  DataSetField = cdsSQLEmployees
end
```

The data of the two ClientDataSet components is displayed in two DBGrid controls. Notice how the program fetches only 5 records (as indicated in the

`PacketRecords` property) in each data packet, and will stop fetching data after the first packet (as the `FetchOnDemand` property is False), even if the grid in not full. You can see this in the following snapshot of the client user interface just after opening the connection:

Following data packets are fetched manually, as the user clicks on the corresponding button:

```
procedure TClientForm.btnFetchClick(Sender: TObject);
begin
  btnFetch.Caption := IntToStr (cds.GetNextPacket);
end;
```

The program shows in the button caption how many records it fetched in each packet. This will be 5 while there are enough records, then the number or remaining records, and finally zero when all the records have already been retrieved. At each fetch request the client DBGrid will show more data, and its scrollbar will be updated accordingly. You can also use the `bntRecCount` button to ask how many records have been retrieved so far.

386 - Chapter 12: DataSnap 2009

The client program has a second form, displayed by pressing the Query button, with another client dataset. This ClientDataSet component is connected with a parametric query defined by the server as:

```
object SQLWithParams: TSQLDataSet
  CommandText =
    'select * from employee where job_code = :job_code'
  Params = <
    item
      DataType = ftString
      Name = 'job_code'
      ParamType = ptInput
      Value = 'Eng'
    end>
  SQLConnection = SQLConnection1
end
```

The client program has a list box, filled at design time with the department names, which is used to pass the proper parameter to the server. Notice that to write this code you have first to update the definition of the parameters, an operation you can do at design time by using the corresponding component editor command for the ClientDataSet component. This is the call used on the client to execute the remote parametric query:

```
procedure TFormQuery.btnParamClick(Sender: TObject);
begin
  cdsQuery.Close;
  cdsQuery.Params[0].AsString := ComboBox1.Text;
  cdsQuery.Open;
  ...
```

On the server, when this query is executed the OnGetDataSetProperties event of the provider adds extra information to the returned data packet:

```
procedure TAppServerPlus.
  ProviderQueryGetDataSetProperties(Sender: TObject;
  DataSet: TDataSet; out Properties: OleVariant);
begin
  Properties := VarArrayCreate([0,1], varVariant);
  Properties[0] := VarArrayOf(['Time', Now, True]);
  Properties[1] := VarArrayOf([
    'Param', SQLWithParams.Params[0].AsString, False]);
end;
```

Notice that the use of variant array parameters still works, even if the transport mechanism used by DataSnap 2009 is now different. On the client side, the btnParamClick event handler has two more lines of code to retrieve these extra properties from the data packet:

```
Caption := 'Data sent at ' + TimeToStr (
  TDateTime (cdsQuery.GetOptionalParam('Time')));
Label1.Caption := 'Param ' +
  cdsQuery.GetOptionalParam('Param');
```

There are a few more features in DataSnap that have been moved over to the new version, but this overview of the ThinPlus2009 program (mostly unchanged from its original version written in Delphi 6) should be enough for my goals: Show you the power of DataSnap and how easy it is to migrate even a complex application to the Delphi 2009 socket-based (and COM-free) version of DataSnap.

The DataSnap Administrative Interface

When you write a DataSnap 2009 server, you can run it, and connect the Delphi IDE to it at design time to get help in writing the client code. This help comes in the form of lists of available methods and providers and also in terms of the generation of the client side proxy classes. To accomplish this every server has an extra interface, internally called DSAdmin. In a deployed server you can disable this interface, to avoid others from writing client applications using Delphi (or at least make their life more difficult). This is accomplished by turning on the `HideDSAdmin` property of the DSServer component and is generally recommended when you deploy an application.

If the DSAdmin interface[156] is active ,though, you can use it to explore a server dynamically. I've written a bare-bones demo that does exactly that. It could be extended providing a full generic calling interface, and even by letting it generate extended client side proxy classes.

The program has a SQLConnection that connects with an available server. You might want to customize the code to connect to the server available at a given IP and port (the demo uses the default values, hard coded). To test the

---

156 For information about the DSAdmin interface refer to the `DSAmin` class (no T in front of the class name) in the DSCommonServer unit.

approach, I've first called the simple `GetPlatformName` method using an SqlServerMethod component configures as:

```
object smGetPlatformName: TSqlServerMethod
  GetMetadata = False
  Params = <
    item
      DataType = ftWideString
      Precision = 2000
      Name = 'ReturnParameter'
      ParamType = ptResult
      Size = 2000
    end>
  SQLConnection = SQLConnection1
  ServerMethodName = 'DSAdmin.GetPlatformName'
end
```

As the method has no parameter and a string return value, the code used to call it is quite simple:

```
procedure TFormAdmin.btnGetPlatformNameClick(
  Sender: TObject);
begin
  smGetPlatformName.ExecuteMethod;
  ShowMessage (smGetPlatformName.ServerMethodName + ': ' +
    smGetPlatformName.ParamByName('ReturnParameter').
    AsString)
end;
```

Most of the DSAdmin methods simply return a dataset. You can open and browse these datasets with simple loops that perform custom processing:

```
smGetMethods.Open;
while not smGetMethods.EOF do
begin
  strLog := '';
  for I := 0 to smGetMethods.FieldCount - 1 do
    strLog := strLog +
      smGetMethods.Fields[I].AsString + ' / ';
  ShowMessage (strLog);
  smGetMethods.Next;
end;
```

However, if your goal is simply to display the information on the screen, what is better than connecting a DBGrid to the resulting dataset? The SqlServerMethod component, in fact, can be opened directly as a database. Still, you cannot connect it to the user interface as it is a unidirectional dataset. The classic approach to display the data is to add a ClientDataSet and a Dataset Provider to the application, connecting them as normal.

The first server method I'm calling this way is the `GetServerClasses` method:

```
object smGetServerClasses: TSqlServerMethod
  Params = <
    item
      DataType = ftDataSet
      ParamType = ptResult
      Value = 'TDataSet'
    end>
  SQLConnection = SQLConnection1
  ServerMethodName = 'DSAdmin.GetServerClasses'
end
```

The result of the call can be displayed by attaching the DataSetProvider component to it, reopening the ClientDataSet and reducing the default size of the DBGrid columns:

```
procedure TFormAdmin.btnGetClassesClick(Sender: TObject);
var
  I: Integer;
begin
  ClientDataSet1.Close;
  smGetServerClasses.Open;
  DataSetProvider1.DataSet := smGetServerClasses;
  ClientDataSet1.Open;
  for I := 0 to DbGrid1.Columns.Count - 1 do
    DbGrid1.Columns[I].Width := 150;
end;
```

Finally, the last method is the `GetServerMethods` method of the DSAdmin interface, which is the most useful one as it returns the methods of each of the available server classes:

```
object smGetMethods: TSqlServerMethod
  Params = <
    item
      DataType = ftDataSet
      ParamType = ptResult
      Value = 'TDataSet'
    end>
  SQLConnection = SQLConnection1
  ServerMethodName = 'DSAdmin.GetServerMethods'
end
```

The code connects the result to the the dataset provider in a similar way to the previous call. The visual effect, in the client application, will look something this:

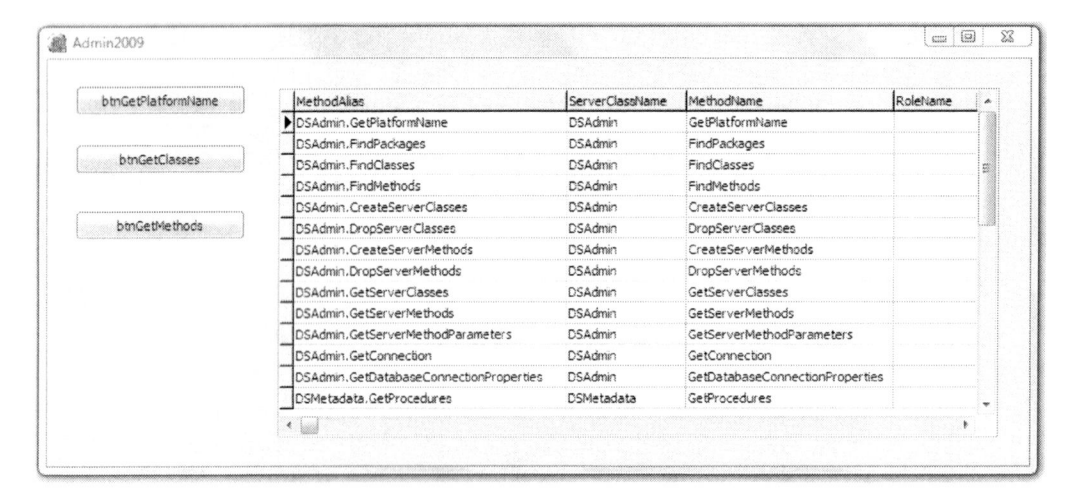

Again, this demo gives only an idea of what can be done using the DataSnap administrative interface. Other methods of the DSAdmin interface will let you retrieve the method parameters and other settings. Finally, you can use a generic SqlServerMethod component and set its name and parameters dynamically to call any server method.

Conclusion

In this chapter I've covered one the most significant updates in terms of the component library in Delphi 2009, the new DataSnap architecture for building multi-tier applications without having to resort to COM. You can use DataSnap 2009 for database programming, but also to easily call any server side method.

As this is the last chapter of the book, there is no "What's Next" section, but only a short conclusion about the product. I don't have much to add to the material presented so far, which hopefully helped you learn about all of the new features in Delphi 2009 and appreciate this version of the product.

Delphi 2009 is certainly an outstanding version, with an incredible number of new features that took me 400 pages to cover. With Delphi having a new owner (Embarcadero Technologies) and such a nice release including support for any language (thanks to Unicode), we can truly hope Delphi will still have a long life. Happy (Delphi) coding, wherever you are in the world!

Index

1995 13	ApplicationMenu 319
211 363	Apply Option Set dialog box 120
Action 306	ASCII 22
Action Manager 269, 304, 306p., 309, 320	Associate 323
ActionItem 315	AsString 336, 341
ActionLink 306	BabelFish 71
ActionList 306	BackgroundColor 265
Actions 303, 305	BalloonHint 249
ActionToolBar 307	Bangla 36
Active Form 294	BarColor 265
ActiveX Control Wizard 294	Barry Kelly 172, 178
ActMan unit 318	BaseException 238, 240
AddRecentItem 311	Basic Multilingual Plane 27, 54
AJAX 200, 204	BCM_SETSHIELD 252
Alan Wood 39	BDE 237, 356
Alignment 256	BitBtn 251
Allen Bauer 196	BLOB 280, 343
Anders Melander 277	Blog 17, 203, 228, 231
Anonymous methods 161, 178, 380	BOM 29, 34, 72p., 91, 233, 268
AnsiChar. 23pp., 44pp., 48, 69pp., 84p., 87	Bookmark 93, 334
AnsiString .... 49p., 55p.	Borland 13
AnsiStrings unit .... 95pp., 243p.	Borland Resource Compiler 126
Application 274, 281	BS_COMMANDLINK 252
Application Menu 310	BS_SPLITBUTTON 252

Marco Cantù, Delphi 2009 Handbook

392 - Index

BSTR	41, 293
Build Configurations	119
ButtonedEdit	259, 261, 318
Byte Order Mark	34
ByteLength	51p.
C++	135
C++ language	137
C++Builder	64
Capacity	230
Capture the execution context	182
CategoryPanel	270, 272
CategoryPanelGroup	270
CF_UNICODETEXT	280
Character literal	70
Character unit	47, 86, 243
Characters unit	48
CharCase	258
CharInSet	45, 85
Chau Chee Yang	351
CheckBoxes	267
CheckWin32Version	274, 281
Chevron	271p.
Chinese	87, 133
Chr	46
Chris Bensen	211, 294
Chris Hesik	133
Class Explorer	127
Class factory	363
Class helper	76
Classes unit	216, 232, 243
ClientDataSet	166, 320, 330p., 339, 364, 370, 379, 382, 384, 386, 388p.
Clipboard	280
ClipBrd unit	280
Closures	178
Coclass	288
Code page	22p., 26
Code point	24, 27pp., 32, 34, 39, 44, 48, 53p., 71, 80
CodeGear	13
ColorDepth	278
Columns	315
COM	283, 365p.
ComboBox	259, 281
CommandLinkHint	252
CommandProperties	316p.
CommandStyle	309
CommandType	312
Common User Access	299
Compiler directive	
G	115
INLINE	115
M	115
MethodInfo	366
POINTERMATH	102
STRINGCHECKS	115
Unit alias	95
VARPROPSETTER	211
Z	115
$HIGHCHARUNICODE	71
$STRINGCHECKS	65
Compiler option	
--codepage	26
--string-checks	65
-$M	115
-$Z	115
Compiler Version	13, 208
Component Object Model	283
Components Wizards	131
Configuration Manager dialog box	122
Configuration Settings	119
ConnectionData	349
ConnectionName	347
ConnectionString	348
Console Applications	98
Constraints for Generics	148
Construct	162
Contnrs unit	157, 163
Control characters	22
ConvertFromUtf32	47, 53
Converting Strings	61
CreatePanel	270
Custom Encoding	76
CustomHint	248pp.
CustomizeDlg	307
Cyrillic	58
Data Pumping	356
Data-aware	357
DataSetProvider	364, 389
DataSnap	361p., 387

DBError..237
DbExpress.......................238, 346, 353, 366
DBGrid...320, 331, 339p., 359, 364, 384p., 388
DBImage..359
DBNavigator...319
Dbxdrivers.ini..350
DbxInterBase unit 351
Debugger..133
Default... 146, 148
Default Constructor..............................155
DefaultFieldClasses...............................339
DefaultFieldDefClass.............................338
DefaultFont..274
DefaultParamClass................................338
Delphi 2007 Handbook......4, 94, 273, 347, 352
Deprecated.....................................209, 334
Description...323
DExplorer...108
DFM Files...80
DialogAction..309
Dictionary..164
Domain Specific Languages..................228
DoubleBuffered.....................................248
Draw...279
DrawText..39p.
Driver...349
DropDownMenu...................................252
DSAdmin..387pp.
DSCommonServer unit.........................387
DSNames unit..373
DSProviderConnection.................364, 382
DSServer................................362, 364, 371
DSServerClass........363, 367, 371, 373, 377
DSTCPServerTransport..................363, 371
Edit...256
Editor...132
ElevationRequired................................252
Email..17
Embarcadero Technologies.............13, 390
EndOfStream...234
EnsureUnicodeString......................64, 115
EProgrammerNotFound.......................242
Equals..217p.

ER/Studio...13
ES_NUMBER...256
Essential Pascal..4
Event Handlers.....................................188
Example...
   AnonAjax..200pp.
   AnonymFirst.........................179, 181, 184
   AppFont..274p.
   BareBoneRibbon..............................302
   ButtonEdits......................................260
   ButtonsDemo..................................252
   CategoryPanels................................270
   CharTest................................45, 48, 84
   CharTroubles.....................................86
   CheckBoxHeader.............................266
   ClassContraint.................................149
   CustomEncoding..............................79
   CustomerDictionary........................164
   CustomFields...................................339
   DataRibbon......................................320
   DbEditPlus.......................................357
   DbxMulti2009..........................347, 351
   DfmTest..81
   DsnapMethods........................374, 378
   DsnapMethodsClient.......................379
   DsnapMethodServer........................370
   EditFamilyDemo......................257, 259
   ExceptionsTest..............237, 239, 241
   First3Tier2009..................................367
   FromAsciiToUnicode..............23, 25, 28
   GenericCodeGen..............................144
   GenericInterface............................168p.
   GenericTypeFunc...........................146p.
   GraphicsTest..................................277p.
   GraphicTest......................................276
   GroupingList....................................263
   HighCharTest....................................70
   HintsDemo.....................................249p.
   IntfConstraint................151, 154p., 169
   IntfContraints..................................168
   KeyValueClassic...............................136
   KeyValueGeneric............................138p.
   LabelsDemo.....................................254
   LatinTest..56pp.
   ListDemoMd2005..........................158p.

Marco Cantù, Delphi 2009 Handbook

ListMonitor	223
MiniPack	80
MiniSize	80
MinorLang	208pp.
MoveStrings	89p.
MyTrayIcon	273
MyTrayIconClick	273
PlainTips	324
PointerMath	100
PointerMathD2007	102
ProjManagerTest	118, 121
RadioGroupDemo	255
RawTest	67
ReaderWriter	233pp.
ResourceTest	124p.
RibbonDemo	315
RibbonEditor	309, 313p., 318
RibbonEditorTips	325, 327
SimpleClient	293
SimpleServer	286, 288
SmartPointers	176
StreamDsDemo	346
StreamEncoding	73, 76
StringBuilder	226p., 229p.
StringConvert	62, 133, 191
StringTest	51, 53p.
SuperProgress	265
SystemObject	218
TestChar	45
ThinPlus2009	381, 383, 387
TypeCompRules	139, 141, 143
UniApiSpeed	37
UniCds	330, 333
UniClipboard	280p.
UnicodeConsoleTest	99
UnicodeData	32
UnicodeMap	32
UnicodeWinApi	35
UniFontSubst	39
UniRichEdit	268
Utf8Test	60
VariantOver	212, 214
VarProp	211p.
WebFind	193p., 201
Exception	236, 238, 241p.
Execute	380
Exit	210
ExpandCapacity	230
ExtCtrls unit	259, 279
Extended Metadata	352
ExtTextOut	38p.
Fabrizio Schiavi	2
FastCode	244
FetchOnDemand	385
File Open	311
FillChar	86
Fluent User Interface	299p.
Font	282
Font Dialog	309
Font substitution	39
Fonts	39
FreeOnTerminate	199
FtWideString	331, 342
Fun Side of Delphi	242
G clef	48
Generate Datasnap client classes	368
Generic Type Functions	145
Generics	135
Generics.Collection unit	243
Generics.Collections unit	157, 163
Generics.Default unit	170p., 243
Generics.Defaults unit	160
GenTLB.exe	284
GetCategoryPanelClass	272
GetCollection	355
GetFieldsList	333
GetHashCode	217
GetNextPacket	385
GetPlatformName	388
GetPreamble	72
GetProcAddress	98, 375
GetServerClasses	389
GetServerMethods	389
GetTableNames	354
GetTickCount	192, 197, 224
GetTypeName	147
GetUserName	37
GetWindowText	35
GIF	277p.
GlassFrame	281

Index - 395

GlowSize 254, 281
GlyFX 278
Google 193
Google group 17
Grapheme 27
GridPanel 272
GroupAlign 315
GroupHeaderImages 262
GroupPosition 316
Groups 263
GroupView 262
Gustavo Daud 277
HeaderControl 266
HideDSAdmin 387
Hint 250
Holger Flick 2
HRESULT 290
HTML 255, 295
HTTP 201
IAppServer 366p., 370, 372
IComparer<T> 160p., 170
IdHttp 193
IDL 284
IEqualityComparer<T> 170
ImageList 262, 276, 307
Images 307
Implicit 174, 214
Indy 193, 200
InfoPower Grid Essentials 359
Inlining 94
InnerException 237p., 240
Installation 108
InstallAware 108
InstanceSize 149
Int8 215
Integral Types 214
Interceptor class 188
Interface Definition Language 284
Interface ID 168
InterlockedIncrement 197
Interposer class 357
Invocation 373
Invoke 185
IsLeadChar 49, 86
ISO 8859 .... 23p.

IsSurrogate 49
IUnknown 289
Jan Goyvaerts .... 2, 38, 65p.
Japanese 71, 81, 280
JavaScript 178
Jeremy North 2, 300
Jeroen Pluimers 2
John Kaster 356
Jon Benedicto 356
JPEG .... 276p.
JQuery 178, 200
Key Tips 313
Keyboard 313
LargeImages 308
Latin-1 .... 25, 56, 62
Lazy initialization 165
LeadBytes 86
LeftButton 260
Length 94
LifeCycle .... 373p.
LinkedActionList 325
LinkLabel 254
ListView 166p., 262pp., 281
Lulu.com 16
MainFormOnTaskbar 281
Marco Breveglieri 2
Marquee 265
Master/details 384
Mastering Delphi ... 4, 15, 80, 157, 177, 286, 293, 305, 381
Math unit 244
MaxThreads 378
Memo 258
MessageBox 36
MessageDlg 275
MessageFont 275
Metadata 352
Method pointers 177
Methods Chaining 228
Micro ISV 15
Microsoft .... 14, 108, 126, 283, 300p.
MIDAS 381
Most recently used 311
Move 89
MoveBy 337

Marco Cantù, Delphi 2009 Handbook

MSBuild..110
MultiByteToWideChar..........................57
Nested types..252
NewRow..316
NumbersOnly.................................256, 357
Office 2007...300
Office Fluent UI Design Guidelines.....300
OnAccept..311
OnAfterConnection..............................382
OnBalloonClick.....................................273
OnClose..375
OnConnect...364
OnCreateInstance.................................374
OnDestroyInstance.......................374, 377
OnDisconnect.......................................364
OnExecute...305
OnGetClass..382
OnGetDataSetProperties.....................386
OnItemChecked....................................264
OnLinkClick..255
OnMouseEnter......................................249
OnSectionCheck...................................267
Open Arrays Parameters......................103
Ord..46
Overloading...212
PacketRecords......................................385
Panel...269
PAnsiChar...............................35, 44, 97
Parallel For..196
ParentCustomHint...............................248
ParentDoubleBuffered.........................248
ParentFont...274p.
PasswordChar.......................................257
PByte..101, 345
PChar...38, 44, 98pp.
Peek..234
Peter W A Wood..2
Philippe Kahn......................................135
PInteger...100, 102
PNG..277p., 359
Pointer Math...99
Polymorphisms.....................................171
PoolSize...378
PopupActionBar..................................269
PopupActionBarEx..............................307

Potential data loss..................................63
Prime number...............................196p., 371
Procedural types...................................177
ProcessMessages..................................197
ProgressBar...................................265, 281
Project Configuration Files.................110
Project Manager................117p., 123, 286
Project Options dialog..................113, 126
Project Options dialog box....................89
Proportional..280
Protected hack......................................357
ProviderName......................................364
Proxy...165
Proxy class..367
Push buttons..251
Put by ref..211
PWideChar..............................35, 44, 97
QueryPerformanceCounter.................192
Quick Access Toolbar...........................313
QuickAccessToolbar............................319
Radio buttons.......................................255
RadioGroup..................................255, 375
RaiseOuterException........................238p.
RaisingException..............................241p.
RawByteString.................55, 66, 90
ReadFromFile...73
RecentItems..312
Reference count.....................................50
Register ActiveX Server.......................290
Registered Type Libraries...................291
RemoteServer.......................................364
ReportMemoryLeaksOnShutdown......174
ResemblesText.......................................96
Resource Compiler..............................126
Resources...123
Resources dialog box..........................124
Resourcestring....................................127
Restricted IDL.....................................284
ReverseString..96
Ribbon....301pp., 307pp., 313, 315, 317pp., 323, 325
RibbonComboBox...............................318
RibbonSpinEdit...................................303
RichEdit..267, 308
RIDL...284, 286

RightButton	260
RoundTo	244
Rows	315
Safecall	287, 289, 382
Screen	275
Screen Tips	323
ScreenTipsManager	323, 325p.
ScreenTipsPopup	323pp.
Sections	266
Server	373
Server Methods	366
ServerClassName	364
ServerMethodName	367
Session	373
Set of Char	45, 84
SetCodePage	52, 56, 62, 66
SetWindowText	38
ShellExecute	255
ShortString	50, 55, 222
ShowCaption	270
ShowHelpButton	302
ShowMessage	275
Singleton	170
SizeOf	146, 149
Smart Pointers	171
SmoothReverse	265
Sorting	159
SQLConnection	347, 352, 354, 364, 366, 371, 387
SqlServerMethod	367pp., 388
Standard actions	308
State	265
Stdcall	290
Steve Tendon	135
String Conversion Warnings	88
String literal	70
StringCodePage	51, 57
StringElementSize	51p., 57
StringOfChar	87
StringRefCount	51
Style	252
SupportsPartialTransparency	276
Surrogates	29
Synchronize	193, 380
SyncObjs unit	244
System unit	46, 51, 57, 214p., 223, 243p.
System.Object	216
System.Text.Encoding	72
SysUtils unit	51, 72, 85, 90, 186p., 237, 242pp.
TAction	306
TActionClientItem	309, 316
TBalloonHint	248p.
TBasicAction	306
TBDXProperties	349
TBitmap	276
TBlobField	343
TBookmark	93, 334p.
TButton	251
TButtonProperties	317
TButtonStyle	252
TBytes	90
TCategoryPanel	272
TCharacter	47, 53
TComboBox	259
TComparer<T>	160p., 170
TConnectionData	349
TControl	248, 318
TCP/IP	363pp.
TCustomAction	306
TCustomButton	251
TCustomEdit	357
TCustomHint	248
TDataSet	332pp., 344pp.
TDBEdit	333, 357
TDBImage	280
TDBXCommand	369
TDBXMetaDataCommands	355
TDBXTable	355
TDictionary<TKey,TValue>	158
TDrawingStyle	279
TDSServerModule	366p.
TEdit	256, 258p.
TEditButton	260
TEncoding	61, 72p., 76
TEqualityComparer<T>	170
TextHint	257, 259, 318, 357p.
TextOut	39, 98
TextOutW	35
TField	332, 342

398 - Index

TFieldDef	341
TFileStream	99, 234
TFunc<TResult>	187
TGraphic	276pp.
Thread Synchronization	193
Threading	223
Threads Status	133
Tiburòn	110
TInterfacedObject	168
TJPEGImage	277
TLabel	254
TLB	287
Tlibimp.exe	285
TList<T>	157p.
TLookupList	339
TMonitor	223, 374, 378
TObject	216, 221
TObjectDictionary<TKey, TValue>	164
TObjectList<T>	163
Tool Palette	130
ToString	216, 218, 227, 238p., 372, 376
ToUpper	48
TParam	344
TProc	186
TQueue<T>	157
TrayIcon	273
TRecordBuffer	345p.
TreeView	29pp., 262, 318
TRemoteDataModule	366, 382
TRibbonPage	302
TRibbonTabItem	302
TScreenTipItem	323
TSingletonImplementation	170
TSQLConnection	350p., 362
TStack<T>	158
TStreamReader	232p.
TStreamWriter	232p.
TStringBuilder	92, 226pp., 234
TStringField	336, 342
TStringReader	232, 234
TStringWriter	232, 234, 236
TSysCharSet	85
TTextReader	232, 235
TTextWriter	99, 232, 235
TThread	193, 223, 379
TUnicodeEncoding	72
Turbo Pascal	13
TVarRec	103
TWideMemoField	343
TWideStringField	335p., 342
TWinControl	248
Type libraries	284
Type library editor	284, 286, 288, 293
TypeInfo	146, 148
Types Compatibility Rules	141
TypInfo unit	79, 147, 222
UCS-2	27
UCS4Char	27, 46, 54, 77
UCS4String	46, 54p., 78
Unicode Consortium	21, 32, 73
Unicode Transformation Formats	28
UnicodeString	49p., 53
UnitName	218
UpCase	48
UpdateRegistry	381
UpDown	378
UpperCase	48, 96
UseCustomFrame	302, 304
UseLatestCommonDialogs	275
User Account Control	290
UseVisualStyle	255
UTF-16	27, 29, 34
UTF-32	29, 34, 76
UTF-8	27pp., 34, 60, 74, 222
UTF8String	55, 60pp., 68p., 92
Variants	103
VER200	13, 208
Video	25
Videos	3
Visual C++	15
VmtParent	221
Wait Chain Traversal	133
Web 2.0 technologies	16
WideChar	44, 49, 85
WideCharToMultiByte	59
WideString	37, 41, 293
WideStrUtils unit	41, 61, 96
Wikipedia	300
Win32	14
Win32 API	34

Marco Cantù, Delphi 2009 Handbook

Index - 399

Windows 9x..35, 39
Windows API..97
Windows unit..38
Windows Vista......252, 254, 257, 259, 265, 281
Windows XP.....39, 251p., 254, 256p., 259, 262, 265, 269, 282
WinExec...375
Woll2Woll Software..359
Word wrapping...255
WriteToFile..73
Yorai Aminov..356
YouTube..25
ZLib unit...244
-idecaption...109
.DPROJ..110p.
.OPTSET..121
.RES..123
€..23, 25, 71

Marco Cantù, Delphi 2009 Handbook

Web Sites by Marco Cantù

here is a partial list of the diverse and somewhat unrelated web sites I manage (or don't manage enough, as some of them are quite old and static) in English language:

```
http://www.marcocantu.com
http://blog.marcocantu.com
http://www.socialwebbook.com
http://www.thedelphisearch.com
http://www.wintech-italia.com
http://dev.newswhat.com
http://delphi.newswhat.com
http://ajax.marcocantu.com
http://www.delphimentor.com
```

Here are other sites in Italian language:

```
http://www.marcocantu.it
http://www.wintech-italia.it
http://shop.wintech-italia.com
http://www.delphiedintorni.it
http://www.piazzacavalli.net
```

Finally, these are personal pages on community sites (not all frequently updated) and micro-blogging sites:

```
http://www.linkedin.com/in/marcocantu
http://www.facebook.com/people/Marco_Cant/600881813
http://www.librarything.com/profile/MarcoCantu
http://stores.lulu.com/marcocantu
http://twitter.com/marcocantu
http://marcocantu.myplaxo.com/
```